PAY, PRODUCTIVITY AND COLLECTIVE BARGAINING

Pay, Productivity and Collective Bargaining

R. B. McKersie
*Dean, New York State School
of Industrial and Labor Relations
Cornell University*

and

L. C. Hunter
*Professor of Applied Economics
in the University of Glasgow*

with assistance from
Werner Sengenberger

Macmillan
St. Martin's Press

First published 1973 by
THE MACMILLAN PRESS LTD
London and Basingstoke
Associated companies in New York Toronto
Dublin Melbourne Johannesburg and Madras

SBN 333 05565 9

Library of Congress catalog card no. 73–75114

Printed in Great Britain by
A. WHEATON & CO
Exeter

To the memory of
DONALD ROBERTSON

Contents

List of Tables   xi

Preface   xiii

List of Abbreviations   xviii

1 A Preliminary View   1
   1 Introduction   1
   2 The concept of productivity bargaining   4
   3 Productivity problems and the growing commit-
      ment to action   10

2 The First Phase of Productivity Bargaining: 1960–6   24
   1 Introduction   24
   2 Evolution   26
   3 The incidence of productivity bargaining   39
   4 Information and opinion   50

3 The Second Phase: 1967–70   54
   1 The impact of incomes policy   54
   2 Growth and incidence   63
   3 Content and coverage   73
   Appendix to Chapter 3   The D.E.P. register as a
      data source   84

4 Effects of Government Policy   86
   1 The N.B.P.I. guidelines for productivity bar-
      gaining   87
   2 Evaluation   97
   3 Conclusions   113

5 The Ingredients in Productivity Agreements 115
    1 Factors involved in the agreements 116
    2 Nature of work (skill utilisation) 118
    3 Hours of work patterns 131
    4 Effort and manning 139
    5 Methods 143
    6 Reward features 151
    7 Achievement and reward patterns over time 156

6 Negotiating the Agreement 160
    1 Introduction 160
    2 Pressure bargaining—the direct approach 163
    3 Integrative bargaining—the indirect approach 168
    4 The role of mixed bargaining 176
    5 Internal consensus 186
    6 Concluding comments 195

7 Implementation of the Agreement 199
    1 Introduction 199
    2 Implementation activities 203
    3 The role of key institutions 214
    4 Synthesis 223

8 Substantive Results of Productivity Agreements 227
    1 Operating results 228
    2 Economic impact 245
    3 Explanatory factors 255

9 An Assessment of Cultural and Organisational Effects 268
    1 Impact on management 268
    2 Impact on the union institution 273
    3 Impact on the work-group and individual 275
    4 Control of shop-floor relations 284
    5 Impact on the bargaining structure 295
    6 Evaluation of the direct versus indirect approaches 301

10 Interpretation 313
    1 Introduction 313
    2 The management function 319
    3 Union orientation 326
    4 The meaning of productivity bargaining for the institution of collective bargaining 333
    5 Control of plant-level relations 345

11 Implications for the Future   351
     1 *The outlook*   351
     2 *The scientific management option*   355
     3 *Technological change*   357
     4 *Manpower planning*   360
     5 *The possibility for a new departure*   362
     6 *The role of productivity bargaining in the fore-
        seeable future*   367

Index   381

List of Tables

2.1 Features of agreements in the period 1963–6: achievement   32

2.2 Features of agreements in the period 1963–6: reward   36

2.3 Productivity-type agreements, 1963–6, by main order heading   45

3.1 Number of agreements and number of workers covered, by main order heading (1958 S.I.C.)   66

3.2 Size distribution of agreements, 1967–9   72

3.3 Agreements analysed by occupational group of workers covered   74

3.4 Frequency of achievement features, 1967–9, and relative importance in first and second phases   76

3.5 Frequency of achievement features, by occupational group   78

3.6 Frequency of reward features, 1967–9, and relative importance in first and second phases   82

4.1 Guidelines for judging productivity agreements   88

4.2 Wages, prices and costs during incomes policy phases: selected indices   99

4.3 Productivity and unit cost increases, 1961–9   102

4.4 Productivity, unit labour costs and productivity bargaining coverage – selected industries, 1966–9   103

5.1 Industry rank order of relative importance for various achievement categories   125

5.2 Work rotations in one publishing agreement   133

5.3 Percentage distribution of reward changes by industry   153

6.1   Ingredients of interest under the two approaches   161
6.2   Characteristics of direct and indirect bargaining   196
7.1   Summary of key activities   213
7.2   Relationship of design features to the implementation
      process   225
8.1   Weekly overtime hours in all industry and in elec-
      tricity supply, April 1964 to April 1969   231
8.2   Time profile of improvement for various ingredients   244
8.3   Labour and equipment costs before and after the deal   248
8.4   Timetable for 'Green Book' in distribution   265
8.5   Timetable for 'Blue Book' at Fawley   265
10.1 Strategies on labour costs   320

Preface

This book has emerged from a study conceived in 1965 when R.B.McK. was in Britain on leave from the University of Chicago. Productivity bargaining was beginning to make its mark on the British industrial relations scene at this time. Its full impact was not yet apparent, however, and this became the theme of the study undertaken by R.B.McK. during 1965–6. Only after the tightening of incomes policy began, and the productivity criterion for wage increases was established as a significant factor in collective bargaining, did the effects of productivity bargaining become manifest. A first draft of the book was completed in 1967. By this time, however, the effects of incomes policy were very much in evidence, and the original plan was scrapped.

At about this time, L.C.H. was invited to join in the study as a co-author, and participated jointly with R.B.McK. in the planning and completion of the project. Combining efforts over the distance between Chicago (subsequently Cornell) and Glasgow had its difficulties, but they were reduced somewhat by annual visits to Britain by R.B.McK. The authors were also fortunate to have had the assistance of Werner Sengenberger, a graduate student of the University of Chicago. His contributions in liaison and as a researcher have been invaluable and his name is thus included with ours on the title-page.

Our intention was to take a broad perspective on the developments in productivity bargaining and relate these developments to the conceptual apparatus of current industrial relations. In this way we hoped to identify the usefulness of these concepts in evaluating the achievements and processes of productivity bargaining. Additionally, it was hoped that the innovations resulting

from productivity bargaining might create new concepts and relationships which would in turn spur new theoretical approaches
to the changed circumstances.

Initially the collection of data was not difficult, for the number
of productivity agreements, though substantial, was still com-
paratively small. As productivity bargaining mushroomed, however, methodological problems arose. And while the detailed
case-study approach had many advantages, it became impractical
to proceed on that basis. Additionally, no satisfactory basis from
which to draw a proper statistical sample existed. We thus turned
to the pragmatic approach, maintaining, developing, and extending where possible the existing contacts in companies employing
productivity bargaining, and relying heavily on the studies and
reports of others. This, we hoped, would provide the broad perspective we were seeking. Such an approach is, of course, open
to criticism. We have, from our own researches and readings,
developed a wide but still incomplete knowledge of productivity
bargaining experience. From that, we moved on to evolve ideas
and concepts which seemed to us to help to explain, or set in
context, particular changes in practice, patterns of development
and variations in techniques. These views are admittedly subjec-
tive interpretations based on our own personal knowledge and
predilections, and others may legitimately draw on different sets
of information and reach different conclusions. Nevertheless, the
analysis presented in the following chapters is in line with the
judgements developed during the course of our study. The test
is not so much whether in the last resort they are all in some sense
correct, but rather whether they prove helpful to others in
interpreting the events of the last decade or so in the productivity
bargaining field, and whether they help to provide a firm base
for general assessment of the accomplishments productivity bargaining has permitted.

While the centrepiece of the study is the analysis of productivity
bargaining at the micro-level, our view is that the significance of
productivity bargaining cannot be fully appreciated unless its
development is seen in the context of the industrial relations and
economic situation of the period. We have, therefore, devoted
several chapters to discussing the key influences which determined
the emergence and development of productivity bargaining, and
in concluding we have also considered its sudden fall from grace

which became apparent in 1969–70. In many respects this rise and fall was associated with changes in government policy, especially incomes policy. The association between incomes policy and productivity bargaining was a close one during the late 1960s – perhaps unfortunately so for the proper evaluation of productivity bargaining. In looking to the future, the book tries to assess the future role of productivity bargaining – for at the time of writing the principles are by no means extinct – and the extent to which some of the lessons learned in the experience of the 1960s may be applied in future, both in Britain and in the United States.

The very nature of our approach presupposes a wide range of contacts in industry, government, and the academic world. A full list of acknowledgements to all those who helped is not practicable, but we would wish to thank most sincerely all those who contributed ideas and materials for our consideration. A number of individuals gave us exceptional assistance and we wish to acknowledge them more fully.

Probably our greatest debt is to management and union officials who provided case-study material or who gave their time willingly to discuss their experience and to comment on our interpretations and arguments. Among these, special mention is due to the following : D. Allison (Purfleet Deep Wharf); L. Archer (formerly of Mobil Oil) and P. McNeilly (also Mobil Oil); the late L. Cannon, J. Haston and other officials of the E.T.U.; G. Eastwood (Printing and Kindred Trades Federation); K. Jones (British Steel Corporation); F. Large (Thomson Newspapers); L. Neal (formerly British Rail and now Chairman of the C.I.R.) and D. Bowick (British Rail); E. Robertson, D. Alexander, J. Bayhylle, and T. Robinson (Engineering Employers' Federation); H. Sallis (Electricity Council); P. Shaw (Post Office Engineering Union); F. Silberman (T.G.W.U.); F. Simmons (N.G.A.); L. Thornton (Esso); E. Vincent (I.C.I.); and M. Viviani (Chemical Industries Association).

Many academic colleagues commented on drafts and engaged in discussion of issues and approaches. Among these, we wish to acknowledge our debt to : G. Bain (Warwick); R. Banks (Michigan State); H. Clegg (Warwick); A. Flanders (Warwick); R. Flanagan (Chicago); C. Lockyer (Strathclyde); T. Lupton (Manchester); W. McCarthy (Oxford); D. MacKay (Aberdeen); G.

Reid (Glasgow); B. Roberts (London School of Economics); J. Seidman (Chicago); A. Thomson (Glasgow) and A. Wedderburn (Heriot-Watt). It need hardly be added that there were issues on which differences of view emerged. While much of the advice we got was taken, there were matters on which our perception was not sufficiently acute to allow us to benefit from suggestions. The remaining limitations in the study are in no way to be taken as a reflection of the quality of the help we received from this quarter.

An important set of data was made available to us for analysis by the Department of Employment. Many officials were engaged in the assembly of the raw data, and to all of them we are most grateful. In particular, we owe thanks to J. Galbraith (now Director of the Office of Manpower Economics) and D. Shearer (formerly Research and Planning Division at the Department of Employment), who arranged for the release of the data and provided assistance in interpretation.

For access to unpublished material, we are indebted to J. Galbraith (Office of Manpower Economics) and Miss I. Lindsay (Strathclyde University). Considerable financial support to cover research expenses was provided by the Graduate School of Business, University of Chicago, and we would like to express our appreciation for this assistance.

Finally, our thanks go to those who had the unenviable task of helping to bring the manuscript to its final form. A great deal of work was involved in the preparation and analysis of the Department of Employment data on productivity agreements, and for this we have to thank Anne Carey, Maureen Robb, Susan Grier and Mary Smith.

For the patient and efficient typing of successive drafts we are indebted to Pat Rennie, Margaret Simpson and (above all) Betty Patterson at Glasgow; and to Barbara Nesbary and Richelle Sessions at Chicago and Barbara Stevens and Ruth Ann Schulte at Cornell. Invaluable editorial advice and assistance in eliminating the rough edges from our final drafts was given by Rachel Goetz (Chicago), Mary Ann Coghill (Cornell) and Anne Carey (Glasgow).

Despite all this help and advice, we have probably failed to make use of all the suggestions we should have, and the remaining flaws must be attributed to the authors rather than to those who gave so willingly of their time and expertise.

A last comment concerns the dedication of this book to the late Donald Robertson, who participated in early discussions on this joint venture. He would perhaps have been surprised – but we think delighted – that this transatlantic co-operation has borne fruit. Our regret is that he is not here to say whether the graft has been truly successful.

R.B.McK.
L.C.H.

The authors and publishers are also grateful to the following for permission to quote from published material: The Institute for Workers' Control for the extracts from 'Productivity Bargaining' from *Trade Union Register*, edited by K. Coates; Royal Van Gorcum Ltd and the International Peace Research Association for extracts from 'Productivity and Conflict', by A. N. Oppenheim and J. C. R. Bayley, from *Proceedings of the International Peace Research Association Third General Conference*.

Abbreviations

N.J.I.C. (N.J.C.)	National Joint Industrial Council (National Joint Council)
C.B.I.	Confederation of British Industry
T.U.C.	Trades Union Congress
N.B.P.I.	National Board for Prices and Incomes
D.E.P.	Department of Employment and Productivity
E.E.F.	Engineering Employers' Federation
NEDO	National Economic Development Office
N.I.C.	National Incomes Commission
C.I.R.	Commission on Industrial Relations
G.P.O.	General Post Office
SCOW	Steel Company of Wales
C.I.A.	Chemical Industries Association
P.O.E.U.	Post Office Engineering Union
T.G.W.U.	Transport and General Workers' Union
G.M.W.U.	General and Municipal Workers' Union
A.U.E.W. (A.E.F.)	Amalgamated Union of Engineering Workers (Amalgamated Union of Engineering and Foundry Workers)
N.G.A.	National Graphical Association
N.U.V.B.	National Union of Vehicle Builders
E.P.T.U. (E.E.T.U./P.T.U.)	Electrical and Plumbing Trades Union (Electrical Electronic Telecommunication Union/Plumbing Trades Union)
N.U.B.	National Union of Blastfurnacemen, Ore Miners and Kindred Workers
SOGAT	Society of Graphical and Allied Trades

1 A Preliminary View

1. INTRODUCTION

Productivity bargaining was essentially a product of the British industrial relations situation in the 1960s. At the time of writing, some productivity agreements are still in operation and others are still being negotiated, but it would be fair to state that the first flush of enthusiasm has passed, leaving in its place a good measure of disillusionment and criticism. In view of this, and the fact that a great deal has already been written on the rise of productivity bargaining and its application in British industry, why should it be necessary to add further to the literature?

The emergence of widespread productivity bargaining was one of the major phenomena in British industrial relations in the 1960s, and as such has to be seen as an important feature in the economic and institutional history of that period. The first productivity agreement is generally acknowledged to have been concluded at the Esso refinery at Fawley in 1960, and it is a measure of the subsequent growth and impact of productivity bargaining that between January 1967 and the end of 1969 around 4000 agreements covering several million workers had been registered with the Department of Employment and Productivity under the productivity criterion of the incomes policy then in force.[1] A development of this magnitude is obviously worthy of thorough examination.

While part of this book is concerned with the development and

[1] Admittedly, not all these agreements could be regarded strictly as productivity agreements, but most of them at least owed their origin to the productivity bargaining development.

spread of productivity bargaining, it is not our purpose to provide a purely historical account. After a full decade of experience, it is possible to embark on a comprehensive assessment of what has been involved and what has been achieved. At this time when the popularity of the approach has declined, what (if any) are the lessons to be learned from the experience and what aspects of productivity bargaining should be preserved? Answers to these questions require a consideration of what productivity bargaining has involved not just in descriptive terms, but in a more analytical way – specifically, the processes and the relationships which occur in the negotiation, implementation and operation of productivity agreements. It is the second purpose of this book to examine the stages, the procedures and the organisational and cultural implications of productivity bargaining, and to put them together in a way that will help to identify the contribution – actual and potential – inherent in the productivity bargaining approach.

With that analysis complete, attention can be turned to the future role of the productivity agreement. If the heyday of productivity bargaining is truly past, two questions of importance arise. First, given the prominence achieved by the productivity approach to collective bargaining at the end of the 1960s, we must ask what will take its place and whether the next important industrial relations development will derive something of its character from the productivity bargaining experience. How far will the passing of productivity bargaining leave a vacuum posing a threat to the stability of the industrial relations and collective bargaining systems?

Secondly, to what extent *should* we be trying to ensure the survival of productivity bargaining? From the points of view of the economic efficiency of the industrial relations system, and the social and cultural health of relationships at all levels within the system, should we be content to let productivity bargaining lapse into obscurity – if that is indeed to be its fate – or should we be seeking to rescue some elements and adapt or modify others?

This study has several objectives, ranging from the descriptive through the analytical to the practical. The core of the book is the analysis of productivity bargaining at the level of the company and plant, and from this analysis we hope to derive a set of conclusions which will allow us to evaluate the need for a productivity bargaining approach in the future, and to suggest the direction for possible modifications. To complete the picture, it is in our view essential to see the rise and subsequent decline of productivity bargaining in the context of the period in which it occurred. Any device for the solution of a problem is relevant only so long as the problem itself remains important, and it might be that the pressing problems of the sixties which gave rise to widespread productivity bargaining are no longer so relevant in the seventies. We shall see that the upsurge of productivity bargaining activity in fact owed much to the circumstances of the time, but that the problems it was designed to tackle are still very much with us.

It is also the case that the sorts of problems tackled by means of productivity bargaining in Britain in the sixties have been increasingly recognised in other countries, most notably the United States, where considerable interest has been shown in the British experience. While this present study is based primarily on an examination of British experience and is set therefore in a very specific – indeed, unique – institutional context, it may be that there are useful comparative illustrations to be made and at least some of the more obvious errors may be so exposed in this treatment that others coming later to the scene may be more able to avoid them.

Three early chapters of the book are concerned with the evolution and spread of productivity bargaining during the 1960s, and with the context of economic and industrial relations policy in which these developments took place. From this 'macro' view of the phenomenon we turn to an exploration of the 'micro' experience, looking in turn at the problems of design, negotiation and implementation, and concluding with an assessment of the experience both from the point of view of the more quantitative or substantive results and from that of the procedural and cultural effects. This section of the book is based mainly on case study material obtained from examination of a number of agreements and from interviews with management and union personnel who have been responsible for the negotiation and operation of these agreements. Finally, in the last two chapters we review more generally the impact of productivity bargaining and draw some conclusions on its role as an element in the national industrial relations scene and as an agent in bringing change to the organisational and cultural milieu of relations at plant and workshop level.

The remainder of this chapter is devoted to a preliminary discussion of productivity bargaining, the kind and the range of problems it was set to tackle and the ways in which it fitted into the circumstances of the time in which it originated, gestated and finally flourished.

2. THE CONCEPT OF PRODUCTIVITY BARGAINING

WAGE PAYMENT AND PRODUCTIVITY

Productivity bargaining means different things to different people. The concept has changed over time, and one's understanding of it is likely to be influenced by the circumstances and the period in which it was first encountered.

Wage bargains adopt different approaches to the relation between rewards and work. Probably the most typical case is where there is a specified rate of payment which is made to all workers in the grade provided certain minimum standards of work are maintained, so that for the given rate of pay workers may produce differing amounts and qualities of output. This situation may be unsatisfactory for a variety of reasons and a good deal of effort has been devoted to devising means whereby payment can be more closely linked to the output or productivity of the worker.

The commonest alternative has been to use the payment system as a means of functionally relating the output of the worker or work-group and the pay received. Approaches based on incentive payments now have a long history. More recently, developments such as the Scanlon Plan have encouraged workers to improve their effectiveness over a wide range of activities, by adopting improved methods and economising on resources. Like the more orthodox incentive schemes, they operate through the payment system, providing a *continuing* formula for the on-going distribution of the benefits of improved productivity.

Productivity bargaining, though concerned with the same problem of relating work to payment, seeks to do so by rather different methods. Instead of operating through the payment system, it places the consideration of ways of improving productive performance directly in the context of wage bargaining. It involves the parties to the bargaining process in negotiating a package of changes in working method or organisation, agreeing on the precise contents of the package, their worth to the parties and the distribution of the cost savings between the reward to labour and other alternative destinations such as the return to capital and the reduction or stabilisation of the product price.[2] In this sense each productivity bargain is a once-for-all method of relating increases in pay to increases in productivity – though this does not preclude the possibility of a sequence of such bargains over time. It does, however, contrast with schemes which work through the payment system, where rewards to labour may fluctuate from week to week as output or productivity varies.

What, then, is so significant about productivity bargaining? First, it is important as an experiment because other approaches by management to the tightening of the pay–productivity link have often been less than successful. Secondly, it opens a whole new source of untapped productivity potential, either by grouping otherwise minor and unimportant changes into a package which becomes worth considering as a source of improved wage payments and higher productivity, or by introducing into the bargaining process a joint attack on difficult problems in the work and payment situation which are unlikely to be taken up with the more conventional approaches, inhibited as they often are by custom and practice. Thirdly, in the productivity bargaining process, the means by which progress to agreement is made and by which the agreement is implemented have afforded opportunities to introduce principles of industrial relations which conform with 'best practice'. Examples include the abandonment by management of a typically defensive posture in favour of a greater initiative in labour relations and the utilisation of labour; greater attention to comprehensive planning, again especially with regard to the workforce and its deployment; and greater involvement and participation by the workers in formulating and applying the wage–work rules which regulate behaviour on the shop-floor.

---

[2] In practice, there may be no separation between the gathering together of the changes and the negotiation on what they are worth, since agreement on what is to be included in the package may depend on the price that is to be paid for them.

FEATURES OF THE CLASSIC AGREEMENT

Perhaps the best way to convey something of the typical form of a productivity agreement, which will serve as a means of pinning down in practical terms some of the more abstract ideas just expressed, is to set out the main characteristics of one agreement. The Fawley agreements of 1960 provide a generally agreed starting point for the species and we shall take this as our reference example.[3]

The initial recognition of problems at the Fawley refinery began with comparisons of its manning levels, labour utilisation (especially in the use of overtime) and costs with those of the Baton Rouge refinery belonging to Standard Oil of New Jersey, the parent company of Esso. The importance of this comparison was heightened by severe international competition in the oil industry and the resulting pressure on costs. Once the problems were properly identified, management became committed to act and subsequently began negotiating with the unions at the refinery a series of far-reaching changes in work arrangements and practices in exchange for substantial increases in rates of pay (about 40 per cent) and reduced hours of work. The changes in working practice included withdrawal of craftsmen's mates and their redeployment to alternative work, relaxation of demarcation rules, new shift-working arrangements, increased freedom for management in its use of supervision, and elimination of unproductive-time allowances.

The crucial factor in the 1960 agreements was the planned reduction of overtime which was to be compensated (and more) by the rise in basic rates. The high level of regular overtime was seen both as the prime cause of inefficiency and high labour costs and the primary means to a solution. With the progressive reduction of overtime and the compensating rise in basic rates, coupled with other changes, it became possible for workers to increase their earnings *and* their real leisure time and at the same time for management to derive the benefit of lower unit costs.

In addition to these changes, it was an important condition of the whole approach and its acceptance that the agreements would

[3] The outstanding description and analysis of the events at Fawley is that of Allan Flanders, *The Fawley Productivity Agreements* (London: Faber and Faber, 1964).

not lead to redundancy, and a guarantee to this effect was given by the company for the duration of the agreements.

The 1960 agreements can be summarised as a package deal, embracing a number of changes in payment and work arrangements, designed to raise productivity and reduce costs. Subsequent agreements in 1962 concentrated on further advances in the same directions. Perhaps the most significant feature of the agreements is not the individual character of the items but the fact that they all occurred together, and that there was an *explicit* link between specified changes in working method and changes in pay and conditions. It is also worth stressing that the changes were introduced not by managerial prerogative or by worker consent but by a sustained process of collective bargaining culminating in a written agreement.

This latter point is significant, for while there had previously been changes broadly similar in style and possibly even in scale to those at Fawley, they had generally been achieved by methods other than collective bargaining. In the end it may be the most significant lesson of the Fawley experience that it opened up a new area for collective bargaining, where, before, the implementation of change by management and its acceptance by unions and workers had been achieved in an *ad hoc*, unsystematic and often tacit manner. This would not have mattered, of course, had the technological and organisational changes that managements wanted to implement always gone forward. That was not the case, however, and in some sectors of industry, like printing and the docks, resistance by unions had resulted in delays in the installation and operation of new machines. Elsewhere there were important areas of effort utilisation and overmanning of plant which were not normally open to negotiation at all. It was the merit of the Fawley negotiations that they showed a new way to tackle such problems.

In contrast to the normal case of industry-wide settlements, the Fawley agreements were negotiated at *plant* level. This was no innovation, for on the refining side Esso was a non-federated firm, long committed to plant bargaining, but it did ease the way for an agreement which could take detailed account of the technical and organisational circumstances of the individual site, in a way not generally possible for the company affiliated to an employers' association.

Although separate agreements were signed by the T.G.W.U. for the process workers and by the group of craft unions for the craft workers, the agreements were simultaneous – as were the negotiations leading to them – and they can be regarded as comprising a single deal covering the whole manual labour force of the plant. Thus the package deal, incorporating a series of changes in work and pay arrangements, was also comprehensive in the sense that it covered the whole plant – a feature which again marked it out as distinct from earlier agreements with some similarities but which were primarily sectional or departmental in coverage.

Was the Fawley deal really the first of its kind? There are many examples of companies introducing changes in technology and the organisation of work or embarking on cost-reduction schemes in a way that might suggest something of the flavour of the classical productivity bargain. However, closer examination shows that they generally fell short of the Fawley experience either in extent of plant coverage or multiplicity of issues. Still more important, a great many of these changes were implemented without ever being the subject of negotiation in a pay–productivity context. Instead, they were introduced by managerial prerogative and with productivity gains exerting an influence on wages only through an incentive payment scheme or, still more indirectly, in a subsequent collective bargaining situation where other bargaining levers would be deployed as well. Thus the Fawley achievement stands out as unique at the time in its coverage of all workers in the plant, its encompassing of a complex of changes at a single step and the direct and explicit link between these changes and alterations in pay through the medium of collective bargaining and according to a deliberate programme of action.[4]

There are several reasons why the pay–productivity link seldom became formally expressed in a collective agreement before the 1960 experiment at Fawley. First, in a collective bargaining en-

---

[4] According to one authority, 'the novelty of the 1960 productivity agreements at Esso's Fawley refinery was not that this was the first occasion on which work practices were mentioned in an agreement, or that it was the first exchange of alterations in work practices for increases in pay. What was new was the negotiation with workshop representatives of all the unions concerned of a series of changes in work practices throughout the plant and their embodiment in a formal agreement with the unions'. H. A. Clegg, *The System of Industrial Relations in Great Britain* (Oxford: Blackwell, 1970).

vironment dominated by the industry-wide agreement, generally concluded by an employers' association on behalf of its member firms, the scope for the development of plant bargaining was reduced. Although the employers' association was not normally powerful enough to prevent members from concluding agreements at shop-floor level to supplement industry-wide basic rates, this degree of freedom for management did nothing to fill the void between the industry agreement and the sectional bargain. As a result, the comprehensive, plant-wide agreement, capable of yielding major gains to both parties, was a rarity.[5]

Secondly, the more usual way to try to give effect to the pay–productivity nexus was by means of the same form of incentive payment system. The limited success of such schemes in many situations is witnessed by a host of critical writings and opinions expressed by prominent observers of the British industrial relations system and we return later to a reconsideration of some of these.[6] In practice, full employment and the growth of shop-floor bargaining power meant that the theoretical niceties of accurate measurement and tight control of standards went by the board, and the perseverance of many managements with one or another form of payment by results simply reflected their inability in the given institutional framework to find an alternative solution to the control of unit labour costs and chaotic wage structures.

Finally, although there was a good deal of propaganda on the need for higher productivity, there was no real impetus to action. As Flanders has put it, 'The fatal flaw of productivity propaganda is also the source of its attraction : it involves no commitment to act.'[7]

In the case of Fawley, there was no industry-wide agreement to constrain independent action, the scope for incentive payments was slight in view of the technological characteristics of the industry, and a commitment to act stemmed from competitive pressures and the unfavourable comparison with American performance. The Fawley experience emerged out of a particular

[5] For evidence on the limitations of employers' associations in respect of plant negotiations, see Royal Commission Research Paper No. 7, *Employers' Associations* (London: H.M.S.O., 1967).

[6] See Chapter 10 below. For a recent study identifying good and bad features, see N.B.P.I. Report No. 65, *Payment by Results Systems*, Cmnd 3627 (London : H.M.S.O., 1968).

[7] *The Fawley Productivity Agreements*, 239.

combination of economic and organisational circumstances at a point of time, and its real lesson was not that a particular formula or design for negotiations could be made to work but rather that the content of collective bargaining could be extended into new areas (notably those of labour utilisation) in such a way as to satisfy jointly the goals of workers and management. It was therefore inevitable that the 'model' would be applied differently in different situations, in line with variations in the problems of labour–management relations, in the objectives of workers and their union representatives, and in the institutional framework.

3. PRODUCTIVITY PROBLEMS AND THE GROWING COMMITMENT TO ACTION

The lessons of Fawley were seized upon rapidly both by other companies and by government because the Esso experiments highlighted two problems of general concern in Britain at the start of the 1960s : low productivity and persistently high levels of overtime work. The three following chapters will be largely devoted to tracing out the spread and development of productivity bargaining, and the role of government policy in fostering this development. But even at this point it is useful to consider in broad terms something of the background conditions which prevailed at the start of the 1960s and the reasons for the growing interest in productivity bargaining and the subsequent commitment to using it as an instrument of change.

Essentially, then, we have to ask about the dimensions of the productivity problem, the processes which allowed it to be conceived realistically and the way in which productivity bargaining was recognised as a novel means of coming to grips with it.

DIMENSIONS OF THE PROBLEM

In a much publicised and undoubtedly influential newspaper article in 1964, William Allen characterised the country as 'half-time Britain' whose symptoms were patent over-manning in many industries and almost universal resort to overtime work.[8] Allen, the architect of the Blue Book proposals at Fawley, laid at least

[8] William Allen, 'Is Britain a Half-Time Country?' *Sunday Times* (1 March 1964).

part of the trouble at the door of industry-wide bargaining. In his view, the introduction of plant bargaining would have made possible an improvement of up to 30 per cent in the efficiency of labour utilisation.

The popular newspaper stories on the theme 'what's wrong with Britain' commonly asserted that labour productivity was anywhere between one-half and one-third of that in some of the more advanced industrial countries. Allen, who had experience on both sides of the Atlantic, claimed that the British worker was only one-third as efficient as his American counterpart. While this characterisation may have been accurate for some of the more aggravated situations, it was probably too pessimistic an estimate for most of British industry when allowance was made for the greater capital intensity of American industry. Nevertheless, the debate over Britain's productivity gap was gradually being moved from a plane of generality to a much more specific appreciation of the size of the problem in particular industries, as the following examples show.

The steel industry, with which Allen was familiar, was operating at a productivity level approximately one-half that in the United States. According to the Iron and Steel Board in 1964 :

> Productivity in the British steel industry is probably only about 50 per cent of the U.S. level. Productivity in the British industry also appears to be lower than in the E.C.S.C. Productivity in the Japanese industry . . . has now overtaken the British level.[9]

On British docks the level of productivity was probably about two-thirds of potential, according to comparisons with the 'model', the Rotterdam docks.[10] Again, in shipbuilding, reliable data from the Geddes Report indicated that the 'country to beat' was Japan with labour costs some 15 per cent below comparable figures in Great Britain.[11] Some of this difference was attributed to lower wage rates but a good portion of it stemmed from more efficient

[9] Iron and Steel Board, *Development in the Iron and Steel Industry, Special Report, 1964* (London : H.M.S.O.).

[10] See Vernon Jensen, *Hiring of Dock Workers and Employment Practices in the Ports of New York, Liverpool, London, Rotterdam and Marseilles* (Cambridge, Mass. : Harvard University Press, 1964).

[11] Shipbuilding Inquiry Committee, 1965–6, *Report*, Cmnd 2937 (London : H.M.S.O., 1966).

methods in the Japanese shipyards. In the automobile industry, the takeover of Rootes by Chrysler dramatised some of the unfavourable comparisons:

> Our investigations had shown us that the number of man-hours in the body assembly, paint, trim and final assembly of a car like the Hillman Minx was around 50% higher than the number of hours in the much larger vehicle like the Chrysler Valiant.[12]

Admittedly, such comparisons do not tell the whole story. Differences in output per head may be due to factors other than differences in the efficiency of labour utilisation (e.g. alternative production techniques, variations in the production 'mix', etc.) while unit labour cost comparisons may need to be tempered by recognition of differences in the real wage levels between countries as a whole. Nevertheless, the cumulative evidence suggests that deficiencies in labour utilisation contributed substantially to a loss of productivity potential in much of British industry.

Not only have productivity *levels* been inferior in much of British industry, but productivity *growth* seems also to have been lagging. At the international level, Denison concluded from a study of nine countries that

> All other countries had higher growth rates of output per unit of input than the United Kingdom in the longer period (1950–62), and all except the United States in 1955–62. The continental countries without exception had substantially larger increases in adjusted output per unit of input than the United Kingdom; France, Germany and Italy experienced increases two or three times as large.[13]

The size of the potential achievements in improved labour efficiency can also be gauged from internal evidence of the time, from the many inquiries into the state of affairs of British industry. For example, the Shawcross Report on the national newspapers, the Devlin Report on the docks, the Geddes Report on

[12] George Cattell, 'Industrial Relations and Efficiency', *Industrial Society Journal*, January 1967, p. 27.

[13] E. F. Denison, 'Economic Growth', in R. E. Caves and Associates, *Britain's Economic Prospects*, a Brookings Institution study (London: Allen & Unwin, 1968), 253. The other countries were the U.S.A., Belgium, Denmark, France, Germany, The Netherlands, Norway and Italy.

shipbuilding, and various early reports of the National Board for Prices and Incomes, particularly those dealing with road haulage, bakery and railways, estimated that productivity in these situations could be increased by anything from 15 to 40 per cent, much of this being attainable by improvements in the use of labour.

Recognition of a productivity shortfall was not confined to 'outside' commentators, as witness the managers' statements reported by W. McCarthy in his nationwide survey of workshop relations undertaken for the Donovan Commission :

> About half of the managers thought there were inefficient labour practices in their plant and that the organisation and arrangement of work could be improved and nearly three-quarters of them thought that workers could put in more effort. Few managers thought that the abolition of inefficient labour practices or the better organisation of work could make more than a 20 per cent difference to costs. Two out of five foremen thought the work they supervised could be better organised, but nearly all foremen said *they* had adequate scope to ensure that it was efficiently done. A majority of managers and foremen thought they could cut at least some overtime without cutting earnings.[14]

These examples illustrate the substance of the productivity problem and the closer definition of the gap that Britain had to make good. But the mere presence of low levels of productivity and high unit labour costs may be an insufficient motivation towards change. The situation just described had existed for some fifteen years before the Fawley agreement was negotiated, even if the dimensions of the problem were less well understood. Why, then, did commitment to act begin to develop in the early 1960s, and why did the productivity bargaining approach to solution seem so attractive?

STIMULI TO ACTION

At the same time as Allen was criticising British efficiency and Flanders was publicising the achievements at Fawley, there was

---

[14] W. E. J. McCarthy and S. R. Parker, *Shop Stewards and Workshop Relations*, Royal Commission Research Paper No. 10 (London : H.M.S.O., 1968) 53.

a fairly constant stream of activity on the productivity front, especially with regard to labour problems, and publicity on a number of important areas kept the issues in the public eye. Some flavour of events may be obtained by enumerating a few of the matters then under review. In 1964, the *Special Report* on the steel industry[15] highlighted the problem of overmanning in the industry in comparison with other countries, and a report of a joint working party on the craftsmen's pay dispute at the Steel Company of Wales emphasised the need for reduction of manning and the achievement of greater productivity. Inquiries into the London Transport dispute[16] and the difficulties that had arisen in the electricity supply negotiations[17] on productivity and status were widely reported and many of the problems that commonly arise in the context of productivity bargaining began to attract attention. In 1965 the Geddes Committee,[18] charged with an investigation of the competitive and organisational problems of the shipbuilding industry, was set to work; also in 1965 the final report was issued of the Devlin Committee[19] investigating labour problems in the docks. A common factor throughout these inquiries was the need for increased productivity through modernisation and the improvement of labour relations and labour utilisation as a means to greater efficiency.

The significance of these activities for the present discussion – and they are only a sample – is that the range of problems which productivity bargaining was seeking to tackle was never far below the surface; while the very existence of these working parties and committees of inquiry was an indication that in government and in private industry the need for active change was being accepted. Productivity bargaining undoubtedly benefited from coming upon the scene at just the time when the public mind was receptive and positively seeking a new approach to long-standing problems.

[15] *Development in the Iron and Steel Industry, Special Report, 1964.*

[16] *Report of the Committee of Inquiry to Review the Pay and Conditions of Employment of the Drivers and Conductors of the London Transport Board's Road Services* (London: H.M.S.O., 1964).

[17] *Report of Inquiry into the Causes and Circumstances of a Dispute between the Parties represented on the National Joint Industrial Council for the Electricity Supply Industry*, Cmnd 2361 (London: H.M.S.O., 1964).

[18] Shipbuilding Inquiry Committee, 1965–6, *Report.*

[19] *Final Report of the Committee of Inquiry under the Rt Hon. Lord Devlin into certain matters concerning the Port Transport Industry*, Cmnd 2734 (London: H.M.S.O., 1965).

There was yet another factor pushing in the same direction – incomes policy – though it was not until 1967 onwards that it was to have its greatest impact. Even in 1962, Selwyn Lloyd's White Paper had stressed that while changes in the cost of living, and trends in profits and productivity could not be regarded as a sound basis for pay increases :

> . . . there may, however, be cases in which an increase could be justified as part of an agreement under which those concerned make a direct contribution, by accepting more exacting work, or more onerous conditions, or by a renunciation of restrictive practices, to an increase of productivity and a reduction of costs.[20]

How far the particular phrasing of this sentence owes its origin to an awareness of what had been achieved at Fawley in 1960 is hard to determine, and it is certainly difficult to believe that the Treasury could have had any conception of the subsequent role that could be (and was) played by productivity bargaining. More probably it was a natural development from the lines of thought that had been pursued by the Council on Prices, Productivity and Incomes in its latter-day reports.

No matter what the connection, the fact remains that the productivity principle was imbedded in the incomes policy almost from the start of the 1960s, and there it was to remain until 1969–70. After the General Election of 1964, an early action by the new Labour Government was to publish a new White Paper on incomes policy.[21] This established a norm for wage and salary increases; one of the few exceptions to the norm was the productivity condition, now repeated in essentially the same phrases as in the 1962 White Paper. Once again it is doubtful how far this 'recommendation' to productivity bargaining would have been taken up if the matter had simply been left there, but of course the main impact of the Labour Government's experiments in the fields of incomes policy was still to come.[22] Still, the productivity theme seemed well established in incomes policy thinking and there was already an awakening of the public conscience in productivity matters.

---

[20] *Incomes Policy: The Next Step*, Cmnd 1626 (London : H.M.S.O., 1962).
[21] *Prices and Incomes Policy*, Cmnd 2639 (London : H.M.S.O., 1965).
[22] For further discussion, see Chapters 3 and 4 below.

In 1965 too the National Board for Prices and Incomes (N.B.P.I.) began its work. Between June 1965 and July 1966 the N.B.P.I. produced eighteen reports, of which ten dealt with wage and salary issues. It became immediately clear that the Board was to concentrate on the alteration of collective bargaining criteria away from the traditional basis in cost-of-living changes and comparability, and towards a link with productivity improvement, especially that sort of improvement that came from new methods of operating and economies in the use of labour. This was true in at least five of the ten wage cases reported on by the Board; of the others, one was concerned with the consequences of the electricity supply productivity agreement and the rest raised other 'test' issues under the incomes policy. Not only this, but in the price references undertaken by the Board, attention was paid to the need to accommodate cost increases – including higher labour costs – in improved efficiency so that price rises would be minimised; and in this area too, the Board made a number of suggestions for improved labour utilisation and cost containment.

We conclude that there was widespread evidence in the early 1960s not only of a productivity gap but of a growing awareness of the dimensions of the problem. Action was stimulated across a wide range of industry by inquiries into efficiency problems, many of them with origins on the labour side, and the initial formulations of incomes policy together with the setting up of the N.B.P.I. were undoubtedly contributory factors in the growing volume of activity. It remains to ask why productivity bargaining in particular became such a popular means of approach to the general problem of productivity shortfall.

ATTRACTIONS OF THE PRODUCTIVITY BARGAINING SOLUTION

Companies may pursue productivity improvement in a variety of ways, and it has constantly been a key activity of industrial management, though varying in scope and intensity from time to time. One possibility is unilateral action by management, and this has been practised with some success by many companies in the post-war period. In a statement primarily about the U.S.A., but possibly applicable to British industry, Garth Mangum has argued : 'Any inefficiencies which cannot be eliminated under the contract within a reasonable time by an alert management are rare.'[23] It has been suggested that demarcation problems can be solved, or perhaps never even arise, when skilful management is on the scene:

> Many large scale employers told me bluntly that demarcation rules . . . do not hamper production if the work is planned properly. Many small employers also contended that if you have good relations with your men, demarcation lines are never strictly adhered to and that most men prefer common sense to rules.[24]

But for one reason or another productivity problems have developed *despite* management's good efforts or in some circumstances because of management's *poor* efforts.[25] In most situations management would have eliminated productivity problems if they could, but for some reason they have *not* done so. While the presence of weak or inexperienced management may explain some situations, it does not appear to be the critical variable in most situations. To the extent that it is, the obvious prescription is to improve the calibre of management.

More commonly, management's inability to deal with manpower utilisation problems on its own has been due to the institutional and informal pressures that preserve the *status quo*. This is the basis of the explanation so eloquently advanced by Allan Flanders, which sees production problems as rooted in the culture of the workplace.[26] It was a critical aspect of the productivity bargain that it explicitly recognised the nature of the problem and activated a process of cultural change – quite apart from its effect in changing specific workplace practices.

[23] Garth I. Mangum, 'The Interaction of Contract Administration and Contract Negotiations in the Basic Steel Industry', *Labor Law Journal* (September 1961), Vol. 12, No. 9, 857.

[24] F. Zweig, *Productivity and Trade Unions* (Oxford: Blackwell, 1951) 17 and 18.

[25] In its report on the docks, the Devlin Committee criticised management in just this way:

> They [the employers] have complained so much about them [time-wasting practices] that it is surprising to find that they have not so far made any systematic study of them such as might show how much they mattered in terms of time or money. Nor do they draw any sharp distinction between practices deliberately created as protective and bad habits which firmer discipline might still cure.

Final Report of the Committee of Inquiry (Port Transport), p. 11.

[26] E.g. in *The Fawley Productivity Agreements*, chapters 2 and 5.

Where restrictions on manpower deployment and effort exist, management cannot embark on a unilateral programme to remove them because the workers and their union representatives will not allow it. It first has to be recognised that these practices fulfil a cultural need, before progress in removing the obstacles to productivity improvement can be made. This hold which the work group has over the work system, and its natural instinct to preserve the *status quo*, are key elements of the situation prior to productivity bargaining.

Union preference for the status quo.   Once customary practices are present (for whatever reason) they are naturally protected by those with vested interests. While trade unions may not always initiate demarcation arrangements, for example, they are certainly quick to use them as defensive arrangements. Generally, unions prefer the existing pattern of working arrangements and express a reluctance to try the unknown simply because the known is more comfortable and secure. As a result they exude suspicion of management and of any overture to change.

Unions may also resist the updating of work rules for more rational reasons because in many cases they stand to lose actual or potential membership as a result of the change. Even where the changeover is gradual and no members actually lose employment, the leadership may resist the development to protect the size and power of their union. For example, in the newspaper industry in London there has been great resistance to the elimination of restrictive practices, even though the companies have guaranteed the continued employment of all incumbents, since the unions involved feel very strongly about preserving the lucrative jobs in newspapers for their 'brothers who will follow in their footsteps'. It has been an established practice for workers to progress from the commercial printing side of the industry to newspapers, and union leaders take a dim view of any programme that does not 'preserve the patch'.

Essentially, then, the response of a union to a proposed change in skill groupings depends upon its own institutional self-interest. If the shift merely entails the reassignment of duties among different sections within the same union, resistance may be less than with a transfer of duties between competing unions. The union response will also be influenced by whether it has been experiencing overall growth or decline in membership. For example, the welders have dropped out of productivity discussions at several refineries because as a trade they have been suffering sharp declines, especially in branches located in shipbuilding regions. Another consideration is the degree of exclusiveness which a union enjoys over a given skill territory. Some job duties can be easily performed by other craft unions; other more specialised job duties are capable of being performed only by one or two craft groups. Finally, some unions find themselves in the predicament where the costs of not engaging in talks are higher than the costs of participation. Consider the dilemma of the painters and the trowel trades. At many refineries they are slowly going out of existence, due to subcontracting and the elimination of maintenance resulting from new technology; consequently, they are forced to engage in productivity discussions 'to make the best of a bad situation'. Yet once they engage in discussions about the flexibility of craft assignments, many of their duties will be taken over by other trades.

The final piece of the picture is the union's ability to resist change, should it choose to do so. Simply stated, working arrangements are preserved through the exercise of union and worker bargaining power, which is most readily available where management cannot afford to take a strike or where the cost of a concession cannot be passed on to the consumer. Thus it is no accident that the industries in Britain which have experienced most difficulty in modernising work rules are also those where the 'lightning' strike is most devastating, as for example in the docks, shipbuilding and newspapers.

Worker interest in the status quo. Just as unions may have institutional reasons for preserving the *status quo*, so may the workers have personal reasons for resisting change. Many rules incorporate or fulfil social ideals or values. The British working class strongly adheres to the notion of equality of opportunity for work and earnings, and this value is reflected in work rules in different industries. It is not uncommon for workers to insist that if one worker is offered overtime, all his colleagues must be given similar offers.[27] In the docks the continuity rule takes its roots in the work group norm that everyone should have the same opportunity for assignment to choice jobs :

[27] Cf. H. Clegg, *The System of Industrial Relations in Great Britain*, p. 280.

The first element in the continuity rule is neither protective nor restrictive, but is designed to ensure that the same men get the rough with the smooth in any job.[28]

Another example of a similar point comes from the newspaper industry :

No pieceworker will start work at the beginning of the shift until sufficient copy is available to enable every operative present to be issued with the equivalent of twelve lines of setting.[29]

These practices can only be explained in terms of the strong social pressures against any individual's gaining an advantage *vis-à-vis* his colleagues. One cannot understand this great emphasis on minimising inequity (even to the point of not maximising total welfare) without reference to the social ideology of the British labour movement and the concept of 'solidarity'.

While such cultural norms may be at the root of much of the reluctance to abandon customary practice, there are other obstacles to change which are more personal : the economic and psychological self-interests of workers. The most frequent reason for resistance to the updating of working arrangements is that workers' needs for earnings and job security are challenged by the proposed changes. They may fear that the new arrangements will erode their skill base and leave them with less recourse to the external labour market. In this sense, the preservation of demarcation arrangements represents an emphasis on skill integrity. While demarcation lines may produce rigidities, they also create a sense of identification between workers and their particular skill groups.

Workers traditionally feel that employers take a short-term outlook in developing skills. Take, for example, the notion of the all-round mechanic, trained to perform a variety of tasks in operation and maintenance, perhaps in a refinery. From management's viewpoint the flexibility achieved is admirable. But what happens to these mechanics when the refinery is shut down or when they receive the 'golden handshake'? Craftsmen, trained in a traditional skill area such as electricity or sheet-metal work, can

---

28 *Final Report of the Committee of Inquiry (Port Transport)*, p. 15.
29 Royal Commission on the Press, *Report*, Cmnd 1811 (London: H.M.S.O., 1962) 225.

seek employment in the larger labour market, but the 'jack of all trades' may find himself 'master of none'.

Moreover, a revision in demarcation arrangements can be especially threatening if the context is one of falling demand for an industry's output. As we have noted earlier, this revision in the scale of production may be a key reason for the restructuring of job clusters; yet, at the same time, the drop in demand raises the spectre of redundancy. It is precisely when a company is under the most pressure to revise job design that the workers are faced with poor prospects for job security.

NEED FOR JOINT INVOLVEMENT

Our purpose in devoting considerable attention to the reasons underlying the defensive attitude of unions and workers and their common support of work rules has been to underline the point that in most situations management can tackle the problems these rules create only by means of a joint approach involving workers or their representatives. *De facto*, the workers and their representatives exercise a power veto. Moreover, the very purpose of a scheme designed to eliminate inefficiency in the use of labour requires that the motivation of the workforce be improved, and this cannot be accomplished without some measure of worker participation.

A great deal of trust is required, for instance, before a programme involving overtime reduction can be initiated. Workers concerned about their take-home pay may not be sure that they are going to receive additional money unless it is guaranteed in some form of negotiated settlement. Thus, some formal way needs to be devised of moving from a high overtime/low hourly rate situation to a low overtime/high hourly rate situation. This requires trust and confidence which can only be realised by joint design and joint implementation of such a programme.

This line of thinking suggests that management, on its own, can hardly solve problems which are so deeply a part of the plant social system. A central premise, then, of this study is that it is essential to understand the historical context within which work rules first arise as well as their economic and cultural significance for workers, unions and managers in order to understand the *change* process that is required to alter these customary practices.

If work rules were merely conventions that could be 'legislated' away or merely economic commodities that could be 'bought out', then productivity bargaining would be either easy or unnecessary.

An underlying assumption is that work rules are functional, and once they are viewed in this light it becomes easier to understand the importance of productivity bargaining as a way of agreeing on methods of bringing about change. Once management recognises that all customs and practices serve a social purpose, they are on the threshold of being able to alter these arrangements by dealing with their underlying causes.

One of the principal merits of the Fawley agreements was that they showed how this approach might be applied. It was not just the substantial rise in wage rates that mattered, but the facts that workers' and union representatives in the plant had been involved in the processes of bargaining and analysis, and that attention was paid to relevant social variables such as the increased leisure which was to accrue and the guarantee against redundancy. Not only was a new source of untapped productivity potential opened up for management, but it was achieved in a way that allowed the worker to participate in decisions affecting his productivity and, ultimately, his pay.

It was also a means of extending the scope of collective bargaining into new areas, and it was quickly recognised that it was not restricted to the problems or to the formula adopted at Fawley. In fact, the predominance of problems connected with the operation of work rules and the widespread problem of systematic overtime meant that many of the early agreements centred on these issues, but as time went on new issues came to the fore. For example, productivity bargaining was turned to deal with the major problem of rationalising wage structures at plant level, where sectional bargaining had led in many cases to a highly complex and often anomalous structure. Work measurement and job evaluation schemes which could help to simplify the structure and put differentials on a more rational footing, were frequently resisted by the workers but productivity bargaining again showed a way round this resistance.[30]

This completes our preliminary discussion of the growing recognition of the dimensions of the productivity gap in many industrial situations and the emergence of a commitment to remedy

[30] For a fuller discussion of the range of issues covered, see below, Chapter 2.

the deficiency. Many of the productivity problems derived from work rules – some dating back a long way – which had become part of the culture of the plant situation and which could not be removed by unilateral management action in the normal case where strong unionism provided the necessary defences. Nor were these problems which could readily be tackled by conventional collective bargaining where the main activity occurred away from the plant in the more remote atmosphere of industry-wide negotiations. The attempts to raise productivity through the payment system by means of incentives could provide some advantage in certain circumstances but it could not really deal with the main problems of worker flexibility and freer assignment of manpower, while it even contributed at times to the creation of further rules, such as output restriction, to the variability of earnings which prompted reliance on overtime as a means of stabilising earnings, and the further confusion of an already complex wage structure.

It was the commitment to a bargaining approach, principally at plant level where the detailed operation of work rules could be discerned and the implications of changes in them appreciated, that marked out the productivity bargaining avenue as an attractive proposition for management and workers alike. Both parties could see in productivity bargaining advantages for themselves, and a means to the achievement of important goals. Only much later did it become recognised that there were also important conflicts of goals which could arise in the process, especially on questions of the locus and balance of control over work and pay. But that is a question best postponed for the present.

Many of these aspects will have to be examined in greater depth in the following chapters, but for the moment enough has been said by way of introduction to convey an impression of what productivity bargaining comprised, the type of problem it sought to tackle and the reasons why these problems had proved fairly intractable in the face of other approaches. The next stage is to explore more thoroughly the way in which the phenomenon spread and developed from its beginnings at Fawley and what were the formative factors which contributed to its rapid growth.

2 The First Phase of Productivity Bargaining: 1960–6

1. INTRODUCTION

We have already indicated that productivity bargaining was a phenomenon of the 1960s and one which flourished greatly in the second half of that period. In this and the next chapter we will investigate in some detail two separate periods, 1960–6 and 1967–70, in which marked differences in productivity bargaining experience are found. The full reasons for this separation will emerge as we proceed but the critical line of demarcation is taken to be the prices and incomes standstill imposed by the Labour Government in the latter half of 1966, after which the influence of a prolonged period of strictly administered prices and incomes policy served to generate a virtual explosion of productivity bargaining. Whereas there was a fairly 'natural' development of productivity bargaining until the middle of 1966, the new situation ushered in by a period of hard incomes policy gave rise to significant changes in the scale of productivity bargaining, generated as a more 'artificial' response to that policy.

If we can establish a causal connection between the mushrooming of productivity bargaining and the particular form of the incomes policy from 1967 on, we must still offer some explanation of events in the first and formative phase between 1960 and 1966. What was the pattern (if any) of the diffusion of productivity bargaining across industry? Did it have an evident economic or institutional rationale? What sort of changes could be observed in the style and content of productivity bargaining in this first wave of agreements? What sort of reaction did the innovation provoke among the interested parties in government and industry?

We begin with an examination of the evolution in the form of the productivity agreement. To conduct this analysis, it was necessary to draw up a comprehensive list of agreements during the period 1960–6.[1] This proved to be a difficult exercise and we have had to resort to an assembly of information from a variety of sources (company contacts, journal and Press articles, etc.) which may result in less than complete coverage, especially in the case of some small agreements which may not have attracted much publicity.

A second difficulty arose because it was not always clear whether a particular agreement should be included in the list. It is quite possible for an agreement to have some superficial elements of a productivity bargain although in practice the application of the productivity principles embodied in it was not taken very far. For example, the 1964 national agreement for the engineering industry, the first long-term (three-year) agreement in engineering, contained a preamble to the effect that the parties recognised the need 'to modernise and improve the productive efficiency of the industry' and to eliminate 'restrictions on the economic utilisation and transfer of labour which are not based on considerations of skill or ability to do the job'. It also emphasised that it was the spirit and intention of the agreement that increases in pay during the term 'should be confined to those which normally take place arising from increased productivity in the industry'. Despite the obvious consciousness of the productivity basis for wage increases, it seems best to omit this agreement since it in no way tried to give operational effect to these clauses.

On the other hand, there are several instances of negotiations at plant, company and even industry level which were strongly indicative of an awareness of the relationship between improvements in the effectiveness of manpower utilisation and compensating changes in payment. Not all of them resulted in productivity package deals of the Fawley variety, but we have decided to include them in the total presentation of agreements because they have themes in common with Fawley or with other agreements reached in the pre-Fawley era, in which pay–productivity links

---

[1] In effect this period begins in 1963 (before which only the Fawley agreements existed) and includes only the first six months of 1966 due to the standstill on prices and incomes imposed by the Government in July 1966. The result of this was to foreclose any agreements which would otherwise have been concluded in the second half of 1966.

were established along a narrow axis or around a single productivity component in contrast to the productivity package that constituted the Fawley innovation. This may result in a somewhat arbitrary list of agreements, but the selection will be justified if it provides a cross-sectional picture of the areas in which the lines of thought central to productivity bargaining were being actively pursued.

2. EVOLUTION

Evolution in this context refers to the way in which the form of the productivity agreement and the prior bargaining process have undergone change to meet the diverse needs of differently organised companies and industries with different types of problem. Significant variations in approach are to be discerned even before incomes policy began to influence the content of agreements. To provide some preliminary account of the form of development in the early years, we will divide the discussion into two parts, one dealing with evolution in the level of negotiation and the coverage of workers under the agreements, the other dealing with the design features of the agreements. Our starting point is the Fawley agreements of 1960.

NEGOTIATION LEVEL AND COVERAGE

Plant agreements. The Esso agreement at Fawley had of course been a plant agreement; the tradition of plant bargaining was well established there and there was no national agreement to restrain the parties from setting their own course. This, however, was not typical and in the context of an industry-wide negotiating body there was much less scope for a company to break out on its own. Almost inevitably, therefore, there was a good representation in the earlier productivity agreements of companies with a plant bargaining tradition. This included other oil companies which were prominent in the early agreements.

Examples were also found in the steel industry, particularly at the Steel Company of Wales, where an agreement was reached in December 1964 resulting in acceptance by six craft unions of greater flexibility and a reduction in the number of craftsmen's mates in exchange for increased wages.[2] The Company was able

---

[2] This was followed up by further productivity negotiations to cover other parts of the workforce.

to proceed independently since it had some years earlier left the employers' association. Elsewhere in the steel industry, progress was possible at works level in spite of national agreements, for (in a complex and somewhat inconsistent system) the tradition of works or district bargaining on matters other than minimum rates and general conditions was well established, and it was usual, for example, for crew size and wages on new plant to be subject to plant-level bargaining. Such agreements along productivity lines were found at the Spencer Works of Richard Thomas and Baldwin and at the Stanton and Stavely Works.[3]

Industry agreements. In a few cases, progress towards productivity agreements proved possible despite the presence of industry-level collective bargaining arrangements. Examples include the national agreement of December 1964 concluded by the N.J.I.C. for the flour milling industry, under which guidelines were laid down for productivity bargaining at *company* level – one of the earliest 'framework' agreements. Again, the Manchester card and ring room agreement of June 1964 covered part of the cotton spinning and weaving industry: it provided higher earnings in return for the introduction of work study, for the introduction of three-shift working, and for a list of agreed job specifications based on job evaluation. Some progress was likewise made in the municipal busmen's agreement of November 1965, negotiated by the N.J.I.C. for the road passenger transport industry.

Elsewhere, the constraints imposed by the national machinery often proved too great and resulted in the company intent on a productivity agreement leaving the national organisation. This was true when Esso proceeded to move from productivity bargaining on the refinery side to a similar venture in distribution. Esso left the Oil Companies Employers' Panel of the Conciliation Committee in 1964 in order to proceed on its own.[4]

---

[3] In 1964, also, the steel industry craftsmen in a national agreement received a ten shillings per week increase in basic rates 'on the understanding of clear and unequivocal support by individual craft unions for the principle of achieving maximum efficiency in the use of skilled craft labour'. Though not in itself a productivity bargain, it was indicative of the interest then being expressed at national level in the need for improved efficiency in the use of manpower. It also illustrates the difficulty of getting positive results from a vague commitment of this kind.

[4] It was followed by other companies, leading to the dissolution of the O.C.C.C. in 1967. Other examples of withdrawal are discussed in Chapter 9.

In a number of cases, productivity bargaining on an industry-wide basis was able to proceed where the employer was virtually equivalent to the industry itself. This was true in electricity supply and also in British Railways, though in the latter it was possible for groups within the industry to be dealt with separately, as in the case of the 1965 agreement on the extension of single manning for diesel and electric locomotives. The 1965 agreement between the G.P.O. (as it then was) and the Post Office Engineering Union covered the whole of the telephone side of the G.P.O.'s business but dealt only with particular groups of workers.

Partial agreements. This restriction of coverage occurred in other cases. Both B.E.A. and B.O.A.C. in 1964 and 1965 concluded a number of separate productivity agreements to cover different sectors of their respective labour forces, and Alcan in its Rogerstone negotiations of 1964 concluded separate agreements for process workers and for craft and associated engineering personnel, following this up with a further agreement for production and service departments signed at the end of 1965. This 'partial' approach could take two forms. In some cases it developed along occupational lines, principally due to the lack of negotiating machinery capable of incorporating joint discussions attended by craft and process unions. Elsewhere, it occurred on departmental or sectional lines, particularly where companies recognised the lags likely to be involved in reaching a plant-wide agreement because of conservatism in certain parts of the plant : in such cases a deliberate strategy was adopted of concluding agreements in sections and departments where rapid progress was possible, and pressure was thereby put on others to fall into line.

Even in this first phase, then, there were indications that 'partial' agreements were a necessary method of approach, though probably most of the early examples were based on occupational groups, with the heyday of the 'sequential' strategy (proceeding from the more tractable to the more difficult sectors) coming later. In some ways the partial approach was likely to prove less satisfactory and more troublesome than a comprehensive or multi-occupational agreement such as at Fawley for it was more likely to disrupt the internal wage structure, to cause comparisons to be drawn between groups covered by such agreements and those that were not, and to generate pressures for compensating wage adjustments on behalf of the latter. If properly harnessed, this pressure could be used to persuade some of the more conservative groups in the plant to become involved and to overcome their suspicions of the innovation. If the pressure could not be controlled, it could end in wage increases unrelated to productivity gain, causing those participating in changes of working practice to feel cheated. This could result in leap-frogging within the plant or non-implementation of agreed changes in working method. Additionally, there was the likelihood that some of the expected gains in the form of an improved cultural environment, involving greater participation and more amenable attitudes to change on the part of hourly paid employees, would never really come into question.

A similar sort of difficulty occurred in companies with a number of different plants. Especially where the number of plants is large, there may be major questions of strategy to be resolved – whether to proceed plant by plant (possibly subject to guidelines laid down from headquarters level) or to seek a comprehensive company agreement, covering all works within the organisation. Much depends on the variety of activities in the company. With a relatively homogeneous product and similar production techniques and ancillary plant, a single agreement is more likely to be feasible, though even in the case of electricity supply the status and productivity agreement mainly created a framework allowing for considerable variation. The more common case of the diversified company presents greater pressures for variation in approach. Esso, for example, found it desirable to negotiate separate agreements not only for its refineries but also for its distributional activities, and again for its maritime branch. Others, such as Shell, adopted a more open-ended approach which allowed full play to the potential of individual units within the group.

Pilot schemes.   A different method of solution to the problems of the multi-plant company was to implement trial schemes, permitting flaws in the agreement to be eliminated and the best ideas to be worked into the final agreement. The classic case of this type was the I.C.I. experience. First proposals for pilot schemes were put forward in April 1965 and an agreement was concluded in October of the same year for trials to be effected at six sites within the organisation. However, the schemes were rejected at site level and it took several years before all of them got under way. The rationale behind this approach, despite its initial lack of success, was clear enough. In a large organisation like I.C.I., with a large number of plants scattered over the country and engaging in very different industrial activities, the principles of a general agreement would have to be differentially applied on different sites. The purpose of the trials was to identify the best ideas and practices that emerged, with a view to building them into the final agreement when the stage was reached of full implementation on a company-wide basis.

Trial schemes were adopted elsewhere, as in the Stanton and Stavely ironworks case already mentioned, where the 1966 agreement with engineering and maintenance workers was introduced by a pilot scheme covering only a section of the works. Again, in the G.P.O., certain changes in the organisation of work and in the introduction of new tools or equipment were tested out in selected locations, the results being reviewed subsequently by a joint Experimental Change of Practice Committee before a decision on full-scale implementation was reached.[5] Pilot schemes were also written into the first proposals for a status agreement in electricity supply, presented to the N.J.I.C. in 1963.[6]

White-collar workers.   Until 1966, the workers covered by active agreements were almost entirely from the hourly paid workforce. The only notable case involving white-collar workers was the Co-operative Insurance Society Agreement of 1966 involving the introduction of work measurement schemes. This example was to prove a starting point for a good deal of activity in the white-collar section generally, and for a much more widespread concern with the introduction of work measurement.

DESIGN FEATURES : ACHIEVEMENT AND REWARD

In turning to the design features of agreements in the period up to 1966 we might expect to find variations from the 1960 Fawley pattern at least equivalent to those just described in the bargaining level and coverage. However, the Fawley agreement of 1960 included a variety of rewards and productivity gains and in fact subsequent agreements in this period tended to incorporate a similar range of items, though undoubtedly with a different

[5] This committee did not, however, deal with wage questions, though there was a fairly firm link between gains in productivity arising out of such changes in practice and increases in wages.

[6] Cf. R. S. Edwards and R. D. V. Roberts, *Status, Productivity and Pay: A Major Experiment* (London: Macmillan, 1971) chapter 6.

emphasis in many cases and with variations in the precise mode of application.

We assume throughout this analysis that work rules exist to serve real needs in the employment relationships, and that their revision and updating in most cases have to be approached as a joint endeavour of unions, workers and management. Both management and labour must then expect to gain from the exercise and we can epitomise these respective gains in terms of improved operating effectiveness, and increased pay and benefits. The managerial goal can be expressed as changes in work method or organisation and these changes will be analysed under the heading of *achievement*. The objective of workers will involve an improvement in the rewards for work and we summarise this under the heading of *reward*.

Both *achievement* and *reward* are capable of further analysis. For this present purpose it is important to have a consistent method of enumerating the design features which can also be applied to

ACHIEVEMENT	REWARD
Quantity of work (speeding up of machinery or track, elimination of teabreaks, elimination of restrictions on output)	*Increased earnings*
Nature of work (greater flexibility between crafts and job enlargement)	*Greater leisure*
Rearrangement of working hours (changes or elimination of overtime, introduction of new shift patterns)	*Ex gratia payments for irreversible changes*
Manning (reduction of numbers employed, elimination of mates)	*Improved fringe benefits*
Change of methods (by introduction of method/work study)	*Redundancy payments* (either statutory or plus a supplement)
Organisation (introduction of new supervision structures, setting up of new work groups)	*Other rewards* (opportunity to make work more meaningful by greater joint consultation)
Responsibility (more share in decision-making by workpeople)	

later data on agreements in the period 1967–9. We have accordingly adopted a classification first developed by the D.E.P., and this is set out above under the main headings of *achievement* and *reward*, with examples of the items included under the various sub-classifications.

Almost inevitably, there are problems of practical application and correct allocation of changes within these headings. However, despite the difficulties, an attempt has been made to classify the features of 73 agreements which met the criteria outlined at the start of this chapter. Although full details on these agreements were not always available there is good reason to believe that the broad pattern depicted in Tables 2.1 and 2.2 is a fairly accurate reflection of the content of agreements during the first phase of productivity bargaining.

Achievement

Table 2.1 indicates the general pattern of achievement as represented in the selected agreements. The most common feature during this period was increased flexibility between crafts (*nature of work*), though this was obviously frequently linked with other factors. This is surely attributable to the difficulties faced by many companies (and even whole industries) as a result of rigid demarcation lines and tightly defined job boundaries, both of which led to discontinuities in production and tended to exaggerate labour

Table 2.1. *Features of Agreements in the Period* 1963–6: *Achievement*

Year	1963	1964	1965	1966	Total
Number of agreements including mention of:					
Quantity of work	1	4	7	5	17
Nature of work	3	11	25	19	58
Rearrangement of working hours	2	7	13	14	36
Manning	3	8	10	10	31
Change of methods	–	3	1	5	9
Organisation	–	1	3	1	5
Responsibility	–	—	—	—	—

shortages already present in a full or over-full employment situation. Furthermore, this had not proved amenable to treatment by more conventional collective bargaining in many sectors so that the new opportunity suggested by the Fawley approach was happily taken up elsewhere.

If greater flexibility and job enlargement were the most important work-change features, *rearrangement of working hours* was not far behind. Restrictions on the amount of overtime working were very common, and in a number of cases the agreement sought to eliminate overtime entirely, reflecting the widespread problem of regular overtime working and management concern over it. Likewise, changes in shift arrangements were important in this category, though they took a number of directions. In the Esso distribution agreement the reduction of overtime enabled the company to introduce double day-shift working and hence achieve much greater utilisation of capital. Alcan, on the other hand, sought a reduction in the number of maintenance craftsmen on shiftwork, to conform with the needs of a new system that was to be introduced with the agreement, involving a move from a 'breakdown' to a 'preventive' maintenance scheme. In general, the need expressed in agreements bearing on shift patterns was for greater flexibility, so that expensive capital equipment was more fully utilised and labour was available when really required, rather than in rigid time periods not adequately related to operational peaks and troughs.

A sizeable number of agreements contained attempts to deal with *manning* problems. The craftsmen's mate issue was a common one, with the agreement in some cases specifying a reduction in their number (as in the initial S.C.O.W. agreement), and elsewhere doing away with them entirely, as at Fawley and the Mobil Coryton refinery. In many instances a more general reduction in manning was specified (e.g. Smithfield Market).

The other categories were of less importance at this stage. Agreements touching on the *quantity of work* (i.e. machinery speeds, break periods and output restrictions) were few in number compared with the categories mentioned earlier, and in most cases these were subsidiary features of the agreement, dealing primarily with tea breaks, grace times and the like. *Changes in methods* and in *organisation* were also sparse, and it is perhaps a comment on the state of productivity bargaining at this time that it had not yet become sufficiently aware of some of the associated measurement and organisational problems.

Overall, then, there is considerable similarity in the *achievement* objectives of the Fawley and other agreements in this first phase of development. Yet the bare classification of issues does not reveal all that was looked for in the way of achievement and some agreements adopted a rather different approach.

The most striking of these agreements was that in electricity supply, which certainly contained a number of achievement features common to other agreements but which differed in its overall conception in a way that was to become increasingly important.[7] The main substantive achievements sought in this agreement, implemented after considerable initial difficulty in 1964, were a reduction in overtime and the introduction of a staggered shift pattern for day workers. These were incorporated in what was termed a 'status' agreement, as a result of which the industry's manual workers were paid an annual salary, and received sick-pay conditions similar to existing staff personnel, plus additional holidays. In short, the agreement was designed to give staff status to the blue-collar sector of the labour force. In addition to the benefits to be derived from overtime reductions and the introduction of staggered work schedules, there was an expectation on the part of management that staff status for manual workers would bring with it a more widespread and wholehearted responsiveness to changes in organisation and technology and the flexibility in work patterns and skill distributions demanded by these changes. This requires some further examination.

The great advantage of plant bargaining is that it can take into account all the circumstances of the local situation in a way that no national agreement is likely to be able to do. It is, therefore, capable of identifying specific changes that can be made and embodying them directly into the agreement. One of the consequences of this approach is that it provides management with a ready-made programme of change and an opportunity of directly controlling the ensuing developments on both achievement and reward sides. But where there is a recognisable diversity of conditions between plants within the same organisation (or in the same industry), as in the case of electricity supply, the adoption of a

---

[7] For a detailed treatment of this agreement and subsequent developments, see Edwards and Roberts, *Status, Productivity and Pay.*

specific approach must be ruled out or, if accepted, must run the risk that potential gains in some areas will be overlooked. The strategy, then, must be in some way to set in motion a process of inquiry at local level that will result in the identification of areas of change leading to improvement in the cost situation, and establishing a means by which such changes can be put into effect. If this is to be accomplished in the form of a collective agreement, there is likely to be a more open-ended approach in place of the more specific listing of changes that typifies the Fawley approach.

In the case of electricity supply, this was done by identifying certain broad objectives in the areas of manpower utilisation and working practice, incorporating these into a joint agreement for the industry in which the rewards for worker co-operation were carefully specified, and then leaving the way open for local management to ferret out and implement appropriate changes in line with the requirements of the local situation. Such an approach involves (at least for the duration of the agreement) acceptance by the labour force of the need for *continuing* co-operation in the introduction of changes of practice, as opposed to the acceptance only of changes worked out in detail and so expressed in an agreement. One of the implications of the open-ended electricity supply approach is that more responsibility is placed on the local management and worker representatives, while the degree of control that can be exercised centrally over plant-level implementation must be correspondingly reduced, and undoubtedly there are risks that uneven progress and lop-sided achievement will result.[8]

In this first phase other companies, notably I.C.I. and Shell, were seeking to work along lines similar to electricity supply. The I.C.I. agreement in 1965 laid down certain broad principles relating to the way in which labour might be deployed, the intention being that detailed changes would be worked out by management and shop stewards at individual trial sites. In return for this, manual workers were to receive an annual salary, with its connotation of greater stability and security of income. Although not quite matching up to the 'staff status' intention of electricity supply, it is evidently a move in the same direction and it was an explicit aim of the move to a salaried status that long-term changes in attitudes to work and innovation would be generated.

---

[8] Cf. Edwards and Roberts, *Status, Productivity and Pay*, pp. 295–6.

These cases indicate that even at an early stage in the development of productivity bargaining there was a good deal of experimentation not just in the form of the agreement but also in the ultimate objectives. The quest for general acceptance of change in a continuous manner rather than a once-for-all exchange of concessions in the use of labour for improved rewards highlights one of the possible disadvantages of productivity bargaining : the danger that strong resistance will develop to any proposals for change not embodied in the agreement and that newly arising needs for adaptation on the part of the workforce will be delayed until they can be incorporated into a new agreement. In other words, where the specific *quid pro quo* approach is adopted, each possible innovation in practice or working arrangements may acquire a price which has to be paid before progress in its installation can be made. The examples we have just considered convey an early awareness of this difficulty, to which we shall return.

Reward

In turning now to the reward side – the gains made by workers in return for acceptance of alterations in the content or pattern of work – we find that most agreements during the period fell into line with the pattern set at Fawley, where the main items had been *increased earnings* and *greater leisure*.

As Table 2.2 shows, virtually every agreement featured some improvement in earnings, which is hardly surprising since it is part of the expectation in any collective negotiation process that the

Table 2.2. Features of Agreements in the Period 1963–6: *Reward*

Year	1963	1964	1965	1966	Total
Number of agreements including mention of:					
Increased earnings	4	14	28	26	72
Greater leisure	1	6	7	8	22
Ex gratia payments	–	1	1	1	3
Improved fringe benefits	–	3	2	3	8
Redundancy payments	–	—	—	—	—
Other rewards	–	—	—	—	—

outcome will include some wage increase. The only major exception was the British Oxygen Company agreement of 1966 in which the theme was continuity of average net pay despite a substantial reduction in overtime hours which had previously comprised an important segment of weekly earnings. Elsewhere, increased earnings were the rule, at times involving new pay structures with a marked reduction in the number of grades and bringing about a change in the wage relativities between key groups of workers.[9]

Table 2.2 also shows up the relative importance of *greater leisure* as a feature on the reward side. In large measure this was a reflection of reduced overtime working, which carried with it a further implication for the wage features of the productivity bargain. Overtime could lead to marked weekly variations in take-home pay, and a number of agreements sought to reduce this source of insecurity by introducing a higher basic wage, consolidating variable components of earnings, and simultaneously reducing overtime. The further extension of this principle to incorporate a salaried payment system has already been commented upon in the discussion of status agreements.

The transition from wage to salary payment usually involved further elements of 'staff' employment conditions, such as additional holidays with pay (an item also appearing under the 'greater leisure' heading of Table 2.2) and sickness payment and pension schemes which were relatively infrequent features at this time. Ancillary changes such as the elimination of 'clocking-in', the granting of time off in lieu of overtime hours worked and absence without loss of pay in certain circumstances, featured in a number of agreements and contributed to a further narrowing of the status differences between white-collar and manual conditions of employment.

The 'no-redundancy' condition. Finally, one of the essential conditions of many agreements was the guarantee that workers would not be made redundant as a result of the agreement. This condition is a 'reward' item in the sense that it implies for workers covered by the agreement an added element of job security which may not previously have been explicit. Its importance is, however, greater than this, for the willingness of employees to co-operate in

---

[9] This latter change was needed in cases where flexibility between two groups of workers removed the historical basis for a conventional differential in their wages.

the introduction of work changes, many of which alter the fundamental content of jobs and directly attack acknowledged situations
of overmanning, must depend on a firm reassurance that their employment will not be threatened. The critical distinction here is
between *job* redundancy, the elimination of existing jobs, and
worker redundancy, the laying-off of present employees. Whereas
the former may be accepted in a programme of change, the latter
is most unlikely to be agreed as part of the price that has to be
paid for gains in other directions. It is perhaps then a significant
point that Table 2.2 shows up no cases in which redundancy payments were written into the agreement.

SUMMARY

From the management side, a no-redundancy condition puts considerable onus on the accuracy of manpower forecasting and
budgeting since gains to the company are reduced to the extent
that expected cost savings from manpower cut-backs are not
achieved. Managements have sometimes needed to reduce the
labour force by more active means than reliance on voluntary
turnover, and a relatively common device has been resort to a
voluntary redundancy scheme whereby workers qualify for sever-
ance payments if they offer to leave the company's employment.
The evidence suggests considerable variation and evolution even
in this first phase of productivity bargaining. This was true in terms
of the level of negotiation, where first attempts were made to conclude agreements above plant level, right up to industry agreements. It was true also of coverage, as indicated by the departure
in some cases from the 'all at once' approach that characterised
Fawley : sometimes it was a section of a plant, sometimes an occupational group, that was covered, and some signs emerged of an
approach that depended on building up a series of partial agreements until they covered the whole of a plant labour force.
Variations also occurred in the mix of features contained in the
agreements, primarily on the achievement side, depending on
the nature of the problems management wanted to tackle. But the
emphasis at this stage was still very much on the same issues as
had been prominent at Fawley : increased flexibility, changes in
working hours, and improved manning ratios. These were areas
which, as the Fawley experience had shown, were able to generate

a high pay-off in terms of achievement and reward, even if the preparation stage was likely to be protracted. Only in the second phase from 1967 onwards, when the requirements of the period dictated more rapid implementation, did there emerge a real attempt to come to grips with some of the other issues. Finally, on the question of variation, we have observed the emergence of a number of agreements which were concerned with a longer-term approach to the same sorts of problems : these were the 'status' agreements which went beyond the direct *quid pro quo* approach to the wage–work relationships.

In a very short space of time, productivity bargaining had not only obtained a foothold but had shown itself susceptible to a wide degree of variation in form and content. In short it had proved an extremely adaptable weapon, capable of dealing with a wide range of problems in the sphere of work-rule revision and the alteration of customary practices such as the reliance of management and workers on systematic overtime as a means of meeting objectives. We must now see how, during this first period, it had spread across industrial boundaries.

3. THE INCIDENCE OF PRODUCTIVITY BARGAINING

Several hypotheses can be advanced to account for industries taking a particular interest in productivity bargaining as a possible solution to outstanding problems. It is worth while exploring how far any of these explanations show up as strong influences on the development, but in advance of this a few notes of caution are in order.

First, the evidence we shall bring to bear for the first phase of productivity bargaining is necessarily somewhat scanty. We shall rely again on the evidence of the 73 agreements analysed earlier in the chapter, and in view of the small numbers statistical testing is out of the question at this stage, though rather more is possible when we come to the second phase. Secondly, some of the 'hypotheses' are susceptible only to a qualitative evaluation in which tendencies can be discerned but no firm quantitative conclusions can be looked for. Finally, it is questionable how far we should *expect* to find any predominant patterns of development. Enough has already been said to indicate the adaptability of productivity bargaining as a general approach and it could be anticipated that alert managements in almost any sector could grasp the importance of the development and explore its relevance for a particular company situation. In practice, too, since the productivity agreement is primarily to be regarded as a means of dealing with the company or plant-level situation, a distinct industrial pattern of development may not be too apparent. Even so, it is relevant to ask whether, in particular industries, this approach to a common set of problems seemed sufficiently fruitful to encourage a number of firms to take it up.

HYPOTHESES

Two contrasting hypotheses may be advanced on the importance of capital and labour intensity.

Hypothesis 1.   Productivity bargaining will be more common in industries with a high capital intensity.

Hypothesis 2.   Productivity bargaining will be more common in industries of a labour-intensive nature.

The basis for the first of these two hypotheses derives from the Fawley agreements, negotiated in a highly capital-intensive situation. It was recognised at Fawley, as elsewhere in Britain at this time, that although labour costs in such an operation might be a small proportion of total costs, they represented a much larger proportion of *controllable* costs, as opposed to costs which were effectively a datum for all companies. In these circumstances we might expect to see a general tendency for productivity bargaining to develop in similar capital-intensive industries. Conversely, it might be argued that the real scope for productivity bargaining with its emphasis on better use of manpower would be in *labour-intensive* situations, where the possibility existed of really major reductions in manning levels by improved organisation of work. Only empirical study can show which (if any) of these opposing hypotheses is more important.

A further hypothesis is that the greatest scope for the application of productivity bargaining will occur in situations where controls over job boundaries and the allocation of work are most jealously guarded. In general, the main historical tradition of such work-rules is found in the craft unions rather than in the general unions

or among unskilled and semi-skilled workers, for whom job territories tend to be more flexible over time, however narrowly defined
at a moment of time. This gives us :

Hypothesis 3. Productivity bargaining will develop more
readily in industries with a strong craft tradition.

Once again, there is a counter-hypothesis, for although (as we
have seen) in this first phase the most important single feature of
productivity bargaining was changes in the nature of work, implying increased flexibility and job enlargement, considerable attention was also paid to changes in manning levels, to the elimination
of idle time and to the control of overtime – all of which may be
at least as important (perhaps more so) for workers other than
skilled craftsmen. Hence :

Hypothesis 4. Productivity bargaining will have a greater
attraction in industries with a high proportion of non-craft labour.

The overtime problem which figured so prominently at Fawley
yields another possibility. Overtime was a problem that was widespread in industry, and it is possible that sectors plagued by high
levels of regular overtime might have seized on the Fawley example
as a means of tackling the issue. Thus we have :

Hypothesis 5. Industries with high overtime levels will be more
likely to have extensive experience of productivity bargaining.

Other possible explanations based on industrial characteristics
are more difficult to test in a systematic way but deserve mention
in passing. One such characteristic is the impact of international
competition. Where such competition, as at Fawley, is coupled
with an opportunity for comparison of manning standards and
alternative methods of work organisation, there is likely to be
greater scope for productivity bargaining as a means of improving
manning levels and deployment. From this, we have :

Hypothesis 6. Industries exposed to international competition
will be more likely to take advantage of the cutting or controlling
of costs made possible by productivity bargaining.

Three other possibilities relate to the resistance of workers to
change and the build-up of defensive practices which offer a challenge to productivity bargaining. First, where the long-term trend
in employment in an industry is downwards, insecurity of employment may generate defensive postures among workers. Secondly,
prolonged or acute technological change very often creates a feeling of insecurity which leads in turn to resistance to the introduc-

tion of new plant or to insistence on the preservation of existing manning levels. Finally, the presence of an important casual element in the workforce will again contribute to the development of insecurity and resistance to change.

In all these cases, the existence of protective practices developed over time by groupings within the labour force presents an opportunity for productivity bargaining. Such practices can seldom be removed by unilateral management action, especially as management often becomes a party to them, implicitly accepting them rather than risk the frictions which might be set up by active attempts to eradicate them. Nor is there much likelihood that collective bargaining above plant level will be effective in dealing with the inefficiencies these practices generate. Productivity bargaining at plant level can, however, provide scope for a solution by involving workers' representatives and management in joint negotiation at a level capable of working in terms of the detailed changes required by a change in working practice. This yields :

Hypothesis 7.   Industries characterised by a high degree of insecurity in the employment relationship will exhibit a tendency to adopt productivity bargaining.

These hypotheses all relate to the *industrial* incidence of productivity bargaining, but they might equally be applied to firms within an industry. To the extent that marked differences exist between firms – in production technique, in their participation in international markets, in their use of overtime, in the degree of security they offer their employees – we would expect differences in their readiness to adopt productivity bargaining. However, once the process is started within an industry, there may be a demonstration effect encouraging other firms to follow suit; and just as this can develop within an industry, so may it develop in a local labour market.

A successful productivity agreement, involving substantial gains in earnings and possibly in leisure time for the labour force, and improvements in cost and productivity performance for management, will put pressure on other firms in the same product market to redress the relative unit-cost disadvantage by engaging in a similar exercise. Also, a need for response may be perceived by firms in the same local or occupational labour market as the initiating firm, since the inter-firm wage relativities will have been altered by the first agreement. In fact, the real importance of such a change in wage structure may be exaggerated, for the typical effect of a productivity agreement is to cut back on employment, or at least employment growth; if job vacancies in the high-wage firm are absent, the state of competition in the labour market will not be appreciably changed. There may, nevertheless, be over-response by employers in a local labour market in which a major employer has struck a significant agreement, due either to fears of increased labour turnover, which may be unwarranted, or to the turning of the screw by local union officials anxious not to see their own members being left behind. From this we obtain :

Hypothesis 8. A major productivity agreement in one company will tend to produce a demonstration effect on other companies in the industry to follow suit : and

Hypothesis 9. A major productivity agreement in one plant will tend to produce a demonstration effect on other employers in the local labour market area.

Two final points relate to the incidence of productivity bargaining within industries. First, the ability of a company to engage in productivity bargaining at plant level may be constrained by its membership of an employers' association and its commitment to agreed industry rates. We might, therefore, expect to find more readiness to enter into productivity bargaining on the part of firms which are non-federated or which are prepared to leave the association to pursue their own objectives along plant bargaining lines. Secondly, companies engaging in productivity bargaining will on the whole tend to be large. The main reason for this is that a big company will often have a better defined personnel policy, the specialist resources which may be needed to identify problem areas in labour utilisation and evolve specific proposals for the solution of these problems, and the capacity to divert specialist management time from day-to-day tasks to the development of longer-term strategy in the personnel field. If the first of these two points is valid (regarding membership of an employers' association) there may be additional emphasis on the point about size since the bigger companies may be better equipped to 'go it alone', outside the aegis of the employers' association and the industry agreement.[10]

---

[10] Towards the end of the 1960s employers' associations in general began to take a more liberal attitude toward productivity bargaining and productivity negotiations within the framework of a national agreement became much more feasible. This is more fully discussed later. Even so, the point made in the text is probably accurate in the context of the period 1960–6.

EVIDENCE

At this point we can consider these hypotheses against the available evidence for the period up to 1966. The following chapter will seek to test them against the evidence for the period 1967–9. Here we turn once more to the information on the 73 agreements discussed earlier in this chapter. Since we are primarily interested in the 'penetration' of productivity bargaining in particular industries, we would ideally wish to have data on the percentage coverage of each industry's labour force. However, the rather crude nature of the data makes this impracticable, though more can be achieved for the second period. We thus have to accept as a rough measure of productivity bargaining activity the *number* of agreements recorded. In some industries, a single agreement might cover a high percentage of the labour force, while conversely a number of agreements might cover only a small proportion of employees. Although this is unsatisfactory, it is less critical for an analysis of diffusion during the early period. Industry-wide agreements, such as in electricity supply, can still be identified among the relatively small total of agreements, while in other industries the varying numbers of agreements serve as a general indicator of the degree of activity.

Table 2.3 sets out an industry analysis of 73 agreements by year over the period 1963 to 1966 inclusive. This shows the increasing number of agreements in each year, the marginal decline between 1965 and 1966 being due to the July 1966 'freeze', which effectively limited productivity bargaining activity to the first seven months. Without that, there would almost certainly have been a greater number in 1966.

There is a considerable industrial spread of agreements, but already certain industries had a strong representation. The signs of greatest activity were in industries like chemicals, passenger transport, shipbuilding (which accounted for all the agreements under the general heading of engineering, shipbuilding and vehicles), metal manufacture and distribution. The question then is whether there is any underlying pattern to this overall picture.

We have seen that both capital intensity and labour intensity could be interpreted as conditions encouraging the productivity bargaining approach (hypotheses 1 and 2). If we relate the incidence of agreements in this early phase to capital intensity as

Table 2.3. Productivity-type Agreements, 1963–6, by Main Order Heading

Year	1963	1964	1965	1966[1]	Total
Number of agreements	4	14	28	27	73
By industry:					
Food, drink and tobacco	–	1	1	2	4
Chemicals and allied products	1	4	7	2	14
Metal manufacture	2	2	1	1	6
Engineering, ship-building and vehicles	1	–	6	4	11
Textiles	–	1	–	1	2
Paper, printing and publishing	–	1	2	4	7
Construction	–	–	1	1	2
Gas, electricity and water	–	1	1	–	2
Passenger transport (including air)	–	4	4	3	11
Postal, telephone and radio	–	–	2	1	3
Distribution	–	–	3	6	9
Other	–	–	–	2	2

[1] January to July.

measured by the percentage share of wages and salaries in net output, we find that there is a strong representation of capital-intensive industries such as food processing, chemicals (including oil refining) and electricity, in all of which the wage and salary bill is less than 40 per cent of net output.[11] Conversely, however, there is also a representation of labour-intensive industries such as shipbuilding, where labour costs are over 70 per cent of net output, as well as in construction, transport and distribution. The remainder of the industries participating in productivity bargaining were close to the all-industry average of about 54 per cent. Thus, overall, there is a sprinkling of industries at both ends of the capital-intensity scale as well as in the middle. Neither of the competing hypotheses in this case is uniquely supported and it is possible that both play a part in stimulating productivity bargaining. In short, they are not mutually exclusive.

[11] Data derived from *National Income and Expenditure* (H.M.S.O.).

A second pair of competing explanations (hypotheses 3 and 4) was based on the importance of craft labour, but here again the scatter is wide. Engineering and shipbuilding are strongly represented, as is printing, and these are sectors with a strong craft element. However, industrial groups such as chemicals, and the food, drink and tobacco sector are also prominent in their adoption of productivity bargaining, and in these the craft element is relatively small. Part of the problem of interpretation here is that agreements, even in sectors with a low craft content, may be designed to deal with problems associated with the craftsmen; thus in chemicals and refining, agreements have dealt with issues of craft flexibility and interchangeability even though the craft element is numerically small. Probably more important is the fact that productivity bargaining was proving capable of dealing with a wide range of labour utilisation problems which were far from being confined to craft areas.

A third suggested impetus to productivity bargaining was the presence of high levels of overtime working (hypothesis 5). We have already seen that in some cases, such as at Fawley and in electricity supply, high levels of overtime were among the most important factors leading to productivity bargaining. At a more general level it is difficult to determine the strength of this relationship for the early 1960s, partly because of data problems and partly because of the fall of normal weekly hours in most industries. However, according to Whybrew, in April 1966,

> All of the 129 industries covered in the Ministry of Labour enquiry showed average hours in excess of the normal week, in 52 the excess was more than 5 hours and in 3 it was above 12 hours. The bulk of industries, however, have . . . an overtime average of between four and seven hours per man per week. This . . . is an industry-wide average using a measure which understates the extent of overtime.[12]

In short, there were few industries which could not be said to have some experience of the persistent overtime problem. Further examination suggests that there is no consistent pattern relating the extent of overtime and the incidence of productivity bargaining. Of 18 industries identified by Whybrew as persistently high over-

[12] E. G. Whybrew, *Overtime Working in Britain*, Royal Commission Research Paper No. 9 (London : H.M.S.O., 1968) 15.

time sectors over a twelve-year period, there is no strong reflection of productivity bargaining experience as measured against the agreements listed in Table 2.3. And again, some industries with a high level of average weekly hours (such as mining and quarrying other than coal; construction; and bricks, pottery, glass and cement) *and* industries with relatively low levels of hours worked (such as clothing and footwear; textiles; and vehicles) are not notable for their early use of productivity bargaining. Thus while many industries could have been encouraged to take up productivity bargaining because of their overtime levels, there does not appear to be any necessary connection between levels of overtime and the incidence of productivity bargaining.

With respect to the 'trigger effect' explanation advanced earlier (hypothesis 6), there is some affirmative evidence, not only in oil refining where we might expect the Fawley example to be followed, but also in civil aviation, metal manufacturing, chemicals and ship-building. Such pressures, however, are largely absent from the transport and distribution sectors, for example, where productivity bargaining had also obtained a foothold. There are some signs, too, that productivity bargaining made advances in areas characterised by employment insecurity (hypothesis 7), such as printing and ship-building, but many other cases in areas of employment growth imply that no unique explanation is to be found in this factor.

In summary, although a number of the hypotheses are consistent with some of the evidence, many of the explanatory factors are not mutually exclusive – no unique or dominant influence seems to be at work. Quite different industrial situations, characterised by different market, technical and manpower conditions, were all amenable to an approach through productivity bargaining.

Apart from the possible influence of industrial conditions, it was argued that the spread of productivity bargaining might be influenced by two types of demonstration effect (hypotheses 8 and 9). How far can these kinds of influence be detected? Certainly the attack on labour costs at Fawley quickly spread to other refineries, and in view of the close connection between oil refining and other branches of the chemical industry it is not surprising to find that these latter featured early in the development phase, undoubtedly assisted by feature articles in trade journals, and personal contacts at conferences and in the normal course of business. It is also worth noting that a substantial proportion of the agreements in distribution were negotiated by the oil companies which, having explored the possibilities in the refining side of their business, turned their attention to the distributive function.

Similarly, there are signs of a strong demonstration effect in shipbuilding during the period 1965–6. For example, Mr Norman Sloan, Director of the Shipbuilding Employers' Federation, argued in 1965 that

> Employers have paid money for the removal of restrictive prac-
> tices and other unions come along and say, 'We have never had
> these restrictions: what are you going to give us?' We are
> finding that one district is played off against another district,
> and one yard against another. Wage costs have gone up by 20
> per cent in the last 12 months. (Reported in the *Glasgow Herald*,
> 24 November 1965.)

Other examples are to be found in passenger transport, civil aviation and the steel industry, though the initial impetus in these cases came rather late in the period. This demonstration effect within the industry is not, of course, the key to the whole picture either, for there were other efforts which appear quite independent.

As for the demonstration effect within the local labour market, the evidence is conflicting. Investigations by the National Board for Prices and Incomes could find no trace of particular productivity agreements having an effect on the pay-rates of other firms.[13] Yet, as the quotation from Mr Sloan shows, employers undoubtedly believed that such a pressure was being exerted. A recent study by John Addison[14] of productivity bargaining in the Southampton labour market area suggests that coercive comparison within the market has caused the primary productivity agreements to act as a standard for others following later, resulting in a narrowing of the overall wage structure. This again must be regarded as evidence of an active demonstration effect, not only with respect to the incidence of productivity bargaining, but also to the level of settlement.

While there may not always be an obvious connection between industrial sectors in which productivity bargaining occurred, there

---

[13] See N.B.P.I., Report No. 123, *Productivity Agreements*, Cmnd 4136 (London: H.M.S.O., 1969).

[14] John Addison, *The effect of productivity agreements on patterns of wages in a local labour market in the period 1960–1970*, unpublished Ph.D. dissertation (London University).

was in many cases a unifying influence from the trade union side rather than that of the employer. Thus unions like the Transport and General Workers' Union and the Electrical Trades Union, which were involved in a number of the early agreements, saw in this mode of approach a means of improving the position of their members to an extent unlikely to be achieved by conventional bargaining, and opportunities to introduce this approach were not likely to be overlooked. Again, reports of particular agreements in union journals and intra-union contacts were almost certainly of importance.

Finally, virtually all the agreements in this early period were negotiated by large companies, many of which were not federated or were, for some reason, relatively free to set their own pace independently of an employers' association.[15] There is a good representation of 'household names' like the oil companies, I.C.I., the shipbuilding firms such as John Brown and Vickers, the Steel Company of Wales, Alcan, etc., while the public sector was also remarkably strong, including electricity supply, the Post Office, B.E.A. and B.O.A.C., and British Railways. While there were exceptions (such as the smaller shipyards), they were very few in number, and there was in addition a small number of agreements negotiated by employers' associations.

This account has inevitably been illustrative and final conclusions must await further examination of the evidence in the second phase of development. For this first phase, however, it must be accepted that none of the various hypotheses on the incidence of productivity bargaining stands out as a unique or even a predominant explanation. We can perhaps see in particular industries a *combination* of factors which led to real scope for applying productivity bargaining techniques – shipbuilding, for example, was subject to strong international competition and unfavourable productivity comparisons, it was marked by employment insecurity and it had a strong craft element in its labour force. Elsewhere the motivating forces were different. Although some clustering of agreements in industrial sectors is evident, we should probably not attach too much weight to the industrial characteristics, and should instead consider whether the impetus did not lie in the circumstances of the individual company or plant. In this connection,

---

[15] By way of caution, however, we should also recognise that similar agreements in small companies are more liable to have gone unnoticed.

there is a fairly strong indication that some agreements have exerted a demonstration effect both within the originating industry and within the local labour market area.

4. INFORMATION AND OPINION

To conclude this chapter, we take up briefly the questions of the dissemination of information on productivity bargaining and initial reactions to it in influential quarters.

Information on an innovation is a necessary part of the diffusion process and we have seen some indications of the transfer process, working out from refining to the chemical industry and parts of the transport and distributive sectors. Apart from this sort of 'trade' dissemination, there was also an important stirring of discussion of the innovation in much wider circles. In this, it is hard to overstate the impact of Allan Flanders's contribution to the understanding of the objectives and principles of productivity bargaining. Already established as one of the leading academics in the field of industrial relations and respected by practitioners as well as theorists, Flanders published his detailed analysis of the Fawley experiment in 1964. The book at once received a great deal of publicity and was quickly followed up by a great number of journalistic impressions and assessments of the Fawley events. It is, of course, true that in areas like electricity supply, shipbuilding, and public transport, events with essentially similar characteristics had been taking place before 1964, to a large extent independently of the Fawley negotiations, so that perhaps even without the publicity given to Esso's efforts by Flanders the phenomenon of productivity bargaining would have developed on a very wide front. Nevertheless, it is difficult to imagine that without the work of Flanders the concept of the productivity agreement would have been so well established in so short a time.

A second wave of information stemmed from the early work of the National Board for Prices and Incomes. In the first year of its work, the Board contributed not only to the general appreciation of productivity bargaining but to advancement of some negotiations already begun on productivity lines. Examples include road haulage, printing, bakery work, bank staff, and bus transport.[16] Even at this early stage, the Board could be said to have begun to act as a catalyst in the process of industrial change, and in productivity bargaining in particular.

These remarks, together with the illustrations at the start of this chapter on the growing awareness of the productivity problem and its relevance to wages, might suggest that these new ideas fell on fertile and receptive soil. Yet there were areas where this was not so. A notable example occurred in the written evidence to the Royal Commission on Trade Unions and Employers' Associations from the Confederation of British Industry in 1965. The C.B.I. evidence alluded to the difficulties posed by plant productivity bargaining for incomes policy, and for the continuation of a strong system of industry-wide bargaining.[17] But perhaps above all it saw productivity bargaining as an aggravation to the already prevalent sore of competitive bidding-up of wages :

> Even where plant productivity bargains were concluded, the higher pay agreed in one bargain would quickly spread to other plants while the more efficient use of labour features of the bargain would not be exported.[18]

Only in 1968 did the Council of the C.B.I. see fit to retract somewhat on this view, having come in the interim to appreciate the 'valuable changes in attitudes and practices' which could derive from 'genuine' productivity bargaining.

Although the Trades Union Congress was much less hasty in putting its evidence to the Royal Commission, its general views on productivity bargaining had become known by the end of 1965 through the medium of a pamphlet in which general approval of the idea was granted, provided it was utilised as a complement to conventional bargaining and not as a substitute for it. It was certainly not to displace the conventional criteria of collective bargaining such as increases in the cost of living, profits and com-

---

[16] It is only fair to note that in its *First General Report* for the period April 1965 to July 1966, the Board intimated its awareness of certain difficulties arising from productivity agreements and explicitly sought a reference incorporating a number of these – a request that was quickly granted.

[17] *Selected Written Evidence Submitted to the Royal Commission* (London : H.M.S.O., 1968) C.B.I. First Memorandum, paras 90–2.

[18] *Selected Written Evidence*, para. 114.

parability. This view was affirmed when the T.U.C. came to present its evidence to the Royal Commission late in 1966. A fair summary of the T.U.C. view is expressed in the following conclusion :

> Whilst therefore there may be much to learn from the techniques of productivity bargaining, the idea that it represents some sort of panacea for Britain's economic problems is mistaken.[19]

Like the C.B.I., the T.U.C. also saw difficulties in marrying productivity bargaining at plant level to the well-established national system of collective bargaining, though – also in common with the C.B.I. – it thought that common characteristics in an industry could be made the subject of an industry agreement. If the T.U.C. was rather more open-minded on the possibilities of productivity bargaining (and it had an extra year's experience behind it) it is still true to say that both the C.B.I. and the T.U.C. had serious reservations about the future development of this sort of agreement, wishing to see it occupy a secondary role in relation to the conventional bargaining at industry level and thereby posing less of a threat to the interests of centralised union and employers' organisations. We will see in the next chapter how some of the individual members of these two bodies tried to tackle the problems thus identified.

This concludes our examination of the first phase of productivity bargaining. It is evident that the productivity agreement had very quickly made its mark on the British industrial relations scene, offering a new means of solution to a long-standing set of problems that were at this time being spotlighted by the general condition of the economy and many of its constituent industries hard pressed by foreign competition. Even in this short space of time, it had been taken up in quite a number of branches of industry and the process of adaptation of principle and technique that was so necessary if the idea was to be diffused had already got well under way. There were many factors working in favour of its widespread application but difficulties were also becoming recognised, as witness the observations of the N.B.P.I., the C.B.I. and the T.U.C. What might have been its future in the absence of the prices and incomes stand-

---

[19] T.U.C. *First Memorandum of Evidence* to the Royal Commission, para. 252.

still of July to December 1966 and the subsequent phase of hard-line incomes restraint is a matter of conjecture. In the event, the development of incomes policy in the period 1967 to 1970 was to have an overwhelming influence on the spread and evolution of the productivity bargain.

3 The Second Phase: 1967–70

Our dividing line between the first and second phases of productivity bargaining is the period of the prices and incomes standstill, from July to December 1966. The standstill itself was the consequence of a major economic crisis which came to a head in the middle of 1966, ushering in a period of stringent government control over the movement of prices and wages. The particular form taken by this strict control led to widespread pursuit of bargaining on a productivity basis, and we look first at the circumstances which attended this development. From this, we turn to an analysis of the characteristics of agreements passing through the incomes policy net, and the processes of growth and evolution, already investigated in the first phase, will be further discussed.

1. THE IMPACT OF THE INCOMES POLICY[1]

With the signing in December 1964 of the Joint Statement of Intent on Productivity, Prices and Incomes by the main employers' organisations, the Trades Union Congress and representatives of Government, it was at once clear that the incoming Labour Government accepted the need for a policy for the control of prices

[1] Our interests in incomes policy in this book are twofold: to examine how the form of the incomes policy provided an impetus for the spread of productivity bargaining, and to consider the nature and efficiency of the control over productivity bargaining exerted by the prices and incomes policy. The latter point will be taken up in Chapter 4, but in this section our main concern is the role played by the incomes policy in diffusing the practice of productivity bargaining. As a result, the account of incomes policy given here may seem incomplete, but it is no part of our purpose to analyse and describe the policy as a whole, with all its variations of content and alterations in supporting machinery and legislation.

and incomes. The Joint Statement served notice of an attempt to carry this policy through on a voluntary and co-operative basis, rather than through direct control by legislation and statutory powers.

THE NEED FOR AN INCOMES POLICY

At this point a brief digression on the reasoning behind this general agreement on the need for an incomes policy is useful as a background to subsequent developments. The British economy in the early sixties was continuing to show the same symptoms of malaise that had plagued it in most of the postwar period : a tendency to inflation, a resultant lack of competitiveness in international markets with obvious consequences for the balance of payments and for sterling and, because of these difficulties, an inability to achieve the levels of real economic growth of which the economy was thought to be capable. The extent to which the inflation was due to demand or to cost factors was a matter of continuing debate, and while this was not resolved, the early sixties were marked by a shift in policy which became increasingly concerned with improvements in the infrastructure of the economy and with the removal of possible obstacles to faster growth in the shape of inefficient operation of markets, factor shortages and misallocations and defects in the institutional framework of the economic system.

Not the least of these new developments was related to the labour market and industrial relations system.[2] In particular, growing concern was shown for the inflationary effects arising from a sellers' market for labour in which wage increases could be relatively easily secured, and a buoyant domestic market for goods and services in which cost increases could be absorbed in price increases without undue inhibition of demand. In this context, the criteria for wage increases were principally those of 'comparability' between groups of workers and cost-of-living changes, with scant regard being paid to the underlying economic relationship between

---

[2] At this point, we need only mention some of the other innovations to be aware of the scope of governmental intervention : items include legislation on industrial training, redundancy payments and conditions of employment; the detailed work of the National Board for Prices and Incomes; the setting up of the Commission on Industrial Relations and the modernisation of the Ministry of Labour, now the Department of Employment; and the introduction of the selective employment tax and its regional variant.

changes in input and output. The operation of the comparability criterion could conceivably have been made less pervasive by a deliberate policy of cutting back on aggregate demand and hence the demand for labour, until the bargaining power of the unions deriving from full employment was neutralised. Instead, the policy-makers opted for the maintenance of full employment and sought to deal with the wage-inflation problems by means of an incomes policy designed to keep the rate of increase of wages and salaries in line with the growth of productivity.

Our main interest is in the form taken by this policy and the reasoning behind it. To devise and implement a purely restrictive policy was not difficult, as the Selwyn Lloyd 'pay pause' (1962) and the Labour Government's 'standstill' (1966) testify. A policy for the control of price increases could also be developed, partly to influence the growth of profits, partly to stabilise the cost of living and so make more acceptable a slower growth of money incomes. But controls of this kind are feasible only for relatively short periods, and it has usually been argued that an incomes policy should provide a programme for the continuing growth of incomes in an equitable fashion consistent with economic efficiency. The problem is to give this operational effect.

Given an objective of bringing about a closer relationship between increases in money wages and productivity growth, the policy-maker could proceed along two paths. First, attempts could be made to divert the parties to collective bargaining away from the conventional bargaining criteria of comparability and cost-of-living changes and towards the relation between increases in pay and productivity improvement. And secondly, the policy could seek to raise productivity itself, thus permitting non-inflationary settlements to be reached at a higher level of pay. In particular, in view of the accumulated evidence on the extent to which productivity could be improved by better deployment and utilisation of labour, it seemed feasible to encourage the bargainers to explore the possibilities for removing restrictive work practices within the context of wage negotiations.

One drawback in this dual approach was that the collective bargaining system as a whole was not well adapted for this kind of negotiation, since the system was formally based on industry-wide bargains that were generally incapable of dealing with plant-level productivity issues. Nor was it easy to see how the supplementary bargaining taking place informally at plant level could be made to accommodate the desired changes so long as the industry-wide agreements continued to restrict individual companies' scope for manoeuvre. What seemed necessary was a more thorough-going revision of the collective bargaining system than could be achieved by an incomes policy *per se*. This task of revision was given over to the Royal Commission in 1965, but understandably, if incomes policy could contribute to the same objective, that would be all to the good.

Given these requirements, we can see why the productivity bargaining innovation offered an attractive prospect to the policy-makers. The productivity agreement directly sought to relate increases in pay to improvements in productivity, principally from increased effort and more adaptability on the part of the workforce. The criteria used in such bargaining were related to the actual conditions at plant or company level rather than some amorphous industrial average, so that many of the ambiguities and sources of disorder in the dual system of collective bargaining could be more clearly identified and dealt with.

Thus it was possible to assign a policy role to productivity bargaining. The encouragement of productivity bargaining, together with other provisions to deal with low-paid workers and possible anomalies arising out of a controlled system, would constitute a policy to control the growth of incomes. Coupled with a policy of price restraint, it would contribute to a stabilisation of the inflationary forces. In the events which followed the Joint Statement of Intent in December 1964, we can detect a fairly close parallel with the line of thought we have just set out.

THE DEVELOPMENT OF INCOMES POLICY, 1965–9

In April 1965 a White Paper on incomes policy[3] established a 3 to $3\frac{1}{2}$ per cent norm for annual wage and salary increases, subject to certain exceptions (to be kept to a minimum and balanced by increases beneath the norm). Increases above the norm would be permitted

(i) where employees made a 'direct contribution' towards increasing productivity;

[3] *Prices and Incomes Policy*, Cmnd 2639 (London: H.M.S.O., 1965).

  (ii)   where a pay increase above the norm was necessary to
           secure a reallocation of labour in the national interest;

  (iii)   where existing wage levels were too low to allow a reason-
           able standard of living; and

  (iv)   where pay had fallen seriously out of line with payment
           for similar work and needed in the national interest to be
           improved.

The first condition is our main concern here, and it is worth spelling out in full. Exceptional pay increases might be allowed

> where the employees concerned, for example by accepting more
> exacting work or a major change in working practices, make a
> direct contribution towards increasing productivity in the par-
> ticular firm or industry. Even in such cases some of the benefit
> should accrue to the community as a whole in the form of lower
> prices.[4]

With occasional modifications, this condition was to remain a
standard element in the successive versions of the incomes policy
in the period down to 1970.

Despite the general agreement about the need for a prices, productivity and incomes policy, the effects of the 1965 version of the
policy were minimal, and there was no very obvious sign that the
general course of collective bargaining was much influenced by
the criteria set out in Cmnd 2639.[5] However, the National Board
for Prices and Incomes was established to provide machinery
for the examination of key settlements and price changes, and
although initially without any real powers, the Board from the
outset accepted the desirability of introducing a productivity theme
into its inquiries.

This phase of policy lasted until July 1966, by which time the
threats of economic crisis present over the previous year or so had
become harsh reality, and on 20 July 1966 a 'standstill' on prices
and incomes was introduced, to last until the end of the year. This
was to be followed by a further six months of very marginal relaxation. The standstill saw the end of the voluntary policy. By
August a Prices and Incomes Act was in force, establishing the

---

[4] *Prices and Incomes Policy*, para. 15.

[5] As witness, for example, the challenge to the policy from the railway
workers and the seamen.

N.B.P.I. on a statutory basis, and providing legal backing to the standstill.

Among its many effects, the standstill intervened in the implementation of a number of productivity agreements. These included major agreements at the British Oxygen Company, Smithfield market, in the baking industry, in electrical contracting and in a number of Clyde shipyards; this last group was allowed to go ahead after only a short delay, the others were held back until at least the beginning of 1967.

This standstill of just over five months provided a breathing space in which it was hoped that productivity would make up some of the ground it had lost to wage and price increases in the last year or so. With the introduction of the period of 'severe restraint',[6] covering the first six months of 1967, the norm for the annual rate of increase of money incomes per head remained at zero but it was envisaged that a limited number of exceptions might be conceded. These exceptions were essentially the four 'gateways' of the 1965 White Paper, though now more precisely stated. The 'severe restraint' document included the statement that :

> Agreements designed to increase productivity and efficiency have an important part to play in improving our national economic performance and *will be given priority* during the severe restraint period.[7]

The significance of this condition was not lost on the parties to collective bargaining. Of the four ways open to any negotiated increase in wages, the productivity gateway offered the best chance of success. Only a small part of the working population could expect to benefit from the 'low-pay' criterion, while arguments that pay rises were necessary either to attract labour for essential work[8] or to prevent 'gross anomalies' in payment would be difficult to sustain. On the other hand, many sectors of industry could see some

[6] *Prices and Incomes Standstill: Period of Severe Restraint*, Cmnd 3150 (London : H.M.S.O., 1966).

[7] *Prices and Incomes Standstill*, para. 27 : italics added.

[8] The early work of the N.B.P.I. had in any case made it obvious that it would not look favourably on wage increases aimed at improving the labour supply position. The way out of this problem, according to the Board, was to examine ways in which existing labour could be more efficiently used. Cf. especially the N.B.P.I. Report (No. 16) on the *Pay and Conditions of Busmen*, Cmnd 3012 (London : H.M.S.O., 1966).

sources of possible productivity gain, and there was now a considerable body of experience and knowledge of productivity bargaining. Admittedly there might be difficulties even here, for not only was the condition of Cmnd 2639 reiterated – that some of the benefit of increased productivity should accrue to the community as a whole in the form of lower prices – but it was now stipulated in Cmnd 3150 that payment of increases on productivity grounds should be dependent on a 'firm assessment' of the improvement in productivity and not paid 'on account'. At the same time, the N.B.P.I. in a report entitled *Productivity and Pay during the Period of Severe Restraint* set out seven tests for agreements seeking to achieve increases under the productivity condition which, if strictly applied, would severely curtail the number of exceptions. Despite such obstacles, it still seemed that the best hope of many groups of workers for an increase in wages was by way of the productivity gateway.

After the period of severe restraint, gradual relaxations in the incomes policy were introduced. From July 1967 until June 1968 *any* increase in pay was expected to be justified against one of the four gateway conditions, with priority being given to agreements designed to improve productivity or improve the relative position of the low-paid sector.[9]

The continued economic problems led to devaluation of sterling in November 1967. Early in 1968 a new White Paper on prices and incomes[10] established a 'ceiling' of 3.5 per cent per year for wage increases in place of the norm, though once more *all* increases were to be justified by one of the four criteria. The 'ceiling' itself, however, was not absolute. It could be exceeded in two ways: where agreements 'genuinely' raised productivity and increased efficiency by a margin adequate to justify a pay rise above 3.5 per cent; and where settlements involved 'major reorganisation of wage and salary structures which can be justified on productivity and efficiency grounds'.

Three points of importance are to be discerned here. First, the productivity gateway was now singled out above the other three as a means to increases above the so-called 'ceiling', and its attrac-

[9] *Prices and Incomes Policy after 30th June 1967*, Cmnd 3235 (London: H.M.S.O., 1967).

[10] *Productivity, Prices and Incomes Policy in 1968 and 1969*, Cmnd 3590 (London: H.M.S.O., 1968).

tions were no doubt enhanced in consequence. Secondly, to this condition was added a new element, again depending on a productivity condition but hinging on reform of the pay structure. Thirdly, a more general form of reference to 'productivity *and* efficiency' was introduced, presumably to cover white-collar and other groups whose work did not lend itself easily to a narrow interpretation of productivity. The effect of these second and third points was to broaden the coverage of workers who might hope to gain increases above the ceiling and to widen the avenues of approach to this end.

These last two points were more fully developed both in the second full report[11] on productivity agreements by the N.B.P.I. in August 1969 (which led to some revision of the earlier guidelines of the 1967 report) and in the final White Paper from the Labour Government[12] on prices and incomes. No formal incomes policy existed between the change of government in mid-1970 and November 1972, although some attempts were made to secure a progressive reduction in the size of pay settlements.

The main conclusion from this retrospective view of the productivity theme in the incomes policy is that there has been from the outset a significant emphasis on the need for wage increases to be directly related to productivity improvement. But the operational effect of this was substantially increased by the highly restrictive phase of the incomes policy from January 1967 to mid-1969, during which some form of productivity agreement was the most probable means to achieve either *any* wage rise at all or an increase above the norm or ceiling. It is a reasonable expectation that this feature of the incomes policy would be reflected in a growing number of agreements based on productivity improvements, compared with the pre-1967 period.

Before we go on to examine the actual course of development, some explanation of the machinery by which these controls operated on wage increases is necessary. Under the Prices and Incomes Act of August 1966, the Minister of Labour had up to 30 days to decide whether to refer proposals for wage increases to the N.B.P.I. If he did so, the increase could be delayed until the Board reported,

[11] N.B.P.I. Report No. 123, *Productivity Agreements*, Cmnd 4136 (London: H.M.S.O., 1969).

[12] *Productivity, Prices and Incomes Policy after 1969*, Cmnd 4237 (London: H.M.S.O., 1969).

for which it was allowed a period of three months. This amounted only to a power of delay, for an adverse finding by the Board could be ignored.[13] The power of delay was strengthened a year later by the 1967 Prices and Incomes Act, which gave government power to delay a proposed increase for up to six months if the Board reported adversely. The 1968 Act further extended this power over a period of eleven months in the case of an adverse report (i.e. up to twelve months in all).

During this period 1967–9, the Ministry of Labour (later the Department of Employment and Productivity) compiled a register of pay cases accepted by them under the productivity criteria of successive incomes policy White Papers. Our examination of the course of productivity bargaining during this period is largely based on data extracted from this register with the kind co-operation and assistance of the D.E.P. although subject to safeguards on the confidentiality of information furnished by individual employers. This procedure provides invaluable information on the development of productivity bargaining but it does raise a difficulty, in that some of the agreements recorded in this register were not productivity agreements in the strict sense of the term as understood before 1966; nor, as the N.B.P.I. noted in its report number 123, did they all come within the 'definition of a productivity agreement' given by the Board.

Many of the so-called productivity agreements between 1967 and 1969 were not preceded by the processes that might be regarded as the hallmark of productivity bargaining in the first phase; such as problem identification, joint negotiation on means to the solution of the problem and mutual development of an acceptable trade-off between changes in practice and changes in pay. However, the whole environment had changed as a result of the incomes policy. Companies were still under as much pressure from unions as before to increase pay and, given the constraints of the policy, the priority became one of first determining an acceptable award and then finding some means of justifying that increase under the policy, rather than identifying desirable

---

[13] Under Part IV of the 1966 Act the Government could impose a standstill on wage or price increases: Part IV was not brought into effect until October 1966: it remained in force until August 1967, by which time Part II had been activated, giving statutory backing to the government's powers of delay over prices and wages increases.

changes and estimating what increases in pay they might be held to warrant on the basis of cost savings.

Without accepting as 'productivity agreements', in the pre-1967 sense of the term, all agreements officially held to have fulfilled the productivity conditions of the incomes policy, it is unrealistic to confine attention only to agreements which would have conformed to the first-phase definition. Such a restriction would fail to recognise that productivity bargaining was a dynamic idea, capable of being adapted to cover new problems and new situations and inevitably, in so doing, taking on new characteristics. We feel justified, therefore, in subjecting the complete D.E.P. register to the same kind of analysis as was conducted for the earlier agreements, though it is only proper to draw attention to the changes in conditions that had occurred between the first and the second phase. Some of the implications of this alteration in scope and circumstance will be more thoroughly explored in later chapters.

2. GROWTH AND INCIDENCE

The sheer volume of agreements in the second phase of productivity bargaining as compared with the 73 agreements in the earlier period makes it possible to undertake a more systematic analysis of some of the questions raised. A description of the D.E.P. data and some problems they presented is given in the Appendix to this chapter. It must be noted that some deficiencies were found in these data and some residual inaccuracies may exist. Extreme care is needed in the interpretation of some figures, especially if used for any purpose other than the present one of observing broad trends and the relative importance of particular features.[14]

[14] One point in particular requires comment. The register was originally intended to be confined, broadly speaking, to agreements in the private sector of industry, presumably on the ground that within the public sector ministerial control or some other form of official surveillance would be exercised to ensure that collective agreements came within the terms of the policy. However, subsequent attempts were made to enlarge the register to cover public sector pay agreements, but these were never completed. After considering whether the information on the register could be accurately extended to include the omitted agreements, it was decided that this was not practicable and the register was analysed as it stood. This does, however, mean that in some industry groups, such as gas, electricity and water, the register fails to record a measure of productivity bargaining activity which undoubtedly took place: on the other hand, the representation of 'eligible' agreements in the transport sector seems to be fairly high.

Our procedure was to allocate each recorded agreement to one of six six-monthly periods between January 1967 and December 1969.[15] As far as possible the date used was the date at which the agreement came into effect. In addition to dating, information was recorded on the location of the firm, the minimum list heading, the number of workers covered by the agreement, the occupational levels of workers covered, and the main features of the agreement, subdivided into achievement and reward changes – these two latter categories being identical to the classification used in the previous chapter.

GROWTH OF PRODUCTIVITY AGREEMENTS

The number of agreements recorded for the three-year period was 4091, distributed between the various sub-periods as follows:

January 1967–June 1968 (18 months)	761
July–December 1968	1107
January–June 1969	977
July–December 1969	874
Date not recorded	372

Set against the results of the previous chapter, the increase in agreements revealed by these figures is dramatic. While the agreements in the first eighteen-month period after January 1967 cannot be accurately allocated to sub-periods, there is enough evidence to show that while 1967 as a whole already saw a marked jump in the number of agreements, compared with the previous four years, the major increase came in 1968, with a peak in the second half of 1968, after which there was a slight tailing-off. In the first half of 1967, the period of severe restraint was in force, to be followed in the next twelve months by a phase of policy in which priority was given to agreements designed to raise productivity or to improve the position of low-paid workers. Cmnd 3590 (of April 1968) introduced the $3\frac{1}{2}$ per cent ceiling, with the exception of cases justifying a higher increase on grounds of exceptional productivity and efficiency improvement. No doubt this has some part to play

---

[15] In practice, due to some defects in the recording of dates of agreements, we were obliged to merge the first three periods, so that the analysis over time is based on the intervals: January 1967–June 1968; July 1968–December 1968; January 1969–June 1969; July 1969–December 1969.

in the explanation of the peak in agreements during the second half of 1968. Incomes policy, therefore, appears to have had a considerable influence on the development of productivity bargaining.

This rapid upsurge in the number of agreements led to a major increase in the number of employees covered. Two alternative measures of coverage are possible, however. Whereas most of the agreements during the first phase had been related to the company or to the workplace, a number in the second phase were negotiated at industry level, taking the form of 'enabling' or 'framework' agreements designed to open up the way for companies party to the industry agreement to negotiate their own detailed productivity deals. The small number of these framework agreements carries a disproportionate significance because, by their nature, they tended to cover large numbers of workers. From the D.E.P. data we were able to identify 76 such agreements which covered a total of 4.5 million workers : the remaining 4015 agreements covered only 3.7 million workers.

The decision whether or not to include the framework agreements in our analysis was difficult. The form of these agreements varied, with some including a concessionary increase in pay as a sweetener to encourage the trade unions to accept the principle of workplace productivity bargaining. A number of agreements, too, included general references to the kinds of change in working practice envisaged as elements in subsequent workplace deals. From this viewpoint, all workers covered by the framework agreements could be held to be subject to the conditions of productivity bargaining. In contrast, it is known that many firms able under the terms of a framework agreement to negotiate separate productivity agreements did not do so, and from this point of view the inclusion of all workers embraced by framework deals would exaggerate the true coverage of productivity bargaining.

In the following discussion, where the *coverage* of agreements seems relevant, we will in general show both sets of figures, leaving some discretion in interpretation to the reader. In any case, there is a margin of error in the coverage figures, since it is known that some workers were covered by more than one productivity agreement during the period, while some comparable agreements in the public sector were omitted from the D.E.P. register. A realistic estimate of the total workers covered at least once during the

Table 3.1. *Number of Agreements and Number of Workers Covered, by Main Order Heading (1958 S.I.C.)*[1]

Main order heading	Number of agreements		Number of workers covered[2]		Percentage of labour force covered[3]	
I. Agriculture, forestry & fishing	8	(8)	3,215	(3,215)	1	(1)
II. Mining & quarrying	13	(12)	14,954	(4,954)	3	(1)
III. Food, drink & tobacco	635	(632)	381,060	(361,060)	48	(45)
IV. Chemicals & allied industries	250	(248)	391,562	(329,562)	78	(66)
V. Metal manufacture	222	(215)	158,997	(73,897)	27	(13)
VI. Engineering & electrical goods	786	(783)	4,263,967	(536,037)	100+	(24)
VII. Shipbuilding & marine engineering	158	(158)	80,402	(80,402)	43	(43)
VIII. Vehicles	319	(319)	511,904	(511,904)	64	(64)
IX. Metal goods	162	(160)	144,243	(128,143)	26	(23)
X. Textiles	93	(83)	200,331	(94,737)	29	(14)
XI. Leather, leather goods, fur	4	(4)	1,439	(1,439)	3	(3)
XII. Clothing & footwear	10	(8)	3,842	(2,342)	1	(1)
XIII. Bricks, pottery, glass, cement	95	(91)	118,704	(98,610)	34	(28)
XIV. Timber, furniture, etc.	37	(34)	78,025	(37,325)	24	(12)

XV. Paper, printing, publishing	328	(311)	286,837	(142,311)	45	(22)
XVI. Other manufacturing industries	125	(124)	64,588	(63,288)	19	(18)
XVII. Construction	30	(28)	37,206	(32,806)	3	(2)
XVIII. Gas, electricity & water	not recorded		not recorded		—	
XIX. Transport & communication	327	(322)	599,638	(369,918)	38	(23)
XX. Distributive trades	202	(196)	319,813	(307,625)	12	(11)
XXI. Insurance, banking & finance	75	(74)	196,905	(187,004)	6	(6)
XXII. Professional & scientific services	12	(12)	2,491	(2,491)	0	(0)
XXIII. Miscellaneous services	66	(60)	275,953	(268,438)	18	(18)
XXIV. Public administration & defence	7	(6)	2,617	(2,617)	0	(0)
Order heading not known	127	(127)	75,398	(75,398)	—	—
TOTAL	4,091	(4,015)	8,214,091	(3,715,523)	36	(16)

[1] All figures in brackets in this table relate to agreements other than those designated as of the 'framework' type.

[2] 58 agreements did not include information on the number of workers covered.

[3] Number of workers covered by productivity agreements as a percentage of employees in employment at June 1968.

[4] In excess of 100 per cent on account of the double counting of workers covered by both framework and plant agreements.

period might be of the order of 6 million, including those under framework agreements, or less than 3 million if the framework agreements are excluded.

Where the *number* of agreements, rather than their employee coverage, is the important matter, little difference is made to the results by the inclusion of the framework agreements, which are relatively few and we have worked with all 4091 agreements. For reasons discussed in Chapter 2,[16] the number of agreements in an industry cannot be taken as a good measure of the penetration of productivity bargaining.

INDUSTRIAL DISTRIBUTION OF AGREEMENTS

In examining industrial distribution, we will confine attention to the main order headings in the Standard Industrial Classification, partly because some information on minimum list headings was missing or obscure, and partly because the broader classification is sufficient for the argument here. Table 3.1 (page 66) presents the detailed results.

The five industries with the largest number of agreements are engineering and electrical goods; food, drink and tobacco; paper, printing and publishing; transport and communications; and vehicles. While these rank among the largest orders as far as employment is concerned, the pattern is not explained by employment size alone : according to the official figures for employees in employment at June 1969, they rank respectively third, ninth, twelfth, fifth and eighth, while some of the largest orders have few agreements. It is significant also that these five leading orders appeared prominently in productivity bargaining in the period 1963–6, while three other industry groups in the forefront at that time (chemicals, metal manufacture and the distributive trades) were only a little behind in 1967–9, ranking sixth, seventh and eighth respectively in the number of agreements struck.[17] Those industries taking an early interest in productivity bargaining were, therefore, most likely to have an extensive experience of bargaining in the later phase. Moreover, virtually all industries had some experience of this type of agreement between 1967 and 1969, even if in some industries, like agriculture and mining, professional and

---

[16] See p. 44.
[17] Cf. Table 2.1.

scientific services, and public administration, neither the number of agreements nor the proportion of employees covered was large.[18] Even in manufacturing there are some examples of low penetration : for example, leather and fur, and clothing and footwear. Likewise construction ranks near the bottom in terms of agreements and coverage.

HYPOTHESES AND EVIDENCE

In the previous chapter, a number of hypotheses were developed to account for the emergence of productivity bargaining in particular industries, but for the first phase no case could be made out for any one of these as a unique or predominant explanation of the pattern. It remains to be seen whether any such explanation can be advanced for the second phase.

Capital and labour intensity

Hypotheses 1 and 2 related to the role that might be played by capital and labour intensity in encouraging an industry to adopt productivity bargaining extensively. In order to see whether either hypothesis was supported by the evidence for 1967–9, we again used the percentage share of wages and salaries in net output as a measure of labour intensity (high shares being taken as labour intensive). The analysis was confined to the fifteen manufacturing main order headings of the Standard Industrial Classification. Rank correlation coefficients were calculated for labour intensity and the *percentage* of employees covered under each heading, separate calculations being made for all agreements, and for agreements other than those of the framework or industry-wide variety. The Spearman rank correlation coefficients were, respectively, $r_s = -0.379$ and $r_s = -0.318$ but neither was significant at the 5 per cent level. The negative sign might be taken as a weak indication in favour of the capital intensity hypothesis.

Skilled labour

Hypothesis 3 suggested that industries with high proportions of

---

[18] Neither in the case of mining nor public administration is this due to undercounting of public sector agreements.

craft labour might have greater experience of productivity bargaining. To test this, we took as a measure of craft representation the number of apprentices as a percentage of the total labour force, with the highest percentage ranked as '1' and the lowest as '14'. Again, this measure was rank correlated with the proportion of employees covered by productivity agreements in the industry. The resulting Spearman rank correlation coefficients were $r_s = 0.253$ (all agreements) and 0.349 (excluding framework agreements). Neither was significant at the 5 per cent level, but the positive sign may be a weak indication of the expected relationship.

Given that result, we must also conclude that hypothesis 4 is not supported: that is, there is no corroboration of the view that productivity bargaining will be most extensive in industries with a high ratio of non-craft labour. (Support to this hypothesis would have required a negative coefficient in the previous correlation.) It is quite possible, of course, that the ability of productivity bargaining to deal with the problems of semiskilled and unskilled labour (over-manning, systematic overtime, output restrictions, etc.) provided an offset to the craft labour correlation, reducing its significance.

High overtime industries

Hypothesis 5 stated that industries with high levels of regular overtime working would be more likely than low-overtime industries to offer scope for productivity bargaining. Satisfactory overtime figures were difficult to obtain for this purpose, but use was made of the list of high-overtime industries identified by Whybrew.[19] For each of these minimum list heading industries, we obtained the number of agreements recorded, and the percentage of the labour force covered by productivity agreements: the expectation was that these eighteen industries would have a consistently greater experience of productivity bargaining than the average. No such pattern emerged. Taking in for this purpose all 4000-odd agreements to give the most favourable condition, we found that 416 agreements were recorded – 10 per cent of the total. This is almost exactly what we would expect if agreements were distributed randomly among industries; and on the hypothesis as stated we

[19] E. G. Whybrew, *Overtime Working in Britain*, Royal Commission Research Paper No. 9 (London: H.M.S.O., 1968), Table 3, p. 16.

would expect more than this. The number of workers covered by productivity agreements in these eighteen industries was just over 0.5 million, out of a total of over 8 million – about 6 per cent, once again very close to what we would expect on a random distribution. On these two counts, therefore, the overtime hypothesis appears to have no special significance. At the individual industry level, however, six of the eighteen industries had high coverage, all in excess of 40 per cent and three very much higher than this: conversely, five had virtually no productivity bargaining experience. While overtime may have been an important motivating force in certain cases, the weight of the evidence is substantially against a consistent relationship of the kind expected.[20]

On the other hypotheses set out in Chapter 2, a briefer comment will suffice. Hypothesis 6, relating to the trigger effect of international competition or comparison, could not be satisfactorily tested in a systematic way. Casual inspection revealed strong representation of productivity bargaining in industries known to be involved extensively in international competition (e.g. chemicals, refining, vehicles, shipbuilding) but counter-examples can be presented (e.g. inland transport), where high coverage is not associated with such competition.

Hypothesis 7 hinged on the influence of insecurity, and here again, because of the diverse causes of insecurity (discussed in Chapter 2), systematic testing was impracticable. One cause of insecurity is technological change, which we might approximate in a very crude way by gross domestic fixed capital formation per employee. Of the six manufacturing industries with the highest ratio,[21] four were also found among the top six with respect to productivity bargaining coverage: chemicals; food, drink and tobacco; vehicles; printing and publishing. Conversely, among those with a low ranking in terms of productivity bargaining coverage, such as clothing and footwear, and metal goods, the capital formation ratio tended also to be low. While the relationship is far from complete – as witness the high coverage in shipbuilding coupled with an exceptionally low rate of capital formation per employee, there is enough evidence to suggest a loose

---

[20] The allocation of agreements and workers to minimum list heading was necessarily rather crude, and conclusions relating to M.L.H. level must be regarded with caution.

[21] Estimates were made for 1967 only, but the ordering does not change significantly for any one year in the mid-1960s.

connection here, which may be worth exploring by more refined methods.

Another source of insecurity identified in our earlier discussion was industrial decline, but an examination of the list of industries with substantial employment declines in the decade 1956–65 showed no clear connection with the list of industries ranking high in productivity bargaining coverage.

The remaining hypotheses related more to the intra-industry and intra-labour market area aspects of productivity bargaining spread and incidence, and the D.E.P. data do not provide any guidance on this.

A final point concerns the size distribution of agreements. It was argued earlier that productivity bargaining might be expected to occur most readily in large companies, and some information can be gleaned from the D.E.P. data, as Table 3.2 shows.

Table 3.2. Size Distribution of Agreements, 1967–9[1]

Size range (number of employees)	0–25	26–50	51–250	251–500	501–1000	1001–5000	5001 & over
Number of agreements (total)	316	307	1417	752	563	533	140
Number of agreements (excluding 'framework' agreements)	316	305	1407	744	555	517	109

[1] Excluded 63 agreements for which size range was not recorded.

Table 3.2 reveals clearly the significantly larger average size of the industry or framework agreements, only a very few specialised industry groups being represented in the lower ranges. Even with the framework agreements excluded, there is a substantial number of agreements (about 20 per cent of the total) covering in excess of 1000 employees. What is not known, however, is whether these are company-wide agreements or plant agreements, and it is impossible, therefore, to make any accurate assessment of whether the large companies are disproportionately represented – as we would expect.

Similar problems occur in the smaller ranges, where it is not possible to distinguish sectional agreements within a plant from agreements covering whole plants or small companies. (Other evidence reveals that many were in fact sectional deals in large plants or companies.)

CONCLUSIONS

Although the examination of the various hypotheses has proved generally negative, the results have some contribution to make to this study as a whole. The fact that generalisation at industry level is not particularly fruitful is a reflection of the versatility of the productivity bargaining format for collective bargaining, indicative of its ability to cope with manpower utilisation problems in different technical and social conditions of employment, and with inefficiencies in the utilisation of different types of labour. It may also be a further indication that, as suggested in Chapter 2, the motivating forces are better identified at the level of the company or plant, rather than on an industry-wide basis where the differences between companies may prevent important relationships from emerging clearly. Later evidence on individual cases will show that most of the factors built into our hypotheses have, at one time or another, had a part to play in explaining the involvement of companies in productivity bargaining, and in accounting for the particular form it took.

3. CONTENT AND COVERAGE

This section concerns the content of agreements and their occupational coverage. Again the D.E.P. information is our main source material. Five broad occupational categories were identified : skilled, semiskilled, unskilled, clerical, and 'other' (e.g. supervisors). Many agreements covered some mixture of skill categories; in fact, only one agreement in three dealt with a single category, while over 50 per cent involved some combination of manual workers. It is significant that, of the agreements covering a single type of worker, the biggest proportion by far, over 40 per cent, dealt with skilled workers, under 25 per cent dealt with semiskilled, and about 15 per cent each with the clerical and 'other' groups. The inference here may be that skilled workers will more often require separate agreements than any other group, either because of the more specialised nature of their work or because the craft union may be reluctant at times to sign a joint agreement with another union, especially if it is a general or process-worker union.

Since more than one occupational group may be covered in a single agreement, the number of observations relating to occupational groups is in excess of the 4000 agreements analysed. In fact just over 7700 observations are registered in the frequency distribution of occupational groups shown in Table 3.3.

Table 3.3. Agreements Analysed by Occupational Group of Workers Covered

Type of worker	Skilled	Semi-skilled	Un-skilled	Clerical	Other	Total recorded
Number of occasions on which included in agreement	2,374	2,524	1,969	411	433	7,711
As percentage of total cases recorded	31	33	26	5	5	100

The two most common groups covered by agreements were skilled and semiskilled but the relatively equal frequencies of each of the three manual groups would seem to confirm the earlier conclusion that there is no special bias in productivity bargaining toward the skilled groups.[22] The predominance of manual workers is not in itself surprising, since their productivity performance has been most frequently criticised in the past.

There was a gradual increase in the percentage of agreements dealing with clerical workers, whose share rose from 4 to 6 per cent between mid-1968 and the end of 1969. Because of the number of agreements without a firm date, the margins of error elsewhere are too wide to be sure of any trend, but the data do indicate a steady growth, over the period, of agreements affecting skilled workers.

ACHIEVEMENT FEATURES OF THE AGREEMENTS

Of greater analytical interest are the data on changes in the achievement and reward features of the agreements. In the limited

[22] Cf. Section 2 above.

analysis for the first phase of productivity bargaining, the most frequent achievement item was changes in the *nature of work*, involving greater flexibility between crafts and job enlargement, followed by *working hours, manning*, and changes in *the quantity of work*. As Table 3.4 shows, this ordering changed markedly in the second phase of productivity bargaining.

To take first the 1967–9 results: *quantity of work*, so defined as to highlight the speeding up of machines, the elimination of breaks and restriction of output, emerges as the most important single factor, occurring in 30 per cent of the cases. There is little to choose between the three categories, *nature of work, manning*, and *change of methods*, which together account for a further 53 per cent of observations. The only other item of major importance is *working hours*.

Between the two phases, the relative rankings have not altered for the two categories *organisation of work* and *responsibility*, which in both periods are of least importance. Elsewhere, with the exception of *manning* changes, there has been a sharp turnaround.

The two biggest categories in the second phase, *quantity of work* and *change of methods*, were formerly fourth and fifth in the rankings, while changes in the *nature of work* and in *working hours* have slipped from the top two places. The significance of this change will be more fully discussed in a later chapter, but some preliminary points may be noted here.

The items comprising *quantity of work* changes are in general the typical ingredients of the workplace effort bargain, having more to do with the pace of the work than with the more deeply rooted attitudes to property rights in work and the preservation of skill boundaries and status. Yet it was these latter items that were the prime ingredient in the first phase, where changes in the *nature of work* ranked most important. The first inference from this is that during the second phase, agreements tended to be based on the 'easier' items for negotiation and (with some important exceptions) steered clear of the more difficult problems associated with traditional craft jurisdictions. Some rationale for a change of this kind can be found in the background conditions of the second phase, for the pressures of the incomes policy were likely to be such that preference would be given by workers (and in many cases managements) to agreements that could be reached quickly. By contrast, during the first phase, this sort of pressure was absent,

Table 3.4. Frequency of Achievement Features, 1967–9 and Relative Importance in First and Second Phases

Achievement feature	Number of times recorded	Number of times recorded as percentage of total observations[1]	Ranking 1967–9	Ranking 1963–6
1. Quantity of work	2499	30	1	4
2. Nature of work	1409	17	4	1
3. Working hours	945	11	5	2
4. Manning	1472	18	3	3
5. Change of methods	1496	18	2	5
6. Organisation of work	322	4	6	6
7. Responsibility	104	1	7	7
Total	8247[2]	99	–	–

[1] Rounded to nearest whole number: hence figures do not sum to 100.
[2] Many agreements had multiple changes in work features so that the total of observations is in excess of the 4000-odd cases.

and while it was not unimportant that negotiations should be prevented from stretching over too long a period, it was easier to fit them into the normal 'wage-round'. In these circumstances it was more practicable to come to grips with the most difficult issues which required a thorough preparation of the ground and very often a prolonged negotiation phase – which in the second phase might simply prove a source of frustration.

It is not, then, entirely accidental that the three most important achievement features during the second phase should have been mostly concerned with 'effort' issues – quantity of work, change of methods, and manning. The rise in the relative importance of 'methods change', incorporating the introduction of work measurement and job evaluation schemes, is perhaps symptomatic of management's growing perception of the need to increase control over production standards and internal wage structures. Wage structure in particular had become a subject of major criticism in the 1960s, culminating in the Donovan Commission's emphasis on the problem. Again, the course of incomes policy may arguably have played a part in this development, for the 1968 White Paper (Cmnd 3590) encouraged agreements involving 'major reorganisation of wage and salary structures' – the sort of problem which could be tackled by techniques such as job evaluation.

Occupational analysis

A separate analysis was made of those agreements which included only a single occupational category to derive an impression of the relative frequency of achievement features for each of the five occupational categories. The overall ranking of features in these agreements was identical to that for all agreements, except that *manning* changes now came second instead of third and *change of methods* third instead of second. Substantial differences did occur, however, in the distribution of features among the five occupational groups, as Table 3.5 shows.

Only in the case of clerical workers did *quantity of work* not occupy first place, but that in itself is significant, especially since the most common category for this group was *change of methods*, followed closely by *manning*. The implication is that in the clerical occupations, the problems perceived by management are primarily those of work measurement and the presence of 'slack' in the labour

Table 3.5. Frequency of Achievement Features, by Occupational Group

Occupational group	No. of cases	Achievement features[1]							Number of features recorded[2]
		1	2	3	4	5	6	7	
Skilled:	473	226	186	125	160	159	31	17	901
as per cent of total number of features for group	—	25	21	14	18	18	3	2	100
Semiskilled:	274	151	67	70	119	103	13	5	528
as per cent of total number of features for group	—	29	13	13	23	20	2	1	100
Unskilled:	99	57	21	23	41	21	6	1	170
as per cent of total number of features for group	—	34	12	14	24	12	4	0	100
Clerical:	169	81	39	9	85	88	39	6	347
as per cent of total number of features for group	—	23	11	3	24	25	11	2	100
Other:	173	87	57	40	57	66	32	11	350
as per cent of total number of features for group	—	25	16	11	16	19	9	3	100

[1] 1 = quantity of work
2 = nature of work
3 = working hours
4 = manning
5 = change of methods
6 = organisation of work
7 = responsibility.
[2] Percentages do not add to 100 due to rounding.

force. In the clerical group, also, *organisational changes* occupied a much more important role than in any manual group. The reformulation of supervision structures and the creation of new work-group systems implied in the process of organisational change is very much what we would expect to find associated with efforts to reduce slack in the white-collar sector.

Within the manual groups some interesting differences are to be observed. While, for example, *quantity of work* rated most importantly in all cases, it becomes progressively more important as we move from skilled to unskilled. In a complementary way, changes in the *nature of work* (reflecting flexibility of skill) are substantially more important for the skilled worker than for the two other manual grades.[23] Thus, rather more attention has been given to obstacles to the full utilisation of skill in the case of the most highly trained group, while efforts to secure more effective utilisation of working time have proved more important in the case of less skilled workers.

Another indication of differences in the manual grades was the much higher proportion of *change of methods* items in the semi-skilled than in the skilled or unskilled groups. This could well reflect the difficulties of many managements in retaining adequate control over the work performance and wage structure of semiskilled workers, and the growing use of work measurement and job evaluation schemes to cope with the problem.

Industry analysis

An examination of variations in the content of agreements by industry produced little of interest. Briefly, it was found that in 22 of the 24 main order headings changes in the *quantity of work* occupied first place, the only major exception being transport and communication, where changes in *manning* took prior place. Changes in the *nature of work* took second place in some industries, including chemicals, metal manufacture, shipbuilding and metal goods – in all of which issues relating to the use of skilled or

[23] Indeed, a rank correlation coefficient was calculated for the percentage of craft labour in an industry (as measured by the proportion of apprentices in the labour force) and the percentage of all agreements in the industry involving a change in the *nature of work*. The coefficient ($r_s = 0.732$) was significant at the 1 per cent level. (Calculation based on data for 14 manufacturing industries).

specialised labour are important. Other variations were minor and of no obvious significance.

CONCLUSIONS

Between the first and second phases of productivity bargaining there is evidence of a shift towards agreements based on 'effort' issues, which we have suggested may be more easily tackled than those involving alterations in job structure and content. A significant increase also took place in the proportion of agreements introducing change of methods, implying closer attention on the part of managements to the difficulties of work control and wage structures known to be prevalent in many industries. An occupational analysis of the work change features revealed a number of interesting differences. In particular, changes involving greater job flexibility and job enlargement figured more prominently in industries with a high proportion of skilled workers and in the skilled category of manual workers; while in the case of clerical workers, work measurement, manning levels, and revised supervisory arrangements were especially important. Industrial variations in content proved insignificant by comparison.

As an addendum at this point, attention is drawn to the increasingly frequent reference to issues of control in the last few pages, especially with respect to work measurement and job evaluation systems. It is useful to highlight the emergence of this issue, since it is one that will occupy a prominent position in subsequent chapters. The use of productivity bargaining as a means of gaining acceptance for systems for work measurement, job evaluation, and measured daywork, was the superficial reflection of a much deeper issue – the extent to which workers and trade unions were prepared to cede control in matters of work rate and pay to management. With growing experience of productivity bargaining involving these sorts of control systems, unions became increasingly concerned over their longer term implications, and resistance to productivity proposals based on such systems emerged as an important obstacle to the continuation of productivity bargaining in a number of sectors.[24]

---

[24] See below, Chapters 9 and 10.

REWARD FEATURES OF THE AGREEMENTS

An analysis of changes in the reward features of agreements proved less useful than might have been hoped, since the overwhelmingly predominant category was *increase in earnings*. Indeed, in 90 per cent of all cases increased earnings were recorded and in relatively few agreements was more than one reward change registered. Of the 4091 agreements analysed, 3445 had only one such feature, 295 had two features, 27 had three and 5 had four features; insufficient data existed for the remaining three hundred or so. The total distribution of changes in rewards is shown in Table 3.6.

So far as the rankings can be meaningfully compared, *leisure* and *fringe benefits* continued to come second and third respectively behind increased earnings, as they did in the first phase. Attempts to analyse the reward changes more fully in the way that was done for the work changes proved worthless due to the small numbers of observations in categories other than increased earnings. The results here are frankly disappointing,[25] but it is probably true that in any case increased earnings would have emerged as by far the most common category. Not only was this already the case in the first phase, but much of the point of productivity bargaining was the desire to relate increases in earnings to gains in productive performance, and added emphasis to this would be predicted during a period of strict incomes policy. While the data have proved disappointing in this respect, the only real loss may be that it prevents us from obtaining a better picture of the reward side of the agreement *other* than the aspect of increased earnings.

[25] Two comments may be made on this. First, the recording of information on reward change features at some stage in the data preparation may have been less carefully done than elsewhere. There is, however, no obvious reason why this should have been so, though it was possibly more difficult to assess the reward aspects and to place them accordingly. For example, detailed examination of data sheets suggests that a substantial number of agreements involved reduced overtime working. While this would be recorded as an achievement feature, it should presumably also have been recorded as a reward change (increased leisure). Yet the number so recorded in the latter is so small as to suggest that this was not done. This raises the second point, that the original Ministry of Labour design for recording reward changes was much less appropriate than it proved to be for the work changes. In practice it might have been more useful to have had some breakdown of the different ways in which increased earnings were given to the workers: for example, by transfer from piecework to measured daywork, by straightforward increases in basic rates, in the form of bonuses, etc.

Table 3.6. Frequency of Reward Features, 1967–9, and Relative Importance in First and Second Phases

Reward change feature	Number of times recorded	Number of times recorded as percentage of total observations[1]	Ranking 1967–9	Ranking 1963–6
Increased earnings	3,718	90	1	1
Greater leisure	194	5	2	2
Ex gratia payments	4	0	6	4
Improved fringe benefits	131	3	3	3
Redundancy payments	14	0	5	n.k.
Other rewards	75	2	4	n.k.
Total	4,136	100	–	–

[1] Rounded to nearest whole number.

This concludes our principal analysis of the D.E.P. data, although some of their implications will be more fully considered later. We have now seen how the need for an incomes policy emerged and the rationale for its particular form in this period. The impetus to productivity bargaining from that policy has been gauged, and the differences in content and style as compared with the initial phase of development have been examined. However, the statistical analysis does not reveal some of the problems that arose during the second phase of development, very largely because of the way that productivity bargaining became identified as a tool of government policy. This is the theme of the following chapter.

Appendix to Chapter 3

THE D.E.P. REGISTER AS A DATA SOURCE

In June 1967, the N.B.P.I. report on productivity agreements[1] recommended that the Ministry of Labour should make an official collection of information about productivity agreements, to be made available to both sides of industry. A register of pay cases was established, covering agreements accepted by the Ministry under the productivity criteria of successive statements of incomes policy. A *pro forma* was designed to record in some detail the main characteristics of such agreements. With the expansion of this form of bargaining and the growth of other claims on the time of Ministry personnel, a less detailed *pro forma* was employed from May 1968 until February 1969. During this period, some 'backlog' cases were written up by N.B.P.I. staff loaned to the D.E.P. for this purpose. Additionally, agreements dealt with at regional level were registered separately in regional offices. Finally, in February 1969, a third form was introduced, which reverted to a more detailed recording of features, and this remained in use until the end of 1969.

For our purpose, it was necessary to devise an information sheet which could be completed for any agreement, no matter which official form of recording had been used. This meant sacrificing some useful information to get a common basis. A form was designed by the authors with assistance from officials of the Department of Employment. Arrangements were made by the Department to transfer data from the original forms to our 'common

[1] N.B.P.I. Report No. 36, p. 47.

basis' information sheet : at all stages, confidentiality of information relating to particular companies was preserved.

At this stage, a number of practical difficulties emerged. Some of the originals had not been fully completed. It was clear also that duplication had occurred, probably due to double recording at regional and headquarters level. Where cross-checking was possible, it was found that the consistency of the records was not complete. For example, the rather broad scheme for the classification of items appearing in agreements, coupled with the number of officials responsible for the original entries, meant that interpretations differed.

Despite these difficulties, we were able with the help and advice of the Department to clear up many of the problems, and a final stock of records was assembled, as free from duplication and inconsistency as could be achieved. Additional information on minimum list heading classifications had to be provided in a number of cases, but in some instances this proved impossible, and a number of agreements could not be allocated accurately to one of the sub-periods adopted for the purpose of analysis.

One other difficulty requires to be mentioned. The register was found on examination not to cover the whole field because the work on public sector agreements was never completed. No practicable method could be found whereby all the gaps could be filled, and it was decided to proceed with an analysis of the register as it existed rather than add further inconsistency to the recording of information. This does, however, mean that in certain sectors with a major public sector component, such as the gas, electricity and water major order heading, the register substantially under-records the coverage of productivity bargaining. In transport, another sector with strong public sector representation, the coverage appears to be almost complete. This deficiency in particular must be borne in mind throughout the discussion of the statistical analysis.

Overall, the register, and hence the results we have derived from the analysis, must be regarded as fairly crude, and the cardinal reliability of some of the figures must be in doubt. We believe, however, that the general pattern of development and the character of the agreements is well represented by the data.

4 Effects of Government Policy

We have argued that the rapid spread of productivity bargaining during the period 1967–9 was due largely to the incomes policy in force at the time. Now, let us consider some of the policy's consequences for productivity bargaining.

The main difference between the first and second phases of development was that in the first the adoption of a productivity bargaining approach by a company was quite voluntary and was not hedged around by any restraints from outside. It was entirely up to the company to get the best deal it could in co-operation with the unions and the workforce. By contrast, in the second period, there is no doubt that companies were often enticed into productivity bargaining when in the absence of incomes policy they would have continued along well-trodden paths. And having been enticed in this way they found themselves subject to certain 'rules of the game' imposed in consequence of the need for incomes policy to retain a measure of control over settlements.

The principal mechanism for control was the vetting of agreements by the D.E.P. and the recourse in critical or difficult cases to inquiry by the N.B.P.I.[1] Inevitably, it was the latter body which seemed to dominate the scene and to have most direct effect on the pattern of settlements, though the Department played an important role behind the scenes in sieving agreements and in many

[1] Mention should also be made of the efforts of the T.U.C. during this period to operate a 'vetting' arrangement for agreements, whereby a special committee of the T.U.C. would be informed of all impending claims. This machinery was set up during the voluntary phase of incomes policy in 1965 and was kept in being after the introduction of legislation. For further discussion, see H. A. Clegg, *The System of Industrial Relations in Great Britain* (Oxford: Blackwell, 1970), chapter 11.

cases providing guidance for negotiators anxious to conclude a productivity agreement. Our starting point in this chapter is a review of the controls on productivity bargaining, not so much from the point of view of the machinery, which has already been described, as from that of the thinking behind the control and the way in which it influenced the development of productivity bargaining. This in turn raises a number of issues highlighted by the pronouncements of the Board and we shall examine these in a preliminary way, though some will require more exhaustive attention in a subsequent analysis. An attempt will then be made to evaluate the success of productivity bargaining in its role as a tool of policy, and in this attention is paid both to the quantitative aspects and to other effects less easily translated into such concrete terms. At that point we will be ready to proceed to a more thorough analysis of the stages and strategies involved in productivity bargaining.

1. THE N.B.P.I. GUIDELINES FOR PRODUCTIVITY BARGAINING

Throughout its life, the N.B.P.I. was almost continually engaged in the evaluation of productivity agreements. Much of its activity in this area arose out of specific references on negotiations or settlements but also on three separate occasions the Board had the opportunity to examine the merits and demerits of productivity bargaining, and the development of its views are instructive in any attempt to understand the problems of productivity bargaining. In general, the Board gave cautious approval to productivity bargaining and obviously accepted it as a valuable constituent of the incomes policy. Its approval, however, was qualified, for it saw a number of dangers in this approach, as a result of which it felt obliged to develop a set of criteria for the evaluation of agreements from the standpoint of the public interest. These criteria took the form of 'guidelines' which were first stated in December 1966, soon after the Board became a statutory agency of government; they were slightly modified in June 1967 and more fully revised in August 1969. A comparison between the first and third versions is presented in Table 4.1.

From this comparison it can be seen that the difficulties that worried the Board remained much the same over the period of

Table 4.1. Guidelines for Judging Productivity Agreements

December 1966	August 1969
(i) It must be shown that the workers are making a direct contribution towards increasing productivity by accepting more exacting work or a major change in working practices.	(i) It should be known that the workers are contributing towards the achievement of constantly rising levels of efficiency. Where appropriate, major changes in working practice or working methods should be specified in the agreement.
(ii) Forecasts of increased productivity must be derived by the application of proper work standards.	(ii) Measurements of efficiency should be based on the application of relevant indices of performance or work standards.
(iii) An accurate calculation of the gains and the costs must show that the total cost per unit of output, taking into account the effect on capital, will be reduced.	(iii) A realistic calculation of all the relevant costs of the agreement and of the gains attributable to the workers' contribution should normally show that the effect is to reduce the total costs of output or the cost of providing a given service.
(iv) The scheme should contain effective controls to ensure that the projected increase in productivity is achieved, and that payment is made only as productivity increases or as changes in working practice take place.	(iv) There should be effective controls to ensure that projected increases in efficiency are achieved and that higher pay or other improvements are made only when such increases are assured.
(v) There should be a clear benefit to the consumer, in lower prices or in improved quality. In some instances 'lower prices' may mean prices lower than they would have been if the undertaking can prove that factors outside its control would otherwise have led to higher prices.	(v) There should be clear benefits to the consumer by way of a contribution to stable or lower prices.
(vi) An agreement covering part of a plant must bear the cost of consequential increases elsewhere in the plant, if any have to be granted.	(vi) An agreement applying to one group of workers only should bear the cost of consequential increases to other groups, if any have to be granted.
(vii) In all cases negotiators must beware of setting extravagant levels of pay which would provoke resentment outside.	(vii) Negotiators should avoid setting levels of pay or conditions which might have undesirable repercussions elsewhere.

almost three years, but some modification or elaboration of the constraints had become necessary by the end of the period. A number of points require extended comment.

PRODUCTIVITY GAINS AND THEIR DISTRIBUTION

The first guideline concerns one of the major bones of contention in productivity bargaining, whether it is proper for *all* gains in productivity to be brought into the reckoning, or whether only those gains should be considered that are due to changes in working practice and improved effort by the workforce covered by the agreement. A fuller statement of the Board's view runs as follows :

> Payment needs to be related to the improved productivity made possible by the contribution of workers and not on the basis of generalised statistics relating to increases in output regardless of whether capital equipment or labour is the source of that increased output.[2]

The conceptual distinction, however, between the contributions of labour and capital is easier than the practical. Productivity improvements, in the sense of increased output per unit of input, may derive from such diverse elements as new technology, improved work organisation, greater collective effort on the part of the workforce and higher quality of labour input, and it is not always possible in a given case to identify the size or value of the contribution from any of these sources. The early productivity agreements centred on changes in working practice and increased effort, and this was the aspect that the Board and the White Papers on incomes policy had in mind in advocating productivity bargaining. Yet from the viewpoint of the workers and unions, productivity improvement, no matter what its source, constitutes a valid argument for increased wages. Even if the productivity gain owes its origin directly to new capital, for instance, labour is still required to operate it and the unit productivity of labour will indisputably have increased.

There are two sorts of difficulty here. The first is that it may prove difficult for company negotiators to resist the claims of

[2] N.B.P.I. Report No. 123, *Productivity Agreements*, Cmnd 4136 (London: H.M.S.O., 1969) para. 118.

unions that they should share in the benefits of increased productivity, whatever its origin. A clear illustration of this arose in a case affecting Post Office engineering grades, where the savings in labour costs deriving from increased labour productivity were estimated and distributed between the engineering workers and the Post Office according to a set formula.[3] The sources of increased productivity were specified as follows :

(i) 'measures which are the subject of specific agreements with the Union' (Post Office Engineering Union);
(ii) 'measures where technical development is the main factor in improving productivity';
(iii) 'steps taken by local managers to improve productivity'.

However, in calculating the amount of savings to be included for the purposes of adding to wages, the Post Office argued that savings from technical development should be excluded and that costs incurred in introducing the changes, such as higher grading and work study, should be deducted. Gross savings, reduced by savings under (ii) and any offsetting costs, would produce a net saving figure, of which the Post Office was prepared to allocate 40 per cent to the union grades for pay purposes.

The P.O.E.U. reacted adversely on three main points : the calculation of labour cost per man, the 40 per cent distribution formula (to which we return), and the omission of savings from technical change. The Post Office's argument for excluding the second category of improvement was that it did 'not result primarily from the acceptance of change of practice or more onerous work by the Union's members, but on capital expenditure, first on research and development of new techniques and equipment, and second to put them into service'.[4] The P.O.E.U. did not, however, accept this view, arguing instead that

Savings resulting from the introduction of technical developments are proper to be taken into account in pay negotiations.

[3] The increase in productivity was derived from the actual man-hours spent by each telecommunications region under all the works orders and headings of man-hour expenditure and this saving in man-hours was converted to a saving in numbers employed. An average total labour cost per man was then estimated, and multiplied by the number of men saved, to give a total figure for gross savings in the period.
[4] This is a union statement of the Post Office argument : P.O.E.U. *Bulletin* (May 1969) 4.

All developments of this kind . . . tend to involve our members
. . . in changes in work content, skill content and in their relationships with other groups of workers. Their co-operation is essential to the successful introduction of new techniques and to the
Post Office obtaining the maximum technical and economic
benefit from them.[5]

Here, then, is the classic statement of the case from each side,
resulting in an antithesis not likely to be resolved except by bargaining even in an example like this where the Post Office believed
that savings from sources (i) and (ii) could be estimated quite
accurately, leaving (iii) as a residual.

Although the N.B.P.I. took a position on this general problem
and tried to insist on the exclusion of savings from productivity
improvements due to technical change, it had to recognise *de facto*
on some occasions that such savings would be included in the
bargaining package. Its unhappiness with this situation was reflected in a plea that it should be given a special reference on this
very issue,[6] but by the time this request came, the Board was near-
ing the end of its life.

The second difficulty is not altogether unrelated to the first. If
the agreement is accurately costed out, and a realistic estimate of
net savings for a given output is available, there is still likely to be
negotiation over division of the gains. Within the bargaining unit,
this may be seen simply as a process of divisive bargaining concerned with the allocation of shares to labour and to capital. In
practice the matter has been less simple, not least because of the
efforts of the N.B.P.I. to extend the benefits of productivity bargaining beyond the limits of the bargaining unit itself.

From the outset the Board wanted to see some part of the gain
being passed on to the community in the form of lower prices or
improved quality,[7] although this was quickly modified to a more
realistic caution that there should be benefits to the consumer in
the form of more stable prices. This suggests a three-way split of
the proceeds of the bargain, and indeed in a number of cases an
equal three-way share-out was adopted. There was, however, no

[5] P.O.E.U. *Bulletin* (May 1969) 5.
[6] Cf. N.B.P.I. Report No. 123, *Productivity Agreements*, para. 139.
[7] Cf. Guideline (v) in the December 1966 report on productivity agreements.

firm guidance on the share-out principle either from the incomes policy or from the Board, which later set out its view as follows :

> We find it impossible to prescribe any hard and fast rules, but suggest that the consumer has a particular claim to a substantial share in parts of the economy where advances in technology make rapid increases in productivity possible.[8]

The difficulties of this approach to the share-out problem should be obvious. In the course of productivity bargaining there are only two main interests represented, the workers and the company, and the consumer has no direct representation. The division between labour and the company is a difficult enough issue in itself, but even when that issue is resolved, there will be the question of whether the company's share of the cost savings should be reflected in reduced (or stabilised) prices or in a contribution to profits, the latter solution being particularly attractive in an era when rates of return on capital are tending to fall. It is in this respect that the Board's anxiety to see some benefit for the consumer becomes important : the Board was in effect indirectly representing the consumer's interest at the negotiating table and simultaneously seeking to bolster up its other policies for price stability via the collective bargaining process.

Both these issues – the 'proper' ingredients of the bargain and the distribution of the gains – are important and difficult aspects of the productivity bargaining process and as such will demand further attention in later chapters, when we will see how the problems were resolved in individual cases. The Board's view on this, however, was a reminder of the externalities generated by the productivity bargain and, as we now see, this was not the only instance of this sort of difficulty.

'SPILLOVER' EFFECTS OF PRODUCTIVITY AGREEMENTS

One of the major fears of critics of productivity bargaining had always been that once an agreement was struck, the increase in wages (which would often be substantial) would be regarded as a target for other workers whether or not they were capable of

---

[8] N.B.P.I. Report No. 123, *Productivity Agreements*, para. 100. This particular quotation clearly recognised that cost savings from technical change *would* enter into the productivity bargain.

productivity gains of equal value. Large rises based on genuine cost savings could lead to claims for similar increases supported only by the 'comparability' argument, and this of course helped to explain the Board's desire to break into the comparability claim and alter the criteria of bargaining. Guidelines (vi) and (vii) were intended as further safeguards against the bidding-up of wages which might follow an agreement, dealing respectively with the impact on the internal and on the external wage structure. Within the plant, that is, an agreement covering a section of the work-force should also take into account the effect on differentials between that group and other groups who might not be able to participate in productivity bargaining, or who might not be able to produce such large cost savings. The Board intended that consequential increases to preserve differentials should be included in the initial bargain, with the effect of spreading the gains more thinly over a wider group.

Similarly, a substantial increase in one plant might have repercussions in other plants of the same company, in other firms in the local labour market area, or in other companies in the same industry, depending on the way the wage comparison mechanism worked in the particular case. Here again the Board was anxious to avoid a chain reaction in which secondary wage increases might be less soundly based on productivity improvement. In fact, as we have already observed, the Board was unable to find positive evidence of such an effect,[9] and it may be that both sectional agreements and individual plant settlements had the effect of encouraging workers outside their scope to engage in genuine productivity negotiations for themselves.

The problem here, as before, is that the interests of the parties to negotiation are bound to be to secure the best bargain for themselves. Modification of wage increases to reduce the effect on differentials inside and outside the plant is not likely to be a popular course, particularly for the workers under the agreement, whose incentive to participate in more onerous work will be reduced as the rewards decline.

This kind of restriction also reduced the room for manoeuvre in some cases. Consider the case of a chemical company negotiating a second-generation agreement and recognising that the initial agreement had given rise to dissatisfaction among white-collar and

[9] Cf. above, Chapter 2 (p. 48).

supervisory staff who had not shared in the agreement and who were conscious of differentials being eroded. The company wished to award a 5 per cent increase to white-collar workers in advance of the manual workers' agreement in an attempt to avoid further dissatisfaction on this score. But this proposal at once ran into trouble at the D.E.P. for, according to the guidelines, the cost of the 5 per cent increase should have been included in the overall costs of the agreement, even though it had not yet been negotiated.

There was in such cases an inherent conflict between the objectives of the negotiating parties and the Board. The latter was charged with the exercise of control in the interests of wage and price stability and to do this it had to try to prevent the dilution of productivity bargaining, whereas the negotiating parties wished to smooth all the possible obstacles in the path to agreement. While the anxieties of the Board have to be viewed sympathetically, the more strictly its precepts were applied, the more likely was it that commitment to productivity bargaining would deteriorate and worthwhile productivity gains would be lost. Undoubtedly, this conflict of public and private interest would be much weaker in a context free from the stringencies imposed by an incomes policy.

EFFICIENCY AGREEMENTS

Perhaps the most significant change between the 1966 and 1969 guidelines was the introduction of the term 'efficiency' into the later statement, in place of the emphasis on 'productivity' in the first version. The difference between these concepts is not easy to summarise succinctly, but in this context there is no doubt that the Board saw productivity as a narrower, more strictly quantifiable concept, and efficiency as an inclusive term, embracing productivity but also improvements in the utilisation of resources which could not be easily measured. Behind this verbal distinction there lay an important change of mind on the part of the Board.

The early statement revealed the concern of the Board that increases in wages should not be given, under the productivity gateway, merely on the promise of co-operation in productivity improvement, or without proper safeguards to ensure that the projected cost savings would be achieved. Hence guideline (ii) insists that productivity changes should be properly measured, (iii) requires that *total* unit costs of output should be reduced, not just labour costs per unit, and (iv) makes it a condition that the scheme should be closely monitored, with pay increases being granted only as changes are actually implemented.

We might expect that such conditions would in any event be insisted upon by managements to safeguard their own interest in the agreement, but in practice the matter may be less simple. For example, forecasts of cost savings may depend not only on the success of changes in work practice but also on whether demand permits output to be kept at expected levels. Again, in some situations management may be prepared to accept some risk, and grant pay increases as a sign that they trust their workers to co-operate in productivity improvement schemes. Indeed, it was one of the notable features of the earlier agreements that they were largely based on mutual trust which in turn could be further developed in the course of the agreement to bring about some of the 'cultural change' effects which Allan Flanders observed as one of the main outcomes of the Fawley agreements.

In the absence of incomes policy, such loose arrangements might be acceptable, for the cost of failure was one that would be borne by management who were in the last resort accountable to directors and shareholders.[10] But with an incomes policy in operation, encouraging productivity bargaining, the public interest came much more into the picture, and the widespread granting of pay increases on the basis of vague expectations, or without attention to the need for monitoring, could have a serious effect on the overall aim of keeping pay and productivity growth in line.

As a result, the Board's concern for the incomes policy led it to take a narrow view of productivity bargaining in which increases in pay were meant to be a very direct *quid pro quo* for realised improvements in productivity. Yet even in the first phase of development, productivity bargaining had been recognised as opening the way to a change of attitudes among workers, as a result of which it would be possible to move away from the strict relation between work changes and rewards, and work towards continuing co-operation by workers as changes in their work became necessary. To adopt this strategy was to embark on a high-risk course, but one which might bring much more substantial benefits to the company in the long run. The risks, however, were at first too

---

[10] In less competitive situations, the customer may share in the cost in the form of higher prices.

great for the Board to accept, and it insisted on quantification of costs and returns *at all stages*, including the first :

> Agreements based on the expectation of changed attitudes without a careful assessment of the gains that are likely to be achieved could be an easy road to competitive wage bidding.

Again, the Board commented as follows on the status agreements in electricity supply, which depended on this more open-ended approach :

> No details of changes in working practices were included in the national agreement, nor were any firm commitments to changes in methods of work negotiated locally before the payments began to be made. We do not think that this method of negotiation should normally be followed by other industries, although on this occasion it was probably unavoidable, given the structure of the electricity supply industry and the circumstances in which negotiation took place.[11]

By the time of its final review of productivity bargaining, in 1969, the Board had come to adopt a more tolerant view, one of the main indications of which is the substitution of 'efficiency' for 'productivity' throughout the guidelines. The Board admitted :

> Experience does however show that it is necessary to revise and broaden our guidelines. It is desirable in particular to give added emphasis to the aim of achieving constantly rising levels of efficiency : this aim can be achieved only with close and continuous co-operation between managements and workers.[12]

This broader interpretation epitomised what the Board referred to as 'efficiency agreements', a concept intended to embrace productivity agreements in the conventional sense, but also to include agreements where it was not appropriate to specify proposed working changes in a narrow sense.[13] This was thought particularly

[11] Quotations from N.B.P.I. Report No. 36, *Productivity Agreements*, paras 65 and 194 respectively.

[12] N.B.P.I. Report No. 123, para. 137.

[13] Cf. the 1969 guidelines (number (i)) above : also N.B.P.I. Report No. 123, pp. 41–3. The alternative interpretation here, attributing to the Board a less positive outlook, is that it was by this stage resigned to making the best of a bad job and this extension was an attempt to salvage what it could from the wreck of productivity bargaining.

appropriate in the case of white-collar workers, for whose work a strict measure of productivity might be difficult to determine. Yet the Board was anxious to see these workers being brought within the scope of its policy and more efficient use made of their particular skills.

This change of mind on the part of the Board came too late to have any effect, for by August 1969, when the go-ahead on efficiency agreements was given, the incomes policy was quickly losing effect and the attention of collective bargainers was turning to other matters. The result is that the scope for this more far-reaching type of agreement, aimed at changing basic attitudes to work, was deliberately restricted during the period when the greatest activity in the productivity bargaining arena was taking place. Some of the implications of this will be seen when we consider the merits of the various strategies on which productivity bargaining can be based.

2. EVALUATION

The guidelines for productivity bargaining represented just one part of the whole policy for prices, productivity and incomes. While it is not part of our intention to assess the success of the policy as a whole, it is important to know how the adoption of productivity bargaining as a tool of the policy worked out in practice, and from that point of view alone we are obliged to pay some attention to the policy's achievements. There are two aspects to this assessment. We can try to determine success in quantitative terms by examining, for example, the rate of growth of wage and salary incomes, productivity, and unit wage costs. We can also regard the policy from a more qualitative standpoint, in which statistical evidence gives way to an impression of the policy's achievements in modifying institutions and changing attitudes in such a way that they serve more efficiently the nation's objectives as set out in the policy framework. In this section we present a brief review under both headings.

QUANTITATIVE EVIDENCE

We must first clarify our objective. The great difficulty in any attempt to assess the impact of an economic policy is to know what would have transpired in the absence of that policy or in the event of a different policy being applied. Incomes policy is no exception but it did to some extent set its own standards. At the most general level, the policy was intended to keep the rate of growth of wages and salaries equivalent to the rate of growth of productivity. A more specific form of the objective can be detected in the norm (or ceiling) for wage increases in each of the various sub-periods of policy during the period 1965–9. This presents its own problems for, as we have seen, neither the norm nor the ceiling was an absolute, because for much of the time there were gateways through the policy, particularly by way of productivity-based agreements. Nevertheless, some appreciation of the success of the policy toward these objectives can be made.

When we come to the efficiency of the productivity bargaining arm of the overall policy, the criteria for assessment need further definition. It is almost part of the expectation in productivity bargaining, especially during a period of incomes restraint, that the resulting agreement will lead to an increase in wages rather above the 'normal' level. Productivity bargaining, then, may actually contribute to a *higher* rate of increase of wages and salaries than conventional bargaining, but this may be acceptable from the standpoint of policy if these increases are accompanied by rises of productivity sufficient to offset their cost. We would then expect to see the effects of this part of the policy in an accelerated rate of growth of productivity and a reduced rate of increase of unit costs, other things remaining equal. Other things do not of course remain equal, and these two variables are subject to a variety of influences quite apart from productivity bargaining. Nevertheless it is worth examining the available evidence for signs of change in the expected direction.

Table 4.2 sets out some of the basic statistical information.

Period I was the phase of voluntary prices and incomes policy, the lack of success of which is quickly seen, when compared with the norm of 3–3½ per cent per year. Not only were hourly wage rates and weekly earnings increasing at an annual rate of over 7 per cent but unit wage and salary costs were rising almost as fast, reflecting little productivity improvement.

Period II was one of tighter control, involving roughly six months of freeze and six months of zero norm. While both rates and earnings rose in Period II due largely to implementation of

Table 4.2. Wages, Prices and Costs during Incomes Policy Phases: Selected Indices

		Percentage Increases at Annual Rates			
Period	Hourly wage rates	Weekly earnings (seasonally adjusted)	Retail prices	Wages and salaries per unit of output	G.D.P. per person employed
I April 1965–June 1966	7.4	7.6	5.1	7.1	1.4
II July 1966–June 1967	2.8	1.7	2.5	0.1	2.9
III July 1967–March 1968	9.2	8.8	2.8	4.7	5.4
IV April 1968–December 1968	4.5	7.9	5.5	0.7	3.2
V January 1969–December 1969	5.6	8.3	5.1	7.6	1.8

Notes:

(a) The percentage increases quoted are those from the average for the quarter preceding each period to the average for the final quarter of the period. Quarterly figures have been used which eliminate random fluctuations in the monthly figures.

(b) Hourly wage rates are taken from the D.E.P.'s index of basic hourly wage rates and relate to manual workers. Earnings figures are taken from the D.E.P.'s monthly index of weekly average wage and salary earnings. They relate to all industries and services and are seasonally adjusted.

(c) The Table is based on one published in *Productivity, Prices and Incomes Policy after 1969*, Cmnd 4237, p. 6. Certain figures have been revised in the light of later data published in the *Employment and Productivity Gazette*.

agreements postponed by the freeze, the overall effect was a sharp reduction in the rate of increase and, due to the 3 per cent increase in productivity, unit wage and salary costs rose only fractionally.

Period III saw a relaxation of constraint[14] and a wage burst occurred as negotiators attempted to regain lost ground. Even then, the effect was moderated by productivity improvements which rose at an annual rate of over 5 per cent between the third quarter of 1967 and the second quarter of 1968. The devaluation of sterling in November 1967 was in part a testimony to the failure of incomes policy in this phase.

Periods IV and V were covered by Cmnd 3590 and marked by the 3½ per cent ceiling for wage and salary increases. While hourly wage rates did not exceed the ceiling by much in the last three quarters of 1968, and by no more than might be consistent with the above-ceiling rises permitted on efficiency grounds, the rate of increase of earnings was much higher. But here again, the effect on unit wage and salary costs was not excessive during Period IV. The final period, however, bears considerable resemblance to the first, except that the rate of productivity increase was somewhat higher. Clearly, the restraints imposed by the sustained application of the policy over the previous three years were proving unacceptable, and the first signs were emerging of the wage explosion which was to continue during the next two years.

It could hardly be said, then, that the rate of wage and salary increases was closely related to the norm or ceiling over the whole period, but comparative success was achieved in Periods II and IV. Still more than this, the time covered by Periods II to IV did seem to inaugurate a new impetus to productivity increases, which did not go unremarked by the N.B.P.I. :

While from the Autumn of 1966 onwards there was some expansion of the economy accompanied by increasing productivity, the rate of increase which developed in 1967 and continued in 1968 was higher than average and singular in that it was not accompanied by a rise in demand reflected in lower unemployment.[15]

---

[14] This was the period when no norm was officially stated : *any* increase had to be justified against the criteria.

[15] N.B.P.I., *Fourth General Report* (No. 122), Cmnd 4130 (London : H.M.S.O., 1969) para. 13.

How was this to be explained? The Board provided a tentative answer :

> It is possible that one factor to have contributed to this rise in productivity has been the emphasis placed on the productivity criterion . . .; the productivity component has always been there, but it has been brought much more to the forefront than in previous phases of incomes policy . . . What may have happened is that the 'squeeze' of 1966 brought about a 'shake-out' of labour and the emphasis on productivity later contributed to stricter manning standards.[16]

This view, which is almost inevitably a hunch rather than scientific assessment, is more firmly stated in the 1969 White Paper on incomes policy :

> One of the main aims of the policy during this period [1968–9] was to stimulate a new approach to productivity bargaining, and its success in doing this undoubtedly contributed to the exceptional increase in productivity which took place in 1968 and which held down unit costs.[17]

It is difficult to know what weight to put on this view. The point has already been made that productivity improvement can be achieved by many routes. There had, for example, been alterations in the labour market situation which could well have influenced productivity : the improved and expanded facilities for industrial training and retraining, the significantly higher level of unemployment and the changed structure of unemployment[18] may be as

---

[16] N.B.P.I., *Fourth General Report*, para. 19.

[17] *Productivity, Prices and Incomes Policy after 1969*, Cmnd 4237 (London: H.M.S.O., 1969) para. 8.

[18] In the later 1960s there was an increasingly common view that changes in the institutional organisation of the labour market, especially as a result of earnings-related unemployment benefit and redundancy payments, were causing a change in the character of unemployment. Such changes could mean that workers were less worried about the financial effect of a spell of unemployment, that workers might even 'volunteer' to be made redundant in order to obtain the lump-sum benefit, that employers might be more willing to pay off labour where previously they might have retained it as a contribution to the social good, etc. If this is so, it could help to explain the higher unemployment rate of the last few years, without *necessarily* implying that the true unemployment situation had worsened. It could mean, for example, an expansion of the short-term unemployed, reflecting the willingness of more workers to register as unemployed and to take longer looking round for a suitable job. For a full discussion of this problem, see J. K. Bowers, P. C. Cheshire and A. E. Webb, 'The Change in the Relationship between Unemployment and Earnings Increases', *National Institute Economic Review* (November 1970).

important in this connection as the productivity criterion of the
incomes policy, while innovations like the selective employment
tax were also apparently contributing to rising productivity.[19]
There is the further evidence that in 1969, when incomes policy
was operating on the same terms as in 1968, productivity improvement slackened off and unit wage and salary costs increased four
times as fast as in 1968, which must raise real doubts about the
contribution of the policy.

At the aggregate level, Table 4.3 compares the behaviour of
G.D.P. per employed person and costs per unit of output for the
whole of the periods 1961–5 and 1965–9.

Table 4.3. Productivity and Unit Cost Increases, 1961–9

	1961–5 (percentage increase)	1965–9 (percentage increase)
G.D.P. per employed person	10.6	12.2
Unit wage and salary costs	11.7	17.0
Total home costs per unit of output	12.8	14.1

Source: *National Income and Expenditure* and *Employment and Productivity Gazette.*

While the rate of increase of productivity rose slightly in the later
period, there was no slackening of the rate of growth of unit costs;
indeed, unit wage and salary costs rose much more quickly during
the second period, which was marked by sustained incomes policy
backed up for much of the time by statutory controls.

Again, at the industry level, the limited data available and presented in Table 4.4 do not suggest that a high coverage of the
labour force by productivity bargaining will mean a relatively low
rate of increase in unit wage costs.

The evidence of this Table is that vehicles, with the highest
coverage by productivity bargaining, experienced the lowest productivity growth and the highest increase in unit wage costs. On

[19] Cf. W. B. Reddaway, *Effects of the Selective Employment Tax: The Distributive Trades* (London: H.M.S.O., 1970).

Table 4.4. *Productivity, Unit Labour Costs and Productivity Bargaining Coverage—Selected Industries 1966-9*

Industry Group	(1) Increase in output per person employed (per cent)	(2) Increase in wage and salary costs per unit of output (per cent)	(3) Percentage of employees covered by productivity agreements
Metal manufacture	9.5	8.5	13
Mechanical, instrument and electrical engineering	13.7	3.2	24
Vehicles	8.1	14.0	64
Textiles	23.1	1.2	29

Sources: Columns (1) and (2) from *Employment and Productivity Gazette*, Column (3) from Chapter 3 above, Table 3.1 (framework agreements excluded).

the other hand, the three other industries, with lower coverage, do suggest some pattern, a higher rate of coverage being associated with higher productivity growth and lower increases in unit wage costs. However, since many other factors undoubtedly influence these indices, we should be very hesitant in drawing from this any strong conclusion about the moderating effect of productivity bargaining on the rise of unit wage costs.

There are indications that over short periods the policy met with some success, notably in Periods II and IV as defined in Table 4.2 above. These successes, however, proved to be short lived, with an apparent holding back of wage and unit cost increases in these periods being compensated by a rapid upsurge in the next period. This dissolution of temporary gains was particularly evident in the period following the end of the formal incomes policy in December 1969, when the pent-up frustrations of the period of enforced restraint finally burst through.[20] In reaching this conclusion, we must bear in mind that even on the most liberal interpretation, no more than one-third of the working population was ever covered by productivity agreements, and it may even have been as low as one-eighth. We should not, perhaps, expect to see *too* great an

---

[20] It is worth mentioning in passing that a number of attempts have been made to evaluate the success of the incomes policy as a whole in restraining the rate of growth of wages and salaries. It is an interesting point that, despite using very different methods of analysis, there is a strong central tendency in these estimates, suggesting that, for all periods of incomes policy during the 1960s (including the Selwyn Lloyd 'pay-pause') the increase of wage and salary incomes was about 1 to 1½ percentage points less than would have obtained in the absence of the policy of restraint. Studies coming to this conclusion include the following: N.B.P.I., *Third General Report* (No. 77) App. A (based on evidence for 1946–66); Frank Brechling, 'Some Empirical Evidence on the Effectiveness of Price and Incomes Policies' (paper read at the Canadian Political Science Association, Montreal, June 1966); R. G. Bodkin, E. P. Bond, G. L. Reuber and T. R. Robinson, 'Price Stability and High Employment', Economic Council of Canada, Special Study No. 5 (Ottawa: Economic Council of Canada, 1967); David C. Smith, 'Incomes Policy', in *Britain's Economic Prospects*, by R. E. Caves and Associates, a Brookings Institution Study (London: Allen and Unwin, 1968); R. G. Lipsey and J. M. Parkin, 'Incomes Policy – A Re-appraisal', *Economica*, N.S. Vol. XXXVII (May 1970); John Corina and A. J. Meyrick, *The Performance of Incomes and Prices Policy in the United Kingdom, 1958–68* (Geneva: International Institute for Labour Studies, 1970). The finding of Lipsey and Parkin has to be qualified by their conclusion that when unemployment lay above 1.8 per cent, the use of an incomes policy would tend to *increase* the rate of inflation above the level that would otherwise have obtained.

effect on national performance, and even at industry level the position is by no means clear-cut, as we have seen.

Despite this rather discouraging finding on the impact of the productivity bargaining element of the incomes policy, it would be invalid to write off productivity bargaining as a whole, for its original purpose was related to company and plant-level problems, not those of national dimension, and not all its objectives were fully quantifiable. We return later to a review of company-level achievements, but now we can take some account of the less quantifiable effects of the productivity arm of the incomes policy.

QUALITATIVE EVIDENCE

The objectives of incomes policy are usually presented in such a way as to include influence not only over the general course of incomes but also over their structure and the means by which incomes are determined. It is true that in later years the policy had come to be dominated by the need for restraint – what Corina has called a 'degenerated' policy[21] – but even if the need for short-term control had largely taken over from the object of managing the progress of incomes, the means to this end has involved a more general effort to reshape the process of wage and salary determination and certain features of the total industrial relations situation. Here we will devote some attention to three topics : the effects on the collective bargaining system, the development of new approaches and new techniques, and the influence of the policy on attitudes. All three topics involve some aspect of productivity bargaining.

Collective bargaining. Our earlier discussion of the problems creating a need for incomes policy suggested that much of the difficulty issued from a collective bargaining system in which the real economic forces at plant level could not be fully accommodated by the industry-wide approach to wage determination. One consequence of that system was reliance on bargaining criteria which could be identified nationally – such as cost-of-living changes and wage comparisons between industries and broad occupational groups. At the same time, the void left by the deficiencies of this system had to be filled in practice by supplementary bar-

[21] Corina and Meyrick, *The Performance of Incomes and Prices Policy in the United Kingdom.*

gaining at local and plant level, usually on an unco-ordinated, piecemeal basis which provided opportunity for competitive, sectional bidding-up of wages without regard to the effect on unit wage and salary costs.

The encouragement given to productivity bargaining by the incomes policy was a means of altering the criteria of negotiation and changing the bargaining structure. For productivity bargaining was seen as a practice most appropriately, though not exclusively, carried on at plant or company level. From the start, the N.B.P.I., which was the main instrument of this part of the policy, took every opportunity to cut the ties of comparability[22] and substitute productivity considerations, and to recommend changes in the bargaining structure which might lead to a greater concern for the economic consequences of wage settlements.

From mid-1967, however, the scope for framework agreements at industry level was appreciated and approved.

Many of the cases referred to the Board covered proposals for a whole industry, the negotiating machinery for which was frequently fragmented and incapable of taking account of detailed productivity questions. A frequent result of the Board's investigations was the establishment of joint committees to discuss the means for productivity improvement in an industry-wide context, while in other cases a modification of the negotiating machinery was introduced to allow productivity and efficiency matters to be brought into the picture. For example, as a result of the Board's investigation into the pay of staff in the gas industry (Report No. 86), a joint working party set up by the National Joint Council recommended the formation of joint productivity sub-committees under each Area Joint Council, to consider ways of involving staff in improvements of working practice – a matter that could only be dealt with in the most general way by the N.J.C. itself. Again, in the case of Bristol docks staff workers (N.B.P.I. Report No. 81),

---

[22] The clearest case of this was in the variety of trades ancillary to the building industry, which were advised either to join the N.J.C. for the building industry or to seek settlements in terms of their own industrial circumstances (see N.B.P.I. Report No. 93). Similar suggestions were made elsewhere, notably in chemicals where I.C.I. appeared to act as a leader, while comparability on a regional basis (e.g. between Scotland and the rest of the United Kingdom in electrical contracting) was also rejected as a valid ground for settlement (see N.B.P.I. Report No. 105, on I.C.I.; and N.B.P.I. Reports Nos. 24, 108 and 120, all dealing with electrical contracting).

the National Joint Council for local authority staffs agreed to set up a ports committee to deal with pay and productivity in local authority ports, this being a special activity not appropriately covered by the N.J.C. with a more general responsibility. Other changes following inquiries by the Board included the amalgamation of employers' associations in the thermal insulation contracting industry, to facilitate negotiations (Report No. 93); the phasing out of the wages council in clothing manufacture (Report No. 110); a single negotiating body for provincial busmen (Report No. 50); and a development of internal negotiating machinery in the larger engineering firms (Report No. 104).[23]

Two general points arise here. First, there is an apparent need at industry level for some kind of intermediate body representative of employers and workers either to develop on a joint basis more detailed proposals for the improvement of productivity or to monitor the progress of an agreement as it is implemented. This will be particularly true where general standards for work study or job evaluation are to be put into effect on an industry-wide basis and where a code of best practice is desired. These are not matters which can be adequately dealt with in the course of industry negotiations, yet neither are they suitable for passing down to company level, where each enterprise would inevitably lose the benefit of others' experience.

Secondly, this does not mean that the importance of central negotiation need be weakened. Indeed, it was not infrequently observed by the Board that it was a condition of progress that strong central organisation should continue, or in some cases, like road haulage, be reconstituted. If, however, the stronger central organisation is to perform effectively, it is likely to need improved supporting services, and again it is one of the features of industries examined by the Board that they often went on to establish an industry advisory service. Examples include electricity supply, gas and local authorities, charged with the task of centralising information, records and work study standards, while in private industry, partly on the recommendation of the Board, the strengthening of the service function of the Engineering Employers' Federation has proved equally important.

[23] The Board also recommended that the national agreement in this industry should only lay down minima and criteria for the industry pay structure, which would then be built upon at company level in the light of internal needs and conditions.

The implications of these observations are that the Board's investigation of productivity negotiations not only gave general encouragement and positive guidance on matters relating to a reconstruction of bargaining arrangements, but pointed out some of the difficulties that would be encountered anyway in a more general switch to a system based largely on plant bargaining – which was, of course, the recommendation of the Donovan Commission. As a result of their experience of productivity bargaining, and in many cases of their being subject to investigation by the Board, some industries were already more prepared, both in attitude and in machinery, for the changes that such a shift would require.

New approaches and techniques. One of the direct outcomes of this sort of intervention by the Board was a more general appreciation of what could be achieved by means of a 'framework' agreement at industry level, setting out general principles which could be used as a basis for subsequent negotiations at plant level. Even in the first phase of development of productivity bargaining there had been some experimentation in this direction, but it was probably the formula adopted by the Chemical Industries Association which most caught the imagination as a useful approach, and this example was highlighted by the attention paid to it in the Donovan Commission Report.

One effect of this was that companies in industries covered by such an agreement[24] found themselves in a situation where there was an onus on them to pursue a productivity bargaining strategy, for which they might be ill-prepared. The consultancy services of their own employers' association or of the D.E.P. might help, but in many cases it was easier to turn to the use of independent consultants. Consultants had, of course, been used in the development of agreements during the first phase, for example in the Esso negotiations at Fawley in 1960. But the new situation may have produced some differences.

Consultants in the earlier period had been used mainly to identify management objectives and to frame the broad terms of approach. Management time was thereby economised and a fresh eye brought to the problems and potential of the organisation. As Esso put the point :

---

[24] For a sample list of industries thus affected, see *Incomes Data Panorama* (March 1968–July 1969) 3–4.

Consultants have . . . acted as catalysts of change and have made it possible to implement ideas which have been circulating in management circles for many years.[25]

However, with the incentives of incomes policy and the emergence of more framework agreements, some managements took to productivity bargaining more as a means of finding a way to satisfy their workers' demands than from a motive based on a desire to solve long-standing productivity problems by negotiation and consultation. When such companies turned to consultants the catalytic role they might perform was probably less vital than the detailed plan of action they could provide. In these cases, some of the benefit of productivity bargaining, especially the joint involvement of workers, unions and management in the drawing up of the package for negotiations, may be lost.

If that is so, there is a parallel with the dislike of the Board for agreements which did not specify changes in practice but relied rather on mutual trust and co-operation to secure benefits – a dislike which persisted down to the middle of 1969 when the broader based efficiency agreement finally gained the Board's seal of approval. This point is an important one, for it draws attention to the potential loss of the cultural change effect which productivity bargaining experience could bring. Once that is lost, and the attention of the parties is focused entirely on the trade-off between increases in pay and specified changes in working practice, much of the prospective benefit of the activity may be eliminated.

This losing sight of the cultural effects was further emphasised in 1968 with the inclusion of wage structure revisions as permissible grounds for exceeding the incomes policy ceiling then in force. For it is in this area, full of scope for the introduction of work measurement techniques and job evaluation schemes, that the need for consultants' advice is likely to be most strongly felt.[26] While no doubt producing worthwhile gains in many cases, this method of

[25] Quoted in Royal Commission Research Paper No. 4 (on Productivity Bargaining) (London: H.M.S.O., 1967) 8. Cf. also Flanders, who wrote that 'the value of the introduction of consultants *per se* was simply that of a catalytic agent: their independent status made it possible to speed up the process of change in managerial attitudes and beliefs'. *The Fawley Productivity Agreements* (London: Faber & Faber, 1964) 100–1.

[26] For an example of the consultants' approach, see D. T. B. North and G. L. Buckingham, *Productivity Agreements and Wage Systems* (London: Gower Press, 1969).

approach is more likely to bring with it preconceived solutions and standard packages of measurement techniques which might do less than justice to the real problems of the firm. This is not to decry the work of the consultants, many of whom gave valuable help, but to point out the consequences of enticing firms into productivity bargaining rather than leaving it to firms themselves to decide whether it offered a reasonable approach to their problems.

The introduction of wage structures as a favoured subject for productivity bargaining was, of course, an important development in its own right. It broadened the scope of productivity bargaining by enabling companies with no real difficulty in the 'traditional' problem areas (persistent overtime, overmanning, demarcation, etc.) to get into the act without requiring them to dress up their case for raising wages for the purpose of getting around the incomes policy. In particular, it opened the way to the inclusion of many white-collar workers, for whom work measurement and job evaluation schemes could be more easily introduced. As we have seen from the evidence of Chapter 3, the second phase of development witnessed a substantial growth in the coverage of white-collar workers, and an increasing use of work study and job evaluation.

There were, then, some indications of new developments and new applications of productivity bargaining deriving from the incomes policy in general and the work of the N.B.P.I. in particular. Not all of these were necessarily for the better, though it was an important achievement to emphasise the need for more accurate measurement of work on the shop-floor and in the office, to spread the net more widely to include white-collar workers, and to introduce productivity bargaining as a means of tackling the widespread problem of inefficient pay systems and structures. It remains for a later chapter to consider the effects of these developments on productivity bargaining itself.

Attitudes and opinions. Finally, we must devote a little space to the effects on attitudes as a result of the official encouragement of productivity bargaining. This encouragement, the efforts of the N.B.P.I. to develop applications of best practice, and the growing commitment to productivity bargaining on the part of many companies, meant that it was increasingly difficult for the C.B.I. and for individual employers' associations to continue their early resistance. To have done so would have been to give up any possibility of retaining a measure of control over individual members' activities in the productivity bargaining field. In the first half of 1968 the C.B.I. began to take a more tolerant view. A policy document, approved by the Council of the C.B.I. and published in the summer of 1968, emphasised the conditions for a *genuine* productivity bargain, based on the N.B.P.I. guidelines but spelling out a little more clearly what safeguards the employer should seek in concluding such an agreement.

While accepting that 'valuable changes in attitudes and practices . . . can spring from the development of genuine productivity bargaining', the C.B.I. maintained that plant-level agreements should not proceed independently of wider considerations, and it recommended that employers' associations and trade unions at industry level should agree on guidelines for productivity bargaining at local level, and on the provision of machinery at national level to ensure that these guidelines were observed. This new role for the employers' associations replaced their former responsibility for national bargaining. It was up to them to accept and define this role, and to acquire the staff and expertise necessary to guide member companies in their efforts to devise and carry through a productivity agreement.

The C.B.I. had, therefore, radically changed its position since 1965. Some employers' associations had moved along the lines advocated by the C.B.I. even in advance of this revision of policy. Apart from the influential Chemical Industries Association case, the Engineering Employers' Federation, before Donovan or the C.B.I. statement, had seriously begun to explore the potential of productivity bargaining in that complex industry,[27] and several other industries negotiated framework agreements providing just the sort of guidelines for plant-level productivity bargaining envisaged in the C.B.I. document.

What of the development of trade union thinking? A general statement of the T.U.C. philosophy is contained in the Annual Report for 1969:

> The aim should be to achieve a structure of agreements each of which is negotiated at the level at which effective action can be prescribed on relevant issues. In this way the industry agreement

---

[27] Cf. for example the conference of January 1968, organised by the E.E.F., and resulting in the publication of a Symposium volume: D. C. Alexander (ed.), *A Productivity Bargaining Symposium* (London: Engineering Employers' Federation, 1969).

(on wages, for example) might lay down minimum rates of pay and set out the principles to be followed, for example in job evaluation and financial incentives; the subsidiary company agreement might govern, for example, the application of job evaluation and deal with the requirements of financial incentives; and agreements at still lower levels might be concerned with details of the use of work measurement schemes including attention to allowances. Each of the agreements would thus deal with productivity issues capable of special definition and treatment at their respective levels.[28]

If the T.U.C. was essentially in favour of plant-level bargaining,[29] it was certainly not at any great expense to the principle of industry-wide bargaining. Instead, it saw in plant bargaining a means of extending the scope of collective bargaining, so that at each of a number of levels there would be an opening up of issues for bargaining previously obscured or difficult to tackle.

This is of course a perfectly legitimate aim, provided there is general agreement on the appropriate issues to be tackled at each stage. But since it possibly would involve a continuous process of bargaining without doing much to reduce the fragmentation of bargaining, it may well be a rather different conception from that in the minds of some advocates of plant-level bargaining – a conception which envisaged both the devolution of bargaining from industry to plant (or company) level *and* the upward concentration of sectional and small-group bargaining at shop-floor level to the works or company level. We might conclude that the expectations of both groups were fundamentally different and that the hopes of bargaining-structure reform leading to less fragmented bargaining were rather forlorn from the outset.

Given moderate encouragement from the T.U.C., the trade unions in general were quite willing to take advantage of the opportunities open to them, no doubt reinforced in their enthusiasm by the pressures of incomes policy. Even so, some unions,

---

[28] T.U.C. General Council *Report* 1969, 304.

[29] A further reflection of this attitude occurs in a 1968 revision of a T.U.C. pamphlet on productivity bargaining first produced in 1965. This pamphlet swung a little to the view that in some sectors the appropriate level for agreements might be the workplace rather than the industry, and it was certainly possible for unions, working within the precepts of this document, to enter into framework agreements as a basis for plant-level agreements.

notably the T.G.W.U. and the G.M.W.U., found it necessary to set out detailed guidelines for their own negotiators, in part to achieve some consistency of approach, in part in opposition to the N.B.P.I. guidelines which were regarded as unfair and unduly restrictive. Similar signs of criticism and unrest among trade unions became more prominent as time went on, and from mid-1969 the favourable attitudes became noticeably less common. The explanation of this must include such developments as the gradual breakdown of incomes policy, the growing awareness of union leaders of the possible dangers of yielding increased control on the shop-floor to employers[30] (even if the reward in the short run was attractive), and the incipient loss of respect for the N.B.P.I. as it struggled to hold the incomes policy intact.

3. CONCLUSIONS

This chapter has shown how the control over productivity bargaining, essential to its new role as a part of the incomes policy in the late 1960s, took shape. It has reviewed a number of issues thrown into relief by the implementation of the control function, and some of these will have to be taken up more fully in the context of particular cases. We have presented some evidence on the way in which the use of productivity bargaining contributed to the objectives of incomes policy, and while the evidence is not wholly satisfactory, it does not encourage the view that the innovation in policy was a great success. It may be that *any* incomes policy of the restrictive type is doomed to failure except as a device to delay wage increases for a time, but in this case the degree of achievement does not appear to have been high, judged as a whole. Furthermore, we have suggested that in the process of being deployed as a policy weapon, productivity bargaining itself may have suffered, as it were, from misuse.

It is true that as a result of being made to play this role, productivity bargaining grew more mature through wider application and more intensive study, and showed its ability to cope with new problems, such as the introduction of work measurement schemes

---

[30] No doubt developed and sharpened by the writings of left-wing commentators such as Tony Cliff, who argued a persuasive if emotive case against productivity bargaining. Cf. T. Cliff, *The Employers' Offensive: Productivity Deals and How to Fight Them* (London: Pluto Press, 1970).

and the reform of disorderly pay structures. But sight was often lost of the important cultural characteristics associated with the genuine productivity agreement, and that represents a serious loss. Furthermore, because of its identification with the incomes policy, productivity bargaining began to meet increasing criticism and began to go into decline alongside the incomes policy, from the middle of 1969 onward.

This brings us back to one of the original questions posed in Chapter 1 – whether productivity bargaining *should* be allowed to lapse into obscurity, or whether it is worth while attempting to ensure that it survives in areas where it can be utilised to good effect. The answers to these questions depend on a more detailed analysis of the approaches to productivity bargaining, the problems of preparation, design strategy, and the issues arising in implementation and control. It is to this more detailed study, based on case material, that we devote the next few chapters.

5 The Ingredients in Productivity Agreements

In the discussions in Chapters 2 and 3 of the evolution and spread of productivity bargaining in the period 1960–70, some attention was given to the changing nature of agreements, but the main thrust was to understand the diffusion that occurred in such bargaining during the decade. In contrast, the present chapter focuses on the content of productivity agreements themselves. Before turning to this content analysis, we would like to comment on the importance of the economic and technological context and of the objectives held by the parties in shaping the ingredients of productivity agreements. Then we can analyse the various aspects of achievement and reward with which productivity bargaining has concerned itself.

Decisions concerning the design of the achievement–reward system are made within the larger contexts of technology and economic outlook. In some cases, such contextual factors will be determining; in others, the interests of the parties will have primary weight. For example, where the skill level of a job is shaped by the production process, it will not be a discretionary part of the work system. However, certain other aspects of that system, such as clustering of skills, manpower assignment, manpower scheduling, may be discretionary and, therefore, may reflect the preferences of the parties.

The technology of production processes and the socio-economic context within which industries function are factors of such pervasive importance as to require special emphasis. They establish the broad limits within which management and unions operate. The impact of these structural variables on the ingredients of productivity agreements will be examined throughout this chapter.[1]

Although management and labour must be governed by the overall economic realities, they are not rendered completely impotent thereby; and their interests must be considered in any study of the ontology of work rules. Certainly, the preferences of the parties can exert a direct influence on the solutions emerging from productivity bargaining. As with technology and economic outlook, the attitudes of the parties to the agreements are ever present forces not to be overlooked. Again, in each section of this chapter we will discuss how such preferences manifest themselves in negotiations.

1. FACTORS INVOLVED IN THE AGREEMENTS

Many key ingredients were mentioned in discussing the seminal Fawley agreement and the others that followed its lead. The list of subjects is imposing, showing as much breadth and variety as employment relationships themselves : reduction of numbers of helpers or mates, alteration of shift patterns, elimination of unproductive time, reduction in overtime, increased earnings, modification of wage payment methods (including streamlined pay structures), institution of staff status, guarantees against cutbacks or redundancy, and elimination of casual employment.

Immediately the question arises of how best to tackle such a range of subjects to reveal coherent and meaningful patterns. We need not undertake an exhaustive enumeration of every feature of all productivity agreements; this aspect of the subject has been already adequately covered. Similarly, we need not develop any new taxonomy of the subjects included in the agreements; already a number of useful classification schemes have been advanced.[2] However, we do believe that it is useful to subject the agreements to analysis in terms of *both* sides of the employment relationship : achievement and reward. These are the categories used in the

---

[1] Several studies have demonstrated the functional connection between type of technology (e.g. process versus assembly versus batch production) and the organisation of work. See J. Woodward, *Industrial Organization: Theory and Practice* (London: Oxford University Press, 1965), and M. Fullan, 'Industrial Technology and Worker Integration in the Organization', *American Sociological Review*, XXXV (1970) 1028–39.

[2] See, for example, K. Jones and J. Golding, *Productivity Bargaining*, Fabian Research Series, 257 (London : Fabian Society, 1966) 7–21.

preceding chapters on the evolution and spread of productivity agreements. Each could be broken down in many ways; for obvious reasons, our analysis employs the subcategories which were used in the D.E.P. tabulations.

ACHIEVEMENT ELEMENTS IN THE WORK SYSTEM

On the achievement side of the equation, the themes with which the agreements concerned themselves are :

  (i) Nature of work, emphasising skill utilisation and worker flexibility
 (ii) Hours of work, including shift patterns and overtime reduction
(iii) Effort utilisation or manning
 (iv) Methods, including work measurement and control, wage payment systems, and wage structure revision

Apart from a slight reordering and regrouping these four themes parallel the D.E.P. groupings used in the analysis of diffusion and evolution in Chapters 2 and 3. Quantity of work and manning have been combined into one category, 'effort utilisation'. Two D.E.P. categories, organisation and responsibility, are not handled explicitly in this breakdown, although much of what is contained under organisation (introduction of multi-craft supervision and new working parties) is associated with changes in the nature of work. But, in any event, the numerical importance of these two themes is not important. As we observed in Chapter 3, they accounted for about 5 per cent of all achievement changes.

REWARD ELEMENTS IN THE WORK SYSTEM

On the reward side we will use a modification of the D.E.P. breakdown :

  (i) Wages or increased earnings
 (ii) Leisure resulting from overtime reduction
(iii) Job guarantees and status

This again is a reduced form of the D.E.P. categories, adopted primarily because of the concentration of the data into these categories, and especially into the first two.

2. NATURE OF WORK (SKILL UTILISATION)

The task of making the most of the worker's skill goes beyond that of finding square pegs for square holes : it includes developing procedures to make possible necessary flexibility and interchangeability in staffing arrangements.

JOB DEFINITION AND DESIGN PROBLEMS

Obviously, the manner in which the production task is broken down into individual jobs – the job design – directly affects both parties. From management's point of view, the job structure determines how work gets done; from the worker's point of view, it determines his basic pay and the nature of his task experience. Two distinctions can be made on job design and worker allocation.

A particular job may be defined either narrowly or widely; however, from the point of view of skill utilisation, the most significant question is what portion of a given job can be performed by a worker from another job. The extent of overlap – the area of potential flexibility – may not be large, but even a small amount of interchangeability can contribute significantly to increased efficiency. Thus, skill utilisation can be explored in terms of the manner in which work components are clustered into jobs and the extent of overlap in these clusters.

The second facet of skill utilisation involves the question of changing the assignment of a given worker. The issue is whether this worker can be transferred to similar work – was he hired to perform a whole class of work or simply to operate a given machine? Since most problems in this area are a result of transferring workers from one physical location to another, worker flexibility can be thought to involve spatial flexibility.

Before illustrating the range of skill utilisation problems tackled by productivity agreements, it is important to underscore the pervasiveness of the subject. A rigid adherence to specific duties can occur in connection with any job area. Such inflexibility occurs most often in the crafts, where the different skill groups jealously guard their respective territories, thereby creating some of the most conspicuous examples of jurisdictional or demarcational rigidities. For instance, demarcation problems were rife in the shipyards before the advent of productivity bargaining. Making a porthole involved the shipwright who marked out the appropriate area, the joiner who checked the marking, the burner who burned out the steelwork, and the caulker who fitted the window; and there were endless conflicts between these different craftsmen. Similar difficulties may exist also between skilled and nonskilled workers (such as semiskilled production workers in many engineering establishments) or among process operators (as in chemicals and oils), or even between groups of semiskilled production workers. Fox and Flanders make the point as follows :

> Craftsmen had always aspired to extend their own unilateral regulation . . . to cover many of the details of job organization and behaviour. . . . Now their example began to be followed by non-craft work groups whose shop floor power awakened new aspirations.[3]

The experience of the Ford company is instructive on this point. Before the redesign of the classification structure, Ford workers tended to think of themselves as 'skilled', 'semiskilled' or 'unskilled'. While flexibility in the use of manpower was limited within each of these groupings, the main problems centred on achieving flexibility between groups. The skilled workers tended to think of themselves as an *élite* and resisted any suggestion of sharing duties with those 'below them'.

WORKER AND MANAGEMENT PREFERENCES

In stable, mass-production situations, management normally prefers specialised skill clusters. Narrowly defined or specialised jobs have the advantages of shorter training periods, greater potential for control, and wage savings that go along with the hiring of semiskilled rather than skilled employees. A study of Fairfields made the point this way :

> We are all for some form of *demarcation*, but in management language we call it *specialisation*. We don't want the electricians to fix our plumbing and we don't want the welders to build our wooden decks.[4]

[3] A. Fox and A. Flanders, 'The Reform of Collective Bargaining : From Donovan to Durkheim', *British Journal of Industrial Relations*, VII (1969) 173.
[4] S. Paulden and B. Hawkins, *Whatever Happened at Fairfields?* (London : Gower Press, 1969) 121.

Workers, on the other hand, usually prefer broader job definitions for the important reason that wages are then appropriately higher; also, job satisfaction may be greater. Moreover, broader job design usually offers the worker wider experience and greater opportunities for skill development.

Situations do, of course, exist where such underlying preferences are not evident. For example, if management does not have the required talents to co-ordinate a highly specialised job structure, it may have to opt for the enlarged job design. Moreover, workers may not *always* prefer broader job categories – especially if they place heavy importance on social contact and minimum involvement in the job. Several studies of the connections between job design and worker needs have concluded that most, *but not all*, workers prefer broader job categories. Frequently, women and certain 'urban', semiskilled workers derive more satisfaction from highly repetitive, narrowly defined job clusters.[5]

Theoretically, there may be no reason to expect the parties to seek either more specialised or broader job categories. Rather, productivity bargaining's main function would appear to be to create a better match between the evolving technological–economic environment and the skill structure. Whether the improved matching represents a 'catch up' or whether productivity bargaining attempts to foster a continuing adaptation between the skill structure and the technological requirements depends upon the strategy adopted (we will distinguish in Chapter 6 between the direct and the indirect approaches to productivity improvement) and the operating results of the different strategies (which we will evaluate in Chapters 8 and 9).

The creation of new skill clusters to keep pace with advancing technology is an important starting point for productivity bargaining. In general, the new skill clusters are likely to be more encompassing than the earlier ones; however, it is still entirely possible that, as production expands into new processes, some refinement in job definition will take place. Thus, the function of productivity bargaining is to find ways of accommodating management's need for adapting skill structures to changing circumstances with the workers' desire for greater occupational choice. In the light of these

---

[5] A. N. Turner and P. R. Lawrence, *Industrial Jobs and the Worker* (Cambridge, Mass.: Harvard University Press, 1965) chapters 4 and 5.

manager and worker preferences, we now examine skill utilisation in actual productivity agreements.

SKILL UTILISATION PROVISIONS

We have been especially interested in the variety of approaches used to tackle the problems involved in skill utilisation. The agreements reveal that increased interchangeability of skills has occurred both *horizontally* (craft-to-craft and craft-to-process groupings) and *vertically* (craft-to-helper or mate). Generally speaking, more work sharing has occurred on a craft-to-craft basis than between craft and process groupings. Such sharing has the appeal of taking place within the 'family' of skilled workers.[6] By contrast, craft workers are reluctant to do process work ('It's beneath our dignity') and usually object to process workers crossing into their skill domain.

Horizontal flexibility. Several approaches to craft-to-craft work sharing can be observed. In many agreements, especially in the oil refining and engineering industries, work sharing between pairs of trades is spelled out. In some cases, inter-craft flexibility is limited to clearly related craft groups. At Philblack, for example, craftsmen were expected to be flexible within the following craft groupings : mechanical and metalworking crafts, instrument and electrical crafts, and building trade crafts. Elsewhere, work-sharing rules have been specified only for selected trades, or where there were rigid job demarcations. For example, in engineering, under the old procedures for the repair or overhaul of plumbing, the pipefitter disconnected pipework, the millwright undertook repair or overhaul, and the pipefitter reconnected the pipes. Under the new procedures, where there is no alteration to pipe-work involved and the connections are simple mechanical joints, the millwright disconnects and reconnects the pipes, completing the work without the aid of the pipefitter.

In those situations where some work sharing has been agreed upon between craft and process personnel, the result has usually been that process personnel have taken over minor maintenance tasks. In the Esso Fawley 1968 agreement it was specified that :

---

[6] It is relevant to note that separate craft groups often negotiate together as part of the same joint craft union committee.

Operators will carry out any [maintenance] work for which they have been trained, or which they are capable of doing, as required by the Chief Operator or Shift Foreman. Additionally . . . operators will use their own initiative and discretion to carry out any such maintenance which enables them to progress with their work.

It has been less common for maintenance personnel to reciprocate by accepting additional tasks of a skilled nature; and the full integration of craftsmen into operating teams, as in the Shell Stanlow agreement of 1969 (JUNC-Agreement), is extremely rare. That agreement provided that :

A number of craftsmen will be integrated into operating departments as members of operating teams. They will be based in departments where, in the Company's view, a major maintenance effort may be expected. Their main duties will be to work on maintenance, but they will also perform operating duties. They will be responsible to the operator in charge of the unit or the appropriate operating supervisor, though engineering technical guidance will be given, where necessary, by maintenance supervision.

Vertical flexibility.   Craft-to-helper or mate work sharing has been generally in only one direction : the duties performed by the helper (if any) have been absorbed into the craft category. Two different approaches can be distinguished. First, instead of each craftsman having his own helper, the helper serves a team of men. Sometimes such teams are in the same trade, as at Stanlow, where:

Instead of one [mate] being allocated to each fitter, a number of mates will act as assistants to a team of fitters.

In other cases, the teams involve several trades, such as the 'general maintenance assistant' at Fison's Fertilizer Company. Second, the skill category of mate often has been abolished. In most instances, the incumbents are transferred to another employment status, such as maintenance assistants. The Philblack agreement of 1968 provided that :

Existing grades of craftsmen's mates will be abolished. Selected electricians' mates and instrument mechanics' mates will be trained as installation craftsmen in one of these crafts. All other mates will be designated as maintenance assistants or building trade assistants.

In a few instances the mates were upgraded or redeployed as process workers. For example, the Mobil Oil Agreement provided that :

> . . . the job of craftsman's mate and electrician's helper will be eliminated and the employees transferred to process shift work, or upgraded as craftsmen.

Worker assignment patterns. A number of agreements have directly confronted the issue of the traditional territorial 'rights' of certain workers and provided for greater flexibility in assignments to more than one location. The Philblack agreement read :

> There will be no geographical restriction on the ability of employees within the Works and any employee will work on any plant, including the pipeline or oil jetty, or any company property within reasonable distance of the Works.

The Esso Fawley 1968 agreement provided that :

> . . . an operator may be released from his crew for certain other activities in the Refinery where recall can be readily achieved in the event of an emergency.

The agreement between the enclosed docks employers and the T.G.W.U. and stevedores and dockers (Devlin Phase II) provided for complete mobility on : (1) movement of employees or gangs of workers to other work within a given shift, including transfers from ship to quay and quay to ship; (2) movement of employees or gangs from discharging to loading and vice versa within shifts; and (3) adjustment in numbers assigned to shed/area crews as required by the employer, with workers being transferred both within and between sheds/areas.

Safeguards and compromises. Productivity bargaining has involved something more than simply an exchange of money for more flexibility. While some agreements may have involved pure and simple 'buy-outs', many have reflected a creative accommodation between management's need for greater flexibility and the workers' need to preserve their skill traditions. An A.U.E.W. official commenting on the Shell Stanlow agreement said :

The aims of JUNC on flexibility and work sharing were very simple : (i) we insisted on safeguarding special craft skills, and (ii) there could be no interchangeability on basic skills that were embodied in the normal craft apprenticeship training, in regard to practice and technical know-how.[7]

In general, the approach of most productivity agreements to the problems of skill utilisation has been to erect safeguards, or at least to enunciate the principles of reserving certain core areas of skills for affected craftsmen. The process workers at Alcan, for instance, resisted a proposal that they should be allotted to one of four broadly defined groups, within which a man could be called on to do any job. They felt that those groups were so wide as to leave no man with a job of his own. It was eventually agreed that each worker should have a normal job, but would be ready to 'range' outside it to perform any process task for which training and experience guided him.[8] Even in the unique 1968 Shell Stanlow agreement, where craftsmen were integrated into process work, the craftsmen identities were protected :

> Craftsmen integrated into operating teams will not be used as operators in charge of process units, nor will they be used full-time as operators, at any level, on a regular basis. The total number of integrated craftsmen will not exceed $7\frac{1}{2}$ per cent of the total number of shift operators at Stanlow.

The thrust of productivity agreements has been integrative, with the parties finding common ground. Instead of simply viewing flexibility in skill utilisation as a suitable trade-off – with workers giving up something and management compensating them for this loss – productivity bargaining has searched for more imaginative arrangements which the parties might prefer, even in the absence of monetary inducements.

INDUSTRY PATTERNS

We were also interested in analysing productivity agreements to uncover industry-wide patterns with reference to skill utilisation.

[7] H. S. Rule before the British Institute of Management Conference (19 April 1969).
[8] N.B.P.I. Report No. 36, p. 5.

Table 5.1. Industry Rank Order of Relative Importance for Various Achievement Categories

Rank order	Nature of work	Hours	Effort utilisation (manning)	Methods
1	Shipbuilding	Paper, printing	Public administration	Clothing
2	Construction	Miscellaneous services	Professional & scientific services	Vehicles
3	Metal goods, n.e.s.	Bricks, pottery	Transport, communication	Engineering
4	Public administration	Chemicals	Leather	Food
5	Chemicals	Transport, communication	Miscellaneous services	Textiles
6	Metal manufacturing	Textiles	Paper, printing	Timber, furniture
7	Engineering	Metal goods, n.e.s.	Distribution	Other manufacturing
8	Paper, printing	Construction	Food	Shipbuilding
9	Miscellaneous services	Leather	Timber, furniture	Metal goods, n.e.s.
10	Bricks, pottery	Shipbuilding	Other manufacturing	Metal manufacturing
11	Vehicles	Other manufacturing	Chemicals	Chemicals
12	Timber, furniture	Food	Metal manufacturing	Distribution
13	Textiles	Metal manufacturing	Vehicles	Professional & scientific services
14	Transport, communication	Vehicles	Engineering	Transport, communication
15	Leather	Distribution	Textiles	Bricks, pottery
16	Food	Public administration	Metal goods, n.e.s.	Miscellaneous services
17	Distribution	Engineering	Bricks, pottery	Public administration
18	Other manufacturing	Timber, furniture	Clothing	Construction
19	Clothing	Professional & scientific services	Shipbuilding	Leather
20	Professional & scientific services	Clothing	Construction	Paper, printing

Table 5.1 ranks twenty major industries in terms of the importance accorded to skill utilisation compared to the other three major categories of the work system : hours, effort utilisation and methods.[9]

With reference to skill utilisation (nature of work – column 1), shipbuilding stands at the top of the list. This rating is consistent with the troublesome nature (both quantitatively and qualitatively) of jurisdictional disputes in this industry. These disputes were well described in the Geddes Report :

> In an industry such as shipbuilding in which a wide variety and range of skills are required, there will inevitably be differences of opinion over the appropriate craft to perform a particular task. The original subdivisions of shipbuilding into crafts took place at a time when production methods in the industry were very different from what they are now and the distinctions between the work and various crafts performed were perhaps much more obvious than now. But, for example, changes in lofting methods have made substantial changes in the work of some shipwrights. Prefabrication has brought the work of the plater and the shipwright much more in line. Riveters can do work that traditionally has been performed by caulkers. Blacksmiths are now trained in electrical welding. In the fitting-out trades some new materials, such as plastics, can do away with the need for painting. Moreover the use of automatically controlled machinery has reduced many jobs from skilled to semiskilled status. But there is a strong tendency to maintain agreed demarcation lines even when they have been slurred, or sometimes obliterated, by technical developments.[10]

It is interesting to note that some of the industries near the bottom of the rank-order list for nature of work have also experienced extensive changes in technology, yet demarcation arrangements have not been a source of difficulty. One possible explanation is that in industries such as transport, food and distribution, work has been organised by function, while elsewhere

[9] It should be noted that the rank order of the industries does not reflect the absolute volume of work changes in a particular category and industry. Rather, it indicates the numerical importance of a certain category of change relative to the other changes in the industry.

[10] Shipbuilding Inquiry Committee, 1965–1966, *Report*, Cmnd 2937 (London: H.M.S.O. 1966) 104.

(particularly in industries at the top of the list), work has been organised by skill or occupational groups. In shipbuilding, for example, the task of fairing a ship has changed with the introduction of modern methods, yet the affected crafts have not adjusted their skill jurisdictions to changing work methods and technologies. Similar attempts to preserve the integrity of skill and craft boundaries (at least until productivity bargaining offered scope for relaxation) might be attributed to such industries as chemicals and printing.

SOME CONDITIONING FACTORS WITH REFERENCE TO SKILL UTILISATION

The last paragraph may have suggested that problems in skill utilisation are simply a function of technology and work organisation. However, at least two other considerations seem equally deserving of attention. Perhaps the most useful way of presenting these various considerations is as hypotheses :

Hypothesis 1: Jurisdictional problems arise as the result of technological change.

Hypothesis 2: The organisation of work into different craft groups creates problems in skill utilisation.

Hypothesis 3: Difficulties in skill utilisation have increased in those industries characterised by economic slowdown and declining employment.

Impact of technological change. The pace of change is certainly a key factor in making traditional practices obsolete; and the industries that have had the most troublesome jurisdictional disputes have tended to be those experiencing the most dramatic changes in technology and materials. Thus, the introduction of web offset equipment in the printing industry rendered obsolete many traditional skill categories. In shipbuilding, the classic distinction between shipwrights and platers proved unworkable as assembly methods changed.[11]

Significance of work organisation. The organisation of work into different craft groups can contribute to tension over skill jurisdictions. Thus, we might expect a high correlation between the

[11] For a good discussion of this issue and a general analysis of disputes over skill issues in shipbuilding, see G. Roberts, *Demarcation Rules in Shipbuilding and Ship Repairing,* Occasional Paper, University of Cambridge Department of Applied Economics (London : Cambridge University Press, 1967).

percentage ratios of craft to total workers and the percentage ratios of jurisdictional to all disputes. For example, shipbuilding, where almost two-thirds of the workers are skilled and where many demarcation disputes have occurred, falls at one end of the continuum; at the other end are such industries as rubber, where craft workers are less than one-fourth of the total workforce. It is interesting that the N.E.D.O. for the rubber industry reported: 'Disputes over demarcation (in rubber) are rare. In every firm visited, there is a tradition of flexible working'.[12]

While the existence of separate work groups creates the potential for the build-up of demarcation problems, the actual result may be quite different because some craft groups have little 'coercive capacity'. They may want to enforce certain jurisdictional boundaries but their bargaining position is weak; the workers may have few employment alternatives or their ability to create pressure through strike action may be quite limited (for example, where operations can be maintained for some time by supervisors). The emergence of skill rigidities depends on both the need or incentive to create and the ability and capacity to defend occupational lines.

Technological change may also intersect with work-group organisation. The presence of separate work groups or jurisdictions tends to exacerbate those demarcation difficulties that have been created by changing technology. The steel industry has seen how changing technology, together with competing union groups, can create major demarcation difficulties, as in the disputes between the bricklayers and the operators over using dolomite to reline oxygen furnaces,[13] and between the engineers and the process workers over the machining of hollows.[14]

Economic outlook and job security. Inertia acting to support existing skill jurisdictions tends to be particularly strong when the economic outlook is uncertain. The decline in employment during the post-war period in the shipbuilding and dock industries con-

[12] National Economic Development Office, *Plant Bargaining* (London: N.E.D.O., 1969) 4.

[13] *Report of an Inquiry into a Dispute Between the Steel Company of Wales and the Amalgamated Union of Building Trade Workers* (London: H.M.S.O., 1967) para. 39.

[14] *Report of a Court of Inquiry into the Causes and Circumstances of a Dispute at the Tube Works of Stewarts and Lloyds Limited at Corby*, Cmnd 3260 (London: H.M.S.O., 1967).

tributed to problems of skill utilisation in these industries. One episode involving such insecurity occurred in the shipyards in 1965 :

> At John Brown, shipyard platers and welders refused to allow seventy-eight sheet metal workers to be temporarily deployed on other tasks so that they could be retained on the payroll.
> The seventy-eight will be dismissed today as redundant. In about nine months, however, they will be needed for the Q4 contract for Cunard, which is already six months behind schedule.[15]

The example just cited points up another dimension of job insecurity in shipbuilding (beyond the long-term decline in employment); namely, the project cycle tends to be discrete with large numbers of workers being hired to handle a contract like the Q4 and then being let go some two to three years later.

The general importance of job security – or more precisely job insecurity – in fostering jurisdictional disputes in shipbuilding has been underscored by Eldridge :

> ... the industry was subject to severe fluctuations. The insecurity which this bred was heightened by the fact that notice to quit the job could be given with less than a day's warning. It was further accentuated by the fact that employment opportunities outside the industry were usually very limited. . . . To exercise effective job control over a specified range of tasks was, therefore, to provide a cushion against shrinking employment opportunities in times of slump.[16]

Even in shipbuilding, job insecurity did not pose a uniform threat across the trades. Some craft workers could find alternative employment and others could not. Eldridge noted that, on the north-east coast, there were more demarcation disputes in fabrication than in finishing. He attributed this difference to greater labour market flexibility for carpenters and the finishing trades as compared to the platers and other fabricating trades whose skills were unique to the shipbuilding industry.

---

[15] *Sunday Times*, 12 December 1965.
[16] J. E. T. Eldridge, *Industrial Disputes, Essays in the Sociology of Industrial Relations* (London : Routledge & Kegan Paul, 1968) 96.

By way of contrast, the motor industry, which has been characterised by almost continual expansion, has experienced little disagreement over skill utilisation matters. In analysing this industry, Turner commented on the absence of demarcation disputes : 'The workers have generally been quite prepared to take on new jobs as automation (or other technical changes) . . . have wiped out their old ones.'[17] Yet technological change has probably been as rapid in the motor industry as in shipbuilding – or, for that matter, as in any other British industry. The difference has been in economic outlook, with the motor industry steadily expanding and the shipbuilding industry steadily contracting.

Contracting employment gives rise to skill problems for another reason. As the scale of operations shrinks, job classifications are often revised to include more tasks. This form of job enlargement is nothing more than the obverse of Adam Smith's principle that as the size of markets increases so also will the division of labour. Just as growth in demand leads to a greater division of labour, so a drop in demand may require a broadening of occupational lines, and these adjustments may not take place readily but provoke extensive demarcation problems.

Pressure to enlarge skill clusters may of course derive from factors other than declining product demand. A rapid increase in productivity (possibly due to new technology or new production methods) can reduce a firm's overall demand for labour and, thereby, induce it to seek a new job structure. For example, in the oil industry, as maintenance has been subcontracted (and that which remains has been concentrated into short periods of intense activity called 'turn-rounds'), the existing classifications have become more and more inappropriate.

STATISTICAL FINDINGS ON SKILL UTILISATION

To examine whether an inter-industry analysis of the relative importance of skill utilisation in productivity agreements could lend support to some of the above stated hypotheses, a series of simple (Pearson) correlation coefficients were computed. The measure of

[17] H. A. Turner, G. Clack and G. Roberts, *Labour Relations in the Motor Industry* (London: Allen & Unwin, 1967) 84. Between 1952 and 1963 employment in the motor industry increased by 50 per cent while productivity rose over 100 per cent. See Turner *et al.* pp. 80–1.

the dependent variable was the same as for the rank order of industries presented in Table 5.1, above. Against this variable we correlated the values for measures of the different independent variables discussed in the preceding sections.

Changes in skill utilisation were positively correlated with the proportion of skilled workers[18] in an industry ($R = 0.52$, significant at the 2 per cent level) and with the proportion of apprentices in an industry ($R = 0.58$, significant at the 1 per cent level), both of which were seen to approximate the importance of craft unionism or separate work organisation in an industry. Skill utilisation changes were also positively associated with firm size ($R = 0.27$) and capital intensity of an industry ($R = 0.25$), but these coefficients were not significant at the 5 per cent level. With respect to measures of job insecurity, employment decline was not associated with the prominence of nature of work issues at the industry level. Unemployment, however, with a coefficient of $R = 0.64$, was significant at the 1 per cent level.

The implication behind the strong positive association of changes in skill utilisation with unemployment rates is that job insecurity leads to the development of such problems and productivity bargaining is a particularly effective mechanism for the development of solutions to them. We will have more to say on this point later in the chapter when we note the impact of unemployment on changes in effort arrangements.

3. HOURS OF WORK PATTERNS

Following the pattern of the earlier analyses, we analysed agreement provisions in terms of hours-of-work patterns in major industries, with special attention to : (1) scheduling flexibility, and (2) control of overtime.

Management's need (in a temporal sense) for labour often conflicts with the workers' attitudes concerning appropriate work–leisure patterns. Generally, the scheduling of workers reflects some form of compromise between management's desire to have workers available as required and labour's desire for normal or regular hours. In many cases, before productivity bargaining the workers' side of the equation had become dominant; they were scheduled

---

[18] Measured as follows: skilled craftsmen as a percentage of total employment. Ministry of Labour *Gazette* (January 1968).

only within normal hours. However, with technological advances and production processes often becoming round-the-clock, seven-day-a-week operations, traditional scheduling arrangements have become less and less appropriate.

One example of a mismatch between the demand for labour and workers' schedules was cited by the N.B.P.I. in its report on the bakery industry : 'The agreement has become interpreted in such a way that all workers in any one bakery have the same rest day in the week, even though the requirements of production may not need the presence of all.'[19]

MODIFICATIONS IN SCHEDULING

One important direction taken by productivity bargaining has been towards the revision of work schedules to achieve more flexibility. Such flexibility in the scheduling can be achieved either on a planned or emergency basis. For planned flexibility in scheduling, the critical question is : within what time horizon must the actual work hours average out to the stated norm ?

'Balancing' periods.   In some instances the balancing period has been extended to an annual basis. For example, in the electricity supply industry, longer hours were scheduled in summer and shorter hours in winter. In air transport, the balancing period for aircrew was one month; and additional flexibility was achieved by shortening rest periods at home base, even though the total number of hours on and off duty remained the same.

In newspapers, where variations in worker demand follow weekly patterns, imaginative work schedules have been developed that concentrate workers towards the end of the week in preparation for the Sunday editions. Sometimes, workers are scheduled for as much as fourteen hours at a stretch – with compensating five-day breaks at set intervals. The schedule in Table 5.2, developed in an agreement with one of the Fleet Street newspapers, provided for a typical worker to move through a ten-week rotation; in some instances he worked ten days consecutively and then had five days off.

One of the beneficial side effects of reducing overtime is that workers are more able to handle irregular work schedules with

[19] N.B.P.I. Report No. 17, *Wages in the Bakery Industry*, Cmnd 3019 (London : H.M.S.O., 1966) 11.

Table 5.2. Work Rotations in One Publishing Agreement

Shift	Sun		Mon		Tue		Wed		Thur		Fri		Sat		Sun		Hours
	am	pm	am	pm	am	pm	am	pm	am	pm	am	pm	am	pm	am	pm	
1									8–5		8–5			4–12		12–6	32
2		10–6		10–6		10–6		10–6		10–6		10–6					48
3									8–5		8–5			4–12		12–6	32
4							8–5		8–5		8–5		8–5				36
5			8–4	4–10	8–5									4–12		12–6	37
6					8–5		8–5		8–5		8–5						36
7	9–4	4–10	8–5											4–12		12–6	36
8		10–6		10–6		10–6		10–6		10–6		10–6					48
9	9–4	4–10	8–4		8–4									4–12		12–6	43
10			8–4	4–10	8–5		8–5										32

AVERAGE WORK WEEK IS 38 HOURS

Twenty-minute lunch break will be adhered to and taken when convenient to the work. No other breaks will be taken. Documentation to be introduced whereby all routine maintenance and repairs carried out will be signed for by the engineer responsible and recorded.

occasional long stints. When workers put in long hours throughout the week, they are not able to handle an assignment of long duration. However, as total leisure increases, the physiological capacity to work a long shift also increases.

Shift work. The printing industry example just mentioned, which introduced flexibility through staggering work and leisure periods, also involved another scheduling device : shift work. Shifts can be designed to adapt working hours to round-the-clock production. Accordingly, shift work involves work at times that are not usually regarded as normal day-time hours; and often the shifts are worked on a rotational basis.

While shift work existed in process-type production before productivity bargaining, the agreements have extended it to occupational groups not previously covered – especially maintenance personnel, as in electricity supply and the Esso Fawley refinery. 'Temporary shift work' has also been introduced; and management has been allowed greater discretion in changing shift patterns (with advance notice), as in the Esso distribution agreement. Such temporary shift work can provide coverage for shut-downs and start-ups which would otherwise interfere with production; they can also be used to speed up work on turn-rounds or deal with major breakdowns. At Mobil Coryton, craftsmen agreed to a maximum of thirty-five cover-up shifts per man per year.

Shift work has been introduced for the first time or extended in volume through productivity agreements in certain other less capital-intensive industries – as, for example, in such engineering firms as Geo. Tucker, Wellworthy, Burroughs Machines, Gullick Dobson, Newton and Chambers.

The use of the 'call-in'. Occasionally, management may also need to mobilize a workforce on short notice; accordingly, many agreements (especially in oil and chemicals) have included provisions for 'calling-in' workers.

In the B.P. Chemicals (U.K.) Ltd agreement of 1969, 'call-in' was defined as :

> Summoning an employee back to work after he has left the factory for the day. 'Call-in' also refers to an employee who is summoned from home on his rest day or on a declared holiday to work on that day.

> When a period of call-in exceeds *four hours* (up to which a

supplementary payment will be made), the hours in excess of four will not qualify for higher payment but will qualify for time off in lieu on an hour-for-hour basis to the nearest whole hour.

In the 1968 interim agreement at Fawley, which involved the craftsmen and the T.G.W.U., a stand-by call-in system was inaugurated 'for selected men who live in the immediate locality of the refinery – in addition to the existing emergency call-in procedure'.

CONTROL OF OVERTIME

Many productivity agreements have made overtime reduction a primary objective, with emphasis on : (1) the amount of overtime to be permitted, and (2) payment schedules for overtime.

While most agreements emphasised the need to reduce overtime, they often allowed for scheduling incidental overtime. A small engineering company agreement provided :

> Employees may be required to work incidental overtime in order to complete jobs on the following basis : Thirty minutes a day totalling not more than one hour per week. Such time shall be treated as incidental overtime and shall not rank for time off in lieu.

A few agreements prohibited overtime entirely. In one instance, cited by Whybrew, the prohibition of overtime was combined with a new incentive system. Normal working hours were the goal, but if the worker completed his assignments in less time, he was to be free to go home without loss in pay.[20]

Where agreements allowed for overtime work, arrangements were also made for payment for such overtime – generally at premium rates, as in the M.U.P.S. agreement of I.C.I. :

> An additional premium per hour will be paid for overtime worked on Saturday and Sunday in the case of employees on a daywork system, on rest days for employees on a shift work system and for work on statutory holidays.

[20] E. G. Whybrew, *Overtime Working in Britain*, Royal Commission Research Paper No. 9 (London : H.M.S.O., 1968) 78.

Several other agreements (including Mobil and Shell) provided for time-off-in-lieu on a one-for-one basis. This latter arrangement of treating all days of the week the same is preferred by management as a means of neutralising any inducement for workers to seek overtime work. For example, at Mobil it was agreed that Saturday and Sunday work could be required for a certain number of shifts per year, with equivalent time-off-in-lieu to be scheduled.

SOME CONDITIONING FACTORS CONCERNING HOURS

The rank order of industries with reference to the subject of hours is presented in Table 5.1, column 2. Generally speaking, the capital-intensive industries appear at the top of the list. However, it is unlikely that technology, *per se*, would explain fully the matter of hours. Worker expectations with respect to satisfactory levels of take-home pay also are clearly involved. In fact, some industries, like the service industries, which are low in capital use, appear high in this rank-order list.

It is desirable to analyse the emergence of the hours issue more systematically. The approach, as with the skill issue, is to correlate certain structural characteristics with the relative importance of the hours issue at the industry level. The D.E.P. data on which this analysis is based grouped together both the shift and overtime subjects into the hours category. Since by far the more pervasive and in some respects more intractable issue has been overtime, most of our hypotheses are based on this facet of the hours subject.

Hypothesis 1:   Overtime occurs as a means of supplementing take-home pay which would be low in its absence.

Hypothesis 2:   Overtime occurs as a mechanism for adjusting national rates to the exigencies of the local labour market.

Hypothesis 3:   Overtime tends to be used where labour is in short supply.

Impact of economic need.   It would appear that in many cases worker expectations, rather than management's need for more hours of work, explain the use of overtime. Thus, where pay is low in relation to going market rates, workers are likely to press for overtime work.[21] Before the advent of productivity bargaining,

---

[21] N.B.P.I. Report No. 161, *Hours of Work, Overtime and Shiftworking,* Cmnd 4554 (London: H.M.S.O., 1970) p. 26, para. 68.

such pressures apparently existed in electricity supply.[22] The industry used the same wage schedule throughout the country, although labour market conditions varied, and overtime arrangements helped equalise these differences. In Birmingham, where electricity supply was a relatively low-paying industry in comparison with others in the area, overtime averaged ten to fifteen hours a week. However, in the South-west, where the relative wage position of electricity supply was quite favourable, five to seven hours of overtime weekly were worked.[23]

The N.B.P.I. study reported that overtime was used less frequently in plants operating on piecework, where the higher earnings decreased the demand for overtime pay.[24] This same study indicated a tendency for industries primarily employing men to make disproportionate use of overtime. Presumably, men need the additional money more than women; and they may also be in a better position, in terms of family responsibilities, to work longer hours.

Overtime can be used either to increase *gross* pay (the point under discussion) or to increase the effective *rate* of pay. Under this latter strategy, overtime hours can be substituted for regular hours through the mechanism of absenteeism. In some instances,[25] absenteeism has developed as a kind of pressure on management to force the scheduling of overtime and/or as a respite from long hours; thus, at Fairfields prior to the advent of productivity bargaining : 'Men were in the habit of going absent and turning up late during the week and then making up their wage packet with the more lucrative overtime rates.'[26] In one of our field studies (Gullick-Dobson) we ran across a similar situation. The company guaranteed forty hours of work and sixteen hours of overtime (three nights and Saturday mornings) at management's discretion

[22] H. Sallis, *Overtime in Electricity Supply*, B.J.I.R. Occasional Paper (London: London School of Economics, 1970).

[23] Care must be taken in interpreting the above findings. The longer hours worked in a low-wage industry may reflect the overall shortage of labour rather than worker preferences. The low wages of the industry may make it harder to recruit and retain workers, and those who are available may be required to work long hours.

[24] N.B.P.I. Report No. 161, p. 27, para. 70. This relationship between extent of overtime and method of wage payment has also been confirmed by some empirical work of Sallis. See Sallis, *Overtime in Electricity Supply*, pp. 6–8.

[25] N.B.P.I. Report No. 161, p. 27.

[26] S. Paulden and B. Hawkins, *Whatever Happened at Fairfields?*, p. 65.

according to the work load; however, due to extensive absenteeism, most workers clocked only thirty-eight or thirty-nine hours.[27]

Impact of bargaining structure. Overtime arrangements might also serve the function of circumventing the terms of the national agreement. When collective bargaining takes place at the central level, the individual plant needs to have some way of adjusting workers' take-home pay without changing the whole national agreement. Thus, overtime pay can become an important way of adjusting rewards locally while maintaining the validity of the national contract.

In this respect overtime provides management with a flexible device to meet the changing circumstances of the local labour market. It could be used to hold those workers who were most difficult to retain, and who often may be the best workers and should be used on overtime. Also, overtime could be withheld in slack times.

The overtime malaise, which characterised much of British industry prior to productivity bargaining, could be characterised by the word 'drift'. In other words, overtime resulted from many of the same forces and fulfilled many of the same functions as did inflated piecework earnings and job classification manipulations, subjects to which we turn later in this chapter.

Impact of labour demand. Quite clearly, overtime would need to be used where labour is in short supply or where a peak demand for labour could not be met by the normal supply. This would describe the classic circumstances for the use of overtime. Where unemployment is low, overtime levels might be expected to be high and vice versa.[28]

STATISTICAL FINDINGS ON HOURS OF WORK

Again, some empirical tests were undertaken to examine the propositions concerning the importance of hours of work as a work

---

[27] However, the N.B.P.I. study did not find a connection between overtime working and absenteeism. N.B.P.I. Report No. 161, p. 24.

[28] For example, in 1970 the Glasgow District Secretary of the Amalgamated Union of Engineering and Foundry Workers recommended that local members should not work more than twenty hours overtime per month. This limitation was reported as being aimed at trying 'to force certain managements to employ more men at this time of grave unemployment crisis. Some companies are using excessive overtime as an alternative to employing additional labour.' (*Glasgow Herald*, 4 November 1970.)

change category relative to other work changes in the productivity agreements of the various industries. Hours of work was positively related to employment growth in an industry ($R = 0.28$) and capital intensity ($R = 0.35$), both of these being rough measures of the need or demand for overtime, and negatively related to earnings from payment-by-result schemes as a percentage of total earnings ($R = -0.38$). The only result significant at the 5 per cent level was the positive association of hours with the proportion of males in an industry's labour force; the payment-by-results coefficient was significant at the 8 per cent level while all other coefficients were not significant. No association was evidenced for such measures as level of earnings and the unemployment rate. It was not possible to test the hypotheses concerning bargaining structure and absenteeism.

4. EFFORT AND MANNING

Management has traditionally dealt with the task of increasing output by intensifying worker effort and/or reducing manpower. Both approaches – in our terms, effort and manning – involve major decisions concerning the ways in which the available manpower is to be used.

The relationship between effort and output can be examined from either side of the input–output equation. Decisions about manning levels presumably affect labour inputs.[29] Thus, if overall output levels remain constant, any reduction in manning means that the intensity of the labour effort of the remaining workers has increased. Correspondingly, any increase in output for a given level of manpower means that effort intensity has also increased.

EFFORT PROVISIONS

Worker effort involves dimensions both of *effort duration* which, as here used, measures the extent to which working hours are productively employed, and of *effort intensity* which measures the qualitative impact of inputs on outputs. This latter aspect of effort

[29] The assumption for purposes of this discussion about the role of productivity bargaining in dealing with the effort–manning subject is that technology is constant. In the instance of introducing labour-saving equipment both manning and effort may be reduced.

has generally been handled by wage payment systems – a subject to which we turn in the next section.

The subject of effort duration includes those arrangements and attitudes that limit the length of time in which the worker is actively involved in productive tasks, such as late starting, early quitting, or long tea or coffee breaks. Whether these practices are *de facto* or *de jure* is probably not as important as how management has sought to eliminate them and how it has tried to utilise worker effort for more of the working day. One of productivity bargaining's tasks has been to identify hindrances to worker effort and to indicate how they can be eliminated.

Agreements designed to obtain a greater expenditure of effort have covered : time keeping (recording starting and finishing times); elimination of idle time (the engineering industry agreement provided that 'all men who find reasonable alternative work shall carry out such work at all times'); regulation of breaks (the B.P. agreement limited breaks to the mid-day meal only and provided tea and washing facilities convenient to the job); and limitations on time devoted to personal matters (the Mobil Coryton agreement established times for washing and changing clothes, and provided for suitably located showers).

In passing it should be noted that idle worker time can be caused by management ineptness as well as by customary practice or worker capriciousness. For example, lack of raw materials and machine failure can increase 'down time' and interfere with effort utilisation. However, such factors have not been the subject of productivity bargaining primarily because, as issues in the province of management planning, they are not as amenable to bargaining action. At best, they have an area of potential that can only be tapped through some participation–achievement–reward system.[30]

MANNING PROVISIONS

The other main dimension is *manning*, and this has been a frequent subject in productivity agreements. The elimination of mates and helpers as well as the specification of smaller working parties and staff groups have occurred in a wide variety of agreements. In B.O.A.C. a seventh crew member, previously thought necessary in busy seasons, was dropped. In other industries, the number of

---

[30] We will return to this aspect of the matter in the concluding chapter.

machines tended by one worker has been increased (e.g. the wool-combers' case). Since this is an important subject, we will give it a closer examination on the basis of the D.E.P. data.

In the ranking of industries with reference to manning (Table 5.1, column 3) the only pattern apparent is that most of the industries near the top of the list are non-craft in character. Perhaps it would be fair to say that the manning problem is for non-craft industries what the jurisdictional or skill problem is for craft-based industries.

One reason for the lack of pattern lies in the fact that technological change can affect effort utilisation in diametrically opposing ways. On the one hand, change might provide the occasion for updating manning requirements. On the other hand, rapid technological change might also create conditions which foster a widening gap between the changing environment and lagging managerial attention to effort utilisation and manning programmes. As we will see, to some extent this latter trend has prevailed.

SOME CONDITIONING FACTORS CONCERNING MANNING

Building on the previous discussion, we can advance two hypotheses :

Hypothesis 1: Manning problems are more likely to exist where technological change has been rapid.

Hypothesis 2: Manning problems are more likely to occur where workers are concerned about job security.

Impact of technological change. Manning problems often reflect management's failure to revise crew sizes when technological change is being introduced. Since such change never ceases, the question can be asked : why are manning arrangements allowed to get out of line? An obvious answer is that at the time that management has the technical – or 'legitimate' – opportunity for revising manning policies the economic climate is far from propitious. When a new process is being developed, management may be least able to stand the dispute that revised manning regulations are likely to precipitate. Instead, the emphasis is likely to be on rushing the new product to market or eliminating 'technical bugs'. Consider the example of railways. With the shift away from steam locomotives, the new diesels' advantages in speed and reliability were so overwhelming that management tended to ignore the manning issues involved in the continued use of unneeded firemen on the engines. No doubt these firemen were of some help to the enginemen when the new equipment was first put into use. But while, from an operational point of view, it made sense to retain such extra manpower to handle unforeseen contingencies in the new operations, after the 'bugs' were eliminated, the extra personnel – true to Parkinson's law – have found various ways of occupying themselves.

Once such manning problems develop, often through sheer inaction, they tend to become habitual and persist over long periods. In such situations, ideas about agreeable manning levels are shaped by traditions within the plant and the local labour market. Worker attitudes toward changes in such standards will depend on their previous experience in the labour market and the atmosphere in the particular enterprise. Foremen and other management personnel who have come up through the ranks may tend to reinforce the traditional standards of effort expenditure; they enforce the general assumption that the existing arrangements are 'legitimate'.

The impact of concern about job loss.   From a personnel point of view, it is quite difficult to cut back on manpower at any time, because of the spectre of lost jobs – redundancy. Rather than allow this endemic fear to harden into opposition to *all* technological change, management often decides to leave the manpower structure intact, and concentrates instead on exploiting the opportunities for increased output and improved quality which the new technology offers.

Workers' fears about redundancy, loss of income, or restricted promotional opportunities are always just beneath the surface. Thus, it could be expected that industries with the slowest employment growth and high unemployment rates would be those where manning problems would be the most severe.

STATISTICAL FINDINGS

The occurrence of changes in manning relative to other changes in an industry was not significantly associated with the industry characteristics of capital intensity and employment change. One significant relationship was found with skill level of the industry ($R = -0.46$, significant at the 4 per cent level). That is, the larger the proportion of skilled workers, the lower was the incidence of manning changes in the industry. The import of this finding is that manning has been a less prominent feature of productivity agreements for skilled workers, where the main focus has been on resolving jurisdictional difficulties. Typically, management's interest has been to expand the effective supply of skilled workers by emphasising flexibility. In view of the general shortage of skilled workers, it would be unlikely that many companies would press for manning reductions of skilled workers.

The relationship between manning changes and unemployment was significant at the 2 per cent level. However, the negative association ($R = -0.54$) requires some explanation. The connection between job insecurity and the tendency for a subject to appear in productivity agreements can operate in two distinct ways. In the first instance, it would be supposed that industries with higher levels of unemployment would harbour more productivity problems and so generate a need for the productivity bargaining approach (a positive association). In the second instance, it would be supposed that industries with lower levels of unemployment would be more amenable to the elimination of these problems through productivity bargaining (a negative relationship). In short, a positive association between the relative importance of a subject and unemployment would suggest that *desirability* of change was dominant, while a negative association would suggest that *feasibility* of change was the more important condition. It is interesting that the statistical work indicates that where skill utilisation was concerned, the desirability aspect was prevalent, whereas with respect to manning changes, the feasibility aspect was the dominant one. In other words, the greater the degree of job insecurity, the more likely are skill utilisation problems to be recognised and tackled by productivity bargaining; and conversely, the more secure the employment in an industry, the more likely is it that manning problems will be tackled in this way.

5.   METHODS[31]

Skill and effort requirements can be examined as substantive areas

---

[31] The organisation of this section of the chapter differs slightly from the preceding sections. Since the D.E.P. data group job evaluation, work measurement and wage payment systems into one category, we could not test hypotheses which were specific to each of these items. Nevertheless, due to the distinctive nature of each of these items, it is important to discuss separately their role in productivity agreements.

in their own right, or focus can be fixed on the methods or tools used to undergird these arrangements. This latter approach deals with the important subjects of : (1) job evaluation in order to arrive at the worth of different skill clusters; (2) work measurement to quantify expenditures of effort and skill; and (3) systems of remuneration (such as payment by results) designed to elicit greater output or intensity of effort.

Before enumerating the detailed role of productivity agreements in introducing various methods, we must introduce a key distinction; namely, unlike the other three categories (skill utilisation, hours, and effort utilisation), this fourth category is concerned *per se* with checking on performance and designing ways to improve it. These methods are tools by which, hopefully, the efficiency of the work system is kept under review on a continuing basis.

Prior to productivity bargaining, internal wage structures tended to lack order, with different rates being paid for comparable work and with no systematic consideration of job requirements. The technique of job evaluation is aimed at rationalising, systematising, and stabilising wage structures; and its use has appeared frequently in productivity bargaining agreements in connection with wage-structure reform.

Similarly, prior to productivity bargaining, standards for measuring effort, for the most part, were established by tradition or past practice, with little attempt to establish 'scientific' norms. The function of work measurement has been to develop effort and manning standards on a more rational basis.

Wage-payment methods also reflected traditions that persisted for some time. The term 'demoralisation' has been used to describe the difficulties that have accompanied many payment-by-results plans.[32] These difficulties included : runaway earnings (often referred to as 'drift'), a downward drag on effort, frequent resort to special allowances or guarantee payments, and increasing disparities and inequities in the relationships between earnings and job levels. Thus, the abandonment of incentive plans and their replacement by measured daywork has been designed to deal with many of the difficulties inherent in payment by results.

While payment-by-results systems had created over the years

[32] S. H. Slichter, J. J. Healy, E. R. Livernash, *The Impact of Collective Bargaining on Management* (Washington, D.C. : The Brookings Institution, 1960) 534.

major administrative difficulties, the absence of any such incentives had created other problems in the form of poor operating results. Unmeasured and unrewarded work systems tended to be even slower and less productive than those covered by payment-by-results. Another theme of productivity bargaining, therefore, has been the introduction into some situations of payment by results for the first time.

WAGE-STRUCTURE REVISION AND THE USE OF JOB EVALUATION

The adoption of new wage structures and the institution of job evaluation have been important in many productivity agreements, especially in such key situations as : British Railways, Rootes (at Linwood), Ford, I.C.I., Esso (both Fawley and distribution), Shell Chemical, and Alcan. Since demoralised wage structures often exhibit contradictory symptoms, in some agreements the wage structure has been elaborated to cover important job differences (as was the case with Ford), and in others – the more frequent case – the wage structure has been simplified. Similarly, promotion has sometimes been tied to a merit system (Imperial Tobacco), while elsewhere (Ford) seniority has been the main criterion.

But regardless of the specific formulation, wage-structure revision has followed one common theme : the design of an appropriate wage structure is a tailor-made affair and reflects the technological and economic circumstances of the particular enterprise; the negotiation of a new wage structure is not the equivalent of adopting a new model plan. Rather, it involves refashioning relationships between pay and jobs in ways that make sense to the affected parties. It is in this latter perspective of wage structures shaped to meet given circumstances that we can develop some hypotheses about the prominence of wage-structure revision in productivity agreements.

HYPOTHESES CONCERNING WAGE STRUCTURE REVISION
AND JOB EVALUATION

Two hypotheses, one on the need-for-change side and one on the feasibility-of-change side, can be advanced :

Hypothesis 1: Wage-structure revision is more likely to be featured in productivity agreements where drift has occurred over a long period of time.

A wage structure is subject to pressures and changes over time. Pay rates for certain jobs may rise more rapidly than those for others. Such changing differentials may be occasioned by technological change, labour market shortages, or pure caprice. The structure can also come under compression from a succession of flat-wage increases. Such flat increases ostensibly treat all employees alike; that is, all wages are raised by a fixed monetary amount rather than being adjusted on a percentage basis. This kind of wage adjustment has been encouraged by inflation and the pressure of rising costs. Flattened wage structures have also come about as a consequence of pressures by junior employees who want higher wages 'now' rather than waiting for seniority and promotion.

By contrast, job evaluation methods attempt to take into account all pay–skill relationships and proceed to develop an organised framework for them. Thus, a major purpose of job evaluation – especially as viewed by the N.B.P.I. – has been to stabilise the wage structure and immunise it from pressures of wage drift. The Board emphasised the value of job evaluation as a check against automatic wage-rate increases, in the face of employee or labour market pressures. Rates determined by job evaluation can serve as restraints on unlimited concessions by management. Instead of moving particular rates upwards and distorting the overall wage structure, management could decide to train its own workers, redesign the jobs, or to take other steps that would not involve the distortion of the wage structure. So argued the Board – the practical validity of this argument will be assessed in Chapter 8.

Hypothesis 2:   Job evaluation will be used more frequently where the staff resources are available to administer the technique.

Job evaluation can be especially useful in large companies with multi-plant operations where it is necessary to develop some consistency across diverse operations. Since workers may need to be transferred between operations and since employees always compare themselves with their counterparts elsewhere in the company, it is obviously important to establish uniformity in pay and skill relationships. But more importantly, it is precisely in these larger scale companies that job evaluation is more feasible due to the availability of qualified staff.

WORK MEASUREMENT

Many productivity agreements have involved the introduction of work measurement procedures, especially in office and clerical operations. In analysing agreement provisions, the N.B.P.I. found that virtually all of those involving office employees provided for the introduction of some form of work measurement, either to revise manning schedules or develop new performance standards.[33]

Work measurement in factories has a longer history, but productivity bargaining has given the technique new publicity and stimulated the development of new approaches. For example, the 1969 Mobil agreement provided for introducing activity sampling studies to estimate work and idle time in various areas of the refinery; and this survey work was to be a joint management and union endeavour. The use of tachographs in transportation has also been fostered by productivity bargaining.

Hypotheses concerning work measurement. Several hypotheses concerning the emergence of work measurement as a theme in productivity agreements can be advanced.

Hypothesis 1: Work measurement will be used more frequently where office employment represents a larger proportion of the total workforce.

This expected tendency hinges on the fact that until the advent of productivity bargaining the question of worker productivity in the office went unnoticed. As a result, effort tended to be low, and manning was frequently excessive.

Hypothesis 2: Work measurement will be used more frequently by larger sized units.

As with job evaluation, a major condition for the successful introduction of work measurement schemes is the availability of trained staff – reflecting a certain degree of management sophistication and commitment.

WAGE-PAYMENT SYSTEMS

As indicated earlier, productivity bargaining has affected wage-payment systems in two different directions. One trend has been away from incentives and a number of companies have used productivity bargaining to secure agreement to abandon existing

[33] Unpublished survey.

payment-by-results plans. Thus, output incentives have been eliminated in the following situations : cars (Rootes),[34] enclosed docks, I.C.I., coal,[35] in portions of the shipbuilding industry,[36] and in the electrical and aircraft sectors of the engineering industry. Mention should also be made of the earlier – but still germane – abandonment of incentive systems at Caterpillar, Glacier Metal, Pet Food, and Vauxhall.

In most cases, the system replacing payment by results has been measured daywork. Under this system, week-to-week variations in earnings are eliminated, and work measurement techniques are actively used. Rates may be adjusted, perhaps quarterly, to reflect changes in individual or group performances, but usually supervisory surveillance, including penalties, or even outright dismissal, are the only 'motivators'. In essence, measured daywork establishes an indirect link between earnings and effort. The system presumes that management is free unilaterally to adjust the work pace, since the company has already guaranteed the worker a high rate of pay.

This presumption is one of the main reasons for union resistance to measured daywork; under such programmes the workers, at least in theory, lose the power they previously exercised under the piecework system to take part in 'mutual' negotiation over effort and earnings. A number of compromise solutions (sometimes referred to as 'controlled daywork') have been initiated. The importance of mutuality and the manner in which this need for involvement on the part of unions becomes reconciled with management's desire for a 'free hand' will be discussed in the final chapters.

At the other extreme, productivity bargaining has often served to introduce payment-by-results systems for the first time; for example, in such situations as electricity supply, local government, gas boards, and individual undertakings (Kraft Foods and Oxford University Press). This interest in output incentives may have been accentuated by the incomes policy and D.E.P. approval of such

---

[34] Also, British Leyland Motor Corporation (B.L.M.C.) are, at the time of writing, embarking on an attempt to move from piecework, which is blamed for an abysmal record of strikes at Cowley, to a system of measured daywork – despite strong opposition to such a move from the unions.

[35] For a discussion of the abandonment of incentives in coal, see R. G. Searle-Barnes, *Pay and Productivity Bargaining* (Manchester: Manchester University Press, 1969).

[36] S. Paulden and B. Hawkins, *Whatever Happened at Fairfields?*

plans. Such incentives provide the workers with opportunities to earn higher take-home pay; and where they have been introduced, it has usually been under the euphemism of 'accepting more exacting conditions of work'.

It is interesting to note that these recent installations mirror the relationships that have generally existed beween environmental characteristics and the use of output incentives. Previous statistical analysis of the extent of incentive coverage by industries has shown that payment-by-results incentives tend to be used most frequently where : (1) labour costs are an important part of total costs; (2) establishments are moderately large (500–1000 employees); and (3) retention of labour has been a problem.[37] Many of the companies newly embracing output incentives fit these criteria.

Although this is not the place to review the complicated and critically important subject of payment by results,[38] suffice it to say that even before productivity bargaining, approximately one-third of all British workers (about two-fifths of all manufacturing workers) were covered by some form of payment by results. The appeal of direct incentives often proved to be irresistible. Management viewed such incentives as a means of controlling labour costs and solving day-to-day problems of supervising workers – though their expectations were not always fulfilled.

Before moving on, we should emphasise the point that the trends may not be as divergent as they may first appear. Payment-by-results systems are being modified in the direction of daywork with the use of ceilings on earnings. For example, in electricity supply incentive earnings cannot exceed $33\frac{1}{3}$ per cent of basic rates. On the other hand, some daywork systems are being modified to allow for more worker and union participation. Whether it is the plan at Philips where workers contract for a pay-performance package for a stated period of time or that at Rootes where mutuality means that workers and their representatives are involved in the setting

[37] R. B. McKersie, C. F. Miller, W. E. Quarterman, 'Some Indicators of Incentive Plan Preference', *Monthly Labor Review*, LXXXVII (March 1964) 271–6.

[38] See R. B. McKersie, *Changing Methods of Wage Payment Systems*, Royal Commission Research Paper No. 11 (London: H.M.S.O., 1968); W. E. J. McCarthy and S. R. Parker, *Shop Stewards and Workshop Relations*, Royal Commission Research Paper No. 10 (London: H.M.S.O., 1968); H. A. Clegg, *The System of Industrial Relations in Great Britain* (Oxford: Blackwell, 1970) 265 ff; and N.B.P.I. Report No. 65, *Payment by Results Systems*, Cmnd 3627 (London: H.M.S.O., 1968).

of production standards, the result is to move daywork systems in the direction of more worker and union involvement in the setting of effort norms (and indirectly in determining pay) – the sort of participation commonly associated with most incentive systems.

Hypotheses concerning wage-payment systems.   The previous discussion has touched on a number of relationships which can now be formalised into hypotheses.

Hypothesis 1:   The subject of wage-payment revision will be more prominent in the presence of incentives than in their absence, i.e. the tendency will be stronger for incentives to be abandoned rather than instituted *de novo*. This presumption is based on the powerful tendency for all incentives to deteriorate.

Hypothesis 2:   The alteration of an existing wage-payment system will be more likely the lower the percentage of an industry's labour force which is organised.

As we will note later (Chapter 9), unions generally have resisted measured daywork. Despite some ideological reservations, union leaders and shop stewards have expressed strong support of incentive systems. One convenor has said :

> In a highly organized factory it (piecework) has certain advantages : it is direct, it can lead to higher earnings and it gives the workers a measure of control over this production.[39]

And there is a more colourful statement by Hugh Scanlon, President of the A.U.E.W. :

> All my life I've attributed most of the ills of the engineering industry to an iniquitous piece-work system. Yet the moment anyone wants to do away with it, we fight with all the vigour we can command to retain it, and correctly so. Because with piece-work you have the men on the shop floor determining how much effort they will give for a given amount of money. In other words there is a mutually agreed contract between operators and management's representatives. Now, with the introduction of new ideas like measured daywork, you have a fixed wage and the only question is – how much work you will do for that fixed wage. This is a developing phenomenon which is meeting with resentment. . . . I would resist to the utmost . . . a scheme that does not contain the fact of mutuality within it. For what is

---

[39] P. Higgs, 'The Convenor', in *Work*, ed. R. Fraser (London, 1969) II 113.

important . . . is that once the piece-work bargain is struck, the worker can work at the speed he chooses.[40]

STATISTICAL FINDINGS

Quantitative measures were developed where possible for each of the hypotheses presented for job evaluation, work measurement and wage-payment systems. These measures were then correlated against the relative importance of method changes in the productivity agreements for the various industries.

The most dominant factor in explaining method changes was found to be the extent of payment-by-result schemes in an industry: it was positively associated with the percentage of an industry's labour force under incentive schemes ($R = 0.47$, significant at the 4 per cent level) and incentive pay as a proportion of total pay ($R = 0.52$, significant at the 2 per cent level).

Although statistically not significant by the usual standards, a positive relationship with the average firm size of an industry ($R = 0.32$) suggests that this category of work change was more likely to occur in larger firms. Such variables as extent of clerical employment and the degree of unionisation proved to be unrelated to changes in methods.

The import of these findings is that the dominant factor associated with methods changes in productivity agreements has been the presence of payment by results. Not all incentive systems have proved troublesome enough to show up on the agenda of productivity bargaining but a sufficient number has done so to produce the above correlations.

6. REWARD FEATURES

Before completing our discussion of the ingredients of productivity agreements we need to consider the reward side. However, our coverage will not be as comprehensive as of the achievement side.

First, pay as such will not be discussed in detail in this chapter. We do not mean to slight its importance. The impact of pay increases on the labour market, and their implications for national income control policies, are matters posing severe problems at the macro-level and have been considered in Chapter 4. We will also

[40] *New Left Review*, No. 46 (1967) 8–9.

consider the subject at some length in Chapter 8 with special reference to changes in pay and pay structure, as aspects of the substantive effects of productivity bargaining. Our immediate interest, however, is in those aspects of the reward picture which present *system*-type issues. While extra pay may provide the important *quid pro quo* in a productivity agreement, it generally does not raise operating or conceptual issues, at least in connection with individual agreements.

A second reason for the abbreviated treatment is that the reward features do not lend themselves to statistical analysis. The main emphasis of almost all agreements is on the same subject of pay and leisure, and a rank ordering of industries for the different subjects as well as any correlation analysis with various economic and technological variables would be meaningless. The uniformity with which the different reward changes were distributed across industries is illustrated in Table 5.3. On first examination, the table might suggest that there is little more to be added at this point concerning rewards. One aspect of rewards, however, while not important in any quantitative sense, remains very important as a basic facilitation of productivity bargaining – guarantees against economic loss. These are included in the table under the headings of fringe benefits and redundancy.

Rewards generally are of two types : (1) 'outputs' that are contingent on the productivity plan itself (e.g. increasing leisure which may result from reducing overtime, or eliminating classification inequities which may not be possible unless job evaluation is introduced), and (2) distributional arrangements that are financed by the overall savings made under the productivity bargaining agreements. Job guarantees and status are primarily examples of the second category.

JOB GUARANTEES AND STATUS

Even in the absence of productivity bargaining, workers worry about job security. However, productivity bargaining, presenting as it does the possibility that fewer workers will be needed, cannot fail to raise the spectre of job loss. Therefore, job security and status guarantees represent key features of any productivity agreement. While the immediate purpose of productivity bargaining may not be job security *per se* (presumably if such means were

Table 5.3. Percentage Distribution of Reward Changes by Industry

Industry order	Wages	Leisure	Ex gratia payments	Fringe benefits	Redundancy	Other Rewards (joint consultation)	Total
03 Food	89.6	5.4	0.2	2.5	0.5	2.0	100.2
04 Chemicals	87.4	6.1	—	5.4	0.4	0.8	100.1
05 Metal manufacturing	92.0	3.8	—	1.4	1.4	1.4	100.0
06 Engineering	91.5	2.5	—	3.6	—	2.4	100.0
07 Shipbuilding	95.0	1.9	—	3.1	—	—	100.0
08 Vehicles	93.1	2.4	—	3.5	—	1.0	100.0
09 Metal goods, n.e.s.	93.8	3.1	—	2.5	0.6	—	100.0
10 Textiles	73.2	13.4	—	7.3	—	6.1	100.0
11 Leather¹	100.0	—	—	—	—	—	100.0
12 Clothing¹	60.0	10.0	—	10.0	—	20.0	100.0
13 Bricks, pottery	94.0	3.0	—	2.0	—	1.0	100.0
15 Paper, printing	80.7	11.2	0.8	5.3	0.3	1.9	100.2
16 Other manufacturing	96.0	2.5	—	0.8	—	0.7	100.0
19 Transport, communications	89.6	6.2	—	1.5	1.5	1.2	100.0
20 Distribution	92.0	3.5	—	2.5	2.0	—	100.0

¹ The percentage distribution in this industry should be considered cautiously because of the small absolute numbers of entries in each change category.

available they would already have been instituted), offers of such
security have been significant factors in promoting such agreements.

In most situations the effectiveness of the entire productivity
bargaining exercise hinges directly on management's ability and
willingness to offer guarantees against redundancy. In one company, management refused to make such assurances, arguing that
some displaced workers might refuse to accept alternative assignments and that the company needed to retain the right to eliminate
their services. As a result, the workers reacted very defensively and
the whole process became embroiled in severe conflict.

In dealing with the problems created by employment instability,
one starting point is a critical examination of those business practices that help to create such instability. For instance, in the case
of Kraft, management agreed to abandon subcontracting; and in
the shipbuilding industry, mergers and other consolidations have
taken place, at least in part to stabilise employment.

Even in the face of adverse environmental factors it may be
possible to guarantee that the economic position of employees will
not be worsened as a result of the productivity agreement. Alcan
gave such a pledge, which went a long way towards securing
acceptance of the agreement.

OTHER GUARANTEES

Various types of income guarantees can be and have been included
in productivity agreements. One such guarantee is the consolidation of the various elements of the pay package into basic rates.
Such a consolidation plays a key part in conferring staff status.
Furthermore, the elimination of 'pluses', lieu rates, and the like,
has occurred in almost every wage restructuring exercise. The shift
from payment by results to daywork also enables workers to count
on a given level of take-home pay. For example, Imperial Tobacco
adopted a proficiency pay scheme, 'under which, subject to improved efficiency and production, fixed weekly payments will
replace the present varying incentive earnings'.

The docks represent a good example of the importance of
establishing a realistic minimum wage as part of the price to be
paid for progress towards productivity deals. In 1969 and 1970,
as negotiations on Stage 2 of the Devlin proposals neared com-

pletion at local level, pressure developed from the T.G.W.U. for a £20 national minimum wage for 40 hours (as compared with the fall-back guarantee of £16 per week, and a minimum time rate of just over £11 per week). This claim led to a national dock strike in July 1970 and a Court of Inquiry was set up under the chairmanship of Lord Pearson. Among other recommendations, the Court of Inquiry favoured a rise in the fall-back guarantee to £20 per 40 hours, and only then did further progress towards the conclusion of deals at docks throughout the country get under way again.[41]

Other guarantees have also been involved in productivity agreements. For employees whose classifications have been downgraded in a wage structure revision, the provision of 'red circle' rates has been considered an appropriate guarantee.[42] The incorporation of staff status also has been a prominent feature in many productivity agreements; it was a key provision in the cases of I.C.I., electricity supply, and Shell.[43] Typically, these companies have proposed staff status after getting the 'religion of human relations'. While staff status may not bolster job security in any real sense (staff workers can also be declared redundant), it attempts to create a closer identification with the company. Consequently, staff status might be termed a career incentive. Whether the acquisition of such status has any motivational value and is, therefore, instrumental in improving worker inputs is something to be examined in greater detail later (especially in Chapter 8).

THE DETERMINANTS OF JOB SECURITY

Where job security is needed it is difficult to provide, and where it is not needed it is easy to provide. In those economic circumstances where workers feel most uncertain, management typically

[41] See: *Report of a Court of Inquiry under the Rt Hon. The Lord Pearson, C.B.E., into a Dispute Between the Parties Represented on the National Joint Council for the Port Transport Industry,* Cmnd 4429 (London: H.M.S.O., 1970).

[42] Ideally red-circle rates tend to be 'washed out' as wage increases are agreed to in succeeding negotiations. However, sometimes it may not be possible to make such a policy stick since the affected individuals over a period of time lose ground relative to others in the plant.

[43] Recently in France the analogous concept of 'mensualisation' has been introduced by the government; essentially it means placing hourly workers on monthly pay schedules and affording them the same status as other monthly paid workers.

finds it difficult to institute the employment and income guarantees that workers so fervently desire. On the other hand, in companies more favourably situated with respect to employment stability – stable product demand, high capital–labour ratio, and fixed manning schedules – the granting of no-redundancy guarantees can be relatively costless. The challenge facing the parties engaged in productivity bargaining, then, has been to design manpower programmes that somehow cope with the vicissitudes of the economic environment within which they find themselves. It has been a special accomplishment of productivity bargaining to have broken new ground in the fashioning of such economic guarantees and manpower plans in a number of important situations.

7. ACHIEVEMENT AND REWARD PATTERNS OVER TIME

So far in this chapter, we have presented a cross-sectional analysis of the ingredients of productivity agreements. By contrast, in the preceding two chapters we looked at the evaluation of productivity agreements over time. At this point we can draw the two perspectives together and in the light of our increased understanding of the substance of productivity agreements we can more adequately discuss several longitudinal patterns touched on only briefly in the preceding chapters.

TRENDS IN WORK-CHANGE FEATURES

As we noted in the chapter on evolution, a fairly sharp shift occurred in the relative importance of skill versus effort issues between phases I and II. Most of this shift probably reflected differences in industry coverages as productivity bargaining spread from the process industries (where it initially emerged) to the engineering and service sectors of the economy.

The industries that first embarked upon productivity bargaining were those where the systems governing skill utilisation were no longer completely compatible with efficient operation of the emerging technology. The existing skill jurisdictions and the scheduling of these skill clusters with respect to time and location were not sufficiently flexible to allow adaptation to the changing technology. Consequently, the starting point for productivity bargaining in these process industries involved redesign of the skill utilisation systems.

By contrast, effort issues in these industries were generally not as important, with the possible exception of manning questions.[44] Certainly, effort in the sense of inducing workers to expend more physical energy did not make sense where the physical output was established by the capacity of the equipment.

However, effort issues were very important in engineering and in other industries where technology was a less dominant influence, but where eliciting worker concern for output had a direct bearing on the level of unit labour costs. Thus, in phase II, as productivity bargaining spread to the engineering-type industries, the subjects of quantity of work and work measurement and wage-payment systems (tools aimed at enhancing quantity of effort) became relatively more important.

These effort-type issues became important during phase II for another reason : productivity agreements were moving in coverage to the indirect side of the workforce. The office, particularly clerical employment, became an additional focus for attempts to improve worker productivity. In such labour-intensive settings the real potential for lowering labour costs was in manpower reduction and increasing output. Whether the emphasis was on eliminating workers directly or requiring the existing workers to increase quantity of output, the effect was the same : effort per worker increased. And the techniques for specifying the new effort standards often involved work measurement and, sometimes, payment by results.

TRENDS IN REWARD FEATURES

During phase I, increased rewards, primarily greater take-home pay and greater leisure, were viewed as important *quid pro quos* for inducing workers to engage in productivity programmes. The rewards represented an important and necessary link in the productivity–pay deal, but they did not provide the impetus nor were they viewed as operating on the achievement side. Management

---

[44] Even then, the manning questions were often related to changes in the utilisation of skilled workers, as in the cases where craftsmen's mates were eliminated or reduced in number in a new system of labour deployment.

generally proposed the productivity plans, and the workers and unions went along because the rewards were sufficiently attractive to make the whole scheme acceptable.

In the light of this premise that rewards in phase I represented the dependent side of the bargain, the role of such subjects as increased leisure and staff status can be readily understood. Generally speaking, workers did not enter productivity bargaining with conscious objectives for realising increased leisure or staff status – these were benefits that management incorporated into the deals to make the productivity programmes attractive.

By contrast, in phase II, the impetus for productivity bargaining emanated more frequently from the reward side – with the workers' desire to maintain and/or improve their economic position. Accordingly, agreements were negotiated that generated enough in the way of additional achievement to justify the pay increases demanded by the workers in the first instance. Because of the priority given to the pay side, it was inevitable that some of the reward features would be viewed as 'achievements' in their own right.

Such items as wage-structure and wage-payment revision came to be viewed simultaneously as both achievement and reward items. The institution of a new job assessment scheme or a revised payment-by-results system usually meant an increase in earnings. Management also counted on such rationalised structures to improve motivation and morale as a result of eliminating inequities and providing direct incentives for increased output.

This new emphasis during phase II on reward-determined bargains can be explained in several ways. For one thing, the pressure coming from the pay side meant that productivity agreements needed to be designed and negotiated quickly, and it is the special character of job evaluation and work measurement procedures that they can be instituted quickly (often with the help of consultants). It was also the case that during the latter 1960s management found itself needing to assert control over wage-payment structures and systems, given the extensive drift and general distortion that had developed in earnings.

Again, this shift in the character of productivity bargaining between phases I and II can be explained by the different mix of industries between the two periods. As productivity bargaining moved to the engineering-type industries, it could be expected that wage-type rewards would be more prominent in comparison to fringes – precisely because in these industries non-monetary rewards have always played a minor role.

This difference in the planning horizons of phases I and II can be seen in the following connection : overtime reduction characterised many phase I agreements (and, by contrast, relatively few phase II agreements) because during this period management and worker/union forces possessed a time horizon that enabled some fundamental restructuring of the work system to take place, such as job enlargement and flexible shifts. These forms of basic work reorganisation made it possible to do the same amount of work in fewer hours. In this sense, overtime reduction was an outcome that depended upon other basic areas of achievement being successfully attacked. In contrast, during phase II, in an atmosphere of much more urgency to execute pay–productivity deals, the parties turned away from overtime reduction and towards the 'quick' achievement areas of wage-structure and wage-payment revision.

In closing, we should comment on the fact that one dimension of rewards, enhanced job security, has been a feature throughout phases I and II. Indeed, it would appear that guarantees against redundancy and other forms of protection against economic loss represent a threshold condition for productivity bargaining. Without such measures, productivity bargaining as a concept has no appeal to the workers.

6 Negotiating the Agreement

1. INTRODUCTION

THE ROLE OF NEGOTIATIONS AND ALTERNATIVE APPROACHES

The purpose of this chapter is to examine the negotiating process by which the parties actually agree on terms for a productivity improvement scheme. In most situations, the negotiation is a logical and necessary step in the overall programme, and takes place after the parties have become sufficiently troubled about existing achievement and reward relationships to seek a revised work–wage system. The parties first agree upon the character of the change and subsequently, after the agreement has been signed, they proceed to put the change into practice. This approach can be termed the *direct* method of productivity improvement.

However, a significant number of productivity agreements follow an alternative sequence of achieving change first, and then codifying it into written agreements or informal understandings. This approach can be called the *indirect* method of productivity improvement. In some respects, it is almost the reverse of the normal productivity bargaining sequence of negotiation and implementation.

Conceptually, the difference in these approaches is with respect to the time horizon involved : the *direct approach* to change with its emphasis on short-run results and the *indirect approach* to change with its emphasis on longer-run results. How these contrasting perspectives relate to the ingredients of a productivity agreement can be viewed as in Table 6.1.

This contrast between the direct and indirect approaches, which will be a theme throughout the remainder of the study, gives rise

Table 6.1. *Ingredients of Interest Under the Two Approaches*

	Direct emphasis	Indirect emphasis
Management	Improved skill and effort utilisation	Organisational change (increased effectiveness)
Workers	Increased earnings	Enhanced status and job security (career rewards)

to differing characteristics in the agreements themselves. Whereas the direct approach leads to a typical productivity agreement, in which the problem areas are specified quite explicitly and removed in surgical fashion, the emphasis in the indirect approach is on eliminating the organisational and motivational rigidities that retard productivity. The aim is to create a climate of continuing improvement and, in this sense, the indirect approach can be realised through what the N.B.P.I. called an 'efficiency' agreement.[1]

How do these two strategic approaches to change relate to negotiation and implementation activities? The direct approach to productivity improvement involves the negotiation of an agreement by traditional *pressure* bargaining followed by the implementation of the agreement in a *compliance* fashion. In contrast, the indirect approach incorporates the *integrative* or problem-solving method to negotiations (to the extent that the planning and design phase can be termed negotiations), an implementation experience characterised by *internalisation* and a change process that involves motivation rather than compulsion.

CHOICE OF APPROACH

It should be emphasised at this point that neither approach can be labelled as preferable in any absolute sense. They represent different strategies towards the same objectives of increased operating efficiency, though the indirect approach sets this in a

[1] See Chapter 4 above.

wider context which might be summed up in the term 'organi-sational effectiveness'. In the chapters dealing with the impact of productivity bargaining we will attempt to evaluate these two approaches.

The choice between the direct and the indirect approach cer-tainly hinges on style or strategy questions and in turn on the orientation of key management officials. Their view of the world may hold that people are moved only by explicit rewards and punishments or they may believe quite keenly in the human re-lations revolution and feel that the road to change is via organi-sational and individual 'restructuring'.

Because the direct approach tends to get results sooner, while the indirect approach works its impact over the long run, the time orientation of the parties plays a role in the choice. Related to this is the attitude of the parties towards risk. The direct method tends to be a low-risk/low-payoff approach. The type of achievement sought is quite specific and the rewards are coupled explicitly. In contrast, the indirect method tends to be a higher-risk/higher-payoff approach. The type of achievement involved, continuous change, is harder to realise but if accomplished the benefits to both sides are likely to be substantial.

The outlook of the workforce also plays a role. For example, if workers feel very strongly about *not* equating monetary gains with changes in customary practices – if such individuals view the con-cept of productivity bargaining as 'selling off their birthrights' – then a direct (pressure bargaining, compliance) process placing primary emphasis on *quid pro quo* exchange would be self-defeating. Also, if workers react negatively as a 'matter of principle' to the types of changes in managerial control often sought through productivity bargaining, such as the introduction of work measure-ment, the institution of time clocks, and the strengthening of man-agement's authority to discipline workers for poor performance, then the change process necessarily would have to involve a basic cultural reorientation and invoke the indirect or integrative and internalisation process.

Within the broad framework of these distinctions, it is possible to analyse negotiations in terms of a few key processes. Two of these processes – pressure bargaining and integrative bargaining – occur at the main table; and they parallel the direct and indirect strategies. Another process, internal bargaining, occurs within the union and management organisations and is a necessary concomitant to both of the basic inter-organisational processes.[2]

2. PRESSURE BARGAINING –
THE DIRECT APPROACH

Most productivity agreements have been reached via the traditional approach of pressure bargaining. By this term, we do not mean to convey the impression that most productivity discussions resemble typical wage negotiations in all respects. There are, however, important similarities, the most significant being the crucial element played by pressure and inducements or various *quid pro quos.*

During phase II (1967–70), when many productivity discussions were triggered from the reward side, that is, from union insistence on wage improvements and from the special exemption given to wage increases based on improvements in worker productivity, almost all productivity negotiations resembled traditional negotiations. The main difference from the historical pattern was that instead of wage determination being based on comparability, cost of living and ability to pay, a new criterion had entered the picture : worker productivity. But the conventional sequence of union demand and management response remained the same.

An examination of the character of productivity bargaining during phase I (1960–6) shows that a large number of these agreements were also negotiated via the pressure approach – with the impetus and insistence usually coming from the management side, however. Several other features differentiate these phase I and phase II pressure-type agreements. The range of subjects considered in phase I was much greater than the limited number of issues discussed in most phase II negotiations. The tendency of the early agreements to be negotiated at the local level as well as the common pattern of discussions getting started at management's behest also set many of the phase I productivity negotiations apart from the normal mode of phase II. But whether we are talking about Fawley-type negotiations of the early 1960s or the pay–productivity deals of the latter 1960s, a common approach, which we have designated as pressure bargaining, can be discerned.

[2] These concepts are elaborated in : R. E. Walton and R. B. McKersie, *A Behavioral Theory of Labor Negotiations* (New York: McGraw-Hill, 1965).

THE APPROACH

The pressure-bargaining approach can be viewed as essentially conservative. Typically the parties want to ensure a certain outcome. For the company, competitive conditions may be so adverse that labour costs must be reduced by a specified amount. For the workers, wage comparisons may be so coercive and compelling that the union is instructed to obtain a specified increase. The essence of pressure bargaining is that one side knows what it wants and approaches the other side determined to achieve its objective.

When the initiative comes from the management side, as was the case during phase I, management, before approaching the union, usually has conducted a detailed investigation of the productivity difficulties and has pushed its thinking to the point of not only being able to state its objectives but also 'finalising' detailed proposals for accomplishing the desired changes. In other words, management first develops the package and then uses collective bargaining as a way of 'selling' the union on the merits of the package.

Before a company can unveil such a package proposal it has to devote considerable time to study and internal discussion. The amount of pre-negotiation activity entailed can be seen by examining the experience of Esso, perhaps the most sophisticated practitioner of this approach to productivity bargaining. At Fawley, management and its consultants studied the operations for a period of eighteen months before placing their proposals before the union. Subsequently, during the 'homework' period leading to the proposals for the distribution agreement, the company's industrial engineers conducted extensive surveys of possible areas for improvement. They focused on forty-five high-cost items and developed alternatives for dealing with them. In this process the engineers conducted many discussions with line management and industrial relations specialists. The probes were very extensive and by the time the 'green book' was placed before union officials, management had formulated a very specific package.

The Esso example describes a company taking the initiative and pursuing a straight line towards settlement. Management was in charge and the unions were asked to accept the obviously attractive programmes being offered. While management in each of these instances took the offensive and knew exactly what it wanted, it also behaved in a reasonably tactful fashion.

TACTICS

In pressure bargaining, the parties move away from their committed positions through the exercise of inducement and coercion. The path toward agreement is a process of getting the opponent to concede as much as possible in as short a time as possible. The gap is closed *not* because the parties formulate new alternatives that allow both sides to obtain their objectives. Rather, the sides alter their stated positions because the costs of not doing so are greater than the gains from continuing to strive for a more favourable settlement.

In some cases the incentive for a concession is provided by information about the positive value of a proposal. For example, Esso was able to move the T.G.W.U. closer to acceptance of its proposals for drivers by revealing that the planned high weekly wage would also improve the level of fringe benefits by an additional £3 or £4 a week. Thus, the indirect gains of the programme were made sufficiently salient for the union leaders so that they, in turn, could explain them to the rank and file.

More often, however, the motivation to grant a concession comes from a desire to eliminate something unpleasant, such as a threatened strike. In many instances negotiations proceed to impasses and involve all the last-minute pressure and drama normally found in conventional negotiations. For example, in the 1965 distribution negotiations at Esso, both sides realised that if an agreement were not reached during the evening of 9 November, then the union spotlight would turn in another direction. Indeed, the T.G.W.U. had scheduled a meeting with Shell for 10 November and the session between the union and Esso had been hurriedly arranged in order to give Esso an opportunity to set the pattern. The union was able to create a deadline atmosphere by playing on Esso's desire to be the leader and by making it known that it was willing to sign an agreement with Shell on 10 November.

Other examples of the use of cross-pressures from the management side of the bargaining table can be cited. In the experience of the Steel Company of Wales (SCOW) at Port Talbot, management played on rivalry among the craft unions to accelerate acceptance of a productivity package.[3] Henry Wiggin and Co. used the pressure tactic of going to the workers directly. In May 1967, after the G.M.W.U. and the T.G.W.U. had rejected a proposed productivity agreement, the company offered similar arrangements to employees who were willing to accept them on an *individual* basis. A substantial number of employees signed such individual agreements, setting the stage for the two unions agreeing to abide by the results of a preferential election (the T.G.W.U. lost recognition) and the eventual signing of a productivity agreement between the company and the G.M.W.U. (except for those employees who continued to retain individual contracts).

As a result of the coercion inherent in pressure bargaining, the number of concessions which are involved in reaching agreement on a productivity deal can be considerable. For example, in the bargaining over the distribution agreement, the T.G.W.U. succeeded in getting Esso to abandon the principle of basing schedules on a speed limit of 40 m.p.h., to reduce the implementation period from 18 to 6 months, to revise the Sunday premium from a straight percentage factor to a flat 2*s* to 2*s* 6*d* per hour, and to abandon the idea of using tachographs on trucks.

This process of extracting concessions from a company can continue for a prolonged period. In the negotiations just cited, serious bargaining commenced in the autumn of 1964 and the contract was not agreed upon until a year later. Bargaining was broken off for most of this period, after the parties stalemated on the speed-limit issue. Negotiations resumed in the autumn of 1965, with the company advancing a substantially better money offer and eventually acceding to the changes mentioned.

Management, of course, can resort to tactics for putting pressure on the unions to end the delaying game. During 1970, negotiations between a large company and several unions bogged down over a number of 'minor' details. The company sensed that the time had come to act, especially since the main craft union (A.U.E.W.) had instituted an embargo against process workers (T.G.W.U.) using tools. The company therefore prepared and released to all employees a statement outlining the details of the proposed agreement :

---

[3] For a description of this episode, see the *Report of a Court of Inquiry under Professor D. J. Robertson into a dispute at the Port Talbot works of the British Steel Corporation*, Cmnd 4147 (London: H.M.S.O., 1969) 12.

The productivity programme has been held up by problems; therefore, to make the situation clearer, management has completed job descriptions, assessments, manning plans and items of work sharing, which management believes to be in the spirit of the proposed agreement. These items are shown in the job descriptions as 'assumed'.

By taking the initiative, developing the job descriptions unilaterally and proposing them directly to the employees, along with an enumeration of the benefits that would accrue to the employees from the proposed agreement, the company put the unions in a position where they were forced to bring negotiations to a conclusion.

ATTITUDINAL ATMOSPHERE

Basically the relationship between the parties engaged in pressure bargaining can be characterised as 'arm's length'. The parties deal with one another in businesslike fashion and seek to maximise their own advantage in the bargain. Within this style of arm's length dealings, there are many variations. On the more accommodative side, we can cite the approach of a small company in the Northeast where the chairman created a friendly and informal atmosphere with union officials. Due to his engaging personality and frank manner the union accepted his proposal at face value. However, it should not be concluded that the parties developed any collaborative attitudes. On the contrary, the relationship remained paternalistic.

At the opposite extreme, we can cite the atmosphere of the early negotiations at Alcan where considerable distrust and open hostility were in evidence.[4] During the initial negotiations the company called upon the unions to honour their 'commitment' to negotiate

---

[4] For an account of the events at Alcan, see M. Walker, 'Productivity Bargaining at Alcan', in *A Productivity Bargaining Symposium*, ed. D. C. Alexander (London: Engineering Employers' Federation, 1969). Walker observes that when the proposals were first put forward by management in 1964, the craft unions rejected them out of hand: 'They said that there were not immediate benefits to a substantial minority of their members. They also thought that the proposed wage levels were inadequate and they objected strongly to being required to negotiate together with the T. & G.W.U. people. . . . The Craftsmen pressed their opposition to a point where we had to withdraw the proposals' (*op. cit.*, p. 86).

a productivity agreement; and the unions attacked the presence of consultants and generally challenged the good faith of the management group. To show displeasure the unions periodically withdrew 'co-operation' and conducted relations in the plant on a strictly legalistic basis. Eventually, however, trust was restored and a successful agreement was later negotiated and satisfactorily implemented.

Just how events can go from 'bad to worse' in the context of pressure bargaining is well illustrated by negotiations during the early 1960s over a manning agreement for a new printing plant. After receiving the company's proposals, the union objected to the manning on the web offset equipment. The company responded with a full arsenal of weapons, writing letters to the Printing Trades Alliance and to officers of the national union (N.G.A.), charging the union with irresponsible actions and threatening to close all printing shops in the area. What started out as a discussion over manning soon became a personal encounter between leading officials. At one point the N.G.A. president used the term 'nonsense' to describe the company's analysis of the economic situation. In subsequent communications the company referred to this phrase and to the 'irresponsible attitude' of the union president. On the union side the officers referred to the petulance of management and to their poor judgement in writing letters to everyone from George Woodcock down.

The above example is not representative but it does indicate the escalation of tension that is involved in some productivity negotiations. More typically, however, in pursuing the pressure approach to negotiating a productivity agreement the parties deal with each other in a careful and calculating fashion. While they refrain from distorting facts, they do not hesitate to withhold information that might jeopardise their position. For example, during discussions about revised crew sizes for telephone installation work, the Post Office refused to disclose cost information for fear such information would give the union a tactical advantage. This example will be expanded later in the chapter.

3. INTEGRATIVE BARGAINING – THE INDIRECT APPROACH

While not so numerically frequent, the integrative-bargaining method of bringing about change has been used consistently throughout phases I and II. It makes heavy use of human relations techniques for achieving organisational change.

THE APPROACH

The important quality of integrative bargaining is the joint process that is involved – the *joint* definition of problems, the *joint* search for alternatives, and the *joint* selection of solutions. This means that management does not approach the union with a highly developed plan – this is left to develop from the process of management–union co-operation. In the case of a large oil company, management entered discussions in a flexible frame of mind and presented a series of 'concerns' to the union. At first, the unions did not believe the company was serious about a common attack on the important problems of the business. They kept asking: 'All right, what is the hitch; when do we find out what the angle is?' The union officials initially were put off by the company's presenting its ideas in terms of broad objectives rather than in terms of specifically formulated programmes, but eventually they joined in on the problem solving.

Quite naturally, it takes considerable time to achieve the reorientation necessary for integrative bargaining to be effectively pursued. In one company most of the sessions were held away from the plant – in a setting that allowed for long and leisurely discussions. Considerable time had been required to allow people to work through their preconceived notions. For example, when management first met with supervisors, a frequent reaction was, 'I think we are getting soft with the union'. After considerable give and take, the supervisors began to appreciate the fact that a collaborative approach did not necessarily entail a diminution of either their supervisory authority or operating efficiency.

TACTICS

The road to agreement is not a straight line when integrative bargaining is used. The process consists of exploring alternatives and it may be necessary for the parties to appoint subcommittees and conduct studies. A lot of 'back-and-forth' activity takes place and usually it is very difficult to discern institutional positions. At

Mobil the parties used a blackboard and both sides attached questions much as students would do in a classroom.

Joint working parties are often used and the effectiveness of this technique is attested to by the experience of Shell at Stanlow :

> Joint management/union working parties were established at Stanlow, with both the craft unions and the Transport and General Workers. Their aim was to look into areas where productivity might be improved in line with the agreed company objectives and philosophy. The joint working parties had a free hand with no commitments. They examined almost anything – work sharing, total salary, clocking-in, the use of modern measuring techniques – as management was anxious to introduce universal maintenance standards. Some of the ideas which emerged were tried out in test areas. The working parties met weekly, and a good feature from the start was the emphasis on communications.[5]

An important characteristic of integrative bargaining is that the parties attempt to avoid taking fixed positions. Instead they spend their time identifying and exploring alternatives. Too often in productivity bargaining, 'solutions' are reached prematurely, before the parties really understand the underlying situation. For example, in the early electricity supply negotiations the parties started talking about the advantages of status (a presumed solution) before either side really knew what the employees wanted in the way of extra rewards or what was needed in terms of better operating requirements. Subsequently, it became clear that the two sides did not have the same concept in mind and what started out as a problem-solving exercise quickly deteriorated into conventional negotiations characterised by work to rule and a court of inquiry.[6]

A good example of how one management stated its position in tentative terms can be seen in the following quote from the Devlin report.

[5] Joy Larkom, 'Planning for Productivity', *Personnel Management*, I, 5 (September 1969) 41.

[6] *Report of a Court of Inquiry into the Causes and Circumstances of a Dispute between the Parties Represented on the National Joint Industrial Council for the Electricity Supply Industry*, Cmnd 2361 (London : H.M.S.O., 1964) 8.

The scheme was criticised – and is still criticised from the trade union side – as lacking in detail, especially in relation to the *quid pro quo*. This does not seem to us to be a sound criticism. The authors of the scheme had to steer a middle course between producing a cut-and-dried scheme, which might have been resented as dictatorial, and an attractive basis for discussion. Reasonably enough, they chose the latter course and made it plain that no deal had yet been concluded. They said :—'We have put the case in the following pages and now we say : over to you. This booklet cannot contain every detail, but we set out the main proposals as clearly as we know how. We hope that you will read them carefully, discuss them with your mates, and raise through the usual channels any points you wish to make.'[7]

The path to agreement may entail considerable organisational change. For example, at one large company the parties designed several socio-technical experiments, the purpose of which was to investigate the nature of optimum man-machine systems. Specifically, the question studied was whether process personnel could assume more responsibility by making required mechanical adjustments to operating equipment. Other studies examined the organisation of maintenance work and the utilisation of labour-saving devices in a packaging department. In addition, sub-committees were established to examine the feasibility of eliminating time clocks and eliminating various demarcation arrangements.

The parties in this instance were also flexible about their own organisational arrangements. Originally the company had planned to achieve consensus within the total management group on the need for a new departure before broaching the subject with the union. However, top management quickly realised that key union officials needed to be involved in the deliberations reasonably early

[7] *Final Report of the Committee of Inquiry under the Rt Hon. Lord Devlin into certain matters concerning the Port Transport Industry* (London : H.M.S.O., 1965) 83. The question might be raised as to why the early discussions on the docks were not more fruitful, given management's exploratory approach. Integrative bargaining was not feasible in an atmosphere of insecurity – as we indicated in Chapter 5, when workers are striving to achieve minimally acceptable financial arrangements, in this instance, adequate weekly guarantees, negotiations will be forced into the pressure-bargaining mode. For a complete discussion of the Devlin Committee and for a general analysis of recent experience on the docks, see Vernon H. Jensen, *Decasualisation and Modernisation of Dock Work in London* (Ithaca, N.Y. : New York State School of Industrial and Labor Relations, 1971).

in the exercise and that the lower levels of *both* organisations needed to be acquainted with the programme simultaneously.

The major inducement or incentive in integrative bargaining is the expectation of a better outcome for both sides. Thus, if both sides 'see' the integrative potential, then they will be motivated to engage seriously in problem solving. One way of revealing the integrative potential in a situation is to embark upon a trial. In the case studied by Oppenheim and Bayley, the success of the experiment provided an important impetus to serious problem solving.

> The Productivity Committee decided to focus on one particular piece of assembly track, and obtained a large number of practical and readily implemented suggestions from employees; when most of these were put into effect a substantial rise in productivity was obtained, which was taken to show what could be accomplished if management and the employees could find a way of working together.[8]

ATTITUDINAL ATMOSPHERE

Problem solving can only emerge in the presence of a trusting relationship. A completely trusting relationship has been evidenced in only a few cases. At the Mobil Coryton refinery the two sides developed trust to the point of allowing the stewards to write out the revised task sheets. In the Post Office (telecommunications) negotiations in 1965 the union displayed its good faith by agreeing to substantial changes in manning arrangements without first demanding large pay increases. The assumption was that the parties would give the experiment a chance and then assess the savings at a later date. The fact that the Post Office was subsequently constrained by the incomes policy from granting more than an average wage increase probably served to negate the development of trust in this situation. In this sense, anything that limits the freedom of the parties limits the potential for the willingness of each party to go on believing in the good faith of the other.

Off-the-record discussions and an absence of publicity are fundamental to the development of trust in integrative bargaining.

    [8] A. N. Oppenheim and J. C. R. Bayley, 'Productivity and Conflict', *Proceedings of the International Peace Research Association Third General Conference* (The Netherlands: Assen, 1970) 87.

Several large companies because of their size and prominence have felt compelled to announce the fact that they are 'engaged in productivity discussions'. The difficulty with such an announcement is that the resulting publicity prevents the parties from working quietly and informally behind the scenes, and gives rise either to fears or to expectations that often have to be resolved quickly, thus introducing pressures that may be inimical to genuine problem solving.

Within the confines of the process, however, the more information that the parties share, the better problem solving is apt to function. Some companies still feel reluctant to reveal the 'inner workings' of the enterprise.[9] Such hesitation makes the definition of problems, the development of alternatives, and the selection of solutions difficult to execute. Without basic data and the overture of trust that is involved in sharing sensitive information, problem solving cannot be effective and attitudes will remain frozen.

Consider the experience of one company, Shell, which would consider itself a practitioner of problem solving, but which in retrospect felt that the process was not sufficiently open and joint:

> In hindsight we feel it would have speeded up the discussion had we exposed the concepts we had in mind at the outset and used the working parties to ferret out other concepts and to graft flesh onto the bones.[10]

Trusting relationships are hard to develop. They develop only when the parties are willing to take some risks:

> One of the tactics that both sides used for generating trust, was to put themselves into 'mortgage' with the other side; negotiators from both sides would give each other detailed information of their goals and plans, thus increasing the state of interdependence that existed between them. In this instance information can be regarded as a form of hostage.[11]

Where such willingness to take a calculated risk is not present, the kind of problems that can be adequately dealt with only via

---

[9] See National Economic Development Office, *Plant Bargaining* (London: N.E.D.O., 1969) 10.

[10] P. H. Rowe before a British Institute of Management Forum in April 1969, London.

[11] Oppenheim and Bayley, 'Productivity and Conflict', p. 101.

integrative bargaining never get solved. For example, as the Scamp report[12] on railways noted, the two sides were unable to come to grips with the manning question because neither side would accept any programme on faith but wanted its gains guaranteed at the outset.

Trusting relationships are also hard to sustain. They require considerable energy and the right kind of personalities. The relationship has to be continually nurtured and reinforced and, if the personalities in the situation change, then the trusting relationship may need to be re-established. For example, in the talks between a large printing firm and the unions a close relationship developed between the managing director and the spokesman for the printing trades. These individuals operated on a first name basis and respected each other's word and understanding of the problems. When other management officials dealt with the same union leader this *rapport* was not present and negotiations generally were not so fruitful.

Another example of the difficulty of maintaining mutual good faith derives from negotiations in a large manufacturing company. Here the parties followed a problem-solving format with exploratory discussions about plant productivity problems, with many of the meetings taking place away from the premises. A major breakthrough occurred when the stewards developed their ideas for reorganising one of the finishing lines. The plan called for a new layout which would enable the workforce to be reduced from 72 to 40 men and spelled out some critical needs for improved working conditions.

The union side was excited with the plan and took it to plant management for approval. Management seized upon the new ideas and proceeded to implement them, meanwhile shelving the proposals for increasing ventilation and improving working conditions because 'they would cost too much money'. The reaction of the union in the face of management's 'rush for the goal' was predictable. It broke off discussion and the process of collaboration ended.

In passing we might reflect on the ability of an 'outside' force

---

[12] *Report of a Court of Inquiry under Mr A. J. Scamp into the Issues arising in Negotiations between the British Railways Board, the Associated Society of Locomotive Engineers and Firemen and the National Union of Railwaymen*, Cmnd 2779 (London: H.M.S.O., 1965).

such as the N.B.P.I. to foster a trusting relationship between the parties. Certainly, the parties themselves must create the basic conditions of trust. However, an outsider, such as a consultant or a government official,[13] can be helpful in establishing one of the prerequisite conditions for the development of trust, namely agreement on facts. As Lord Devlin in his analysis of newspapers commented :

> Negotiations can be simplified if they can be conducted upon an agreed basis of fact; indeed they can break down, as they have in the past simply because there is no common agreement about what the relevant facts are. The main purpose of the Joint Board is to provide this basis of fact in a form that is understood by and acceptable to both sides.[14]

Beyond the function of 'fact finding', an outsider can perform a type of mediation function by specifying a compromise position. In the case of British Railways, the N.B.P.I. performed this very role. By reducing the official work week to 40 hours the Board did two things : it gave the workers an implied increase in take-home pay, if working hours which were then well above 40 were not reduced; and at the same time it gave the railways an incentive to reduce overtime, in which case the workers' gain would come in the form of increased leisure.[15] A similar deadlock characterised the bakery industry with the unions demanding 'without strings' an increase in money and the employers similarly demanding without a *quid pro quo* a reduction in overtime. In this instance, the N.B.P.I. stepped in and recommended an interim wage increase.[16]

While the N.B.P.I. in these instances could not foster, on its own, integrative bargaining, nevertheless, it helped the parties take the first step *together* – which is essentially the essence of building trust : the parties take calculated risks and subsequently experience constructive results.

[13] The Manpower and Productivity Service of the Department of Employment and Productivity performed this 'outsider' role, particularly during the period of formal incomes policy.

[14] Joint Board for the National Press *Report* for the year ending 31 December 1965.

[15] N.B.P.I. Report No. 8, *Pay and Conditions of Service of British Railways Staff*, Cmnd 2873 (London : H.M.S.O., 1966) 10.

[16] N.B.P.I. Report No. 151, *Bread Prices and Pay in the Baking Industry, Second Report*, Cmnd 4428 (London : H.M.S.O., 1970) 9.

In passing, we should note that another function for outsiders is to serve as 'scapegoats'. This role can be important as a way of dealing with antagonisms which may develop even in integrative bargaining. In one instance, rather than letting these negative sentiments undermine the relationship, the consultants, who provided the initial impetus to the productivity talks, withdrew, thereby serving to absorb the hostility that many of the union people felt towards the programme of change.

The work of regrading, the implementation of suggestions for improvements, the developing of new incentive pay schemes, etc., was tackled by the men themselves with such enthusiasm that the consultants were no longer perceived as necessary and their services were dispensed with about midway through the negotiations. . . . The success of the enterprise which they helped to set in motion made their rejection both necessary and unavoidable.[17]

4. THE ROLE OF MIXED BARGAINING

The central challenge in negotiating a productivity agreement is how to take advantage of both processes, that is, how to increase the joint gains through integrative bargaining while at the same time guaranteeing a minimum share through pressure bargaining. Such an assignment might be quite straightforward if the behaviour required by one process coincided with that required by the other. But this is not generally the case. To maximise joint gains the parties need to behave co-operatively and to search for solutions that are in their best joint interests. In contrast, to maximise their respective shares, the parties need to deal with one another in a circumspect fashion and with an eye for the tactics of the situation. Several examples can be cited of the questions arising from this inherent tension between the tactical requirements of the two processes :

1.   In pursuing a productivity agreement, at what point in the planning process should a company contact the union ? The direct approach and its primary negotiating process of pressure bargaining dictate that the union be contacted only after the programme has been crystallised and the company is in a position to present it

---

[17] Oppenheim and Bayley, 'Productivity and Conflict', p. 88.

to the union as a fully developed package. Hopefully, the package is sufficiently attractive for the union and its members to accept it readily. On the other hand, the indirect approach and its negotiating process of integrative bargaining suggest the involvement of the union and its representatives very early in the design of the agreement so that their ideas can be incorporated. If approached early enough in the planning process the union feels that it can exert some influence on the means chosen to reach the new goals. In contrast, if management does all of the homework, develops the plan in great detail, and then approaches the union, the potential for integration of interests is diminished considerably.

2. In a situation of multiple union representation, should the company encourage all the unions to come together to discuss productivity change in a concerted fashion or seek to deal with them separately? Pressure bargaining dictates that the unions be approached separately. By this tactic the company may find one union that is interested in moving ahead, thereby creating cross-pressures on the other unions to fall into line. On the other hand, integrative bargaining suggests that all of the unions be involved in the discussions, especially if the productivity improvement sought involves skill flexibility and co-ordination across different work groups. Only by including all interested parties in a joint exercise of discussion and exploration would an agreement be fashioned that would make sense in terms of the operating exigencies.

3. In making contact with a union, should the company place primary emphasis on discussions at the top, middle, or bottom levels of the organisation? Pressure bargaining suggests contact at the top where key spokesmen are more sensitive to institutional interests. Integrative bargaining, which flourishes on facts, is executed more effectively at the bottom by workers and stewards who have a first-hand feeling for the situation.

Most instances of mixed bargaining occur by default rather than by design. Unlike the pressure and integrative bargaining approaches, which are usually pursued in a clear and consistent manner by the parties, especially the management side, the emergence of mixed bargaining can usually be attributed to different styles or confusion within the management organisation. In this sense much of what passes for mixed bargaining is, in reality, 'muddled' bargaining.

It is not our purpose to illustrate the inept combination of pressure and integrative bargaining that often characterises productivity discussions. Instead we would like to analyse how the two basic processes might be combined in a skilful fashion in order to capitalise on the strengths of each. Much of the material that follows is normative and a guide to more effective negotiations rather than an analysis of actual practice.

THE APPROACH

While the requirements of pressure and integrative bargaining are at many points diametrically opposed, it is the special function of mixed bargaining to create a synthesis. Mixed bargaining is in part pressure bargaining because an important element in this approach is the concern of each party over the final allocation of resources. In this sense, pressure is used in a direct way to ensure a favourable outcome. However, the process is not pure pressure bargaining and considerable time is spent in a joint search for new solutions. In a game-theory sense, mixed bargaining can be described as the process wherein each party seeks to maximise the joint *sum* (through collaborative efforts with the opponent), while at the same time striving to obtain as large a *share* of these joint payoffs as possible (through coercion and other pressure tactics).

Several examples of this synthesis can be given. On the question of when and with what finality of planning the company should approach the union, a mixed tactic can be devised. One balance between no initiative and too much initiative is for the company to spell out to the union general objectives and problems, having first convinced itself that some solution is possible to the productivity predicament, and then to leave it to the bargaining process to develop the detailed plan.

Similarly, on the question of level of contact, a mixture of approaches can be used. The union may need to be approached on a multi-level basis. Most leaders at the top recognise the inevitability of change and often hold a point of view quite close to that of management. To cultivate their co-operation the company may need to sit down with these leaders in general, off-the-record discussions such as B.O.A.C. tried with its key union people. But where top union officials do not have too much influence over people at the bottom, most of the details of the agreement may need to be worked out at the lower levels.

TACTICS

Operationally, the skilful mixing of conflict and co-operation can be handled in the following manner : co-operation takes place over the size of the joint gains and conflict over the shares. In other words, the parties spend their time making the 'pie' as large as possible, and then at some point turn to the difficult question of allocating respective shares. This differentiation of negotiations into sum and share constituents can be achieved along a number of dimensions : organisational levels, agenda items, time phases, and settlement criteria.

Differentiation by organisational levels. One way of separating the two processes is for subcommittees to engage in integrative bargaining and for the chief negotiators to engage in pressure bargaining. This means that staff experts and the subordinate members of an organisation maintain a professional approach while the top officials, those vested with responsibility for protecting institutional interests, hammer out the respective shares. This approach appears from our investigations to be typical of mixed bargaining.

Sometimes the arrangement is reversed, as illustrated by the case discussed earlier of the large printing company and the printing unions in which integrative bargaining occurred at the top and pressure bargaining at the bottom. Management chose to discuss broad principles at the top and after several months of high-level co-operative discussions a tentative package was agreed upon. The translation of these principles into operating arrangements was left to the individual unions and the local plants. This meant that the hard bargaining over how the settlement would affect individuals took place at the local level. This same separation, by level, occurred in the Scottish east coast shipyards. The principles were negotiated at the top and included enabling agreements, while the details were negotiated on a yard by yard basis.

This differentiation by levels is well documented in the Oppenheim and Bayley study.

On two occasions during the following months private after-dinner meetings took place in a country hotel between the five key men mentioned earlier, in which the senior shop steward of the minority union was included; the senior author was also invited. These meetings were important in that the parties felt themselves able to exchange ideas freely in a frank atmosphere.[18]

In some respects this organisational differentiation of negotiations into problem solving and hard bargaining already exists in British industrial relations. However, the difficulty with the bargaining/consultation dichotomy that has pervaded many industries is that important industrial relations issues get categorised *incorrectly*. Specifically, wage matters and efficiency matters are considered within bargaining, while morale and welfare matters are considered within the consultation process. The result is that key subjects tend to be handled in a pressure or power way and unimportant subjects tend to be handled in an integrative or collaborative way. While it is important to have a separate forum for creation (integrative bargaining) and another for allocation (pressure bargaining), important issues involving pay and productivity need to be considered in *both* and not channelled by tradition exclusively into one or the other.

Differentiation by agenda items.   Another way to differentiate negotiations is to separate a complicated agenda into smaller elements. It is easier to develop a relationship in steps rather than in one big jump. In other words, if the determination of the sum and the allocation of the shares takes place in sequential steps, then the parties may be able to 'feel' their way into a situation that is in their best interests, both in terms of the sum and the share payoffs.

For example, in the docks the decasualisation subject has been handled first; secondly, the weekly guarantee; and eventually, work rules. The dock situation also suggests the advisability of linking problems that are naturally related. In the first phase the parties hammered out a package that was in the best interest of both sides in terms of stabilising the workforce and eliminating the inefficiencies that went with that tradition. Thus, one way of executing mixed bargaining is to fashion package solutions to related problems.

While many issues exist which cannot be linked naturally with others, in most instances they can be subdivided – and this applies

---

[18] Oppenheim and Bayley, 'Productivity and Conflict', p. 87.

to many of the so-called issues of principle. For example, the question of single manning of trains during the 'deep night' hours can be viewed in terms of specific schedules and relief periods rather than just in terms of the emotional consideration of safety.[19]

Differentiation by time phases. Mixed bargaining is also facilitated by the phases through which negotiations typically proceed. During the first phase the parties usually devote their attention to 'reconnoitring the range' and trying to answer the question : can a bargain be struck? The second phase involves the process of exploration, the use of sub-committees – this is essentially the problem-solving phase. The third phase brings the parties towards convergence and to the task of agreeing on terms. This involves a heavy element of pressure bargaining and share allocation.

Inevitably, some type of final 'crunch' is required, even for negotiations that have followed the integrative bargaining process. Consider the experience of Shell at Stanlow :

> The working parties went on through 1966 and 1967 . . . but they finally bogged down in dreariness. First the unions, then management, felt they had turned into long discussions which were getting nowhere. At one point, the joint union negotiating committee banned overtime in protest. No one could see any chance of bringing about change. (Eventually this stalemate proved to be a turning point, and the parties moved to an agreement by the end of 1968.)[20]

A second example of problem solving followed by hard bargaining can be taken from the Oppenheim and Bayley study :

> Even so, the negotiations fell somewhat behind and in the end the Managing Director took over the chairmanship of the negotiations and the final agreement was hammered out in two marathon sessions which lasted until well into the night.[21]

Interestingly, Oppenheim and Bayley attribute the emergence of hard bargaining to the structure of British society : 'When it came to the crunch, the unions insisted on making a distinction between communication and negotiation. . . . Thus the caste system served a function in "maintaining the boundaries" of the

---

[19] *Report of a Court of Inquiry under Mr A. J. Scamp* (negotiations between the British Railways Board, A.S.L.E.F., and the N.U.R.) p. 14.

[20] Larkom, 'Planning for Productivity', p. 41.

[21] Oppenheim and Bayley, 'Productivity and Conflict', pp. 87–8.

union organization.'[22] Our interpretation would be quite different: hard bargaining or the power resolution of shares during productivity negotiations is inevitable and chief negotiators inevitably adopt this style during the final phase.

The time phase dimension enables each party to interpret with some accuracy the meaning of his opponent's tactics. In other words, what may seem like inscrutable behaviour can be understood if one knows the time setting and particular phase of negotiations. In the first phase it is essential for both sides to 'talk up' the advantages of a presumed productivity agreement in order to arouse interest and to stimulate motivation. For example, in the Post Office telephone negotiations, management spent a long time talking about the importance of the proposed changes and how much money might be saved by the new working procedures. However, in the final phase, when hard bargaining was taking place over shares, it suited management's purpose to downgrade the value of the new arrangements, as illustrated by the following statement : 'Where mates are necessary for the work, there is no reason to assume that they will, in many cases, be more efficiently employed than at present'.

Another example of seemingly conflicting behaviour is the tendency for a union to drag its feet early in negotiations and then at the end to press for implementation of the agreement as rapidly as possible. During the first phase of negotiations, a union needs to 'feel its way' because of possible rank and file opposition; while during the last phase, speed is of the essence since the rank and file want to receive the benefits as quickly as possible. At the outset of the Post Office negotiations, the union pressed for a variety of 'experiments' and generally seemed to drag its feet, at one point forcing management to make additional concessions before negotiations could be resumed. When an agreement was finally reached, the union asked that implementation take place immediately.

Settlement criteria.   If the parties agree on the criteria for allocating shares at the outset, they are thereby freed to concentrate on integrative bargaining, knowing in advance the principles governing the share-out. Irrespective of the exact division, however, there may need to be some early indication that the potential gains are likely to be large enough to support this approach. The union especially will not be motivated to engage in productivity

[22] Oppenheim and Bayley, 'Productivity and Conflict', p. 92.

bargaining unless it sees an expectation of gains large enough to make the exercise worth the trouble, both in terms of the time involved in negotiating the agreement and the difficulties inevitably encountered in implementing a new programme. Even a 50–50 division rule may prove inadequate if the total dividend is small, or if the resulting wage increases do not keep pace with gains in wages achieved by other groups.

A good example of this can be seen in the experience of a large insurance company. This particular company had negotiated a productivity agreement with a 50–50 split of manpower savings. The main element in the programme involved the introduction of work measurement. To get the programme started the parties had agreed on a wage improvement of 3 per cent. At the one-year point, the company proposed another 3 per cent wage improvement. For its part, the union indicated that 3 per cent was not enough and threatened to impose sanctions : a ban on overtime, selective strikes, and no further co-operation in the introduction of work-measurement techniques. In the face of this 'ultimatum' the company agreed to distribute the remainder of the savings – which produced a wage increase of approximately 6 per cent. However, the union still objected and demanded more, and at the time of our investigations the matter was still hanging in limbo between the reluctance of the D.E.P. to approve the 6 per cent increase, the displeasure of the union, and the frustration of the company.

In this example, the workers felt compelled to abandon the principle of a 50–50 split of the savings, which had emerged as a rational solution to the allocation issue, once it became clear that their wages were lagging behind general developments. They engaged in power bargaining as a way of satisfying economic needs in a situation of 'scarce resources'. However, in most cases the principle of equal shares provides an acceptable basis for dividing the gains,[23] and the parties are able then to turn their attention to making the savings as large as possible.

CASE STUDY OF MIXED BARGAINING

The experience of Mobil at Coryton is a particularly good illus-

[23] In fact, where other splits have been agreed to, the rank and file have voiced opposition. For example, considerable tension has been generated by the 40 per cent formula used by the Post Office and the 43.5 per cent worker share used by the Steel Company of Wales. In each case the unions have exerted pressure to move the formula to a 50–50 arrangement.

tration of mixed bargaining (leading to the signing of the agreement) and at this point it is useful to present this impressive example of productivity bargaining in an organised fashion.[24]

The first step by management was to conduct a feasibility study of productivity bargaining. This was aided by an outside consultant, who made various recommendations about the operations at Coryton. This phase took considerable time and involved a frequent exchange of ideas between front-line supervision and top management. Management was anxious to assure itself that it would be possible to execute a productivity plan that involved no cash payment for overtime. To do this it designed *pro forma* maintenance schedules and estimated the impact of other changes to make sure that the assumptions about the new working arrangements were realistic.

After management had convinced itself that the programme was worthwhile and identified the key targets for potential change, it approached top union leadership and outlined its thinking. Several subsequent meetings were held with the top union leadership, and as a result the company improved several provisions in its proposal, especially those dealing with annual earnings.

In effect, during the first phase the company created a favourable union response and clarified the range of mutual advantage. By improving the yearly guarantee, the company dealt with the key threshold issue and induced the union to participate in the design of the agreement. By contacting the union at the top, the company secured the commitment of key officials, although the actual design and implementation of the agreement was to be carried forward at the local level by stewards and rank-and-file employees.

Once the design process actually got under way, the parties established at the plant level two subcommittees : one for maintenance, and one for process. Approximately fifteen shop stewards out of a total of eighty served on these two committees. Typically, two or three sessions were held each day. The committees were chaired by operating people with the industrial relations group performing a co-ordinating function.

Over a fifteen-month period the subcommittees tackled a wide

[24] This account is based on our own fieldwork at Mobil. For a separate perspective, that of a consultant, and one that essentially parallels our own, see F. E. Oldfield, *New Look Industrial Relations* (London, 1966) pp. 49–53.

range of problems. One of the first was deciding on the redistribution of the seventy-five mates whose positions were scheduled for elimination. Of these, fifty-five were easily handled. Another ten needed to be looked at carefully, and only three or four cases proved troublesome. The company agreed to keep on several electricians' mates as 'special situations', thereby accommodating the plan to an important political need of the union (the mates were eventually made electricians).

The main subject for the subcommittees was flexibility and the extent to which job duties could be rearranged between process and maintenance workers. As negotiations went forward and trust developed, the company followed the procedure of merely submitting the job sheets to the committees and allowing the stewards to write out the new flexibility arrangements.

Towards the end of the negotiations some conflict emerged as the parties talked about 'shares'. Specifically, considerable tension developed over the amount of pay to be guaranteed in the new contracts. After the start of discussions and the preliminary agreement on the yearly guarantee, wages in the general labour market had moved ahead. Consequently, the company found it necessary to go beyond its original guarantee of maintaining take-home pay and offered an additional 5 per cent. The union demanded 12 per cent, pointing out that cost of living alone had increased by 6 per cent during the fifteen-month design period. Eventually, the company expressed a willingness to move up the effective date of a 4 per cent increase to six months after the start of the agreement. This increase had been scheduled to be paid at the end of the first · year. As a result the parties reached agreement.

In general, very few people lost any money under the operation of the agreement. Nevertheless, considerable opposition to the agreement was expressed within certain groups, such as the pipe-fitters, painters, and some of the other civil engineering trades. The Electrical Trades Union was initially opposed but was brought round especially in the light of the special arrangement that had been made for their mates. Considerable 'selling work' had to be done by the company and eventually consensus emerged in favour of the productivity agreement.

The experience of Mobil is an interesting blend of increasing the gains for both sides and some hard bargaining over respective shares. In this instance, the differentiation of pressure bargaining and integrative bargaining took place by level. The joint gains were created at the local level by the stewards and management officials. The division of the 'fruits' into respective shares was handled by the union officials from the district and top company officials. It would have been difficult and counterproductive for the stewards, who were behaving quite co-operatively, to have tackled the question of shares – this was done by the district officials who had remained aloof from the problem-solving activity.

5. INTERNAL CONSENSUS

So far, our analysis of negotiations has considered only the 'main table'. We have assumed implicitly that each negotiating team has acted with perfect internal co-ordination and fidelity with respect to the wishes of its principals and constituents. This is clearly not always the case and regardless of whether the parties approach each other in a pressure bargaining, integrative bargaining, or mixed bargaining mode, considerable bargaining activity occurs 'within the ranks'.

On the management side the problem of achieving internal consensus exists throughout negotiations, but it is especially severe during the *pre-bargaining* phase – during the period when management is forming a proposal and making ready its presentation. In one nationalised industry considerable difference of opinion existed within the management ranks over the feasibility of productivity bargaining. In order to crystallise commitment and to galvanise the organisation into action, the chief management negotiator agreed to an immediate wage increase with the union on the condition that a productivity agreement would be signed two months later. Confronted with increased labour costs and given a specific time deadline, the management organisation swung into action and an agreement was signed on schedule.

On the union side bargaining within the ranks also takes place throughout the negotiations, but it is especially intense during the *ratification* phase. Within the union internal differences occur in many directions. A difference of opinion may exist between a negotiator and his superiors. For example, the officials of the Boilermakers' Society who participated in the productivity negotiations at I.C.I. found themselves at odds with the President, Daniel McGarvey. The latter had made strong statements in the Press about not 'selling the rule book', whereas local officials felt quite strongly that productivity bargaining presented an attractive opportunity for increasing member benefits and for controlling the inevitable : organisational and technological change.

Usually, however, the focus of internal differences is between the union negotiator and his members, or between competing factions. In some instances the disagreement is over objectives, in other instances, over strategy and tactics. The integrative bargaining approach, for example, can create considerable disagreement within a union. The rank and file may assume that the only way negotiations can be conducted is through pressure, deadline crises, and an exhibition of militant behaviour. The activities which are required in problem solving, namely, subcommittee work and a constructive exchange of ideas, may violate the expectations of the rank and file about the appropriate behaviour of their representatives.

In several productivity bargaining exercises the achievement of consensus within the union has represented the major task facing both parties. Consider the following sequence that occurred in the negotiation of a productivity agreement at the Shell refinery, Stanlow.[25] Productivity discussions had been proceeding for some twelve months when the workers called an unofficial mass meeting and demanded that the productivity discussions be terminated and that conventional wage bargaining be instituted immediately. While the full-time union officials rejected this point of view, they found it necessary to speed up discussions and to place productivity bargaining on a more formal basis. The company, in turn, appreciating the seriousness of the challenge, co-operated. One result was that more management officials participated in the discussions.

Soon after, however, the discussions received another jolt with the withdrawal of the Boilermakers' Society over the issue of work sharing. This departure almost terminated the discussions. The breakaway, however, did produce one benefit in disguise, by creating substantial impetus to achieve convergence. Efforts concentrated on reaching agreement before other unions developed cold feet. Within several weeks a productivity agreement was ready – but when it was presented to the craftsmen for ratification, it was rejected overwhelmingly. The company then made a number of

[25] Much of this material is taken from the speech by H. S. Rule to the British Institute of Management Forum in April 1969, London.

changes : work sharing and flexibility arrangements were softened and some modest improvements were made in salaries. The package was accepted after a vote at a mass meeting of craftsmen in August 1968, despite the continued opposition of some shop stewards.

Divergent expectations such as those in the preceding example can produce severe repercussions if they are not confronted and minimised. The risk that any negotiator runs in ignoring such gaps is that he may have underestimated the opposition of the membership and he may find the agreement being rejected and his leadership repudiated. Certainly, not all productivity agreements have been automatically ratified. A case in point was the 1963 negotiations on the docks when the rank and file vetoed the 'new deal'. Consider the commentary of the Devlin Committee :

First, there was no preparation of the ground for the rank and file. It is, as we have already noted, a difficult matter for a trade union leader to decide at what point in the negotiations he takes a plan to his constituents. There can be little doubt that in the case the secrecy was excessive. Mr O'Hare did not take even his principal officials into his confidence and he did not confide in the National Docks Secretary until the scheme was on paper and ready to be issued.[26]

Another example comes from the study of productivity bargaining by the Engineering Employers' Federation. In a discussion of Tubes Ltd[27] the example is given of a setback to a productivity bargaining exercise because the shop stewards presented the package to the rank and file prematurely. In addition, the company allowed the union to handle all communications with the workers about the plan. No doubt this was done out of respect for the authority and leadership of the union; however, the plan was reasonably complicated and in retrospect both sides agreed that the stewards needed the assistance of the company in gaining acceptance from the rank and file.

[26] *Final Report of the Committee of Inquiry under the Rt Hon. Lord Devlin* (concerning the port transport industry) p. 82.

[27] D. C. Alexander (ed.), *A Productivity Bargaining Symposium* (London : Engineering Employers' Federation, 1969) 92.

STRATEGIES FOR ACHIEVING INTERNAL CONSENSUS

Achieving internal consensus can be viewed as a process of bringing the outlook of the rank and file into line with that of the leadership, both with respect to behaviour and with respect to substantive results. Broadly speaking, a union leader can either deal *openly* with the discrepancy and arrange his tactics to change the outlook of the rank and file; or he can *ignore* the gap, either leaving it unresolved or taking steps to neutralise the consequent repercussions.

Since the achievement of internal consensus represents a form of negotiation, we can utilise the concepts introduced earlier to describe this process. In essence, the open approach represents a type of integrative bargaining – the problem being that the organisation will not be able to achieve its aspiration. The approach involves opening up the subject for internal discussion and agonising reappraisal. By contrast, the alternative approach of ignoring the gap or minimising the organisational perception of the gap resembles the manipulation tactics of pressure bargaining.

The open strategy can entail, for example, the use of such a tactic as putting militant members of the union on the negotiating committee so that they can see the futility of their approach and better appreciate the need for problem solving. Such a step was taken in the dock negotiations when the T.G.W.U. officials allowed 'militants' to participate in high-level discussions. Minutes were also posted for those who could not attend the meetings so that they could be 'educated' about the potentialities of problem solving. In addition a series of bulletins were issued by the National Modernisation Committee to acquaint the membership with the issues of decasualisation and restrictive practices. Significantly, these bulletins were sent to the men's homes rather than being distributed at work.

In some instances, a mass meeting may be used to achieve more understanding and consensus within the ranks. We can cite one very interesting example :

The next stage was a works meeting. This was a remarkable step, unique in the history of the firm and the first of its kind in the United Kingdom. It took place during the second half of a Saturday morning, in a local cinema, and was extremely well-attended – certainly attendance was much better than even the more optimistic management estimates had suggested. The employees were paid £1 per head for their attendance. The meeting was addressed by the Managing Director and by several others, including the principal Union leaders, and broke up in what was hoped would be an atmosphere of mutual confidence.[28]

The approach of ignoring the gap can entail such tactics as limiting the opportunity of the membership to follow what is actually taking place – as a result they are not aware of the discrepancy between their expectations and the bargaining process as it is being conducted. Eventually members may realise what has happened, but by then negotiations may be over. The presumption is that the membership will accept the results and the associated behaviour of the negotiator as a *fait accompli*. This is essentially the strategy that district officials of the Boilermakers' Society used at I.C.I. They did not keep the President informed and when the productivity agreement was finally announced, McGarvey was not in a position to repudiate it openly, even though he was unhappy about the settlement.

In other instances the leadership may have to confront the disappointment or opposition of the rank and file through persuasion, education and possibly even coercion, in order to gain a satisfactory ratification vote on the contract which has been negotiated with the employer.

In general, both management and union officials can help the other side gain consensus within his respective organisation. While this activity represents a very delicate assignment – indeed, it is the type of co-operation that the parties can attend to only after they have developed a close working relationship – it often accompanies the negotiating of a productivity agreement and makes final acceptance possible.

CASE STUDY OF INTERNAL CONSENSUS

The negotiations between the Post Office Engineering Union (P.O.E.U.) and the Post Office during the early 1960s illustrate many important dimensions. A description of these fascinating

---

[28] Oppenheim and Bayley, 'Productivity and Conflict', p. 86.

negotiations is instructive both for understanding the process of achieving internal consensus and for relating this process to the other processes which we have been exploring in this chapter. We will present data obtained from our fieldwork and then comment on its significance for each of the major phases of the negotiations.

Initiation of discussions. The story starts with a letter written by the union to the Post Office on 13 December 1960.

Dear Engineering Department
We have indicated to our conference the views about the inappropriateness of the existing engineering instructions (covering the size of working parties) and we have been aware of the evidence from experiments aimed at widening the scope of duties performed by two-man working parties.

The union has been sensitive to the point expressed by telephone subscribers when they have criticised the need for three- or four-man installation parties to visit their houses to complete a telephone installation. There is also the possibility of reducing the cost of installation.

It is our intention to make such a recommendation at next year's annual conference. It would be pointless, however, in making such a recommendation if this idea did not have the general support of the engineering department.

Several days later, on 30 December, the Post Office responded as follows :

Dear Post Office Union
We are glad to hear the interest you have expressed. We also have recently been considering the need for increased flexibility.

We would like to meet you on this subject and the 20th of January is satisfactory.

On 17 and 18 of January the union negotiator met with his committee, entitled the Experimental Practices Subcommittee. At the meeting he reported on the above exchange of letters. However, he did not indicate that he was holding a meeting with the Post Office on 20 January.

The top officials met on 20 January and a general discussion ensued about the feasibility of increasing gang flexibility. During the meeting the company provided a breakdown of work being done by different types of gangs. In turn, this information was discussed at the next meeting of the Experimental Practices Subcommittee on 28 and 29 March 1961.

Analysis.   During the opening round the union and the company established a range of mutual interest. They determined to their own satisfaction that something mutually advantageous might result from pursuing the subject of flexibility. The union negotiator handled his internal relationships very carefully. He kept his committee apprised, but only partially. He did not tell his committee about the key meeting with the company until after it had been held, for fear that some of them would have wanted to participate. In other words, he preferred to keep them apprised after the fact in order to report progress rather than having some of the militant members disrupt discussions with the company.

Rebuff from the delegates.   In early March the union negotiator distributed the minutes of the 20 January meeting to all members of the union in a monthly newspaper. At the Annual Conference subsequently held in the spring of 1961, the negotiator asked for formal authority to proceed with productivity discussions with the Post Office. The conference 'referenced back' the proposal, indicating that they did not want anything to do with flexibility or reduction of gang sizes.

Analysis.   The union leader suffered an obvious setback. The rank and file and their delegates were not prepared for change and the abrupt submission of a proposal to proceed with a productivity discussion aroused instinctive opposition.

Cultivation of a climate within the union.   Between March 1961 and March 1963, the union negotiator and his subcommittee spent considerable time discussing the subject of flexibility and reduced gang sizes. They also discussed the subject with various branches. As a result, at the Annual Conference in the spring of 1963 the top union officials successfully introduced an 'emergency resolution' to reopen discussions with the Post Office on a possible productivity agreement.

One reason for the changed outlook was a developing realisation within the union that the Post Office was moving ahead with its own studies at the local level. Specifically, in September 1962 the Belfast branch had reported that management had proposed an experimental programme for operating two-man gangs. While the union negotiator had taken the position that these matters should be settled centrally, he knew it was only a matter of time before the self-interest of the local members would lead them in the direction of co-operating with management.

Analysis. The union moved as quickly as possible to create a climate of acceptance for change. The leaders knew that some local branches were co-operating informally with management in establishing two-man gangs. Thus it was imperative that the officers push a resolution through the Annual Conference which would allow the union to reopen discussions with management on a productivity agreement, thereby keeping control of the change process.

The quest for agreement: integrative bargaining. During the summer and early autumn of 1963, the Post Office and the union held many meetings devoted to a discussion of different crew arrangements and a dissemination of information about savings and benefits associated with the different schemes. During this same period the union negotiator held many briefing sessions with members of his own subcommittee – most of whom did not participate in negotiations. One reason was that they were working members of the union and could not travel to London very frequently, and it was also easier for the union negotiator to engage in problem solving with the Post Office in the absence of the 'rank and filers'.

The only point of conflict during this period occurred at a meeting in early September when the management negotiator showed the union a draft of a memorandum soon to be released for internal communication within the Post Office. It talked about a reduction in the three-man groups and implied the eventual elimination of a key classification. The union negotiator expressed surprise and strongly urged that the memorandum not be disseminated until the union had had a chance to review the matter fully. The Post Office agreed to delay the bulletin; and when it was finally released in early October (after some important changes had been incorporated, such as a pledge of no redundancy), the union asked for eleven hundred copies for distribution within its own organisation.

However, as soon as the memorandum reached the locals, the union negotiator received many vehement complaints. In fact one of the branches called an emergency meeting to express its opposition. Other branches forwarded letters demanding more information or asking for visits by union officials to 'explain' the development. The union leadership answered all these letters and spent considerable time visiting different branches.

Analysis. The Post Office erred in its plan to release an internal document on classification changes. An engineering study group had been proceeding on its own during the two-year hiatus (1961–3) and its work had *not* been co-ordinated with the group seeking a productivity bargaining agreement. Once the Post Office had gone half-way to meet the union by incorporating certain guarantees such as no redundancy, the union negotiator then had to deal with his own organisation. He found it necessary to spend considerable time educating his organisation about the impending changes.

Reaching agreement: mixed bargaining. By the early part of 1964, discussions were moving to a conclusion. The Post Office asked the union whether it was planning to make a report to its spring conference. The union indicated that it wanted more time since the projected changes were very important and would entail considerable adjustment for the membership.

While the discussions were generally constructive during this period, a couple of tense moments occurred during the preliminary discussion of the concept of two-man crews. The parties had tentatively agreed that these streamlined teams would not erect poles – however, subsequently in a survey of practice the Post Office found, much to its surprise, that in a number of local situations poles were being erected by two-man crews. Accordingly, management asked the union to relax the previously agreed limitation. The union negotiator refused and said that he was sticking by the earlier understanding that two-man crews could not erect poles. On the positive side the parties agreed to undertake several experiments in order to observe at first hand how the new working arrangements might be effected.

During the summer and autumn of 1964, the final details were agreed upon and the union released to all branches a copy of 'The Organisation of Installation Working Parties' and a master plan detailing the duties of the technical grades. Again the branches demanded more information and requested the presence of top officials. Since many aspects of the plan could only be agreed upon locally, the union negotiator turned many of the issues back to the branches for thrashing out with local management.

Agreement was reached within the union and the agreement was signed in early 1965.

Analysis. The final portion of negotiations contained elements of hard pressure-type bargaining, integrative bargaining, and internal consensus making. The employer's request on the two-man crew duties vividly illustrated how difficult it can be to develop a master plan for productivity change. Practices differ considerably throughout an organisation as diverse as the Post Office.

The union negotiator also had to spend considerable time dealing with the objections of the rank and file. One technique was to throw the burden back on the branches to resolve their own difficulties and the details of implementation with local management.

All in all, the union negotiator handled his difficult position quite skilfully. He generally used the integrative bargaining approach. He was more circumspect, however, with respect to his own subcommittee, although he kept them fully apprised of developments – usually after the fact. With respect to the rank and file, he announced developments only when there was something concrete to communicate. He then dealt with their opposition and the consequences of their resistance rather than conducting an educational campaign in advance.

6. CONCLUDING COMMENTS

The purpose of this chapter has been to analyse the various activities that are involved in negotiating a productivity agreement. By dividing the complex process into conceptually separate processes, we have been able to differentiate the direct and indirect approaches and their respective negotiating counterparts : pressure and integrative bargaining.

The essential characteristics of the two bargaining approaches can be summarised as in Table 6.2.

The pressure-bargaining approach is most often used where the parties do not enjoy a co-operative relationship and/or where the parties seek the type of productivity change that can be readily identified and executed. If much investigation is needed into the source of the productivity difficulties or if a good deal of imagination is required in formulating solutions, pressure bargaining is not appropriate. Pressure bargaining usually becomes dominant

Table 6.2. *Characteristics of Direct and Indirect Bargaining*

	Pressure or direct bargaining	Integrative or indirect bargaining
Basic approach	Careful planning and development of programme by management	Joint discussions on problems and possible solutions
Tactics	Concessions as a result of *quid pro quos* and deadlines	Characterised by creative detours and unstructured search
Attitudes	Arm's length	Co-operative

as an approach when the workers feel insecure about obtaining a minimally acceptable economic outcome. To raise the probability of obtaining a desired wage improvement, they engage in pressure bargaining to compel management to honour their expectations.

The main advantages of pressure bargaining or the direct method are that the agreement is likely to be signed relatively quickly and that it represents a lower-risk strategy. The main disadvantage in pressure bargaining is that the parties may fail to solve any problems and devote all of their attention to dividing up the existing 'pie'.

Integrative bargaining, by contrast, focuses attention on creating solutions and on conducting a fundamental search for organisational arrangements that benefit both sides. In a game-theory sense, the two sides view the world as holding potential for increasing their joint payoffs. Minimal attention is placed on the division of the resources since each side can satisfy its primary needs by collaborating with the other to increase the total gains. The big advantage of integrative bargaining is that fundamental change processes can be set in motion and some very basic problems solved, or at least explored.

Considerable manpower is required to carry on integrative bargaining. It is no accident that the companies that have practised this approach have relatively more staff personnel and tend to be characterised by longer planning horizons. Thus, integrative bargaining can be more readily pursued in such industries as oil and electricity supply than, for example, in engineering where the personnel or the time are less available for problem-solving activities.

The disadvantages of integrative bargaining or the indirect method are more subtle. The big drawback is that one side may take advantage of the other. Since integrative bargaining requires the disclosure of sensitive information and the adoption of a flexible posture, it is possible for one side to be victimised. Usually such treatment is not apparent until after the negotiations have been completed, until the moment when it becomes clear that what seemed like co-operative behaviour on the part of the opponent was nothing more than treachery in disguise. Pressure bargaining avoids this pitfall, since in arm's-length bargaining each side remains on its guard and behaves in a way which guarantees for itself a minimum return.

Another drawback stems from the high-risk nature of the integrative approach. It takes considerable time to show results. The extensive time requirements of problem solving can create difficulties, especially those arising from unfulfilled expectations. In a number of cases, workers have shown willingness at an early stage to co-operate in changes but enthusiasm has waned when implementation becomes delayed, either because of difficulty in completing other parts of the deal or, in a few instances, because of incomes policy constraints.

It is not sufficient for integrative bargaining to take place at the top level of the organisations, for a bright new programme for change to emerge, and for the 'problem solvers' to assume that everyone will accept it. All levels of the organisation must eventually become involved in the design process itself. It is at this point that 'staff' types often take their biggest tumble. They assume that any issue in the industrial relations area can be resolved by problem solving at the top. 'Just get people together and produce a better solution and then everything will be all right.' This mythology most commonly occurs at the top of many large corporations (and also in the higher ranks of some unions). Staff specialists may develop a brilliant approach to productivity change and worker rewards, but fail to realise that a technical masterpiece is no substitute for a better relationship. This can only be achieved by full participation at all levels.

For these reasons, integrative bargaining or the indirect approach has emerged as an infrequent approach to productivity change.[29] Great skill is required on both sides, and the issues themselves must contain the potential for problem solving. Beyond these requirements, the parties must be willing to wait for a considerable period of time before the process begins to show results. An orientation that emphasises short-run results is not compatible with integrative bargaining.

[29] During much of phase II (1967–9), the anxiety of the National Board for Prices and Incomes over the effects of the more open-ended type of agreement was a further inhibiting factor: see Chapter 4 above.

7 Implementation of the Agreement

1. INTRODUCTION

Stripped to its essential features, the implementation of a productivity agreement involves the activities pursued by management and union officials to bring about change in worker behaviour. As with negotiations, the emphasis is on process. Whereas the negotiating process leads to some form of understanding, the implementation process leads to some form of operating results. The steps taken by both sides to secure desired results are the concern of this chapter; the nature and effectiveness of the results will be discussed in the next two chapters.

One distinguishing feature of the implementation process is that it necessarily takes place at the local level. Agreements can be negotiated either centrally or locally, but implementation cannot be executed from the top in a complex organisation. Practices and underlying conditions vary so substantially among local units that the productivity change process can only take place where productivity itself is determined.

A second distinguishing feature is the importance of job design and job satisfaction. During the negotiation of the agreement, workers are interested primarily in wages and benefits (what we have termed 'rewards'); however, once the agreement is signed, these items are taken as given and the workers' attention turns to questions of the agreement's influence on their day-to-day work experiences.[1]

The third distinguishing feature is the amount of diligence and tenacity that is required. Since the implementation phase can cover

[1] See W. W. Daniel, *Beyond the Wage–Work Bargain* (London: P.E.P., 1970) 59.

a period of years, the parties find themselves involved in an intense experience of prolonged duration. Curiously, the parties often find it easier to mount the energy that is required for negotiating an agreement than to bring about change and to administer a fluid situation over an extended period of time. It is easy for co-ordination to falter when other matters press upon the officials, and their attention is taken away from administering the productivity agreement; during the negotiating period the officials can direct all their energies to hammering out the agreement.

In the records of implementation, there are many instances of this lack of co-ordination. In the Post Office example discussed in the preceding chapter, management wanted to set up experimental groupings; the union quickly agreed and then nothing was heard on the subject. Only after the union had pressed the point was the programme launched. Similarly, the union held up a management letter about a new job classification, saying it wanted to examine the duties in practice. Only after the Post Office had pressed the union for an answer did action take place. Such instances dramatise the day-to-day challenges that are perpetually a part of the implementation experience.

INTERNALISATION AND COMPLIANCE

Throughout this study, heavy emphasis has been placed on the notion that most rules and practices existing in industrial relations have some functional value for the participants, even though in some cases the reasons for the practices may have become obliterated by change. For the most part, the rules governing the work system are held in place because they continue to fulfil specific needs of the persons involved in the workplace experience. In many cases, a conditioning process has taken place so that people have come to understand and to 'need' the arrangements that are already present. This mutual reinforcement or equilibrium is an essential characteristic of the employment relationship.

Such a perspective is appropriate for understanding the process by which worker behaviour is changed. Generally speaking, workers will alter their behaviour and adopt new modes only if they are induced to do so for either intrinsic or extrinsic reasons.

The intrinsic rationale for changing behaviour stems from the fact that all workers, in varying degrees, hold ego and other self-fulfilment needs which the work experience may or may not satisfy. Productivity bargaining, then, can be a means for creating more satisfying and fulfilling work experiences. For example, as a result of introducing a flexibility programme, skilled workers may be able to think of themselves more as true craftsmen and as important contributors to the success of the enterprise.

In some cases, the intrinsic benefits of the work experience may not be readily apparent to the workers and certain educational processes may be required before such aspects of the work scene become salient to the workers. And once such sensitising has been accomplished, the workers may adopt the new work procedures because they are preferred in their own right; not just because some financial rewards are made contingent on accepting them.

By contrast, the extrinsic rationale for the alteration of worker behaviour depends upon the linkage of rewards and punishment to the new pattern of work which is sought. This type of change is best understood in terms of traditional psychological theory with its emphasis on reinforcement. The assumption is that people do not change their behaviour unless they are rewarded or punished. Presumably, people are pulled toward the new work arrangements by the associated rewards or are moved away from the old forms by the increased costs incurred by adhering to the *status quo*. This method of facilitating productivity improvement involves the manipulation of the structure of rewards and costs in a way that motivates workers to accept change. If the rewards and costs specified by the agreement are not subject to manipulation or alteration on the shop-floor, then it is necessary for management to engage in tactics for securing compliance, e.g. the institution of 'side bargains'.

At this point, we can relate these two types of need to two distinct change processes. The process of enlisting intrinsic needs can be referred to as *internalisation*. Under this approach workers internalise, for one reason or another, a desire to change. This drive may stem from their own preference for the new working patterns or from a feeling of obligation to honour the commitments made by their leaders in negotiating a productivity agreement. For example, workers might engage in more flexible working practices because they identify with their union leaders who have espoused the new principles. Similarly, foremen might carry out their side of a productivity agreement because of their organisational loyalty.

The second change process can be labelled *compliance*. It is the process by which worker behaviour is changed because of the prospect of additional benefits or costs, such as pressure and discipline. This can be referred to as the extrinsic rationale for altering the behaviour of workers.

These change processes can be compared in several ways. Both compliance and internalisation work with the attitude–behaviour linkage but they start at opposite ends. The compliance process aims to secure change quite directly, either ignoring attitudes or assuming that they will change once the new behaviour is set in place. In contrast, internalisation starts with attitudinal change, based on the premise that if the basic orientation of the workforce can be realigned, then new forms of behaviour will quickly follow.

The compliance process invokes the techniques of traditional management and hardly needs elaboration at this point. The internalisation process represents more of a departure from the normal style of administration and consequently some additional comments are in order. The basic aim of internalisation is to resolve the fears and 'hang-ups' that workers harbour towards new working arrangements. The assumption is that once these fears have been dealt with, workers will move to the new arrangements because they appreciate the value of them. Management and, to some extent, union officials, play a facilitating function rather than the traditional one of active leadership involving the overt manipulation of inducements and pressures.

One final point which should need little spelling out is that the design features of the agreement are themselves likely to be related to the question whether the approach will lean towards either compliance or internalisation. For example, where the design is characterised by concentration on a narrow range of specific changes in the organisation of work, where a short time horizon is adopted for giving effect to change, and where the agreement affects only a section of the workforce, the method of implementation is almost bound to be one of compliance. Conversely, where a broad range of issues, loosely defined, is adopted as the agenda, where no fixed time-limits are set, and where the level of employee coverage is plant or company wide, the possibilities for internalisation are much greater.

This does not mean that the choice of design features will necessarily *determine* the course of implementation : the direction of determination may easily be reversed. That is, in some cases the initial steps in the design will derive from attention being focused on certain items regarded as critical, usually by management, and once these have been selected, the method of implementation may follow naturally. In other cases, management may decide explicitly to adopt either a compliance or an internalisation method, because of organisational or technical factors, for example. That decision will then become influential in determining the subsequent choice of ingredients and the tactics to be adopted in negotiation. We will return to this inter-relationship in the synthesis at the end of this chapter.

2. IMPLEMENTATION ACTIVITIES

The process of implementing a productivity agreement can be thought of as entailing two basic steps : the specification of the new terms of the work system, and the creation of some impetus for the organisation to adopt these new arrangements. These steps and their related activities will be considered in the following sections, using the alternative approaches of compliance and internalisation as organising concepts.

The first step of spelling out the new elements of the work system largely occurs during the negotiation of the productivity agreement (especially under the direct approach). However, many details must be hammered out during the implementation period itself and an important technique for specifying standards is work measurement. The other activities which we will discuss relate to the second step of achieving a climate and desire for change. These activities include but are not limited to participation, communication, incentives and experimentation.

WORK MEASUREMENT

Work measurement, an important tool in the hands of skilful management, can be used to establish goals and pinpoint progress towards the implementation of the agreement. The contrast between the compliance and internalisation approaches arises around

the establishment of performance standards and the communication of information on results (compared against the standards).
The compliance avenue to change usually employs *attainable*
standards, spelling them out *explicitly*, and linking rewards and
punishments to the realisation of these targets. On the other hand,
internalisation usually involves *ultimate* or long-run standards,
using them implicitly and as guidelines rather than as indicators
of required performance. These distinctions can be elaborated as
follows.

Type of measurement standard. Performance standards can
be thought of as expressing either attainable or ultimate performance. The attainable standard, which is the type necessarily used
in systems that reward workers for extra results, implies that a
typical worker operating under typical conditions can meet the
targets. On the other hand, an ultimate standard describes an ideal
level of performance and is used to highlight the difference between
actual and optimum results. Allowances for such factors as delays,
poor materials, unforeseen handicaps, and the like, are built into
the attainable production standard because they are, by and large,
beyond the control of the individual worker; however, there are
no such adjustments in the development of an ultimate standard.

Use of standards. Management can make either explicit or
implicit use of measurement information. An explicit use involves
the disclosure of the standard, communication of results, and
possibly the payment of contingent rewards or punishments, depending upon the relationship between standards and results.
Alternatively, management uses measurement information only for
the guidance of the organisation, as a means for highlighting problems rather than for actively controlling the workforce. In this
method, more emphasis is placed on inputs and on eliciting a 'fair
day's effort' than on the specification of particular results for which
workers are held accountable.

PARTICIPATION

Since the negotiation of a productivity agreement is a joint exercise, it would seem essential to make its execution similarly a joint
endeavour – indeed, most companies would not have embarked
upon productivity bargaining if they did not believe in worker–

management co-operation or if they thought they could achieve acceptable results unilaterally.

While most companies favour some measure of participation, the variations are considerable. For example, in the N.B.P.I. report on job evaluation, different degrees of participation are cited. In the coal industry, a joint committee of representatives from the National Coal Board and the National Union of Mineworkers was established to evaluate and grade jobs. In another case, some participation by employees occurred in ranking jobs but neither employees nor union officials were involved in relating these rankings to pay levels.[2]

Examples also can be found where companies have attempted, for the most part, to implement agreements on a unilateral basis. In a car manufacturing company, union representatives were not allowed on the work measurement committee, despite the fact that work measurement as a technique and effort intensity as a problem area represented major themes of the productivity improvement. This company followed the direct approach and its complement, the compliance method of implementation, in the belief that management could get results by specifying standards and insisting on performance.

On the other hand, some companies have placed such importance on participation that the whole exercise from start to finish has embodied the theory of joint optimisation – in this sense the process is what we have called integrative bargaining and internalisation. Such an approach is described in the study of productivity bargaining at Tubes.[3] In this instance, both a departmental productivity panel and a works advisory council were established to help implement the productivity agreement. The Work Sharing Committee established at Shell, Stanlow, in 1968 represents another case in point :

After implementation of the agreement a joint committee will be established with agreed terms of references. This will consist of representatives of the Company, the Craft Unions and the

---

[2] N.B.P.I. Report No. 83 *Report on Agreement Relating to the Pay of Surveyors and Wood-cutting Machinists in the Saw Milling Industry,* Cmnd 3768 (London : H.M.S.O., 1968) 13.

[3] D. C. Alexander (ed.), *A Productivity Bargaining Symposium* (London : Engineering Employers' Federation, 1969) 92–7.

T.G.W.U. Its function will be to ensure that the working practices developed are in accordance with the principles and spirit
of work sharing as set out in [the agreement.][4]

Perhaps the most extensive programme of grass-roots participation has taken place at the Gloucester works of I.C.I., where
internalisation has been the theme of the implementation experience. In introducing the agreement, management established a
number of working parties to carry out detailed analyses and to
review suggestions for changes. And management set up shop
discussion groups to involve the men and themselves directly in
the design and planning of the changes in organisation and
methods of working. Every operator attended at least one discussion group and each group included shop stewards and supervisors,
as well as operators.[5] The exact style of participation depends upon
the orientation of management and its willingness to allow some
form of joint decision-making on a day-to-day basis. The more
management emphasises compliance, the less likely is it that participation will be extensive. Of course, unions favour participation,[6] and even where management is compliance-oriented, the
reality of union insistence will bring about some measure of joint
involvement.

Most situations fall somewhere between the extremes of a
unilateral and a totally joint determination or implementation of
agreements. In these situations management sets the pace and uses
participation to check out plans and to test reactions before initiating a new piece of the agreement. The operation of the Experimental Practices Committee in the telecommunications branch of
the Post Office fits this description. The specific ideas for new
working practices usually have emanated from management,
although as we noted in the last chapter, the impetus for change,

---

[4] Productivity agreement between Shell U.K. Ltd, Stanlow Refinery/
Thornton Research Centre, and The Joint Union Negotiating Committee
(JUNC), 1969, Section IV.
[5] Evelyn Glor, 'I.C.I.'s New Process', *Industrial Society*, Vol. L (November,
1968) 6.
[6] Tony Topham in his spirited essay argues for the establishment of pay and
productivity committees to monitor agreements. He takes a very forthright
stand in favour of direct involvement by these committees and criticises
arrangements where joint productivity committees are only advisory, such as
at British Petroleum. See T. Topham, in *Trade Union Register*, ed. K. Coates,
T. Topham, M. B. Brown (London, 1969) 89.

on occasion, might also come from the union side. Generally speaking, the committee has been used to work out the feasibility of new ideas and to develop methods for testing these concepts – rather than developing the programmes from scratch.

COMMUNICATION

Short of having everyone participate in the fashioning of a productivity agreement, the next best thing is the creation of vicarious involvement. The object is to share with the rank and file the rationale as well as the essence of the new system. By communicating the details of the agreement and spelling out the benefits, top officials from both sides can create an atmosphere wherein groups lower in the system will be motivated to make changes because of the obvious advantages. Of course, the advantages may not be so 'obvious' to everyone. Moreover, some workers may feel that their work practices are already efficient. And in some instances they may be right. In large multi-plant companies many situations are bound to exist where the 'new' arrangements envisaged in the productivity agreement do not improve upon existing work practices; in other work situations, practices may be quite inefficient but the workers fail to realise that the world is different from their 'little corners'. Such parochialism can be changed only through communication and education.

Eldridge, in his study of shipbuilding, has documented the critical role of communication in fostering a readiness to accept change. He notes that many managements have run into trouble because they have been too secretive. 'Workers live in a twilight zone, where some things are known, others half-known and rumoured about, where they are prepared for some changes but not for others.'[7]

By contrast, in one yard, systematic communication and consultation took place and management even took the stewards and shipwrights to London to see a new computer profile burner in operation.

A senior manager also described how, before the initiation of an extensive modernisation scheme, he spent six months meeting men and stewards in the canteen 'over beer and pies'. (This

---

[7] J. E. T. Eldridge, *Industrial Disputes, Essays in the Sociology of Industrial Relations* (London: Routledge and Kegan Paul, 1968) 121.

same company also introduced changes in periods of expanding activity.) . . . Certainly this yard was remarkably free of demarcation disputes. Indeed, management went to some pains to point out that, to some extent, the outside world had a misleading picture of the worker's attitude to technical change. In some cases, it was noted, the workers themselves press for new equipment when the old is not working properly.[8]

The status agreement in electricity supply also illustrates how important the communication system is in getting results. Shortly after the signing of stage II of the agreement in February 1965, members of the council travelled around the country, meeting managers at district level. The purpose of these briefing sessions was to acquaint all members of local management with the potentialities of the new agreement. Local management, in turn, held meetings with supervisors and the communication process continued downward and eventually reached all employees. On the other side, the unions held some meetings but these were not as effective, because they faced the problem of not being able to disseminate information to their organisations as quickly as management. In retrospect, management felt that the two communication channels might have been merged to good advantage, with management attending the union meetings and union officials attending the supervisory briefing sessions.

To carry out a communication programme, various techniques have been used. In one instance, as we noted in the last chapter, a local cinema was rented, and on a Saturday morning all the workers were brought together to have the productivity agreement discussed. The workers were each paid one pound for their time and trouble. Thomson House has used a system of cost targets which are promulgated to the various departments. This information provides the different groups with specific knowledge about goals and progress. In other instances, management has prepared bulletins, progress reports, and indices of progress – all to the end of communicating with the workers where things stand and what remains to be accomplished.

While a good measure of communication appears necessary for both the internalisation and compliance methods of change, certain important differences in emphasis can be noted. When

---

[8] Eldridge, *Industrial Disputes*, p. 122.

internalisation is the mode, communication is as complete and as extensive as possible. Since in the indirect approach it is difficult to separate the negotiation and implementation phases, much of the activity that we discussed in the last chapter in connection with integrative bargaining also applies here.

In contrast, when compliance is the mode, communication appears to be more circumspect and guarded. In the Fawley study, Allan Flanders noted how management hesitated to report too much progress for fear it would provide the union with a basis for another wage claim.[9]

Beyond these tactical considerations, a reluctance to confide in the rank and file in some situations probably stems from fear about 'leaks' to competitors, the class tradition of British industrial life, or the feeling that the 'boys' should only know so much i.e. 'they would not understand the complexity of the enterprise even if we told them the facts'.[10]

Regardless of whether management's desire to withhold information stems from the dictates of its compliance orientation, from fear, or from certain myopic attitudes, as a practical matter it has little choice but to release *some* information. Both union and 'outside' pressures tend to force disclosure. For example, several key unions that have been most active in productivity bargaining have insisted that full information be made available about the agreement and about the progress of implementation. The following statement presents the thinking of one large union on the question of communication and information :

In order to maintain confidence in the workings of this agreement and in the spirit thereof, the Company will make available to the members of the Joint Works Committee and/or their advisors all records, accounts, forecasts, statistics and any other information requested, whether relating directly to productivity or not. On the specific request of the Company, the members of the Joint Works Committee shall undertake to keep secret any information so obtained which would clearly prejudice the

[9] A. Flanders, *The Fawley Productivity Agreements* (London: Faber and Faber, 1964) 151.
[10] The latter argument was reported in the N.E.D.O. study of the rubber industry. See National Economic Development Office, *Plant Bargaining* (London : N.E.D.O., 1969) 10.

Company's competitive position, but such requests will be kept to an absolute minimum by the Company.[11]

Similar expectations about disclosure of information are beginning to be held by the political parties and by governmental agencies. Illustrative of this are the following statements by the Labour Party:

. . . workers' representatives should have the *right* [in italic] to adequate information covering all aspects of their company's affairs, provided that this does not seriously jeopardise the firm's commercial interests.[12]

and D.E.P. under the Conservative Government:

The Government considers that it is an essential part of the successful conduct of collective bargaining that the employer should not unnecessarily withhold information about his undertaking that the trade unions need in the course of negotiations. . . . In the Government's view the employees of the larger employers should be entitled to some basic information about the undertaking, just as shareholders are in the case of public companies. The provision of this information to employees would recognize the interest which they have in the progress of the undertaking for which they work, and would acknowledge its obligations toward them.[13]

THE DEVELOPMENT OF INCENTIVES TO CHANGE

The creation of some motivation or impetus to change is the key activity in the implementation experience. This is especially so when the compliance approach is being used. Since this approach emphasises the alteration of behaviour through *quid pro quos*, it is important during the implementation phase to have 'carrots' (or possibly 'sticks') available for use. By contrast, the internalisation process which works primarily through changed attitudes does not

[11] Transport and General Workers' Union, draft of an 'open books clause'.
[12] See *Industrial Democracy*. A Statement by the National Executive Committee to the Annual Conference of the Labour Party, 1968, p. 2.
[13] See D.E.P., *Industrial Relations Bill, Consultative Document* (London, 1970) p. 20.

rely on the structuring of rewards, but more on the intrinsic attractiveness[14] of the new work arrangements (more responsibility, more variety, fewer anomalies, etc.).

A complete discussion of this subject of incentives to change would carry us into a full-fledged enumeration of day-to-day administrative techniques, as they are normally practised, even in the absence of productivity bargaining. The range of appeals and pressures used by foremen to motivate employees are varied and the subject has received considerable attention in the literature.[15] Consequently, our purpose is only to present a few points that will give special meaning to the task of day-to-day administration, in the context of implementing a productivity bargaining agreement via the compliance approach.

The ideal arrangement for motivating workers via the compliance approach would be to design an agreement that pays rewards soon after achievement and pays them in direct relationship to the contributions of small groups of workers. In most cases, however, such an optimum reward–reinforcement system is not possible. The timing of changes in monetary reward is usually set by the agreement and the parties take this feature of the agreement as given.

Nevertheless, in some situations it is possible to manipulate the positioning of rewards. For example, management may be able to arrange the payment of premium money for certain schedules in such a fashion as to give the maximum inducement to the acceptance of such new working arrangements. In electricity supply, supervisors in certain instances used the higher payments of special rotas to put the productivity programme across.

Other possibilities exist. In the case of Esso Distribution, management withheld planned increases for several depots that had not made their targets – this financial penalty quickly increased motivation.

In general, however, the implementation experience must be

---

[14] This does not mean that money is not important as a motivating device under internalisation – but rather than using it as an immediate *quid pro quo* for improved performance, it can be structured into yearly guarantees and longer-run career rewards.
[15] See, e.g. M. Haire, *Psychology in Management* (New York: McGraw-Hill, 1964); P. F. Drucker, *Technology, Management and Society* (New York: Harper & Row, 1970); A. S. Judson, *A Manager's Guide to Making Changes* (London: Wiley, 1966).

handled without resort to any restructuring of rewards. Foremen and others directly involved in the implementation experiences must motivate people to change by other means. Consequently, they have to 'reach' for other rewards and sanctions. One important non-financial reward is the offering of additional free time. Some companies have dealt with the overtime problem by specifying a fixed number of hours that can be used to get the job done, and then permitting employees to quit early if they complete the assigned task in shorter time. This arrangement has its origin in the classic practice of the 'stint'.

Moreover, most foremen are not without the option of putting the onus on the individual. This can be done through competition between work groups, mass appeals, or even moving to some form of pressure and discipline.

EXPERIMENTATION AND THE PACE OF CHANGE

It is with respect to the dynamics of change that the two approaches to implementation differ most sharply. Internalisation, which requires considerable time, is characterised by a steady pace. Since major alterations in the work system are usually involved, a phased pattern is often used : each piece of the programme is digested before the next piece is tackled. Pilot projects and the introduction of the scheme on a plant-by-plant basis are especially appropriate for internalisation. I.C.I. has followed this method. As a result, a record of success has developed and the improvements are allowed to lock in place at each plant before the design is filled out by moving on to another plant.

The pilot scheme device implicitly means that the organisation can return to the *status quo* should the new arrangements prove unworkable. This can have considerable advantages. If the workers realise that they can return to the earlier work system without prejudice, they are more likely to be willing to try new patterns. To achieve this safeguard some companies have calculated earnings under alternative methods, and then paid the greater amount to ensure that no workers would be disadvantaged by the agreement. Such a procedure is particularly relevant where the productivity programme calls for the revision of an incentive system.

By contrast, the compliance approach generally calls for implementation on a quick or even 'crash' basis. Usually the design is applied throughout all units of the company, to avoid the cross-pressures that inevitably develop when some units go first and others are waiting and watching. For example, at Coryton overtime was eliminated *immediately* when the agreement became effective in January 1965. As a result when the summer maintenance period arrived with the requirement of scheduling several major overhauls everyone assumed that the tasks would be performed without resorting to overtime and such was the case.

In Esso Distribution, the implementation period was compressed from the planned eighteen months to less than twelve months. While some officials felt that the company had been pressured into the shorter time period purely as a bargaining proposition (to accelerate the receipt of the productivity payments by the workers), with few exceptions the agreement was implemented on schedule. The N.B.P.I. in one of its studies emphasised the importance of quick implementation.

> In the case of a company in a continuous process industry the agreement appears to have had too long a time scale for implementation. Job evaluation and work study, two changes that were to be implemented successively, could with advantage have been introduced concurrently with redeployment payments.[16]

Consultants also can help in this 'dash for the finish'. They can provide the extra manpower that is required to move people through a difficult transition. Once the transition has been completed, the consultants can depart and the parties can cope with operating the system over the long run.[17]

Despite the desirability (from the compliance viewpoint) of implementing change as rapidly as possible, the administration of most productivity agreements tends to be a drawn-out exercise. Many companies have found that progress is slower than expected. For example, Esso at Milford Haven estimated that it would take an additional two years beyond their initial time budget to reach the target of complete flexibility. Specifically, they were finding that it was taking much more time than had been anticipated to train craftsmen to handle process work.

16 See, N.B.P.I. Report No. 161 (supplement), para. 24, p. 25.

17 As we noted in the last chapter, the consultants can also serve the function of 'scapegoats'. They are in a position to absorb the hostility generated by the changeover and then they depart, leaving the parties to develop a working relationship within the new environment.

214   *Pay, Productivity and Collective Bargaining*

SUMMARY OF KEY ACTIVITIES

Before discussing the role of unions and management in the implementation process, it is useful to summarise the activities just discussed with respect to the contrasting approaches of compliance and internalisation. This is done in Table 7.1.

Table 7.1. Summary of Key Activities

	Compliance	Internalisation
Work measurement	Use of attainable standards with explicit disclosure and enforcement.	Use of ultimate standards, primarily as guidelines.
Participation	Limited involvement of workers/union representatives with management holding the 'upper hand'.	Joint design and implementation of productivity programme.
Communication	Some limitation on the amount of information released to the organisation.	Full and open dissemination of information.
Incentives	Use of contingent rewards and side payments where possible.	Motivation to change not dependent upon immediate *quid pro quos*.
Experimentation and the pace of change	Implementation across the organisation and as rapidly as possible.	Use of pilot projects and a steady approach to change.

3. THE ROLE OF KEY INSTITUTIONS

This section of the chapter will discuss the role of union and management institutions in the implementation process. Our premise is that once a basic capacity has been developed within the union and management organisations, involving a positive attitude towards change and the leadership resources necessary for executing the change, the actual process of shifting to the new arrangements can be handled quite readily. Shortcomings either in commitment or in resources can, however, make the whole process much more difficult. As we shall see, the organisation of resources can also play an influential part in determining the ease of implementation.

THE ROLE OF UNIONS

Two features of the union organisation can be singled out for their key influence on the implementation process. They are the general *posture* of union leaders towards the change experience and the overall *capacity* of the union to get involved in the implementation experience.

Posture of unions. Union leaders tend to endorse those programmes that they have helped to formulate. Thus, their posture is generally positive during the implementation phase.

An example of such positive support is reported by Cliff (although his purpose is to criticise the T.G.W.U. for having become a 'tool of management'):

> For the first time in the history of the docks the T.G.W.U. employed what was known as 'flying squads' to travel from dock to dock to explain the more attractive parts of the scheme, i.e. the security of permanent employment, increased unemployment pay, and the (minimal) improvement in pensions. . . . At the same time the unions collaborated with the port employers for the publication of a new newspaper (*The Port*) which was used on a grand scale to propagate the advantages of Devlin.[18]

Occasionally, the initiative for the agreement has come from local officials and stewards. In such cases, top officials will usually take a neutral stance, not wanting to fight something that is a *fait accompli.*

Apart from pride of authorship, union officials tend to support the implementation of productivity agreements for practical reasons. As Chapters 2 and 3 indicated, productivity bargaining during most of the decade has been an instrument of change blessed by public policy and sought after by the rank and file. Thus, most workers expect that their union representatives will be involved in the process to secure the 'fruits' and to safeguard

[18] T. Cliff, *The Employers' Offensive; Productivity Deals and How to Fight Them* (London: Pluto Press, 1970) 167.

their rights. For example, at Gullick-Dobson the rank and file insisted that stewards be involved in the implementation of the productivity agreement : first, to explain the meaning of the changes and secondly, to be their spokesmen in the changeover experience.

Capacity.   In most instances the important determinant of union involvement is not so much a matter of posture as a question of available resources. Unions tend to be generally understaffed and not equipped to deal with the scope and intensity of change involved in the implementation experience. Since the alteration of working practices is a time-consuming process, requiring attention to many local details, a union without adequate resources is hard put to exert sufficient influence over the course of events.

In the Post Office telecommunications case, discussed earlier, the top union officials were able to learn about reactions at local level only through the *management* information system. While local officials were not behaving belligerently – in fact, some of them acted more reasonably than central leadership – central officials were unable to exert any influence and the implementation experience reflected local arrangements between supervisors and local union officials rather than the policies of the central union organisation.

Certain techniques have enabled some top union leaders to exert considerable influence over developments at the local level. In the case of one large union, the central headquarters maintained a 'hot' telephone line to all locals involved in implementing productivity agreements. Problems were thrashed out 'live' over the telephone and not allowed to pile up as would have been the case if written communications had been used. On some occasions the queries coming in from the locals could not be answered within the knowledge of the central union staff. In these instances the top officers referred the issues to the company and asked them to help formulate the responses. Thus, the union officers were able to maintain an effective degree of control over the situation by calling upon the resources of the employer.

THE ROLE OF MANAGEMENT

Management probably represents the most important single influence in the implementation process. Accordingly, it is appropriatc to examine the state of managerial competence generally existing prior to productivity bargaining and the changes that are often the prerequisites or concomitants of successful agreements.

The state of management. While managerial incompetence is ccrtainly not unique to the British context, a number of unique conditions have existed that bear some special discussion. These peculiarities tend to become especially salient when an attack is made on productivity problems.

One set of difficulties derives from the peculiar position that junior management, in particular the foreman, hold in many industries. Although the foreman is expected to function as a manager, he is usually not equipped to do so. Not infrequently, he simply lacks the administrative skill or the authority to do the job, having been selected from the work group on the basis of his skill as a craftsman. In newspaper printing, for instance, the shop-floor supervisors were generally found to be technically competent, but had very little or no executive authority or were untrained in the techniques of management.[19]

In some industries unions and work groups exert considerable control over the recruitment and activities of foremen, thus helping to preserve the status and craft tradition of their trade. For example, in sectors of the printing industry it has been the practice that the printer with top seniority automatically assumes the job of overseer. If he keeps his union card, as is the practice in newspaper printing, he is especially vulnerable to the chapel's disfavour since his card can be withdrawn.

A lack of managerial skill combined with voluntary or enforced loyalty towards the work group tends to induce the foreman to comply with pressures from stewards and workers. A rich vernacular characterising this acquiescence can be found in many industries, e.g. 'ducking and diving' in printing. To the extent that the foreman seeks to maintain his position *vis-à-vis* the workers by accommodating to their pressures, for example by systematically providing opportunities for earnings improvements such as through the provision of overtime work, he inverts his management role to become a 'quasi' shop steward.

One consequence of the positional weakness of foremen is that shop stewards tend to 'short-circuit' the managerial line of com-

---

[19] The Economist Intelligence Unit, Ltd, *The National Newspaper Industry, A Survey* (London, 1966) 105.

mand by side-stepping the foreman and often his superiors, to deal directly with higher managers. This sort of action is capable of upsetting the entire management machinery. Stewards defend the practice by pointing out that junior management typically has not been vested with enough decision-making power to solve the problems at hand, and that, therefore, it would be a 'waste of time' to deal with front-line supervisors.

There exists a large gap between the talents that are available and those that are required of front-line management to make productivity bargaining successful. Productivity bargaining presupposes strong junior management. Foremen, if they are to be crucial agents in administering change, need to be well trained. And yet in many situations, foremen, embarking upon productivity change, possess very little formal preparation; at best, they have some natural talent for leadership or have learned some administrative skills on the job.[20]

Companies embarking upon productivity bargaining have attempted to deal with these deficiencies in several ways, ranging from comprehensive formal reorganisation of the management hierarchy to a few hours of foremen training.

Reorganisation of the management structure. Before setting out to implement a productivity agreement, a great many companies have re-aligned or streamlined their management organisations. Quite often this restructuring has taken place well in advance of discussions over productivity, since it is easier to approach the union about the productivity of manual workers after management has 'put its own house in order'.

In the case of Mobil, Coryton, for example, the organisation was altered over a period of several years before the onset of productivity discussions: the number of people reporting to the refinery manager was cut from nine to five, a new maintenance department was established, and an overtime reduction programme was inaugurated. By the time the productivity agree-

---

[20] A study of the foreman in industry, published in 1951 by the National Institute of Industrial Psychology, reported that 40 per cent of supervisors they interviewed had formal supervisory training. The Royal Commission study, more than 15 years later, found a very similar proportion. See N.I.I.P., *The Foreman*, 1951; and Government Social Survey, *Workplace Industrial Relations: An Enquiry Undertaken for the Royal Commission on Trade Unions and Employers' Associations* (London, 1968).

ment was signed, the company had achieved an organisation that could initiate and cope with change.

Similarly, at Fairfields, major alterations took place in the management organisation.

The new Fairfields management first gave some added status to the foremen by putting them on salaries instead of weekly wages. They then reduced team sizes down to fifteen on a ship and twenty-five in a workshop. Training sessions were instituted at weekend and week-long courses. It was also made clear that the foremen were the main line of communication down from the management.[21]

Many firms approaching productivity bargaining have deliberately decentralised control. I.C.I. provides a good example of this move. 'With responsibility shifting down the line under an agreement, called the Manpower Utilisation and Payment Structure (MUPS), the number of supervisors is reduced, but the role of the supervisor becomes more crucial.'[22]

In some establishments, special staff positions have been created as a prelude to productivity deals. Thomson House brought in four professionals to form an industrial relations department, with this staff assuming a watchdog function over the productivity agreements. At I.C.I., central staff have been made available to local plants involved in implementing productivity agreements. Their role is one of advising, enlightening and monitoring the process of change at local level.

At Rootes, several senior-level managers were added to strengthen resources likely to be critical in the application of high performance standards :

They [the foremen] were singularly well-equipped to deal with minute-to-minute crises of the kind arising from material shortages or sudden labour disputes, but they had not been trained in advance planning techniques or to get results from people without the sanction of fluctuating wage packets. It was essential to bring in one or two people at senior level who had had experience in planning manpower utilisation and controlling

[21] S. Paulden and B. Hawkins, *Whatever Happened at Fairfields?* (London : Gower Press, 1969) 128.

[22] Evelyn Glor, 'I.C.I.'s New Process', p. 26.

production performance in an entirely different environment and without using the carrot as a regulator.[23]

In other firms, the industrial relations function has been formally separated from personnel administration. At Fawley, which had a large employee relations department at the beginning of the 1960s, the number of professional staff in this department was steadily reduced and personnel management gradually 'redelegated' to line management.

A concrete way of demonstrating the high value of foremen is through salary improvements. At Shell's Stanlow refinery, there was considerable dissatisfaction among the supervisors after the pay improvements for workers in the 1964–5 agreement. Consequently, in advance of the 1968 round of productivity bargaining, staff up to supervisory level were granted a 5 per cent salary rise. At the same time, overtime payment for these workers was replaced by a system giving equivalent time off in lieu : this put the supervisors on the same basis envisaged for manual workers in the productivity bargain plan.

Improving administrative competence. A further step in improving the ability of the organisation to execute change is to enhance the calibre of management by training. Virtually all companies involved in productivity bargaining have invested in training for managers, as well as for shop stewards. Consider the following quotation taken from a report on Shell Chemicals :

> Training programmes were also arranged for supervisory staff with the object of introducing them to the new conditions under which they, and the personnel responsible to them, would be working and also to give them the opportunity to discuss the implications of the agreement, as they saw them, with senior staff who had been responsible for the conduct of the negotiations. Introductory courses in productivity improvement techniques for senior staff, involving operational research, mathematical models, computer programming and statistics, have been held concurrently.

The Electrical Trades Union School at Esher has served as a training ground for productivity bargainers. This school has run joint courses for several trade unions as well as for managers and

[23] George Cattell, 'Industrial Relations and Efficiency', *Industrial Society* (1967) 29.

stewards, during which typical problems in the implementation of productivity agreements have been discussed and analysed.

In addition to technical skills, the implementation of a productivity agreement requires other skills, of a more temperamental quality : persistence, calmness, and firmness. The implementation experience often involves a heavy emphasis on talking through problems and slowly bringing about change. During this critical period the quality of management exerts a direct influence on results and the absence of effective management inevitably produces a poor implementation.

Several examples of skilful management in action can be cited from the experience of Esso. At Milford Haven during the summer of 1964, considerable tension developed as the new productivity agreement was being implemented. Whenever a craftsman objected to taking orders from a non-craft supervisor, the company would have a craft-trained supervisor repeat the order. The union remained adamant for a while, but eventually it realised that the company's orders were the same whether they were initiated by a craft or non-craft supervisor. In effect, the company waited patiently for resistance to diminish and for the workers to grow accustomed to the new supervisory arrangements.

A similar approach was taken by Esso in the introduction of tachographs in distribution. During the negotiations leading to a productivity agreement this subject had evoked considerable controversy. The company wanted to use tachographs to collect relevant data for determining schedules, while the union felt that such surveillance was an invasion of the drivers' privacy. Consequently, in the agreement no mention was made of tachographs except to say that the subject would be worked out locally. Subsequently, when management at one depot asked the union to allow tachographs to be installed on several trucks, permission was refused. The company then proposed to have an outsider perform the monitoring exercise. After a period of time with this arrangement in force, the drivers said that they would prefer to have their own supervisors do the observing rather than an unknown outsider. Eventually the men accepted tachographs, feeling even more comfortable with an impersonal device than with supervisors on the scene.

The crucial role of managerial skills and style is also evident in the experience of I.C.I. :

It was accepted . . . that MUPS could not be given a fair trial without major attitude changes at every level. It was striking and impressive to hear hard-headed managers, results-oriented men whose progress depends on meeting production goals, stress again and again in the informal seminar sessions the need for open two-way communication channels, for receptivity and patience, for restraint on their own part and the encouragement of 'managerial' functions such as planning and organisation at shopfloor levels. And not simply preaching the gospel from I.C.I. headquarters, but giving specific examples of their own actions to achieve these purposes in specific situations.[24]

A combination of tact, patience, and firmness characterised the manner in which these companies handled the problems of implementing productivity agreements.

It would be misleading to assume that the difficult task of gaining acceptance for new working arrangements can be handled merely through the exercise of tact and persistence. Numerous cases can be cited where resistance to change is so intense that implementation with 'deliberate speed' is not possible. The parties may stalemate and management may have to bide its time, try again in a different way, or even use the facilitating role of outsiders. A case in point is the experience of Rootes at Linwood when management sought to apply new production standards. For this illustration we draw heavily on the report of the Court of Inquiry, headed by D. J. Robertson.[25] Briefly stated, the company had successfully negotiated a comprehensive productivity proposal with the N.U.V.B. and T.G.W.U. However, the engineering union[26] and a number of smaller craft unions refused to sign. The company then attempted to implement the agreement.

As part of their implementation of the Agreement from 6 May, the Company informed the shop stewards in the press shop that they intended to apply the work measured standards which had been in dispute for some time. This would involve a reduction of personal allowance time from 55 minutes – which the press

[24] Evelyn Glor, 'I.C.I.'s New Process', p. 26.
[25] *Report of the Court of Inquiry under Professor D. J. Robertson into a Dispute at Rootes Motors Limited, Linwood, Scotland*, Cmnd 3692 (London: H.M.S.O., 1968).
[26] At the time known as the Amalgamated Union of Engineering and Foundry Workers (A.E.F.), now the A.U.E.W.

shop had hitherto enjoyed – to 35 minutes, which had been accepted in the remainder of the plant. The shop stewards were told, at a meeting on 10 May, that if co-operation was obtained, the increase due under the new agreement would be paid. After discussion with the men, the stewards replied that, in accordance with A.E.F. policy, they were not prepared to work to the Company's new conditions, which their Union had not accepted. They were told that if they took the break from 11:00 to 11:10 a.m., they would not be paid for it; most press operators nevertheless stopped work for this period. On returning, they refused to work on a line where the new standards had been posted. The Company explained that they would not be forced to achieve the standards laid down, and that no disciplinary action would be taken against anyone who was considered to be making a fair effort. Nevertheless, the press operators maintained their refusal to work on this line until the standards had been removed and 55 minutes personal allowance restored. Work therefore ceased at lunch-time on that day, about 200 men being involved.[27]

In this case, as in a number of others, the problems of implementation were initially beyond resolution by purely internal negotiation, and the need emerged for an outside agency to suggest new approaches or to exert the pressure of another opinion in order to loosen up the rigid position taken by one of the parties.

4.   SYNTHESIS

We are now in a position to summarise and to organise the themes of this and the preceding chapters. Most productivity improvement exercises follow the traditional format of negotiation, followed by implementation of the agreement. This is what we have termed the direct approach and it usually entails pressure bargaining and compliance processes. By contrast, the indirect approach reverses or merges the steps, and implementation often precedes codification or negotiation (especially where trials and pilot projects are used). The appropriate processes for this approach are

[27] *Report of the Court of Inquiry under Professor D. J. Robertson at Linwood*, pp. 10–11.

integrative bargaining and internalisation. The following scheme summarises these combinations:

Choice of approach	*Negotiation process*	*Implementation process*
Direct	Pressure bargaining (one-off)	Compliance
Indirect	Integrative bargaining (continuing)	Internalisation

The question immediately arises whether any other combinations are theoretically possible or empirically observable, e.g. could pressure bargaining be followed by internalisation? Such a sequence could naturally occur in a two-tier situation. For example, a common path to productivity bargaining is to negotiate a general agreement at the top level of the organisation (often via pressure bargaining) and then to remand the agreement to the local level for implementation. At the local level considerable clarification and elaboration may be required before the agreement can be put into practice. In some instances, the size and nature of the rewards will only have been prescribed in general terms in the framework agreement; and the parties at the local level will find it necessary to devote considerable attention to hammering out specific details before implementation can begin. Clearly, such activities may (but need not) come close to what could be termed internalisation. Except for this one variant, most productivity bargaining exercises follow the sequences outlined in the schema above.

Before leaving the subject of implementation, we should comment on the factors that lead the parties to choose a particular approach. Certainly, structural factors, such as economic conditions, as well as attitudinal disposition bear on this choice – in the same manner as they do for the choice of negotiating approach.

No purpose would be served in repeating the discussion contained in the previous chapter on the determination of negotiating strategy. However, as we observed at the start of this chapter,[28] there is one additional factor that exerts a direct bearing on the nature of the implementation experience, namely, the substantive nature of the agreement itself. In effect, the design features of the

[28] See pp. 202–3 above.

Table 7.2. Relationship of Design Features to the Implementation Process

	Compliance	Internalisation
Nature of productivity improvement	Achievement that can be accomplished, in large part, on the 'shop-floor' (e.g., elimination of tea breaks).	Achievement that requires top-level management involvement and total organisational commitment (e.g. new schedules).
'Expected value' of productivity improvement	The size of potential improvement is correspondingly smaller and the probability of success correspondingly larger.	Since the exercise is long term and addressed to basic problems, the size of potential improvement is large. However the probability of success may not be large.
Specification of productivity improvement	Highly detailed and specific enumeration of improvement.	General statement describing the type of improvement being sought.
Scope of change	Several ingredients or possibly only one issue, such as alteration of wage payment system.	Many ingredients combined into a 'package'.
Size of the achieving unit	Smaller grouping such as plant or department or just manual workers: a partial approach.	Total organisation: a comprehensive approach.
Time horizon	The time horizon is short and the process may be repeated; that is, several productivity agreements may emerge over a period of time, such as at Fawley.	The time period is much longer and generally the parties view the exercise as one massive and intensive change experience, such as at I.C.I.

agreement serve as a type of mediating mechanism or bridge between the bargaining room and the implementation experience, although the causality may run either way, from the primary selection of bargaining level or issues for negotiation, to the method of implementation; or vice versa.

Table 7.2 illustrates the relationship between the various design questions inherent in a productivity agreement and the alternative methods of implementation, compliance and internalisation. We have selected those design elements which were important themes in our discussion of ingredients and negotiations.

8 Substantive Results of Productivity Agreements

The purpose of this chapter is to examine the substantive results that have emerged from productivity agreements. In the next chapter we will consider the impact of productivity bargaining on the institutions and culture of the workplace. This division of subject matter is close but not exactly parallel to the contrast we have drawn in earlier chapters between short-run and long-run goals sought by the parties to the agreement, and it is also possible to see some respective reflection of the direct and indirect strategies.

The immediate task is to develop a *scheme* for evaluating the substantive gains. An initial distinction must be made between results as viewed by management and those which are of primary importance to the workforce. Secondly, there are two sorts of effect each of which will be weighed up by the parties against the objectives they have set themselves in embarking on this course of action. One effect is the *economic* impact. For management, what will matter most is the effect on unit production costs, the expectation being that these will be reduced or at least stabilised; and, in view of the emphasis on improved utilisation of labour, special attention may be given to the effect on the wage bill and on unit labour costs. For labour, the economic effects to be measured will be largely the change in earnings together with any other monetary rewards and any changes which affect, for example, the security or stability of income.

The second effect relates to changes in *operational practice*, again bearing on both management and worker interests. These alterations in working practice and plant organisation are the means to the reduction of unit costs, although they will very often be identified in the eyes of management as highly desirable goals in their own right, quite apart from their cost effect. For example, greater flexibility may reduce demarcation disputes and so remove a problem which management is reluctant to tackle for fear of aggravating inter-union wrangles. From the management side, therefore, we have to include under this heading all changes relating to improved operating effectiveness, and we will discuss these largely in terms of the skill/effort framework developed earlier. These changes in operating practice also have significance for the worker. Although there is some tendency to regard the effect on the worker primarily in monetary terms, it has to be remembered that alterations in the use of a worker's skills and changes in the spatial or temporal deployment of his work may be just as important. The substantive effects of productivity agreements must, therefore, include the impact on the nature of the work performed, hours of work, methods of effort regulation, and job security.

In addition, we will consider some of the factors which appear to have an important influence on the degree of success achieved. A partial explanation will be found in the ingredients of the particular agreement depending, for example, on the emphasis given to skill as opposed to effort issues, or to manning changes versus work-measurement programmes. In addition the important measures of success and failure can be associated with management, union, and structural variables. Finally, an additional 'layer' of explanatory factors is to be detected in the more general character of economic and social circumstances, such as the presence of an incomes policy; and here it is important to distinguish between phase I and phase II agreements.

We first proceed to assess the operating results of productivity bargaining. With this qualitative evaluation completed, we then examine the quantitative picture. Finally, we turn to an analysis of substantive results in terms of various institutional and environmental variables.

1.   OPERATING RESULTS

Assessment of operating results requires us to ask several questions : Did the agreement produce any changes in operating programmes and practices? Did the ingredients or inputs of the agreement materialise into the desired outputs? These questions are examined with respect to the elements of achievement and reward identified in earlier chapters.

SKILL UTILISATION

In general, it appears that substantial gains have been realised in the flexible use of manpower. While craft workers have maintained their skill base, considerable interchange of duties has occurred at the periphery. This marginal expansion of work jurisdiction can have substantial effects, because it allows not only more intensive utilisation of relatively high-cost labour, but also in the use of ancillary labour (such as craftsmen's mates) whose effective work-time is notoriously low. In the Fawley case, the 1960 agreements resulted in craftsmen spending 5 per cent of their time performing new tasks as a result of greater flexibility, but the total cost savings were undoubtedly much more than proportional.[1]

In some cases, management has not been able to increase the flexible development of craftsmen as far as desired. Safety regulations have acted as a limiting factor, making it possible for management in the oil refining industry to move only very slowly towards instituting the 'all-round mechanic'. For example, it has not been feasible to have a process operator reassemble a piece of equipment that operates at high temperatures and pressures, even though the *dismantling* of such equipment can be done by the operator rather than by the fitter.

Another limitation, of course, has been the practical one of economics. An all-round mechanic has not been feasible in the oil industry because a 'superior' type of employee would be required to perform the wide range of skills involved, and such an individual has not been easy to find or very economical to hire. Consequently, it has been necessary for management to hire talent within the traditional (and narrower) skill groupings, even though these classifications may be somewhat outmoded by new technology.[2]

Generally speaking, changes in the patterns of skill utilisation take considerable time to implement because the new working

---

[1] The Blue Book at Fawley contained an estimate that mates were only about 40 per cent as productive as the craftsmen they assisted. Cf. A. Flanders, *The Fawley Productivity Agreements* (London: Faber & Faber, 1964) 170.

[2] For a discussion of this subject, see L. C. Hunter, G. L. Reid, D. Boddy, *Labour Problems of Technological Change* (London: Allen & Unwin, 1970).

practices need to be accepted and digested, and this process requires considerable 'education and cultivation'. For example, the success of work sharing between maintenance and process personnel depends upon the interest of the receiving side in acquiring the wider range of duties and the willingness of the granting side to forgo exclusive jurisdiction over the shared duties. Significantly, maintenance-to-process work sharing has been harder to implement than craft-to-craft work sharing. Maintenance workers tend to be loath to acquire process work because they deem it dirty and low-skilled (even though process workers may be quite willing to cede part of their territory). All of these sensitivities take considerable time to overcome.

HOURS OF WORK

Productivity bargaining has influenced hours of work in two ways: by permitting a readier acceptance of shiftwork, and by reducing the level of overtime. In both cases, the underlying problem has been the need to improve the scheduling of labour inputs relative to the pattern of demand.

Shiftwork. A recent survey[3] has shown that about 25 per cent of full-time adult workers in manufacturing are now on shiftwork: for all industries and services the figure is a little lower, at 20 per cent. This represents an increase of about 100 per cent since 1954. Various reasons can be advanced to explain this growth, notably the growing capital intensity of industry, and the emergence of a number of factors which have made it more important to intensify the utilisation of capital. Overlying the long-term trend, there is evidence of an acceleration in the adoption of shiftwork[4] in recent years, and it is probable that productivity bargaining has played some part in this. Certainly, industries such as chemicals, engineering and shipbuilding, with widespread experience of productivity bargaining, were prominent among industries with a significant expansion of shiftwork between 1964 and 1968: in these three cases, the proportion of shiftworkers increased respectively from 28.6 to 35.7 per cent, from 11.4 to 18.0 per cent, and from 4.8 to 17.7 per cent.

[3] N.B.P.I. Report No. 161, especially pp. 64–7.
[4] N.B.P.I. Report No. 161, p. 66.

Productivity bargaining, by placing new importance on the full and effective use of capital and labour, forced management in many industries to re-examine the potential of shiftwork. Even where the potential was known, and management wished to see it introduced, however, difficulties were often raised by workers and unions. The N.B.P.I. survey already quoted found that of firms that have abandoned shiftwork, 28 per cent had done so because of recruitment difficulties or union and worker resistance; while of firms that had abandoned plans for introducing shiftwork, as many as 60 per cent mentioned these reasons in explanation. The opportunities opened up by productivity bargaining, both for the breaking down of resistance by consultation and for improving the attractiveness of shiftworking by enhanced compensation, were readily grasped in many companies. Elsewhere, the opportunity has been taken to adapt the existing shift system to changing requirements.

Table 8.1. *Weekly Overtime Hours in all Industry and in Electricity Supply, April* 1964 *to April* 1969

Date	All industry (U.K.)	Electricity Supply		
		As a whole (U.K.)	C.E.G.B.[1]	Area Boards[2]
1964 April	5.7	7.3	8.8	7.1
October	5.9	7.1	8.5	6.8
1965 April	6.3	3.1	1.3	4.1
October	6.3	1.8	−1.0	3.3
1966 April	6.1	1.8	−0.9	3.4
October	5.7	1.8	−1.1	3.4
1967 April	5.8	1.7	−0.6	3.1
October	6.0	1.5	−1.0	2.9
1968 April	6.0	1.0	−1.7	2.5
October	6.2	1.7	−0.8	3.2
1969 April	6.2	1.7	−0.8	3.2

[1] Generation
[2] Distribution
Source: H. Sallis, *Overtime in Electricity Supply*, B.J.I.R. Occasional Paper (London: London School of Economics, 1970) 31.

Management at Mobil, for example, rated as one of the big gains from productivity bargaining the ability of the company to schedule employees for 10 continuous shifts (including weekends) without paying overtime. In a more recent agreement, provision was made for 24 continuous shifts, plus 8 weekends to be worked by any craft employee, and voluntary work in excess of the agreed amount.

Similar gains were achieved in electricity supply, where flexibility in scheduling has involved monthly and seasonal adjustments, as well as adjustments in hours of the day and days of the week. The results are summarised in Table 8.1 which shows a comparison of weekly overtime hours in electricity supply and in all industry in the United Kingdom.

Weekly overtime in electricity supply during the five-year period between 1964 and 1969 fell from 7.3 to 1.7 hours. Most of this decline can be attributed to the introduction of flexible scheduling and the greater use of shiftwork. During the same period, overtime in all industry increased from 5.7 to 6.2 hours per week.

Overtime reduction. While the introduction of shiftwork has contributed to overtime reduction, the moderation of overtime working through productivity bargaining deserves treatment in its own right. But before presenting the evidence, it is important to put the subject into some perspective. The national overtime average of 5–6 hours during most of the 1960s probably overstated the amount of *real* overtime that was being worked. This point can be confirmed by examining the statistical changes in overtime. During the late 1950s, average overtime amounted to only 4 hours – the difference between an official working week of 45 hours and an actual working week of 49 hours. By the mid-1960s, average overtime amounted to 6 hours – the difference between an official working week of 40 hours and an actual working week of 46 hours. One interpretation of these figures is that overtime was merely a *result* of reducing the official working week in order to enhance pay, i.e. it was a statistic rather than a symptom of workplace inefficiency. The N.B.P.I. report made this point in its analysis, *Hours of Work* :

The evidence is therefore that at least so far as men in manual work in manufacturing are concerned, the last two reductions in normal hours, in contrast with immediate postwar experience, have been treated only in part at their face value as measures intended to reduce actual hours and have to an equal extent been treated as changes affecting pay.[5]

But, to dismiss the overtime situation as a measurement artefact is to miss the point that in many situations unnecessary overtime was being worked, especially in such industries as oil refining, electricity, railways, bus transportation, and printing. In these industries, hours were considerably higher than the national average and higher than would have been expected purely on the basis of technical or labour demand considerations. It is in these industries particularly that overtime reduction has represented an important accomplishment of productivity agreements. Of the seven agreements examined by the N.B.P.I. in their first report on productivity bargaining, 'five . . . had substantial cuts in working hours as a central objective',[6] and the Board found that this objective had been realised.

In one of these cases (Fawley), overtime reasserted itself during 1965 and 1966.[7] A similar development has also occurred in engineering, where a steady fall was arrested in 1968–9 and an increase in average hours worked was recorded. In one engineering firm the immediate effect of the productivity agreement was a reduction of overtime by two to three hours a week, while total production remained fairly constant. Although basic rates were increased by 5 per cent, total earnings declined for a number of employees. As a result, workers who felt underpaid for the changes that had taken place either left the firm or exerted pressure on management to reinstate overtime. Management conceded and overtime reverted to its pre-productivity agreement level of four to five hours a week.[8]

Moreover, in several of our case studies, the administration of the overtime reduction programme has produced some difficulties. At one printing house, the time-off-in-lieu clause did not work properly. Very little of the overtime scheduled has been compensated by time off, and claims for monetary payment have been increasing. In other instances, turnover has increased and employee morale has declined. In the case of electricity supply, when

[5] N.B.P.I. Report No. 161, p. 17.
[6] N.B.P.I. Report No. 36, p. 3.
[7] N.B.P.I. Report No. 36, p. 27.
[8] N.B.P.I. Report No. 161 (Supplement), p. 21.

overtime was cut back, earnings fell approximately £6 a week behind the motor industry and the gas industry (due in the latter case to an emphasis on piecework). As a result for a period of time in the Midlands area, unfilled vacancies in the industry ran at almost 12 per cent, absenteeism at 7 per cent, and the turnover of journeymen electricians was about 40 per cent within three years of having finished apprenticeship. Because of these effects, operations had to be subcontracted even more frequently than was normally the case.

In another company[9] in which shiftwork was introduced without difficulty, management also had hoped to reduce the amount of overtime worked by maintenance craftsmen. The overtime was reduced initially but eventually crept back to its previous level of 30 hours a month. Management tolerated that overtime level because the maintenance crew was only a small proportion of the workforce and the relative cost of 'manufactured' overtime was very slight when compared, for instance, with the consequences to production of a ban on overtime. An additional disincentive to overtime control in the maintenance section was the pressure from production managers for prompt repair and maintenance services.

Despite these counter-examples, there have been many instances where productivity agreements have succeeded in cutting overtime hours; the N.B.P.I. report on hours of work attests to this fact. In one capital-intensive firm where a series of informal productivity agreements were concluded with factory shop stewards, the previous average of about twelve hours of weekly overtime was virtually eliminated. Simultaneously, turnover and absenteeism dropped and the previously experienced problems of labour recruitment have eased over the last few years. The transition to a forty-hour week was accomplished through the introduction of new equipment and rationalisation of work.

EFFORT UTILISATION

Important areas in which progress has been made toward improved effort utilisation include manning changes, work measurement, the adaptation of wage-payment systems and job evaluation.

Manning.   The prospect of substantial reductions in manning

⁹ N.B.P.I. Report No. 161 (Supplement), p. 24.

while maintaining or increasing output has been one of the most attractive features of productivity bargaining from the management point of view. In practice, the anticipated gains have often proved more difficult to achieve, but even so, substantial reductions have been accomplished in some cases. Two outstanding examples may be cited. The first comes from the newspaper industry where, within the space of several years, Thomson House simultaneously expanded and introduced greater mechanisation while cutting back on previous manning standards at the highest pagination size by about 28 per cent. The result was a significant reduction in unit labour costs in the machine room.

The second example is from the Steel Company of Wales :

The redeployment (of mates) began in January 1966 . . . by June 1966, 800 mates having been redeployed, the result had been to reduce the overall labour force by that number of men.[10]

The total manpower reduction envisaged at the Steel Company of Wales was 5200 men (almost half the labour force) over a five-year period, and just under half of this was estimated to be due to technological change and the remainder due to major changes in working practice.[11]

More generally, manpower reductions through productivity agreements have probably averaged out at much less than the 20 to 30 per cent reductions achieved in the more spectacular cases. It has to be noted, however, that economies in the use of manpower in some instances were aimed more at enabling labour shortage problems to be overcome, rather than removal of surplus labour.

Work measurement.   The elimination of manpower has frequently been fostered by a work-measurement system. This involves the specification of expected production performance and the planning of operations to achieve these results. Targets and goals are set for various units and members of the organisation are

[10] Royal Commission Research Paper No. 4. *Productivity Bargaining* (London : H.M.S.O., 1967) 18. By early 1969, the number redeployed stood at 1500. See E. O. Smith, 'Demanning South Wales Steel', *Management Today* (June 1969) 106. For a fuller discussion of the problems of reducing SCOW manning, see E. O. Smith, *Productivity Bargaining – A Case Study in the Steel Industry* (London : Pan, 1971).

[11] E. O. Smith, *Productivity Bargaining*, p. 170.

held accountable for their performance measured against these targets.

The labour-saving effects of work measurement have been impressive. For example, at a large car company it resulted in elimination of 20 per cent of all white-collar employees. The dramatic impact of work study (often associated with the introduction of incentives) was observed by the N.B.P.I. in its second report on water supply :

We noted (in our earlier report) that work study was little used in the industry although substantial improvements in labour productivity could thereby be obtained. The picture now is very different. One hundred and nine undertakings have applied or propose in the near future to apply work study to distribution operations. . . . These 109 undertakings together employ nearly three-quarters of the total number of employees in the industry.

A sufficient number of undertakings had introduced work study based on incentive schemes for us to judge how effective they had been in raising productivity and reducing unit costs. . . . Enquiries made in 17 undertakings indicated that the improvement in labour productivity from such incentive schemes could be of the order of 100 per cent. Unit labour costs have been reduced by 20 to 35 per cent.[12]

Similarly, the introduction of work measurement (in this case *without* incentives) at Stanton and Stavely achieved the following :

The results of the reorganisation show a considerable increase in individual and team productivity. Before investigation 71 men worked an average of 52 hours per week. After implementation, 53 men are working 42 hours per week on average. Plant workload is higher than before, and in addition some work previously done by outside contractors is being carried out by the maintenance department. Individual men's gross earnings have risen, but the department payroll is about 15 per cent lower.[13]

What is behind the increase in productivity that often accompanies the installation of work measurement? Part of the increase

---

[12] N.B.P.I. Report No. 152, *Pay and Productivity in the Water Supply Industry* (London: H.M.S.O., 1970) 14.
[13] C. H. Wilson and A. Shaw, 'How to Make Productivity Pacts', *Management Today* (August 1967) 118.

comes as a result of the better planning and scheduling that the measurement system introduces, thus representing as much a contribution of management as of the workforce. Nevertheless, the workers also contribute directly to the increased productivity by being able to work at their accustomed pace for the *full* day, as a result of the improved rationalisation of plant operations fostered by work measurement.

A second part of the explanation for the dramatic increase of effort in the presence of measurement is what might be termed the 'knowledge incentive' and the reinforcement that goes with the setting of targets and the publication of information on results.[14]

While the introduction of work measurement has generally produced impressive results, the point should not be overlooked that in a number of instances workers have shown considerable resistance to the concept. Apart from the fact that work measurement can result in the elimination of jobs, it also raises issues of status and treatment, especially for white-collar workers. For example, if the introduction of work measurement, as part of a programme of improving effort levels, suggests to white-collar workers that they are being treated like factory workers, their resistance may be as intense as that expressed by craft workers to changes in demarcation arrangements.

Wage-payment systems. To continue our analysis of effort utilisation, an evaluation is required on the operating results of different wage-payment systems. This complex subject is difficult to deal with in any abbreviated fashion, but as a general rule an alteration in wage-payment methods exerts a salutary effect on productivity, if only in the short run. And this may be the most important point about wage-payment revision: it is the opportunity of change rather than the particular characteristics of the new system that is important. Thus, I.C.I. abandoned incentives and increased productivity while electricity supply instituted incentives and also increased productivity.

The proponents of measured daywork (and the number seems to be growing) point to the demoralisation tendencies that are often associated with payment-by-results systems, very frequently because they are used in situations where worker attitudes are

---

[14] A. Abruzzi, *Work, Workers, and Work Measurement* (New York: Columbia University Press, 1956); E. S. Buffa, *Readings in Production and Operations Management* (London: Wiley, 1966).

generally not conducive to eliciting effort by monetary inducement. A good example of this decay can be seen in the experience
of a large food company. The state of affairs before the introduction of the payment-by-results scheme could be characterised as
uncontrolled effort. Crew sizes were often twice as large as they
needed to be, and generally the level of effort was very 'relaxed'.
In addition, attitudes were bad, and generally management exercised little control over the workers. While the installation of the
incentive system produced dramatic results, at least in the short
run (overtime was reduced substantially and crew sizes were cut),
the new system slowly began to deteriorate, as workers found ways
of achieving higher earnings without expending the required effort
and as they concentrated their energies on qualifying for special
payments.

The supporters of measured daywork argue that while the
system may require more inputs on management's part, in return
for this, management benefits from more *certainty* about results.
'A day-rate plan probably requires 25 per cent more supervision
than . . . payment by results, but this is a small price to pay for
freedom from disputes and control over cost and methods.'[15]

On the other side, the supporters of incentive systems point to
an important problem inherent in measured daywork; namely,
management has to 'overwhelm the workers with attention' to get
satisfactory results. Moreover, it is unlikely that a measured daywork system will realise a level of overall effort that can be achieved
under the best incentive installations, at least in the short run. Over
the long run, it may be possible to achieve effort levels on measured
daywork comparable to those on piecework, but this requires considerable supervision – both quantitatively and qualitatively. A
good example of these tradeoffs is the coal industry where, after
the 1966 agreement calling for a transition from piecework to
daywork, productivity fell and it took two years of management
'inputs' before productivity reached prior levels.[16]

The options for management comprise a pursuit of acceptable
but not optimum results with a high degree of certainty (measured
daywork) or a quest for better overall results which may entail a

---

[15] Comment of Leslie Blakeman, formerly labour relations officer at Ford,
as quoted in T. Cliff, *The Employers' Offensive: Productivity Deals and How
to Fight Them* (London: Pluto Press, 1970) 54.

[16] K. G. Searle-Barnes, *Pay and Productivity Bargaining* (Manchester:
Manchester University Press, 1969) 161ff.

higher risk of non-attainment (incentives). On balance, results under the two systems are likely to be roughly similar and this conclusion was confirmed by the N.B.P.I. in its thorough investigation, *Payment by Results*.[17] Productivity sometimes may be higher with incentives, but the higher earnings and administrative costs result in overall unit labour costs that are about the same as with measured daywork.

Job evaluation. One final matter relating to effort utilisation merits some discussion – job evaluation. Here the influence is quite indirect, since job evaluation has played a key supporting role in the process of wage-structure rationalisation, by introducing consistency into relationships between money and skills throughout the job structure. It has, in effect, served the purpose of 'clearing the air' and allowing the parties to refashion the job structure into a more intelligible set of relations, based on common criteria. The relevance of this to the effort problem is that inefficient wage structures will fail in their main purpose of attracting, retaining and motivating employees, and overhaul on a more rational basis should yield important benefits by stabilising the workforce and drawing increased efforts from it. Although some short-run benefits may be derived, the chief results will be achieved over the longer run, in the shape of increased morale, greater interest in promotion, and improved recruitment and retention of labour. Inevitably, the measurement of these consequences is difficult, though the qualitative improvement should be obvious to management if the restructuring has been successful.

As with work measurement, management must accept the costs involved in job evaluation. The N.B.P.I. estimated that a wage-structure overhaul might cost from 2 to 12 per cent of the wage bill[18] – a substantial cost, given the probability that the main returns would be long term. Also, this cost may not be a once-for-all occurrence, since as the underlying conditions change, so may the system of evaluation need to be amended. The pursuit of stabilisation does not mean that job evaluation can be made into a rigid determinant of wage rates. The tool must serve the larger goal of achieving viable relationships between different skills and the pay attaching to them.

---

[17] See N.B.P.I. Report No. 65, pp. 23 and 38.
[18] N.B.P.I. Report No. 83, *Job Evaluation*, Cmnd 3772 (London: H.M.S.O., 1968) 16.

REWARDS

Most of the benefits accruing on the workers' side represent straight economic gains, and these will be considered in the next section of this chapter, dealing with quantitative results. However, some reward features contained in productivity agreements can be viewed more properly as qualitative outcomes of the overall programme of change and may be commented upon briefly at this point.

Staff status. One feature to which productivity bargaining has given some prominence and which operates primarily on the reward side is staff status. The institution of staff status can produce intangible feelings of increased position and worth, and such results should not be minimised.[19] Staff status can also play a facilitating role for productivity bargaining. By dealing with some basic needs for recognition, staff status may 'release' workers to engage in productivity improvement. On the other hand, Robinson concludes that staff status is rather inconsequential and represents a change in form rather than substance, eliminating a type of negative influence without releasing any positive motivations.[20]

In some respects, staff status may be the dream of industrial relations theorists rather than a practical wish of workers. In examining some of the situations where staff status has been introduced, we gained the impression that management may have idealised the concept and beguiled itself into the belief that workers desire to be treated as members of the company staff. For example, in the electricity supply negotiations, management insisted on talking about staff status as a very important reward arrangement that the company was willing to institute; but as discussions unfolded, it became clear that what the workers really desired was more money and the regularisation of their pay and working hours. The notion that they would derive some intrinsic benefit from thinking of themselves as members of the staff did not receive much support.

---

[19] The honour system that goes with salary status may have some positive effects on employee morale. An interesting example of this was evident in the experience of one company which found that with provision of personal time for workers to attend grandmothers' funerals, fewer grandmothers 'died'. When workers were not paid for personal time (the prior arrangement), the men felt that absence was their own affair.

[20] R. T. Robinson, 'Manual Workers on Staff Conditions', unpublished manuscript (Engineering Employers' Federation), p. 6.

Quite to the contrary, after the agreement had been implemented, the engineers, who always had staff status (and felt the 'compression' created by the improvements granted to the manual workers), asked to be compensated for call-in pay.

No doubt the positive impact of staff status, if it exists, is to be seen over the long run as the following quotations from two studies indicate :

It could readily be predicted that a simple change of formal status is unlikely radically to change work attitudes that have been formed over long individual and collective experience. It would be more reasonable to expect that it would be only over a period of time that changes in formal status would begin to change attitudes, and only then if coupled with more radical change in management.[21]

Labour stability and turnover are probably affected by individual attitudes and labour market phenomena, rather than the employee's status, and it seems likely that absenteeism, time-keeping and 'sickness' are improved only by a two-stage process: Staff conditions may cause the employee to adopt attitudes which are conducive to a more responsible work place behaviour pattern.[22]

Union rewards. Unions have experienced a number of positive gains from productivity bargaining. These benefits have been evident primarily in the white-collar sector where unions have been struggling to gain membership and to consolidate their positions. Generally speaking, where productivity agreements for white-collar workers have been negotiated, union membership has increased, local associations have joined national groups, and in general the rank and file have shown much more support for their organisations. The explanation is that productivity bargaining represents a very important and sometimes traumatic experience for white-collar workers; and unions tend to benefit from such experiences. If the agreement goes well and produces important improvements for the workers, the union reaps the benefits from being associated with the good results and more people join the

[21] W. W. Daniel, *Beyond the Wage–Work Bargain* (London : P.E.P., 1970) 30. He is reporting on some unpublished work of Dorothy Wedderburn.
[22] Robinson, *Manual Workers on Staff Conditions*, p. 6.

ranks; if, on the other hand, workers feel that they have given up more than they have received, then they reach for the union's help to stabilise the situation and to counter management's thrust for improved productivity.

In a number of instances, agreements have provided explicitly for measures designed to strengthen unions. Some agreements have instituted compulsory union membership.[23] Others have instituted full pay for the convenor,[24] and in some instances office space has been provided. Another important principle, which has been incorporated into a number of agreements, has been the 'balance of trades'. This approach ensures that any rundown in employment will affect competing unions similarly. Such an arrangement does not lessen the threat of job loss but makes it more tolerable since the unions know that all groups will be treated similarly.

No redundancy and other guarantees. The guarantee that no worker redundancy will occur as the direct result of a productivity agreement has been an important element in many instances. In practice, these arrangements have been handled quite straightforwardly by reliance on normal wastage, but in some cases changes in economic conditions have created difficulties. For example, at I.C.I. the number of surplus workers was higher than anticipated for a period of time, because national wastage rates dropped, partly on account of a worsening of employment opportunity elsewhere, and partly due to the enhanced attractiveness of employment in the company as a result of the agreement. In the case of Alcan, too, where a no-redundancy guarantee applied, a period of slack business made a cut-back desirable. The company decided, however, to retain the surplus personnel since it realised how difficult it would be to disentangle overall demand and productivity factors or to explain this distinction to the workers.[25]

In both cases, the results in purely economic terms may seem worse than expected, but in the longer run, when attrition has allowed the extra employees to be absorbed, and when the morale effect of the companies' willingness to maintain the guarantee is

---

[23] This occurred at Fawley. See Royal Commission Research Paper No. 4, *Productivity Bargaining*, p. 29.

[24] S. Paulden and B. Hawkins, *Whatever Happened at Fairfields?* (London: Gower Press, 1969) 111.

[25] See D. C. Alexander (ed.), *A Productivity Bargaining Symposium* (London: Engineering Employers' Federation, 1969) 85, 88.

taken into account, the results may be impressive. Indeed, the N.B.P.I. commented on the situation at Alcan as follows :

The Rogerstone agreements of Alcan went into force at a time when demand was declining and for some time this hindered assessment of their effect on costs; but it is now clear that unit costs are fewer than they would otherwise have been, and the outcome should be very satisfactory if demand continues to pick up.[26]

Other companies, faced with excess labour, have chosen to induce the requisite reduction through early retirement and the 'golden handshake'. This procedure has the advantage of maintaining a no-redundancy programme while at the same time reducing the size of the overall workforce. But it has the disadvantage of making it possible for any worker, if he so chooses, once he meets certain eligibility requirements, to leave the employment of the company. Often, these individuals are the 'best' workers – precisely those with higher ability and experience, who feel most confident about securing employment elsewhere in the labour market.

Apart from the no-redundancy condition, guarantees relating to maintenance of earnings have sometimes been used, either by the device of red-circle rates or *ex gratia* payments to workers whose earnings situation is threatened by the agreement. While these represent costs in the total agreement which have no apparent economic return, they may have the same general effect as the no-redundancy clause, maintaining the morale of workers and providing a sympathetic atmosphere for the implementation of the agreement.[27]

TIME PATTERN OF RESULTS

Finally, a number of key distinctions can be made about the time profile of achievement and rewards. First, there is the issue of whether a particular programme of change aims at bringing arrangements up to date or whether it focuses attention on the future and the elimination of problems on a continuing basis. A

---

[26] N.B.P.I. Report No. 39, *Costs and Prices of Aluminium Semi-Manufacturers*, Cmnd 3378 (London: H.M.S.O., 1967) 13.

[27] For a discussion of the part played by these devices in the Steel Company of Wales negotiations, see E. O. Smith, *Productivity Bargaining*.

second issue is whether a programme, once in place, has a natural stability or whether a process of (gradual) reversion takes place. These two dimensions of results are suggested for each of the major ingredients in Table 8.2.

Table 8.2. *Time Profile of Improvement for Various Ingredients*

Ingredients	Catch up or continuing improvement	Stable or reversion in improvement
Skill	Catch up, or continuing	Stable
Hours	Catch up	Reversion
Effort	Catch up	Reversion
Work measurement	Continuing	Stable
Wage-payment systems	Continuing	Reversion
Job evaluation	Continuing	Stable

The contrast between the 'back-slide' effect, which characterises some issues, versus the 'locked-in-place' quality of certain other issues is best illustrated by examining the contrast between skill and effort ingredients. The effort system constantly experiences pressure to change – the so-called effort bargain is ongoing – while the skill or job-structure system generally remains in a state of equilibrium. While the job structure may be difficult to change due to economic and psychological resistance associated with any alteration in skill clusters, once the system has been altered, the new job structure tends to remain in equilibrium since both sides have their own reasons for operating within the new skill juris-dictions : workers desire occupational identity, while management has the objective of maintaining a viable arrangement of duties yielding acceptable results.

By contrast, the effort–earnings system tends to be less stable. The positive aspect of this characteristic flexibility is that the effort–earnings system can be more readily adjusted, if it moves too far away from the acceptable range of labour costs. For example, management can tighten up its supervisory organisation, introduce work-measurement techniques, even introduce different wage-payment systems, all with fairly immediate results on effort levels – and these steps can be taken much more readily than would be the case with the alteration of jurisdictions or the enhancement of management control over work assignments.

The other side of the picture is that the effort–earnings system is likely to drift over time. It does not possess built-in stability – each side holds objectives which are in conflict. For a given level of earnings, management wants to increase effort in order to reduce unit labour costs and labour wants to reduce effort in order to minimise the expenditure of energy and the extent of fatigue. Similarly, for a given level of effort expenditure, management and labour hold divergent preference functions with respect to the level of aggregate earnings. It is this conflict of interest that leads to drift, often in a direction that entails a reversion of the improvements achieved in the productivity agreement.

2. ECONOMIC IMPACT

NATURE OF THE DATA

'Hard' economic information, especially relating to costs, has been obtained for only a portion of the eighty agreements we have examined closely. Several reasons account for the paucity of firm information. Chief among these is the lack of knowledge on the part of companies themselves. Either the requisite information for assessment has not been collected or it has not been analysed in such a way as to permit an evaluation of their experience to be made. Surprisingly few companies had developed machinery for *ex post* assessment.

A second factor, perhaps closely connected, is the sensitive relationship between companies and government, especially the D.E.P. and N.B.P.I., whose influence was still present when the majority of our investigations were undertaken. Companies were hesitant to release information, even to academic researchers, for fear that their position with respect to the public authorities would be jeopardised. This is not to say that these companies violated the precepts of incomes policy; rather, it suggests that they were anxious to preserve for themselves the flexibility that went with anonymity and lack of disclosure.

Aside from the lack of information, three points need to be made about the data we have been able to obtain. One serious problem is that we have found it impossible to control for what would have happened in the absence of productivity bargaining. In order to evaluate the economic significance of a particular agreement, it would ideally be desirable to compare achievement and rewards under a productivity agreement with what would have occurred had the agreement not been signed. We have not found it feasible to do this.[28]

A second important qualification about the information in hand is that the margin of error is undoubtedly quite high. When information was available, it was usually provided in very general terms. For example, we were able to learn whether a productivity agreement paid for itself or lost money, and even, in some instances, to calculate the proportions of the savings allocated for distribution to employees, but estimates more precise than these were impossible to obtain.

Finally, there is the problem of premature timing of evaluation *vis-à-vis* the time profile of achievement. The results realised in the short run may be unrepresentative of the long-run picture. In the Alcan and I.C.I. cases discussed above, economic conditions in the short run caused events to diverge from the plan, but in the longer run there is a greater likelihood that they will get back in step. Conversely, we have seen examples where in the short run considerable success has been achieved, only to be followed by deterioration and reversion to old – and bad – habits of operation.

Then, too, the strategic approach taken to productivity improvement may make an assessment of short-run results quite inappropriate. While most agreements purport to make an impact within a year or two, some agreements quite deliberately take a much slower approach to improving productivity. Such a style is consistent with what we have identified as the indirect strategy for achieving change.

British Rail, for example, followed a strategy in 1968–9 of 'setting the stage', with the consolidation of grades, elimination of piecework in the shops, and the modification of the disputes procedure. While some concrete gains were realised and management endeavoured to achieve a break-even between savings and additional costs, the real fruits will presumably be harvested in the first half of the 1970s. Consequently, an evaluation of British Railways from the standpoint of 1970–1 would reveal some changes in

[28] Future research might very well investigate this question by using a matched-pair approach.

attitudes and pay structures and some modest improvements in operating efficiency. Should productivity bargaining at British Rail then be judged only a limited success? Such a verdict would be premature, given the five- to ten-year time horizon of the key strategists at British Railways. We will attempt to assess the impact of the indirect strategy in the next chapter.

ECONOMIC RESULTS : PHASE I (1960–66)

Most first-generation (1960 to 1966) agreements produced substantial gains for the workers. Of some forty agreements that were analysed closely, take-home pay typically increased some 5 to 7 per cent, and in about one-fifth of the agreements, hours were shortened. In several cases, staff status and other manpower guarantees were instituted. For approximately one-third of the agreements, increases in take-home pay were substantial (in terms of that period), in some cases, running as high as 10 per cent. Increases in hourly rates where overtime reduction was involved were often of the order of 15 to 20 per cent on an annual basis.[29]

With only a few exceptions, the increased rewards became a permanent part of the compensation structure. 'One-shot' payments occurred very rarely.[30] One instance involved United Glass and *ex gratia* payments for 90 weeks to cushion a drop in weekly hours from 48 to 42.[31] A second instance occurred at Alcan and again involved *ex gratia* payments to provide 'once-for-all' compensation for loss of earnings accompanying the transfer of maintenance workers from shift to daywork.[32] A third instance took place at SCOW in 1964 and involved a lump-sum payment of £31 10s (made just before Christmas) for agreement 'to the principle of working with or without mates as required by management'.[33]

---

[29] These generalisations on the extent of rewards are corroborated by the work of the N.B.P.I. and the Royal Commission. See Royal Commission Research Paper No. 4, *Productivity Bargaining*, pp. 24–5, and N.B.P.I. Report No. 36, pp. 25, 26.

[30] The tabulation of reward features for phase I agreements which we discussed in Chapter 3 showed only four cases of *ex gratia* payments.

[31] See Royal Commission Research Paper No. 4, *Productivity Bargaining*, p. 14.

[32] N.B.P.I. Report No. 36, p. 69.

[33] See E. O. Smith, 'Demanning South Wales Steel', p. 106.

Returning to the general case of permanently improved earnings, we must ask the question : what happened on the cost side? On admittedly limited evidence from information supplied by ten firms, it would seem that during phase I many companies were at least able to break even and, in some cases, they were able to reduce unit labour costs significantly. Essentially the same conclusion was reached by the Royal Commission :

> It is difficult to conclude otherwise than that productivity bargaining has on the whole led to reduced costs for employers, and even where companies have only aimed to break even as a result of agreement this has been in return for benefits which can be assumed to be likely to result eventually in reduced costs.[34]

In view of the fact that during the early 1960s both hourly and unit labour costs generally increased substantially,[35] a stabilisation (and, in some instances, a decline) in unit labour costs accompanying productivity bargaining represented a significant achievement.

Table 8.3. *Labour and Equipment Costs before and after the Deal*[1]

	Before Deal	After Deal
Men	1000	815
Units	500	312
Wages cost per year	£1,065,000	£1,021,000
Total cost per year	£2,017,000	£1,670,000
Average hours worked per week	54½	42
Average earnings per year	£1065	£1255
Capital committed in units	£5,000,000	£3,120,000
Reduction in men		18.5%
Reduction in units		37.6%
Reduction in capital committed		37.6%
Reduction in hours worked		23.0%
Reduction in total cost		17.2%
Increase in average earnings		17.8%

[1] Esso Petroleum Company, *Memorandum of Evidence submitted by Esso Petroleum Company Ltd.*, *to the Royal Commission on Trade Unions and Employers' Associations*, May 1966, p. 21.

[34] Royal Commission Research Paper No. 4, *Productivity Bargaining*, p. 38. The same conclusion was reached by the N.B.P.I. in Report No. 36, pp. 21, 22.
[35] See Chapter 4 above.

The important point is that the parties attempted to finance reward improvements from increased savings coming from the productivity agreements – and were generally successful in this aim.

The experience of Esso is illustrative of the economics of many first-generation agreements. The example in Table 8.3 is taken from Esso's testimony to the Royal Commission, and while it represents only 'hypothetical' calculations, our own investigations of the Esso experience suggest that the numbers are reasonably accurate.

ECONOMIC RESULTS : PHASE II (1967–70)

When we move our attention to the second phase of productivity bargaining (1967 to 1970), the economic gains are less clear. Important examples can be cited of agreements that appeared to be successful on both the cost and reward sides. For example, as a result of second-generation agreements at Coryton, Mobil estimated that the workforce had been cut by 16 per cent, with over half of this reduction stemming from the phasing out of the civil trades. Moreover, during this same period large capital investments occurred and physical plant capacity increased substantially with an associated increase in workload estimated at approximately 25 per cent – for an overall increase in *worker* productivity of over 50 per cent for the four-year period 1965 to 1969. During the same period wages at the refinery rose considerably.

A second example of a phase II agreement that appears to be 'on all fours' is drawn from an unpublished report by one of the governmental agencies, analysing the introduction of payment by results. Since this subject has played such a prominent part in phase II agreements, it is instructive to examine the performance of such a 'model' agreement.

The overall effect of this agreement can be gauged by examining the 'debits and credits' to the labour cost account. Since output remained the same (the firm's markets did not increase, at least in the short run), we can confine our attention to changes in total compensation. Weekly earnings remained relatively constant at about £20 since increases in hourly rates of about 40 per cent were almost balanced by a reduction in actual hours from 65 to 44 per week. Thus, the savings accruing from this element of increased productivity were shared in total with the workers, as is typically the case when overtime reduction is involved. In addition, the workforce was reduced through attrition by approximately 30 per cent. Nevertheless, output targets continued to be met, mainly due to the higher effort stemming from the introduction of piecework and the lessening of fatigue accompanying the drastically reduced hours. The company's labour costs dropped substantially as a result of the reduced manning.

Unsuccessful cases. By contrast, we can cite several cases where productivity bargaining failed to produce the expected gains, at least in the achievement sense. One such case was Ford. The 1969 agreement, which involved the introduction of a new wage structure, provided for increases of between 7.5 and 10 per cent, yet the company received in return very little in the way of increased productivity. One defence is the argument that wages would have gone up as much even in the absence of such an agreement; and another defence is that over the long run the improved job structure might increase morale and motivation.

While in the case of Ford, difficult, and in some respects intractable, labour problems explain much of the lack of success on the achievement side, in other cases, the failure of the agreement can be attributed to the initial orientation of the parties in cloaking themselves in a productivity agreement in order to walk through the gateway of incomes policy.[36] In two cases, which we examined at first hand, the companies signing these 'pseudo' productivity agreements were American owned. In both cases, they signed agreements without any solid expectations of obtaining improvements in operating practices or reductions in labour costs. One of the agreements provided for introduction of piecework, which would enable the workers to realise their demands for increased earnings, but which, given the automatic technology involved, was not necessary or even appropriate. The second company entered into a flexibility-type productivity agreement, but management indicated that few of the 'intended' changes in manpower utilisation were either desirable or practical. In fact, when the firm was challenged by the D.E.P. to justify the wage increases in terms of concrete changes, it could not make a convincing case.

---

[36] For an example of a productivity agreement which was 'inspired' by wage pressures (and which proved unsuccessful), see Case A in Kevin Hawkins, 'Productivity Bargaining: A Reassessment', *Industrial Relations* (Spring 1971) 10–34.

In other instances, the inability to achieve acceptable results stems from confusion on management's part about the proper way to pursue productivity bargaining. For one company, engaged to a large extent in the rubber industry, results were disappointing because the company had been led into plant productivity bargaining via a national framework agreement, but despite some efforts from headquarters to suggest a consistent plan of approach to negotiation or agreement design, little attempt to follow this lead was made by management at plant level. The result was that plant-level agreements were heterogeneous in content, and diverse in coverage – most of the agreements being based on sections or departments and the potential advantages of plant-wide, comprehensive agreements were passed over in the process. Nor was there any real attempt to establish machinery to secure implementation of agreements actually concluded. As a result, wages increased by almost 37 per cent over the period 1966–70, more than two-thirds of this being due to plant awards; while productivity, as measured by a range of formulae, increased at a very much slower rate. The net outcome was that the productivity bargaining development, far from being self-financing, added substantially to the wage bill in a period of slow output growth.

Most of the failure to realise reductions in unit costs must be attributed to good intentions gone astray or to good ground preparations with the harvest still to come. An excellent illustration is the electrical contracting industry. In 1963, the National Incomes Commission (N.I.C.) examined a three-year agreement containing a key provision for the reduction of the working week from 42 to 40 hours without loss of pay. On the achievement side, increased productivity would presumably come as a result of 'full co-operation' : (a) full utilisation of hours of work which shall not be subject to unauthorised 'breaks' (time permitted for tea breaks shall not be exceeded); and (b) the achievement of maximum output and the elimination of all forms of time-wasting.[37]

The N.I.C. concluded :

In the face of what we accept is the genuine determination of both sides of the industry to co-operate in producing the fundamental and necessary change, we are not prepared to hold that

[37] National Incomes Commission, *Agreements in Electrical Contracting*, Report No. 2, Cmnd 2098 (London: H.M.S.O., 1963) p. 39.

this agreement looked at as a whole is contrary to the national interest.[38]

Then in 1966, the N.B.P.I. reviewed the new three-year agreement that provided, among other things, for a 13 per cent wage increase during the first year. The achievement side of the agreement provided for the reclassification of electricians according to skill, elimination of craftsmen's mates, and the establishment of joint industrial boards.

In examining experience under the 1963 agreement the Board concluded :

> The negotiators of the 1963 agreement had two declared aims: to improve the pay of the industry's employees relative to that of other workers and to increase the industry's productivity. They did not achieve the first and there is no firm evidence that they have achieved the second.[39]

But, in its recommendation to allow the new 13 per cent increase, the Board took note of the fact that :

> This agreement [1966] was settled after a long period of negotiations; the parties gave joint evidence to us and, in the words of that evidence, the agreement is to be 'viewed as a constructive attempt to foster improved productivity, greater efficiency and general prosperity, not only to the employee and management in the industry, but also to the Nation'.[40]

The Board also urged that 'priority should be given to the introduction of a uniform method for measuring output and performance so that improvements in productivity can be assessed'.[41]

In 1969, the Board once again reviewed pay and productivity relationships in the electrical contracting industry and reached mixed conclusions. It had always thought the productivity provisions of the 1966 agreement to be its 'weakest aspect' and now it found this view confirmed by the negligible impact on work practices. The Board accepted, however, that the two successive three-year agreements of 1963 and 1966 were designed 'to lay the

[38] Ibid., p. 45.
[39] N.B.P.I. Report No. 24, *Wages and Conditions in the Electrical Contracting Industry*, Cmnd 3172 (London: H.M.S.O., 1966) 13.
[40] N.B.P.I. Report No. 24, p. 13.
[41] N.B.P.I. Report No. 24, p. 27.

foundations for lasting productivity advances' and this had been successfully done by means of wide-reaching changes in organisation and the wide scope of the agreements covering education and training, improved work methods, better welfare provisions for employees, and so forth. Although the agreements had not yet proved successful in releasing productivity potential, the Board was optimistic that the industry was now in a position to achieve this, having created the requisite industrial relations and organisational environment for such a step.[42]

The course of productivity bargaining in electrical contracting could be termed a 'failure' in view of a succession of agreements that have not produced positive results on the achievement side in the shape of reduced unit costs. The expectations that various statements of co-operation would produce substantive improvements have been, so far, unrealised. We say so far because it is possible that the improved atmosphere, on which all sides are agreed, may contribute to big improvements in the future (and in this regard the electrical contracting industry may be putting an emphasis on the indirect strategy), but for the time being the experience viewed from a purely economic standpoint must be characterised as a failure.

These examples can, of course, act only as somewhat random indicators of economic achievement, and it is regrettable that we have not been able to obtain more systematic data which would allow a better appreciation. However, all the evidence we have been able to muster does not produce so favourable a view of productivity bargaining during the period 1967–9 as that advanced by the N.B.P.I. :

> Despite inadequate information in many cases, in three-quarters of the companies we examined we were able to conclude that the net effect of the agreement was the achievement of lower costs per unit of output.[43]

Some explanation for this discrepancy may be due to the fact that the N.B.P.I. analysis included agreements negotiated and implemented during phase I as well as agreements from phase II.

---

[42] N.B.P.I. Report No. 120, *Pay and Conditions in the Electrical Contracting Industry*, Cmnd 4097 (London: H.M.S.O., 1969), see especially chapters 4 and 8.

[43] N.B.P.I. Report No. 123, p. 28, para. 97.

Our own experience with companies involved in phase II agreements suggests that relatively few companies even had the basic accounting data and monitoring machinery to assess the direct impact of the agreement on unit costs, except in the roughest way. It might also be added, not altogether unfairly, that if the N.B.P.I. was correct in its judgement[44] it is surprising to find that many companies were so prepared to opt out of productivity bargaining when the pressures of incomes policy dissolved.

Further evidence for our less sanguine view of economic results derives from a study of phase II agreements in the engineering industry, conducted by the Engineering Employers' Federation and completed in mid-1971. From a sample of about 50 firms, half were found to have entered into some form of productivity agreement. Of these, about half were characterised by the study as 'phoney' agreements. Altogether, only one-quarter of the 25 or so productivity agreements were considered to have achieved any substantial results. Thus, in contrast to the N.B.P.I. estimate of 3 out of 4 agreements reaching a satisfactory conclusion, the E.E.F. study would suggest a ratio closer to 1 in 4.[45]

Of course, the question again needs to be asked whether, in the cases where productivity bargaining produced no direct economic payoff, the parties were any worse off than in the absence of productivity bargaining. At the micro-level, the answer is probably 'no'. For any individual establishment, wages would in any case tend to move ahead in response to pressures from the general labour market and if a pseudo-agreement was signed, it is *unlikely* that it would add to the expectations for wage improvements that the workers brought to the bargaining table. This point was explicitly recognised in some industrial sectors. In our conversations with the Chemical Industries Association, for example, the point was made that there was little difference in earnings improvement between cases where productivity bargaining had been tried

---

[44] And even a one-time member of the Board has offered a more pessimistic estimate. He said that as many agreements were spurious as were soundly based. Hugh Clegg, *How to Run an Incomes Policy and Why We Made Such a Mess of the Last One* (London : Heinemann, 1971) 38.

[45] An interesting point can be made out of the downward trend of estimates. The N.B.P.I. estimated the proportion of soundly based agreements as 75 per cent in early 1969. Clegg estimated the proportion at 50 per cent in early 1971 and the E.E.F. at 25 per cent by mid-1971. No doubt, the passage of time has made more accurate appraisal possible and the earlier optimism and rhetoric has given way to more honest assessment of results.

unsuccessfully and those which had not involved productivity bargaining at all. However, from the macro point of view the assessment might be quite different in that the higher rates of wage increase often associated with productivity bargaining would tend to set the tone for wage expectations right across the board. Such high levels of expectations might be kept in check so long as a strong incomes policy existed, but with its dissolution, the release of frustration would be almost bound to be mirrored in a spate of substantial wage claims.

3. EXPLANATORY FACTORS

It is appropriate to turn now to an analysis of various factors that appear to be associated with these direct results of productivity bargaining. The variables under examination are generally the same ones that have been used throughout the study : management, union leadership, and bargaining structure.

ROLE OF MANAGEMENT

Without much question management plays a key role in determining the operating effectiveness of a productivity agreement. Since management usually provides the impetus for productivity bargaining, if the quality or intensity of this impetus should falter, then the results are likely to be commensurately poorer. We can cite two examples from the same region of Scotland where management's skill and lack of skill played a critical role in explaining the outcomes.[46]

A case of failure. The company and union agreed in 1965 to a productivity agreement providing for elimination of restrictive practices and introduction of a work-measurement scheme. The latter was aimed at providing a basis for determining future wage increases. In practice, however, wage increases were not related to productivity. The failure of the plan was due to the lack of adequate staff to perform the task of work measurement and to unreliable norms which made it impossible to base wage determi-

---

[46] These two case studies are based on information supplied by Isabel Lindsay, of Strathclyde University. We are indebted to her for providing this material, and allowing us to summarise it.

nation on them. As a result of the unsatisfactory experience with work measurement, the workers resisted the use of the stop-watch, even though provision for its use had been included in one of the agreements. The cause of the failure can be summed up as follows. Management attempted too much and went about it in too complicated a fashion – with the result that the men felt that 'the whole point of the exercise was to use "fancy agreements" to disguise a reluctance to pay wage increases'.

A case of success.   In this instance productivity bargaining began in 1968, prompted by the need to get a wage increase approved by the D.E.P. Negotiations took place only with the engineering and boiler shops. On the engineering side the cranemen's functions were extended and fitters were allowed to work machines. In the boiler-shop there was failure to reach agreement on platers doing welding but it was accepted that burners should work profile-burning machines. The principal stress was laid on 'improvement in timekeeping' and 'full utilisation of working hours'. While such vague expressions of intent may be often valueless, in this instance the experience was quite positive – specifically, management exercised authority in these matters in a way that they had not done previously. Moreover, their right to do so was generally accepted by the men. Here, management sought to increase productivity in only a limited way. As a result it was able to handle the change and set the stage for additional productivity bargaining.

In most cases, the 'management problem' is not incompetence but inability to cope with the complex administrative task of co-ordinating activities at many levels of the organisation. Many productivity agreements deal with such problem areas as skill regrouping and rescheduling which cannot be executed without considerable planning and co-ordination by both middle and top management. A good example of this comes out of the experience of London Transport. The productivity agreement specified new working schedules, but implementation proved difficult due to management's inability to procure new buses when needed. This prevented the execution of the new schedules and in turn affected hours of work and rewards of the bus crews adversely.

A similar experience was reported by the N.B.P.I. in their first report on productivity bargaining. The case in point is Esso Distribution :

Several obstacles had to be faced in carrying out the agreement. For various reasons the Company's vehicle replacement programme had fallen behind, and the larger vehicles for which the agreement had been partly designed were not available in the expected numbers. Because of resistance from customers the introduction of shift-work was much slower than the Company had forecast, and against a target of 60 per cent of vehicles on shift, only 30 per cent had been reached by the end of the year. Consequently to maintain services, and to meet new demand which was growing faster than expected, the Company had to employ more vehicles on a contract basis, and overtime levels fell less rapidly than had been hoped. By the end of 1966, however, large vehicles were coming in, the proportion of vehicles on shift was rising, fewer contractors' vehicles were employed and overtime was close to target. It could reasonably be hoped that the expected cost-reductions would be achieved by the end of 1967.[47]

The need for competent management extends down the organisation and involves front-line supervision as much as top management. I.C.I., for example, has deemed this factor of such crucial importance that it has put all its supervisors through special training programmes and has instituted a series of follow-up and support procedures to ensure that foremen perform effectively.

To summarise : good management will not guarantee a successful result but without it, poors results are bound to occur. In other words, good management is a necessary, but not sufficient, condition to obtaining satisfactory results from productivity bargaining.

THE ROLE OF THE UNION

The other key participant in productivity bargaining, the union, can exert almost as critical an influence on results as management. Strong union leadership can help immensely. Productivity bargaining appears to have been successful where union leaders have 'indoctrinated' their subordinates and taken an active part in the implementation of the new rules. This certainly was the case on the West Coast Docks in the United States where Harry Bridges and the leaders of the International Longshoremen Workers'

[47] N.B.P.I. Report No. 36, p. 56.

Union (I.L.W.U.) exerted strong control downward through the union organisation to have the new agreement accepted and implemented by the rank and file, and this has been the experience in many similar situations in Britain.

Relationships within the union. Stewards play an important role in determining the overall results of productivity bargaining. In most situations, stewards view themselves primarily as agents of the work-groups in the plant and, if the attitudes of this primary group are primarily resistant to change, which is often the case, relations at plant level will not be conducive to productivity improvement. For example, at the Stanlow refinery of Shell, the 1964–5 productivity agreement which had been signed by district officials was implemented only with some difficulty, and the changes in working practice which were achieved tended to deteriorate relatively quickly in some departments. Thus although some gains were made, the start was somewhat shaky and it was only when the parties signed a second agreement in 1968 – this time with full involvement of the workers in the specification of the flexibility programme – that more substantial and permanent gains began to emerge.

Clearly, the nature and intensity of the interaction between union officials and stewards determines in large part what happens at the local level. If top officials are in favour of productivity bargaining, and authority in the union is centralised, then there is a greater chance for union support at the local level; the E.P.T.U. would appear to fit these circumstances. Interestingly, a union like the T.G.W.U., which purports to be highly decentralised, has also shaped local union thinking through its cadre of some 500 full-time officials. Thus, in the E.P.T.U. it is central commitment and the telephone, while in the T.G.W.U. it is 'staff presence' that has influenced (usually in a positive direction) the attitudes of local leaders towards productivity improvement.[48] The favourable experience in electricity supply can be attributed in large part to this

---

[48] In some situations, however, the members and their stewards operate reasonably autonomously. One example is the Boilermakers' Society (A.S.O.B.). While in recent years this union has taken a more positive attitude towards productivity bargaining over flexibility, in one firm in the Liverpool area the A.S.O.B. stewards were only able to sign a flexibility agreement by acting completely independently from the district officials in Birkenhead who had not approved the changes. See 'How the Boilermakers Dismantled the Barricades', *The Financial Times* (8 December 1969).

variable of union leadership. The E.P.T.U. has involved itself very directly and positively in the implementation programme.

Not every union would accept on philosophical grounds the approach of the E.P.T.U. and T.G.W.U.; nevertheless, many unions, as a practical matter, have become involved in the implementation process, and the extent to which they have supported the agreement determines, in large part, the degree of success.

Relationships among unions. Beyond commitment and organisational cohesion within the individual union, the structure of representation in different unions plays an important part in explaining overall results. The importance of whether productivity change comes to a situation of union rivalry or co-operation can be illustrated in the following way. At Mobil, the craft unions and the T.G.W.U. did not see 'eye to eye', while at Philblack, extensive collaboration existed between the craft and process unions. As a result, the overall success of the agreement was more pronounced at Philblack because issues of manpower utilisation on a plant-wide basis could be considered, while at Mobil most of the increased flexibility which occurred took place within the craft ranks.

The experience of SCOW at its Port Talbot works probably represents one of the most dramatic instances of how union rivalry thwarted productivity bargaining for a considerable period of time. The events leading up to the Court of Inquiry,[49] held during 1969, involved the signing of a productivity plan between SCOW and seven craft unions. The plan called for reductions in manpower, a simplified wage structure, the use of work study and job evaluation techniques, and compensation and retraining for redundant employees. However, the National Union of Blast Furnacemen, Ore Miners and Kindred Workers (N.U.B.) refused to sign. Union rivalry and competitiveness among the three N.U.B. lodges played a large part in their unwillingness to sign a productivity bargain.

The mere presence of several different unions at the plant level is not as crucial as the tenor of their relationship. The N.B.P.I. concluded that little connection existed between the number of unions involved and the degree of success achieved.[50] While com-

---

[49] *Report of a Court of Inquiry under Professor D. J. Robertson* (at Port Talbot). For an extended treatment, see also E. O. Smith, *Productivity Bargaining*.

[50] See N.B.P.I. Report No. 123, p. 5.

petitiveness is bound to occur more frequently in the presence of several unions than in the case of exclusive representation, a number of instances can be cited where unions have formed joint councils, often as a concomitant of productivity bargaining – with the result that labour–management relations at the plant level have become more conducive to productivity improvement. Fairfields was a case in point.

A second interacting variable is location. For some geographical regions, where the tenor of unionism is 'moderate', multiple representation may not produce any problems. However, for a region like the North-west, the result will usually be quite different. For example, our fieldwork involved a visit to a plant in the Liverpool area where craft rivalry, reflecting the generally militant atmosphere of the labour market, prevented progress towards relaxing demarcation lines.

In closing this section, we might note that while union support (like management involvement) is not a sufficient condition, it certainly is a necessary condition. Without it, poor results are assured. By way of illustration, consider the difficulty experienced during the mid-1960s by the bakery industry in improving productivity. The problem can be traced to the aloof posture of the union and its assertion that a programme for overtime reduction was 'management's worry'. The leaders held that management, and management alone, had the responsibility to obtain results; and the union's only obligation under a productivity agreement was not to interfere.[51]

ROLE OF BARGAINING STRUCTURE

Bargaining level.   The shape of the bargaining structure can exert a strong influence on operating results. Generally speaking, the most successful bargains have been those negotiated and executed at the plant level. Since productivity agreements must be related to local problems (otherwise no change will take place) and since practices and problems differ so much among companies and even among plants of the same company, it is difficult in centralised dealings to specify the kind of improvements that can take place in each individual situation.[52] Not surprisingly,

[51] N.B.P.I. Report No. 17, p. 2.
[52] See Nora Stettner, *Productivity Bargaining and Industrial Change* (Oxford: Pergamon Press, 1969) 125.

several of the bargains that have been struck at industry level or at the top level of large multi-plant companies have given the most trouble : for example, at Ford, on the docks, and in the engineering industry.

In the docks, working conditions and wages varied quite dramatically from place to place. While some of the lower paying docks were able to make quite rapid progress in the implementation of Devlin phase 2 (leading to new, improved wage structures coupled with modernisation in the context of local productivity deals), the high-paying ports, and notably London, encountered much greater difficulty in finding a solution. The result was highly uneven progress towards implementation, a series of disputes in the London docks, and anxieties (leading to a strike in 1970) on the part of the trade unions over those dock workers who were unable to be fitted into the Devlin approach.

A special problem of central agreements is the difficulty in arriving at specific terms (assuming the parties are following the direct approach to productivity improvement). Commenting on the 1964 engineering agreement, the N.B.P.I. said :

> As we have indicated, the 1964 agreement contained a general exhortation about increased productivity. While some employers consider they gained advantage from this, we consider it preferable that national agreements for manual workers should contain specific guidelines on productivity.[53]

Even the December 1968 agreement, which was more specific about the form to be taken by productivity change, failed to exert much influence on developments at the local level except in a small fraction of cases.

Centrally negotiated agreements also tend to cost more because the issue of comparability is magnified and attention is focussed on the conflicting principles of parity (which we will discuss in the next chapter). When all units of an industry are brought together, a feeling of competitiveness is bound to exist if arrangements are not made uniform, even though the economics of the situation calls for differentiation.

The effects of this approach were clearly stated by the N.B.P.I. in relation to the 1964 package agreement in engineering, just

[53] N.B.P.I. Report No. 49, p. 32.

discussed. The deal added $9\frac{1}{2}$ per cent to the wage bill of firms belonging to the E.E.F., but earnings rose by about 20 per cent, due to wage drift. Productivity growth was much slower, and costs rose – quite the opposite of the intention. The responsibility for this was placed by the Board on the two systems of negotiations, at national and workshop level, together with the fragmented bargaining at plant level, and the absence in most cases of a coherent wage policy. In this type of structure, comparability at sectional, plant and company level will almost inevitably raise the total wage cost above the levels planned at the centre.

In the case of oil distribution a different effect was observed. The parties eliminated the London differential, but were not able to institute a Midlands differential, even though it was probably called for in terms of supply and demand. The problem, in the context of centralised dealings, is that once a differential is given to one group, all other groups demand comparable treatment.

The early I.C.I. experience illustrates some further problems of conducting negotiations at the top. Company and union officials tended to 'get carried away' in designing a very imaginative agreement which was signed in 1966. Union officials indicated that the plan was acceptable; and everyone assumed that with such a brilliant plan and with such enthusiasm being expressed by the top leaders, the rank and file would accept it readily. Much to the surprise of the top leaders, considerable resistance developed at the bottom when the plan was promulgated initially. After rejection of the plan at local level, the parties then moved to a plant-by-plant shaping of the productivity package. Over a period of several years, the parties engaged in discussions at the various plants about the design and implementation of productivity plans in these locations. Good results were achieved[54] and by early 1971 most of the operations were or were about to be covered by the Weekly Staff Agreement. The point of the I.C.I. story is that productivity improvement could not be *executed* from the top and progress was realised only as each plant hammered out its own agreement –

---

[54] The evaluation of the N.B.P.I. was phrased as follows: 'These figures indicate not only that there has been a substantial increase in productivity but that earnings seem to have been reasonably contained within the settlement of October 1967'. N.B.P.I. Report No. 105, *Pay of General Workers and Craftsmen in Imperial Chemical Industries Ltd*, Cmnd 3941 (London: H.M.S.O., 1969) 5–6. A more complete evaluation of the I.C.I. experience is given in Chapter 9.

admittedly within the framework of the master agreement, but in essence a unique and local plan.

The importance of the I.C.I. lesson of moving away from the company to the plant level to make productivity bargaining succeed was duplicated in the experience of the shipbuilding industry. Rather than negotiating a national agreement, the Amalgamated Society of Boilermakers sought local agreements, first for the Upper Clyde in 1966 and then during the next three years for Tyne, Belfast, Merseyside, Barrow, Lower Clyde and Wearside. Commenting on this strategy, the union said :

> If we had tried to carry this through on a national basis, we would have been slowed down to the speed of those employers who wanted to drag their heels.[55]

Other aspects of bargaining structure.   The critical importance of bargaining structure is reflected in more than just the level or vertical locus at which the productivity agreement is negotiated and implemented. Bargaining structure also involves certain horizontal forces which impinge on the union–management relationship and, in turn, affect the outcome of productivity bargaining.

Consider, for example, the Fleet Street newspapers where productivity bargaining has taken place on a decentralised basis. This characteristic alone would suggest satisfactory economic results. But the evidence casts some doubt on this expectation. In its study of seven newspapers during the period 1967 to 1969, the N.B.P.I. found that manning had been reduced by 5 per cent, earnings increased by 18 per cent, and output increased by 9 per cent, for an overall increase in unit labour costs of 2 per cent.[56]

The less-than-satisfactory results could be attributed to a very fragmented structure wherein productivity agreements were signed with individual chapels covering relatively few workers. In this situation, the pressures of comparability were intense and management found itself using productivity bargaining more as a device for wage accommodation than as a device for cost reduction.

Another illustration of how pressures emanating from the larger industrial relations context impinge upon productivity bargaining

[55] *Financial Times* (8 December 1969).

[56] See N.B.P.I. Report No. 141, *Costs and Revenue of National Newspapers*, Cmnd 4277 (London : H.M.S.O., 1970) 13.

can be seen in the experience of Esso. The company has conducted productivity bargaining on a decentralised basis,[57] but the results have been quite different across the three sectors. Generally speaking, the best results have been obtained at the Milford Haven refinery where, because of its remote location in western Wales, the parties have been able to work on a programme of productivity improvement without the interference of outside pressures and comparisons.

By contrast, in its distribution agreement, the company barely broke even. Under pressure to be the first one to sign a marketing agreement in the industry, the company increased its offer to such an extent that the benefits accruing to the workers during the eighteen-month agreement equalled the estimated savings from the first five years of the programme. While in practice the agreement met its productivity objectives, a high 'price' was paid for these improvements.[58]

The experience at Fawley falls somewhere in between the extremes of Milford Haven and distribution. While Esso has not been hooked into an industry-wide or area-wide agreement in the Southampton area, nevertheless, the pressures emanating from the labour market affected the enthusiasm with which workers implemented the various agreements. The first agreement, the Blue Book, was implemented quite successfully because the wage increases and other benefits afforded under the agreement allowed the workers to spurt ahead in the 'local-league tables'. However, as other groups caught up and even passed the Fawley workers, the enthusiasm for productivity bargaining waned.

One empirical manifestation of the difference in bargaining structures within Esso is the sharply different pattern of negotiating timetables between distribution with its complicated and competitive orientation and Fawley and Milford Haven with their more local arrangements (see Tables 8.4 and 8.5).

The significant point about these two timetables is that management developed the Green Book faster than the Blue Book – three months compared with approximately eighteen months – reflecting the 'hurry-up' atmosphere in distribution. However, once the

---

[57] In the one case, distribution, where the agreement was signed at the company level, implementation has been on a plant-by-plant basis.
[58] See N.B.P.I. Report No. 36, pp. 16–18, for data that parallel our evaluation.

Table 8.4. *Timetable for 'Green Book' in Distribution*

June/September 1964	Discussions in the field with managers, supervisors and men to draw together proposals for negotiations.
September 1964	First proposals put before the trade union 'Green Book'.
January 1965	Informal negotiations with the trade union.
February/October 1965	Continuous discussion with trade union at national and local level to find solutions to problems that had been identified nationally and locally.
November 1965	Formal negotiations with trade union.
November 1965	Agreement.

Table 8.5. *Timetable for 'Blue Book' at Fawley*

Mid-1957	Work started at the refinery on identifying areas of inefficiency.
November 1958	Memorandum from the consultant.
November 1958/ December 1959	Development period: discussion at plant and shop floor level, involving stewards, supervisors, management and men.
February/May 1960	Formal negotiations.
July 1960	Agreement.

Source: Memorandum of Evidence submitted by Esso Petroleum Company Ltd. to the Royal Commission, pp. 4–5.

respective proposals were put to the unions, the bargaining process for the Green Book consumed twelve months compared with less than six months for the Blue Book, reflecting the tactics and pressures of the drivers' branch of the T.G.W.U. to get the best monetary settlement possible.

Industry-wide agreements. While fashioning a productivity agreement to reflect the unique characteristics of each undertaking is quite desirable, often such an approach has not been feasible. The need for uniformity and central co-ordination of pay and benefits has made the design of company-wide or industry-wide agreements absolutely essential, and in some cases, the results have been quite noteworthy. Both electricity supply and the Post Office (telecommunications) have realised substantial gains in productivity and their agreements have been company-wide or, for that matter, industry-wide. The good results can be attributed to standard (though not identical) technology throughout the systems and strong management.

When we move, however, beyond the single-company agreement to the framework agreement covering an entire industry, such as chemicals, engineering, and rubber, we encounter operating results that are often only marginal advances at best. In each of these three industries, we have visited situations where productivity bargaining at the level of the individual company could be characterised as confused, poorly executed, or nonexistent.

The experience of the engineering industry is a good case in point. As we noted earlier, only about one agreement in four could be termed *bona fide*. This finding was based on a survey conducted by the E.E.F. itself in 1971. Earlier (1967), the N.B.P.I. had evaluated the 1964 package deal as follows :

> While the agreement helped to secure some increase in productivity, it is questionable whether the general declaration of interest had any significant effect. . . .
>
> Only about 20 per cent of the plants replying to our inquiries said that this preamble had been of any help in negotiations to increase productivity. . . .
>
> In individual firms we found that very few had implemented the provisions of the package deal in the manner intended by the bargaining parties.[59]

This is not to say that operating results need always be inferior under framework agreements. Instances of success could emerge as management and union officials develop greater sophistication in harnessing local programmes to master agreements.[60] But the achievement of acceptable results at the local level under the banner of a framework agreement remains a standing challenge.

Incomes policy.   We should append a final brief comment on another factor that has often influenced the success or failure of agreements – the presence of incomes policy. We have been critical of management in a number of cases cited in this chapter, and in some instances management has, in fact, been deficient. In other cases, management has been persuaded by the incomes policy to

[59] N.B.P.I. Report No. 49, *Pay and Conditions of Service of Engineering Workers*, Cmnd 3495 (London: H.M.S.O., 1968) p. 21, para. 63.

[60] N.B.P.I. Report No. 123 describes a number of framework agreements and some of their ramifications but presents little in the way of results or general evaluation.

adopt a productivity bargaining approach to wage determination not as a matter of conviction but as a way of keeping workers happy in a time of overall wage restraint.

Despite the efforts of the incomes policy and the N.B.P.I., agreements did at times result in wage increases that were well out of line with the norm, and the larger the increase, the greater the publicity it was likely to attract. These increases then became a sort of target for workers and union negotiators, and wage expectations gravitated towards the more extreme levels at which settlements were reached.

Managements, faced with such examples and presented with union cases built on exaggerated expectations, may at times have been too anxious to match these claims, putting perhaps disproportionate weight on morale and retention of labour. As a result, they responded to pressures to build up a productivity justification for an 'expected' level of settlement, perhaps taking the most optimistic view of achievement that might be realised under the agreement when in the event a more cautious view would have been warranted.

This sort of response cannot be put down to poor management in the sense that management was devoid of ideas or incapable of control, though it might be said that its judgement of the situation was at fault.

9 An Assessment of the Cultural and Organisational Effects

In this chapter we turn to the impact of productivity bargaining on the cultural and organisational setting of workplace relations. First, we examine the influence of productivity agreements on the key institutions of the workplace : the management and union organisations. Attention then moves to the cultural effects and especially the impact on the individual and the work-group. This discussion leads naturally to the control issue and an analysis of shop-floor relations. The next step is to present an assessment of the effect of productivity bargaining on the structure of collective bargaining. Finally, an evaluation is made of the direct and indirect strategies.

In one sense these sorts of effects may be regarded as more long term than the effects discussed in the previous chapter. This does not necessarily mean that the effects now to be discussed take longer to show themselves – some may occur instantaneously – but rather that their effect is more likely to be long-lasting since they will bite more deeply into the processes and attitudes underlying the conduct of industrial relations.

1. IMPACT ON MANAGEMENT

MANAGERIAL INVOLVEMENT

The impact of productivity bargaining on management can be distinguished by level. Senior management has generally been much involved, usually in providing the impetus for the movement into productivity bargaining. Front-line management, particularly foremen, have been involved extensively in the implementation process, though it has been a frequent complaint that they have not been brought into the picture early enough and are left to implement a series of changes for which they have had little responsibility. The role of middle management, such as departmental heads, is less clear and there is some evidence that they have been kept rather aloof from the proceedings, both at the planning and the implementation stage. In some cases this was undoubtedly due to the responsibilities taken by the personnel or industrial relations department, using its specialist staff to liaise with senior management and with those involved at the supervision/shop-floor interface. Smith, for example, noted in his study of the SCOW agreement that

> Many foremen, *and some of their immediate superiors*, claimed that their shop stewards had been better informed of the progress of negotiations and therefore understood the Green Book agreement far better than themselves.[1]

Yet, in view of the great range of activities for which management has to take responsibility – from the general design stage, through the preparation of manpower targets and their planning, the negotiation and specification of enlarged mobility and flexibility, the organisation and running of management and joint working parties, to the elaboration of work measurement or job evaluation schemes – it seems that if productivity bargaining is to be successfully accomplished, it must involve middle management just as intensively as junior and senior staff.

IMPACT ON FRONT-LINE SUPERVISION

Operating under a productivity agreement makes the jobs of lower-level management inevitably more demanding, perhaps more challenging, and certainly entailing more commitment and energy. Foremen, whom we interviewed, generally commented that productivity agreements brought major changes in the nature of their jobs. The agreements asked them to be creative and innovative and to meet specified targets and to exert control. Under most agreements the foremen were expected to manage the same work with less people, with different people, or in less time.

[1] E. O. Smith, *Productivity Bargaining* (London: Pan, 1971) 411.

For example, at Mobil, Coryton, the institution of activity sampling to determine the adequacy of manpower utilisation and multi-craft supervision meant that the supervisor's job became more demanding. Adding to the challenge was the fact that the number of foremen was reduced, as a way of lowering costs. Within these constraints, the foremen at Mobil had to turn out more work in 40 hours with only occasional resort to overtime.

As a result of these increased demands arising out of productivity bargaining, many foremen have been less than enthusiastic about implementing productivity agreements.[2] This opposition to productivity bargaining on the part of foremen has other roots, however. Beyond the difficulty of coping with a more demanding job, foremen often feel a threat to their relative income position from productivity bargaining, especially when the workers they supervise gain considerably more in the way of increased take-home pay. Many agreements, indeed, have the effect of diminishing or removing pay differences between workers and foremen.

Loss of 'status' can pose another threat to foremen. Some productivity agreements have elevated blue-collar workers into 'staff' status (e.g. electricity supply), and in so doing have eradicated the symbolic difference between workers and their supervisors; and where the function and importance of stewards have increased, foremen may feel threatened. In an engineering firm studied by the Commission on Industrial Relations, the role of stewards expanded considerably as a result of productivity bargaining with the effect that 'foremen thought their authority was being undermined as the relative status of the stewards grew in relation to their own'.[3] Then, too, a greater reliance on the rational tools of work measurement and job evaluation has meant that certain staff groups have come to play a greater role in shop-floor decision-making. This development has also tended to weaken the stature of supervisors.

[2] Daniel comments on this tendency for foremen to prefer the 'old way'. See W. W. Daniel, *Beyond the Wage–Work Bargain* (London: P.E.P., 1970) 28. Hawkins discusses the impact of productivity bargaining on foremen with such words as 'victims' and 'left out in the cold'. See K. Hawkins, 'Productivity Bargaining: A Reassessment', *Industrial Relations* (Spring 1971) 10–34.
[3] Commission on Industrial Relations, Report No. 17, Cmnd 4668 (London: H.M.S.O.) 55–6. Similar findings of a diminishing role of the foreman and increasing strain experienced on his job as a result of productivity bargaining were reported in three case studies. See K. Hawkins and C. Molander, 'Supervision Out in the Cold', *Personnel Management*, III (4) (April 1971).

In the face of these dislocating forces, some foremen have responded with anxiety and hostility. When the agreement passes into their hands they adopt what might be called a 'white charger' approach. Some companies have found supervisors over-eager to implement the agreement. They have used the productivity agreement to 'get even' and to vent their resentment at having been hemmed in by union pressure over the years. Flanders mentions such an incident at Fawley, when supervisors acted over-zealously in eliminating wash-up time.[4]

Another example occurred at Mobil, Coryton, where some supervisors said, in effect, 'It says here in the agreement that you are supposed to work this turn – well, go ahead.' In general, such a reliance on the letter of the law can breed counter tactics : the union and the workers do only what they have committed themselves to and no more. The whole spirit of searching for better working arrangements and solving problems as they occur can be lost.

In other instances, foremen press demands for the restoration of their relative income positions, choose to seek other employment, or just 'sulk'. An example of this comes from the Fairfields experience :

> In the early days of the company the management concentrated much of its efforts on getting the support of the workers for their proposed changes. Foremen were regarded as part of management and, as such, were assumed to support the changes. This assumption, while understandable, was invalid. The foremen . . . had little idea of their own part in the proposed changes. They did not feel part of management, and when the workers' representatives were constantly being consulted by the senior managers, they felt that they were being ignored. . . . Senior management reassured foremen about their status and their place in the company, but foremen wanted a more tangible form of recognition – increased salaries. Senior management had other priorities and resentment built up around this issue which affected the performance of the management function.[5]

[4] A. Flanders, *The Fawley Productivity Agreements* (London : Faber & Faber, 1964) 144.

[5] K. J. W. Alexander and C. L. Jenkins, *Fairfields: A Study of Industrial Change* (London : Allen Lane, The Penguin Press, 1970) 127.

Management, of course, is not an innocent bystander and as we outlined in Chapter 7 many steps can be taken before and during productivity bargaining to strengthen the standing, morale and competence of front-line supervision. The action by one company in attempting to cope with the 'foremen problem' has been outlined by Oppenheim and Bayley :

> Particular attention had to be paid to men on the boundary, if they were not to become marginal. The supervisors, of whom much was demanded in the form of role change, were at times in danger of becoming the scapegoats for both sides and could have become a focus of discontent. Their reintegration through retraining was only partly successful and they required a disproportionate amount of communicative effort.[6]

Our purpose has been to indicate that productivity bargaining exerts quite a 'traumatic' impact on foremen. Some foremen do not make the transition, while others cope reasonably well. The foremen who appeared most capable of making the transition were generally the younger ones (the older foremen expressed apprehension over the new procedures and the formal training involved) and those with general or multi-craft backgrounds (those with single-craft backgrounds often felt insecure in handling the expanded scope of the supervisor's responsibilities).

GENERAL EFFECTS

Aside from the important organisational effects, productivity bargaining has produced some very important changes in the calibre of management and the attention given to professional administration. Even in instances, such as Ford, where productivity bargaining has not been a resounding success, it is agreed that one of the most important by-products has been an increased awareness on the part of management concerning the importance of planning, technical competence, and an ability to 'get the job done'.

Such awareness about the value of good management seems to apply especially to line supervision. For example, in the case of the Post Office (telecommunications), as a result of productivity

---

[6] A. N. Oppenheim and J. C. R. Bayley, 'Productivity and Conflict', in *Proceedings of the International Peace Research Association, 3rd Annual Conference* (Assen, The Netherlands, 1970) 115.

bargaining, local management has been exposed to various training programmes and given considerable stature by top management. Even though productivity bargaining in the Post Office has been ensnarled periodically at the national level, for instance over the allocation of savings between capital and labour accounts, at the local level the impact has been clear and decisive, in that some very important cultural changes have taken place in the role and posture of line management.

2. IMPACT ON THE UNION INSTITUTION

UNION STRUCTURE AND LEADERSHIP

The impact of productivity bargaining on the union can be differentiated by level of leadership. Top officials have participated in productivity bargaining, either in the formulation of policy or in the negotiation of industry-wide agreements. Similarly, stewards at the bottom have been directly involved, sometimes in the actual development of an agreement and certainly in its day-to-day implementation. By contrast, full-time district officials have been much less involved, reflecting the fact that they fall between the two tiers of the typical collective bargaining structure. More importantly, most district officials, already busy with regular assignments, have been unable to devote the time that is required to help negotiate and implement a productivity agreement.

Aside from the structural changes that productivity bargaining has fostered within union organisations, a very important impact in many instances has been a changed outlook on the part of full-time union leadership. For example, union leaders during their 1971 negotiations with British Rail were much more willing to listen to arguments concerning the 'economics of the situation' than they had ever been in previous negotiations. While productivity bargaining as a subject was dead in the British Rail talks of 1971, some of the appreciation for relationships between pay and productivity within the individual enterprise had carried over and management reported that the discussions (however heavily infused with the traditional arguments about comparability and cost of living) were much more constructive than had been the case before the advent of productivity bargaining.[7]

[7] For further discussion of the railways case, see the final section of this chapter.

A further striking effect of productivity bargaining on the union institution has been the fostering of more working co-operation among unions. In many instances councils have been formed to co-ordinate the demands of different craft unions, and in some instances process unions have been included in these plant-level councils.[8]

OUTLOOK OF STEWARDS

One outcome of working coalitions among different unions has been a widening of horizons for many stewards. Rather than feeling primarily responsible for small 'fiefdoms', stewards have tended in many instances to identify with the total plant and to feel a much greater sense of involvement. In a study of shop stewards, the C.I.R. noted : 'Where comprehensive productivity agreements had been installed stewards' functions were much enhanced.'[9] Hawkins concluded from his study : 'The shop stewards in all three companies found their *de facto* influence and authority being accorded *de jure* recognition as a result of productivity bargaining.'[10]

However, this broader view, stemming from productivity bargaining, can produce some unforeseen problems for shop stewards. Some managers have commented that each productivity agreement has cost them several stewards and, in some cases, a convenor. The basic factor behind this leadership turnover is the difference in time span between a productivity agreement and the term of office held by union officers. A productivity agreement often requires several years before all the 'costs and benefits' have been sorted out and during this period, while the men are waiting to decide whether they have entered into a 'good deal', the stewards come up for re-election. It is not hard to imagine how voices of dissent from the sceptics can create political casualties.

Again, in the transition to more positive attitudes, which can accompany productivity bargaining, stewards are apt to move into this constructive stance more rapidly than their constituents.

---

[8] Kevin Hawkins discusses the importance of a multi-craft bargaining committee in explaining the success of Case X. See K. Hawkins, 'Productivity Bargaining: A Reassessment', pp. 10–30.

[9] Commission on Industrial Relations, Report No. 17, p. 79, para. 179.

[10] K. Hawkins, 'Productivity Bargaining: A Reassessment', p. 25.

The men may still feel hostile towards management and hold beliefs that nothing can be gained from conciliatory behaviour; while stewards, who have seen the results of problem-solving activity in the negotiation of the agreement, may be more disposed to collaborative behaviour. This 'boundary' position that stewards find themselves in can create considerable difficulty. As we noted in Chapter 6, especially in the section on 'bargaining within the ranks', some union officials are able to cope with this position of being in 'no man's land', while others remain ambivalent, receive 'static' from both sides, and eventually retire from office.

3. IMPACT ON THE WORK-GROUP AND INDIVIDUAL

Change of the magnitude and variety normally envisaged in a productivity agreement could be expected to exert a dramatic impact on the social structure of the workplace. This impact can be observed with respect to the structure, outlook and norms of work-groups, and the attitudes of individual workers.

IMPACT ON WORK-GROUP STRUCTURE AND STYLE

Productivity bargaining has, on occasions, exerted an unsettling impact on work-groups. In oil distribution, management, invoking a clause in the agreement, reorganised several work teams. Similarly, at many process plants new working parties composed of craftsmen and process workers have been formed. Such reorganisation may result in a collision between the new format and existing informal shop-floor groupings.

An example of this effect can be seen in the experience under the 1968 shift agreement at Fawley. The T.G.W.U. workers refused to implement the so-called 'job-release item' of the agreement. This provision enabled management to assign a worker of a certain team for a short time (few hours) to other groups in case these groups could not meet their performance targets. The work teams, being very cohesive and having developed a spirit of group loyalty, refused for twelve months to comply with this rule. Because there was a degree of competition between the teams they were not willing to assist other groups in satisfying their targets.

Another example comes from the agreement with the Amalgamated Society of Boilermakers in the Fairfields experiment :

The cornerstone of the agreement and probably its fundamental weakness was that it permitted flexibility only where this would progress (the tradesman's) own work. It became an easy matter, particularly for the less craftbased trades, to ensure their future survival by 'protecting' their work. For a man of one craft to 'progress own work' it was necessary that no specialist service trade was readily available. After the implementation of the agreement some foremen complained that 'welders were refusing to allow other trades to weld for any length of time'. Eventually the management was able to overcome such reservations by forming special service squads.[11]

All such changes in group relationships can be disruptive, can create negative attitudes, and impede productivity – at least until new work-group stability has been achieved. As we saw in the last chapter the net impact of the agreement on work-group relations may be quite favourable, especially if basic frictions, such as demarcation problems and pay inequities, have been eliminated, but such a positive result is likely to be evident only over the longer run.

By far the most significant impact of many productivity agreements on work-group relations can be characterised as a change in style : the endorsement and pursuit of problem solving. In the Oppenheim and Bayley study,[12] stewards, as a result of participating in many small-group discussions, came to realise that more could be created by seeking to change underlying conditions than by always asking for 'nuisance pay'. Stewards responded to problems as common causes and common tasks to be solved rather than as crises of confidence and battlegrounds for class warfare. Sociologists would characterise such behaviour as one of joint endeavour, and considerable research exists to substantiate the fact that people engaged in common tasks are likely to develop positive attitudes towards each other.[13]

In turn, these positive attitudes can feed back on the productivity programme and serve to improve results even further. At Mobil, Coryton, the group attitudes changed dramatically from

11 Alexander and Jenkins, *Fairfields*, p. 127.
12 Oppenheim and Bayley, 'Productivity and Conflict'.
13 G. C. Homans, *The Human Group* (New York, 1950).

those of creating overtime opportunities to those of getting the job done within the stated schedules. The test of the new outlook came when a major fire required working long hours by regular employees and by outside contractors. For the inside workers, the long hours meant only the generation of eligibility for time off. For the outside contractors, the long hours meant substantial premium pay. Despite this disparity the inside workers expressed a preference for the time-off-in-lieu arrangement and indicated that the new arrangement, consisting of a high standing yearly salary, coupled with normal weekly hours, was preferable to a system of fluctuating pay and extensive overtime.

PAY NORMS

In the preceding example, the positive value of the new work and salary arrangements more than offset any temporary disparity in take-home pay between the inside and outside workers. However, in many other situations, disparities, especially those generated by the agreement itself, exert a direct influence on work-group and individual attitudes. In line with the adage that 'it is not the amount but the difference that hurts', any alteration of pay relativities can generate considerable dissension and resistance. Workers accept existing wage relationships merely because they have existed for a long time, even though they may not reflect significant skill differences, and to the extent that the structure embodies certain rules of the game. For example, workers gravitate to the better-paying jobs on the basis of experience, and any change in the wage structure is bound to distort relationships between seniority and pay.

One reason the reward side of productivity bargaining can be so disruptive is that any pay change restructures existing relativities and calls into play a variety of attitudes about pay. Any change in pay relativities within the plant is bound to be viewed by some group as inequitable, especially given the range of principles which can be involved. We will touch on three of these.

Exchange parity. This principle can best be illustrated by an example. In printing, as productivity bargaining proceeded, management found itself in the middle of the following argument. The managers of the machine rooms demanded increases comparable to those received by the machine crews who had negotiated productivity agreements. For their part, the machine operators represented by the Society of Graphical and Allied Trades (SOGAT) insisted that if the managers (represented by N.G.A.) received increases without a productivity deal, then their productivity bargain would be nullified. What the SOGAT crews presumably were saying was that the managers should not receive more money unless they were asked to work to more exacting conditions.

The point of view implicit in the preceding example can be termed the principle of exchange parity. Rewards should be increased for those who are asked to contribute more achievement. This principle is violated when some workers under an agreement are able to move to more lucrative reward arrangements while others are not – all of this in the face of equal sacrifices or inputs. A good example of this can be seen in the experience of electricity supply. Earnings went up faster for the generating personnel than for the distribution workers because certain stagger patterns (with higher differentials) were more easily executed in the round-the-clock operations of the power stations than in the daytime operations of distribution : reading meters and conducting service calls in private homes. Disparities also developed between the fully and under-utilised workers. The individuals who had worked high overtime prior to the agreement were often precisely those with more motivation. Consequently, they felt that the 'lazy old timers' had won a windfall, while their own take-home pay in some extreme cases fell by as much as 30 per cent after the two-year transition period.

The principle of exchange parity has several cutting edges – not only does it guide which groups should receive increases and which groups should not, it also implies a one-for-one relationship between extra achievement and extra earnings. The notion that a given percentage improvement in effort should be accompanied by the same percentage improvement in earnings is strongly imbedded in the industrial relations fabric.

Outcome parity.   In addition to exchange parity, the parties, in fashioning the reward side of an agreement, usually attempt to incorporate another principle, outcome parity : similarly situated workers should receive similar outcomes. This norm has been termed by the Royal Commission 'the desire for equality of improvement'[14] and the importance of extending similar benefits to

[14] Royal Commission Research Paper No. 4, *Productivity Bargaining* (London: H.M.S.O., 1967) 34.

comparably situated workers has been discussed in some detail by the N.B.P.I.[15]

In several companies, which have been introducing payment by results, the expectations emanating from the principle of outcome parity have led to the development of 'lead in' payments for workers *not* on incentive. In the case of electricity supply and local authorities, lieu payments of £2 and 10 per cent, respectively, were agreed to in order to deal with both the fact and the feeling of inequity on the part of workers not on incentive (in both these instances workers who were put on incentives generated increases in take-home pay of between 25 and 35 per cent).

Personal parity.   Another norm by which workers judge the efficacy of any productivity agreement is the notion that after a change, a worker should not suffer economic penalty, especially if he continues to work as hard as before.

A restructuring of wage and salary systems often calls this principle into play. After job evaluation, some workers may be told that their rates of pay have been 'inappropriately' high. At one large company, workers reacted very negatively to such downgradings and even talked about affiliating with an outside union when the results of the job evaluation exercise became known. In an objective sense (based on job evaluation factors or perhaps even in terms of labour-market considerations of supply and demand), the results of the exercise may have been valid; nevertheless, the workers viewed their prior rates of pay as legitimate. Over time the workers had tended to magnify the job requirements to equal their rates of pay.

In the face of such resistance to change, several companies have made it possible for the individuals who have been 'down-graded' to receive the same take-home pay for a period of time through the provision of 'red circle rates'. In addition, if promotional opportunities can be provided for these individuals, then they can 'earn' their accustomed pay and enjoy the status of the more demanding jobs.

A second and perhaps more frequent situation of reduced earnings arises under various schemes for reducing overtime. Generally

---

[15] N.B.P.I. Report No. 5, *Remuneration of Administrative and Clerical Staff in the Electricity Supply Industry*, Cmnd 2801 (London: H.M.S.O., 1965) 15.

speaking, people do not like to have their take-home pay cut, even if they work proportionately fewer hours. In the study by Whybrew, there was no evidence that workers preferred leisure to the extent of being willing to take home less money.[16]

A good example of this can be seen in the experience of one of the companies which the N.B.P.I. studied :

> The immediate effect of the agreement was to reduce overtime to about 2–3 hours a week (from the previous 4–5 hours). . . . Commensurate with this was an increase in bonus earnings but a fall in total earnings for some operatives despite a 5 per cent increase in basic rates. . . . Employees' dissatisfaction with earnings opportunities was soon reflected by increased labour turnover; in particular the more highly skilled tended to leave. Shop floor pressure for overtime was re-exerted. . . . Currently, overtime is near its pre-productivity agreement level of 4–5 hours.[17]

A further example of the difficulties presented by a drop in take-home pay can be cited from the experience of Esso distribution, where about 10 per cent of the drivers suffered pay cuts as a result of the implementation of the Green Book. These men, primarily from the tight labour market areas of Birmingham and London, had been working considerable overtime prior to the agreement; consequently, in these areas there was considerable resistance to implementing the new programme. A similar problem was encountered in the Midlands where enhancements under the electricity supply status agreement were not large enough to compensate some workers for large cuts in overtime earnings.

One solution is to link the cuts in hours and the increases in hourly rates on a group-by-group basis. The N.B.P.I. advanced this idea in its report on British Rail, suggesting that productivity increments be paid on a depot-by-depot basis as hours were cut.[18] In other words, each unit would be allowed to maintain its take-home pay. While this approach of matching productivity changes with changes in basic rates (so as to maintain take-home pay) may

[16] E. G. Whybrew, *Overtime Working in Britain*, Royal Commission Research Paper No. 9 (London: H.M.S.O., 1968) 78.

[17] N.B.P.I. Report No. 161, *Hours of Work, Overtime and Shiftworking*, Supplement, Cmnd 4554–I (London: H.M.S.O., 1970) 21.

[18] N.B.P.I. Report No. 8, *Pay and Conditions of Service of British Railways Staff (Conciliation, Salaried and Workshops Grades)*, Cmnd 2873 (London: H.M.S.O., 1966).

conform to the principle of exchange parity, it does not fulfil the principle of personal parity nor for that matter the principle of outcome parity.

Another solution tried by a number of companies is to put sufficient money into the overall increases in basic rates so that most employees do not suffer a drop in take-home pay. Certain high-overtime individuals may experience some reduction in pay, but if the new guarantee is high enough to capture a majority of the workers, the plan may be acceptable. For those individuals who do experience a drop in take-home pay, it may be possible to introduce some compensating adjustments through the wage-payment system. For example, some companies in the Midlands have introduced incentive arrangements to allow workers facing overtime reduction to maintain their accustomed take-home pay.

Reconciliation of the principles.   As the preceding points have indicated, the parties attempt to design productivity agreements so as to reconcile the various principles governing rewards. However, this reconciliation can go only so far. The basic point is that productivity bargaining, which changes the pattern of rewards, is inevitably going to be a disruptive process and even an imaginative design of the rewards cannot eliminate a period of tension which lasts until the new pay relativities become accepted.

Generally speaking, the best way to summarise the handling of the conflicting principles would be as follows. The principle of personal parity has been maintained as far as possible because workers will not be induced to enter into productivity bargaining if, on balance, they end up worse off. Therefore, no-redundancy guarantees and other assurances that the workers' position will not be affected adversely have been a *sine qua non* of most productivity agreements. As between the other two principles, namely, exchange and outcome parity, there has been a tendency to give more weight to outcome parity. As mentioned, this has been a particular emphasis of the N.B.P.I. which has urged the parties to design the reward side so as to include all affected or similarly situated workers, even though they may not be making a direct contribution to higher productivity.[19] Recognising the pressure of coercive comparisons, the Board has required the parties to con-

[19] N.B.P.I. Report No. 36, p. 41, para. 138.

sider, in the costing out of an agreement, the additional rewards that will have to be given to workers who are on the 'sidelines'.[20]

CHANGE IN OUTLOOKS AND ATTITUDES OF INDIVIDUALS

As demonstrated, productivity bargaining can be a disruptive experience, but it can also produce substantial gains for the individual. On balance, then, we might expect worker response to tend in a positive direction; this should certainly be the case after the transition to the new working arrangements has been completed. In fact, many of the achievements, which we described in Chapter 8 in terms of operating results, must also be considered as having positive influences on worker attitudes, job satisfaction, and morale. These effects may even be more important than any short-term productivity increase specified by the bargain. For improved worker satisfaction – although of a more intangible quality – may produce more lasting productivity enhancement than the specific changes incorporated into the agreement. Turning the argument around, if productivity bargaining were to cause significant and permanent damage to worker attitudes and satisfaction, no short-term savings could be sufficiently large to make the agreement viable.

Apart from the emergence of positive attitudes towards the experience of productivity bargaining in a number of instances, there was the significant result of workers changing their general outlook and orientation. Managers have commented how, as a result of productivity bargaining, individuals have become much more knowledgeable about the economic situation. Along with more awareness of what the enterprise system is all about, this new orientation can lead to some very direct changes. For example, management at Esso acknowledged that it would have been impossible prior to productivity bargaining to have introduced larger trucks or to have instituted computer control in the refinery. As a result of productivity bargaining, a new climate developed wherein important economic changes were more readily accepted.

The importance of these intrinsic factors is supported by the work of Daniel.[21] In one study of a petrochemical plant, the

---

[20] This point was developed in more detail in the discussion of incomes policy. See Chapter 4, p. 93.

[21] Daniel, *Beyond the Wage–Work Bargain*, p. 25.

reason most often mentioned by the workers involved for favouring the agreement (the majority of them were favourably disposed to it) was the greater job interest and satisfaction emanating from the various changes undertaken. Money gains and better conditions of employment ranked only second and third as sources of favourable orientation.[22]

Clearly, then, job enrichment is one sort of change that has boosted satisfaction. Where tasks have been rearranged into new, more inclusive job classifications or where greater inter-job flexibility has been achieved, workers have usually experienced a gain in satisfaction. One worker in a chemical plant whose job duties were amplified and whose versatility increased under the agreement expressed his satisfaction this way :

> You are more flexible now – before you were confined to just one job – you were the only one that could do that job and you were stuck – now nobody is indispensable – you are not stuck forever on the job – the more people that know the job the easier the running, the safer the job and the more interesting it is.[23]

In a survey of worker reaction to a productivity agreement in a nylon spinning plant, 72 per cent of the respondents experienced benefits from the agreement as it had led to wider areas of activity and responsibility, more rewarding relationships with workmates, and more freedom, particularly from supervision.[24]

A second major source of enhanced satisfaction has come from rationalised pay structures, even though, as we noted in the preceding section, there have been instances where these alterations produced initial turmoil and unrest. Quite often, these initial responses dissipated quickly. Where pay structures were brought more in line with what was generally accepted as fair wage relationships, morale was heightened. The importance of wage relations can hardly be overstressed for a country like Britain where norms of equity are deeply inculcated in the social fabric and the thinking of labour.

Reduction of hours, due either to a cut in regular weekly hours or to less overtime, is another source of greater worker satisfaction

---

[22] Daniel, *Beyond the Wage–Work Bargain*, p. 55.
[23] Daniel, *Beyond the Wage–Work Bargain*, p. 54.
[24] Daniel, *Beyond the Wage–Work Bargain*, pp. 74–5.

derived from productivity bargaining. There are two elements to this increased satisfaction. One, of course, is that the shortening of hours results in an equivalent lengthening of leisure time. But probably as important is the release of the worker from the persistent concern about achieving a satisfactory take-home pay that was at the root of what has been termed 'overtime manufacturing'. One maintenance manager described how the taste for overtime vanished after productivity bargaining:

> It is now as difficult to persuade craftsmen to work overtime as it was previously to dissuade them from overtime working.[25]

4.   CONTROL OF SHOP-FLOOR RELATIONS

The long-run institutional impact of productivity bargaining is most likely to be observed in the control of shop-floor relations. Since the control system directly affects the extent to which the parties realise their achievement and reward objectives, the impact of productivity bargaining on this function ought to be quite manifest.

Clearly, management has strong reasons for being interested in the control system of the workplace. Whether workers are as interested in this subject is more debatable. Control of the work system may or may not be a key objective for workers – to the extent that the employment relationship adequately meets income and security needs, little practical reason may exist for exerting control over the work system. Ideological reasons may exist for resisting management's unilateral influence over the work system, however, and these are most likely to be felt and vocalised by union representatives.

Stewards and full-time trade-union officials are vitally interested in the question of who runs the workplace and are likely to resist quite strenuously any alteration in the control equation. The rationale for their existence depends upon their ability to influence the outcome of the work system; and they must maintain for themselves a participating position in the key decisions of the workplace.

[25]   N.B.P.I. Report No. 161 (Supplement), p. 19.

OBJECTIVES OF THE PARTIES

One way for each side to realise its primary objective with respect to achievement and rewards on a continuing basis is to seek arrangements that ensure control over the work system. This approach, with its emphasis on control through continuing procedures, stands in contrast to that which focuses on the negotiation of specific changes in achievement and rewards, where the workers and their negotiators participate in the formulation of new job descriptions, revised effort standards and new shift schedules, but where the control issue is never explicitly raised.

Where control is an important objective, and the 'tools of management' are a key issue, participation is still present, but the emphasis now is on designing and sanctioning a procedure which will continue to function after the signing of the agreement. The balance of control will then depend on the character of this procedure. If management's wishes dominate, the procedure will tend to operate in such a way that the on-going participation of workers is minimal : if workers and unions maintain a share in the control function they will be intimately involved in the progressive application and adaptation of such tools as job evaluation and work measurement.

These two perspectives, one emphasising substance and the other procedure, can be depicted as follows, with respect to the key ingredients of the bargain :

	Negotiated Improvements	Control Procedures*
Skill	Enlarge job content; if necessary revise in demarcation arrangements	Determine management's authority for assigning and transferring workers
Hours	Establish new schedules and shifts	Govern management discretion to determine work schedules
Effort	Eliminate tea breaks; reduce crew sizes	Institute work measurement; introduce measured daywork
Earnings	Realign wage structure	Introduce formal methods of job evaluation
Security	Institute special guarantees (no redundancy); realign basic rates to reflect earnings	Eliminate casual employment and increase worker attachment

* Control procedures may work towards greater authority for management or towards limitations upon it, depending on the balance of power within the procedure.

THE IMPACT OF PRODUCTIVITY BARGAINING

Many assertions have been made about the role of productivity bargaining as a device for shifting control away from workers and union institutions and into the hands of management. Two experts can be cited who support this view. Tony Topham, a union spokesman, has written an eloquent essay[26] in which he has characterised productivity bargaining as a device for eliminating the power of stewards and giving management a free hand in the operation of the workplace.

All this is of course a very old theme indeed; it reaches back right through the history of employer–union relations in the engineering industry for example, finding its classic expression in the procedure agreement of 1922 : 'The employers have the right to manage their establishments and the Trade Unions have the right to exercise their functions.' The control conflict has taken a sharper turn, however, in the context of incomes policy and the new aggression with which management and the state now approach industrial relations, as compared with the permissive atmosphere of the 'fifties. At national level, and as institutions, the trade unions are not well-placed, either structurally, or philosophically, to stress control questions. They are bargaining agents, accustomed (since the slump of the inter-war years at least) to work in the narrow field of wages and conditions. The idea of *control* is a political one, which used to flourish certainly at all levels of trade unionism, but which has given way, since the Mond–Turner talks after 1926, to the idea of joint agreements, a co-operative approach, and a statesmanlike detachment from wider political issues. The *practice* of control, however, has remained a daily problem for the shop stewards. The effect of productivity bargaining, with its assault upon shop-floor control, has been to increase the awareness of control questions at all levels.

The same characterisation (although with a completely opposite evaluation) has been made from the management side. George Cattell states the case for the 'management must manage' adage

26 T. Topham, 'Productivity Bargaining', in *Trade Union Register*, ed. K. Coates, T. Topham and M. B. Brown (London, 1969), p. 85.

and calls upon unions to help in this endeavour : 'The greatest contribution which organized labour can make to efficiency and its own future is to permit, or even promote, good management.'[27] The implication of the Topham and Cattell statements is that the power of stewards over the activities of the rank and file will be reduced considerably as a result of productivity bargaining. Stewards will continue to represent the men on matters of wages, but with respect to the day-to-day issues of shop-level control and manpower utilisation the primary initiative will pass to management.

Other experts have characterised the 'battle' for control as much more complex. William McCarthy has observed to us that the answer to the question whether stewards will remain influential depends on whether they have been influential in the past. In other words, productivity bargaining does not have any special impact on the control function. Another view is that the best way to characterise the state of control is one of 'confusion'.[28] Productivity bargaining upsets the normal modes and regulations and it is not clear what the net impact will be.

Our own position on the control issue follows from this. The evidence we have been able to collect suggests that productivity bargaining does not change the *locus* of the control system as between management and labour, but that it exerts a dramatic impact on the *kind* of control that is exercised. Prior to productivity bargaining, decisions were made in terms of precedent, customary practice, or the dictates of stewards and foremen. Such a control system could be characterised as haphazard and *personal*. By contrast, under productivity bargaining, the control system becomes much more deliberate, rational, and *professional*. It remains just as much a product of joint influence, but the process of joint regulation has been placed on a much more systematic and impersonal basis.

Changed attitudes and changed styles for handling the decision-making process provide evidence for this 'new look' on the shop-floor. At Mobil Coryton, for example, the stewards said, 'We are the managers of the agreement.' In addition to viewing themselves as group leaders, they viewed themselves more and more as pro-

---

[27] *The Times* (3 February 1969) 23.
[28] This idea was expressed by Professor Andrew Sykes, of the University of Strathclyde, in a personal interview.

fessionals in the administration of a rational plan. Before productivity bargaining every new event precipitated an embroiled discussion : the union asked for 'condition' money and management attempted to implement the changes without the payment of such 'penalty' money. Decisions were made on a very haphazard basis, as stewards, men and foremen argued out solutions. As a result of productivity bargaining, however, various principles have been established about the utilisation of skills. When a new situation develops, the parties at Mobil choose a course of action by reference to these new understandings.

This move to rationalisation has been fostered by the introduction of new systems, such as work measurement and job assessment, which have enabled both sides to approach decision-making in a framework of agreed principles and procedures.

Many spokesmen, especially on the union side, do not accept our conclusion that the techniques of scientific management have not represented a change in the power equation of the shop-floor. Consider an excerpt, again from Topham :[29]

Writing in the T. & G.W.U. Journal, *The Record*, in January 1968, that union's then Education Secretary, Tony Corfield, discusses the switch of management initiative from piecework and incentive systems, to measured day work.

'. . . it is essential that our shop stewards appreciate what they are giving up when management proposes going over to fixed day wages. The loss may not be in earning capacity. The change may involve a loss of workshop participation and control over the payments system.'

These opinions reflect a growing awareness of the problem at shop-floor level. Shop stewards at the B.M.C. have explained very clearly the implications of measured day work for their situation.

'It is the strength of our shop stewards backed by our readiness to take militant action that has won us our present wage levels. Much of the power of shop stewards comes from their negotiations over piece rates and lieu rates. By doing away with these negotiations the B.M.C. bosses hope to be able to break our factory union organization.

'Once we lose control over wage rates the bosses hope they

29 Topham, 'Productivity Bargaining', pp. 85–6.

can determine the line speed and the labour loading, i.e. the number of men engaged on a particular job. At Vauxhalls the line is constantly being speeded up as a result of measured day work and there is a higher degree of labour mobility within the factory. Workers, including stewards, are constantly being pushed around from one job to another. This way they hope to isolate potential "trouble-makers" and prevent us getting together with our mates and doing something about it.'

Measured day work is in fact one of the more important devices, along with flexibility of labour, abolition or curtailment of overtime, etc., which, when incorporated into a grand management strategy in a productivity deal, have the effect of weakening shop steward controls and sanctions on the job. The engineers' principle of 'mutuality', with the stewards and workers *bargaining* from an independent position, is replaced by *unilateral* management control over jobs, speeds, and conditions of work. The aim is to eliminate the contractual element in local bargaining.

The concern expressed by Topham about the impact of measured daywork on the control function may be ill founded. His point might be true in the short run while workers are gaining experience of the new system.[30] But if American experience is any guide (where measured daywork has been used for several decades), workers will develop their own devices for controlling the effort bargain involved in measured daywork to the same extent as they have for the wage bargain involved in traditional payment-by-results systems.[31] Superficially it might appear that management exerts much more control over worker effort under

[30] During this transition it is likely that the stewards may feel some loss of power. Having been used to the open field of fragmented bargaining provided by piece rates, it may take some time for stewards to assert effectively their role in the establishment and implementation of production standards under measured daywork.

[31] S. H. Slichter, J. J. Healy, E. R. Livernash, *The Impact of Collective Bargaining on Management* (Washington: The Brookings Institution, 1960), chapter 18. Compare also the view of the T.G.W.U. on measured daywork: 'The important issue on measured daywork, however, is that employers often seek to accompany it with a reduction in bargaining rights. . . . There is in fact no reason why mutuality cannot be maintained on a measured daywork system, and the Union's policy is that not only pay but also performance levels, time speeds, rest periods, job specifications and manning are always negotiable.' T.G.W.U., *Plant Level Bargaining* (London: Transport House, 1970) 15.

a measured daywork than under a payment-by-results system; workers, however, develop as much interest in the performance standards that determine effort requirements as those that dictate take-home pay. The principle of *mutuality* – meaning that all aspects of working conditions and pay should be permanently negotiable – presumably applies to the determination of work standards regardless of whether these norms are used for piecework or measured daywork. Given the strong feelings held by the labour movement about the worker's prerogative to participate in determining expected as well as actual performance, it is unlikely that management will achieve much in the way of unilateral control as a result of introducing measured daywork.

We can attempt to sum up the subject of control and the impact of productivity bargaining in the following way. In the act of negotiating a productivity agreement, union participation is active and complete, since presumably a productivity agreement does not go into effect until the unions involved have agreed to the terms. But this is where the difficulty begins. Precisely because the agreement may provide for the institution of new methods, such as work measurement and job evaluation, management may gain from the agreement a charter to move unilaterally to change the work system as the need arises. But while management may gain an edge in the short run, the point that we have been making is that over the long run, workers and the union representatives will be just as involved in the operation of the workplace, either because they develop tactics and procedures for influencing the day-to-day use of such systems as work measurement and job evaluation, or because they return to the bargaining table (perhaps in the context of negotiating another productivity agreement) to revise these systems. Thus, bargaining continues to take place over the design of the systems (although on an intermittent basis), while involvement and participation take place continuously over the day-to-day implementation of these systems.

Productivity bargaining represents more of a change in the *qualitative* aspects of the power equation than in the *quantitative* dimensions. There is no reason to assume that because a worker as a result of decasualisation, for example, has increased his time horizon and identified with his place of employment for a period of years rather than weeks, he is in any way a captive of the company, and that his union representative has relegated all authority to management. While it is true that confrontation may *not* occur on a day-to-day basis – because many decisions will now be handled directly by the new systems – nevertheless, confrontation will still take place at key intervals when important principles of the systems are being revised or when new systems are being introduced.

EMERGENCE OF AN ADMINISTRATIVE SYSTEM OF CONTROL

Before leaving the subject of control it would seem desirable to put our conclusions about the shift in style (rather than locus) of control into a more comprehensive perspective. What is really involved in the impact of productivity bargaining on the control of shop-floor relations is the emergence of an *administrative* system. To trace out this development we need to separate the control function into its main activities. When the phrase 'control of shop-floor relations' is used, various constituents might be envisaged. Without any pretence of completeness, we would identify the following decision areas as important and note their alteration as a result of productivity bargaining: (1) supervisory authority, (2) control of labour costs, and (3) control of manpower (hiring, promotion and retention).

Supervisory authority. Prior to productivity bargaining, first-line supervisors were more likely to be the 'front lines' of the union; they held union cards and could supervise only men of their own union. This requirement enabled unions to exert control over the allocation of work and the clustering of skills and to ensure that traditional jurisdictions were preserved. Consider an example from printing.

> The lower level of management is drawn almost solely from the craft trades and all possess a union card. . . . Holding union cards, which can be withdrawn, they are vulnerable to union pressure, and for this reason their authority is limited, or even non-existent in some departments.[32]

Productivity agreements contain many examples of important changes in supervisory authority, generally aimed at increasing the professionalisation of foremen. As a result of a productivity agree-

[32] The Economist Intelligence Unit, Ltd, *The National Newspaper Industry: A Survey* (London, 1966) 185.

ment with the engineering craftsmen (A.U.E.W.), management at Thomson House was able to change the rule that overseers were appointed by the union and to secure the right to appoint the overseers in consultation with the union. Similarly, in other instances, craftsmen have given up in productivity agreements their insistence upon craft-specific foremen, agreeing to multi-craft supervision or even to non-craft supervision.

This move to general supervision represents a sufficiently important trend to merit specific examples, selected from productivity agreements.

Philblack

Technicians and craftsmen in the absence of their technical supervisors will be responsible for the technical aspects of their work, but may be supervised by non-technical supervisors in all other aspects.

Esso – Milford Haven[33] (electrical maintenance)

At times members of this group may be detached to work under the supervision of a specific area, either on electrical work or other maintenance tasks.

I.C.I.

Tradesmen and general workers can be given supervision by men of any background.

Control of labour costs.   Productivity bargaining has exerted a direct impact on the control of labour costs as a result of the introduction of various devices for minimising drift, specifically job evaluation, work measurement and measured daywork. The intricacies of these techniques have already been discussed;[34] here, our purpose is to indicate the importance of these tools for controlling labour costs.

As we indicated earlier, the use of these industrial-engineering techniques does not remove the worker and the steward from a position of influence. They still participate in vital decisions of the work system but against a framework of jointly agreed principles and procedures. Whereas prior to productivity bargaining, performance standards were determined more by tradition, rule books, and outside forces, with the use of the new tools they are

---

[33] It is interesting that Esso unsuccessfully sought to obtain acceptance of the concept of general supervision in its negotiations at Fawley.

[34] See Chapters 5, 7 and 8.

determined more by a methodology. The shift is more from a style of 'haggle' to one of rational determination – stewards continue to take an active part in the settling of pay and performance issues, but the tenor is more objective and less characterised by pressure.

We do not want to imply, however, that some sort of new era has been realised. It is easy to overemphasise the rationality of the new systems and their power in controlling labour costs. These new systems can foster rationality *if the context is right*. Merely abandoning piecework will not eliminate wage drift if pay scales are too low. Similarly, the realignment of the wage structure via job evaluation will not eliminate leapfrogging if labour is in short supply. The firm must be in balance with these basic and underlying economic factors before 'the tools' can be effective.[35]

Control of manpower. As we noted earlier in the study, the achievement side of productivity bargaining can be distinguished broadly between skill and effort issues. Where skill (or nature of work) has been a primary focus, productivity bargaining has exerted a very important effect on the control of manpower. In these situations, productivity bargaining has brought about a new emphasis on the internal labour market. The move to new skill groupings with an overriding emphasis on flexibility has meant that job duties reflect more the exigencies of the particular situation than the dictates of the external labour market.

Productivity bargaining in such circumstances can alter the structure of a firm's labour supply from an essentially occupational-type organisation to a task-oriented organisation, defined by enterprise rather than craft objectives. Milford Haven can be cited as an advanced example of this shift, in this instance from a work structure based on traditional occupations to *teams* organised by area of the refinery.

Job titles have been used which refer to craft or operating background of the job concerned. It is proposed, however, to improve common identity by simplifying job titles. For example, day workers (craftsmen and day operators) would be known as Day

---

[35] The reports of the N.B.P.I. dealing with job evaluation and productivity bargaining discuss this point in passing. The tenor of these reports is that the tools *per se* will not control wage drift. See: N.B.P.I. Report No. 83, pp. 37 and 42; and N.B.P.I. Reports Nos 37 and 123.

Technicians, and shift workers (operators and craftsmen) known as Shift Technicians.

Each shift will be divided into a number of working groups. Initially, these will be Pipestall, Power Former Steam Plant, O.M. & S., and Marine Terminal. Operators will be fully flexible within each work group and in addition will be trained to work in other groups as necessity dictates.

Rotation between groups will continue to take place but movement will be less frequent than at present. The frequency of rotation in the various areas would be determined by shift supervision in consultation with the Marine supervisor and the shift crew.

A craftsman will eventually provide operating backup coverage. Therefore, he is required to be fully conversant with all aspects of steam plant operation. He will receive, as required, refresher training to ensure that he is always familiar with steam plant operations. In addition, he will be able to work anywhere in the refinery and carry out maintenance work as required by the agreement.[36]

Similarly, with respect to career paths, productivity bargaining has fostered a greater emphasis on vertical movement within the firm and less on a horizontal movement among firms within the labour market. For example, in a number of agreements the position of mate has been abolished and the incumbents trained for other positions within the company – in some cases the movement has been to craftsmen status. A second step has involved the development of upgrading programmes available to all employees. At Shell, Stanlow, the 1968 agreement provided: 'The present system of advertising vacancies will cease. In its place a system of career development will be introduced.'

Supporting this trend has been the emergence in several agreements of the concept of industry craftsmen, i.e. a shift in the training of workers toward specific rather than just general skills.

Shipbuilding

The great breakthrough was the acceptance of the unions to reduce the apprentice training period from five years to four years and the agreement for all apprentices to be trained in

[36] Excerpt from Milford Haven agreement, 1967–8.

the first year, not for any specific trades, but as 'shipyard workers'.[37]

Steel

Up to now, craftsmen in particular have tended to think of themselves, not primarily as workers qualified to work in the steel industry alone, but rather as people of general skills who can transfer their allegiance overnight. The new skills which craftsmen will acquire as they become steelworkers grade 7 will be more specific to steel. Further, although the engineering grades will tend to become more skilled through retraining this skill will also be of a specific kind.[38]

Increased worker attachment to the individual enterprise has been fostered especially by programmes of decasualisation, as in the docks and printing, and by various fringe benefit schemes which have encouraged career employment with one company. Such 'fruits' of productivity bargaining as sick pay, improved holidays, and retirement schemes can be characterised as moving the labour market of the individual firm from an open to a closed system. Under an open system, workers flow in and out of employment with a particular firm and these flows take place for various skill areas. Under a closed system the port of entry is at the bottom and workers stay with one firm and gradually progress upwards.

5. IMPACT ON THE BARGAINING STRUCTURE

Productivity bargaining has brought about a number of changes in bargaining structure. In particular, it has been associated with a trend away from industry-wide bargaining in favour of plant bargaining. At the same time a great many industries have continued to rely heavily on collective bargaining at national level, though the impact of productivity bargaining experience has enforced some changes in the general approach. Both aspects require some comment at this stage.

MOVEMENT AWAY FROM INDUSTRY BARGAINING

A number of companies have found it necessary to leave indus-

[37] S. Paulden and B. Hawkins, *Whatever Happened at Fairfields?* (London: Gower Press, 1969) 123.

[38] E. O. Smith, 'Demanning South Wales Steel', *Management Today* (June 1969) 105.

try associations, as a means of acquiring the freedom to fashion productivity agreements. To justify such a conclusion that productivity bargaining has contributed to the trend away from industry-wide agreements, several citations are in order. Esso, for example, pulled out of the conciliation machinery in oil distribution in 1964 as a prelude to negotiating the 'Green Book', as did the other major oil distribution companies as they each became involved in similar agreements. About the same time Alcan withdrew from membership in the South Wales and Monmouthshire Iron and Steel Manufacturers' Association on the grounds that its proposals for a productivity agreement conceived of work and pay arrangements so different from the rest of the industry that its continued membership would have caused embarrassment.[39] In 1968, the N.J.I.C. for the trawler fishing industry was dissolved on the ground that the diversity of local conditions could be more appropriately dealt with by local settlements. Dunlop has announced its intention to leave both the E.E.F. and the Rubber Industry's National Joint Industrial Council, to allow it to co-ordinate the pay and conditions of all U.K. employees in its rubber plants and ultimately, it hopes, to negotiate jointly with the 'appropriate' recognised unions.

One of the fullest statements on the reasons for leaving an employers' association – in this case the E.E.F. – is given by Henry Wiggin & Company Limited, which withdrew from the Federation in July 1966. In evidence to the Royal Commission, the Company stated its view of the engineering national agreements :

Specifically, it is the Company's view that these agreements – some of which date from the 1920s – suffer from the following disadvantages which make them unsuitable for modern industrial conditions and which hamper rather than encourage legitimate efforts to improve efficiency :
    – the provisions relating to piecework make the revision of anomalous standards difficult and time-consuming;
    – the drafting of the agreements is often imprecise;
    – the procedural machinery they provide beyond plant level sometimes places more emphasis, at least in the Company's experience, on the achievement of a settlement rather than on the independent adjudication of the merits of the case;

---

[39] N.B.P.I. Report No. 36, pp. 35–6.

and
- the rights of recognition that the agreements automatically
  give to all but one of the signatory unions, without a proof
  as to representation, promote rather than solve problems
  of inter-union competition and overlapping recognition.

In addition, an agreement made for a whole industry, however
well it is drafted, is unlikely to satisfy completely the individual
requirements of any of the companies on whose behalf it is
made; still less will a remotely made agreement give individual
employers and union representatives that sense of personal
involvement and responsibility which is essential if it is to work
well at plant level.[40]

While most companies leaving employers' associations would
probably not fully subscribe to *all* these points – and certainly
some would place less weight on the 'representation' issue – this
extended critique provides a valuable illustration of the range of
reasons why companies wished to pursue their own individual lines
of exploration through plant bargaining. This sort of approach
explicitly recognises that the terms of agreements have to be
applied in a particular context, with its own production standards
and its own mix of technology and pace of technical advance.
Only in the relatively rare circumstances where technology is
virtually standard across the industry and where the experience
of technical change is common to firms at the same time, is it
likely that an industry agreement could begin to cope with these
needs; and as we have seen, quite apart from such technological
aspects, there may be other considerations which cannot easily be
satisfied except by a plant-level agreement.

ADAPTATIONS IN CENTRAL MACHINERY

While the most dramatic impact of productivity bargaining on
structure has been the emergence of more plant bargaining, in a
majority of the cases the negotiating machinery has remained
centralised and productivity agreements have been signed at the
company or industry level. Where there has been a desire both to
maintain a strong central authority and to capitalise on the potential of productivity bargaining, those concerned with the conduct

[40] Document supplied by the company.

of industrial relations at the centre have had to give thought to some adaptation of the structure. The following excerpts from, or comments on, industry agreements reveal some of the innovations that have been introduced :

Chemical Industry (1968 agreement)

You will see that a Joint Standing Committee has been set up to encourage and guide the development of local Productivity Bargaining. This will have 6 employer, 3 JIC Union and 3 Craft Union members. Firms wishing to provide in a local bargain for some variations in conditions of employment specified in a national agreement are asked to seek the approval of this Committee. You will shortly hear more of how it will operate.[41]

The Joint Standing Committee on Productivity Bargaining has now been operating since January 1968 during which time it has provided an advisory service on Productivity Bargaining which is administered by CIA. A disputes procedure has also been established by the Committee both to resolve difficulties arising during the course of negotiating a productivity agreement and to settle disputes arising from existing agreements.

Multi-union courses have been set up under the Committee's aegis for training shop stewards in the principles of productivity bargaining. These courses are complementary to those organised for senior management by CIA.

By February of 1971 the Committee had received notification of 54 completed agreements, covering 27,000 (40%) of JIC employees, as well as notifications of productivity agreements in the various stages of development, covering another 14,000 (20%) of JIC employees.[42]

The 1970 national agreement for the chemical industry provided that 'each productivity agreement shall include a clause determining the manner in which national wage increases shall be applied', and the 1971 agreement, reflecting the pressures for large wage settlements at the national level and at the same time the desirability of continuing to negotiate productivity agreements at the local level, included this clause :

---

41 Chemical Industries' Association Circular No. 1760.
42 Communication from Chemical Industries' Association.

Where local negotiations take place resulting in improvements to wage rates laid down in the national agreement such local arrangements will contain a clause relating such improvements to future changes in the national agreement.

The relation between nationally negotiated increases in the base rate and the amounts payable as the result of plant or company productivity bargains shall be defined in the productivity bargain.

The fashioning of a better balance between central machinery and local determination can be examined further in the following industries.

Rubber took an important step in 1967:

In July of 1967 the Rubber industry replaced basic rates by minimum rates of £13 per man and £9 15s for women, leaving the settlement of actual pay structures to individual plants where it was hoped that productivity agreements could be negotiated.[43]

The 1968 agreement went further and stated:

Wages, rates and systems of payment for all workers, including earnings for skill, responsibility and productivity, shall be determined at the local level and any increases made shall relate to increases in productivity or efficiency or to changes in job evaluation or similar assessments.

Biscuit Manufacture

The J.I.C. set up a standing productivity committee to make recommendations on areas of activities in which progress might be made, give help and advice to individual firms, to encourage negotiation of productivity bargains wherever appropriate, and to ensure that productivity agreements are entered into within the framework of the national agreement.[44]

Civil Air Transport

The negotiating structure for civil air transport was radically changed by the three year pay and productivity agreement effective 1.1.68. This agreement, the first to cover all grades

[43] H. Clegg, *The System of Industrial Relations in Britain* (Oxford: Blackwell, 1970) 153.
[44] *Incomes Data Panorama* (1968–9), p. 21.

of employees (except pilots) affiliated to the NJC, is the first to be negotiated under the new 'two-tier' system . . . (which) established a negotiating procedure with the first tier responsible for determining increases for everyone employed in the industry and the second tier (on a sectional panel basis) dealing specifically with negotiations associated with individual productivity agreements.[45]

And even in the wages council sector, innovations were made :

Brush and Broom Manufacture
A Commission of Enquiry concluded, in December 1967, that this Wages Council should stay in being for the present, but urged the establishment of voluntary machinery for negotiations, and suggested a three-year rundown. Since then the principal trade union, the National Society of Brushmakers, has concluded productivity agreements with a number of major companies in the industry and also has submitted proposals to the employers . . . which it is hoped will lead to a national agreement incorporating productivity guidelines.[46]

These examples provide some indication of the way in which national negotiating bodies have responded to the challenge of productivity bargaining. A fairly typical approach has been the use of some kind of framework agreement, by which member companies are enabled to pursue their own agreements without breaching the traditional rules of the formal negotiating machinery for the industry.

ADAPTATIONS AT THE LOCAL LEVEL

Aside from changes in national machinery, in a number of instances productivity bargaining has fostered some changes in local arrangements. One important development has been the movement of the tone and locus of discussions more in the direction of policy issues affecting the total factory rather than just the individual or small work-group.[47]

[45] *Incomes Data Panorama* (1968), p. 78.
[46] *Incomes Data Panorama* (1968–9), p. 46.
[47] In his analysis of Case Y, Kevin Hawkins rates the shift from the individual to the factory-wide arena as the most important result of productivity bargaining. See K. Hawkins, 'Productivity Bargaining: A Reassessment', pp. 10–34.

Another significant development has been the merging of the historically separate procedures for bargaining and consultation. Just this development is taking place in electricity supply, an industry that has previously handled issues through the separate channels. The need for change was emphasised by the difficulties the parties experienced in implementing the status agreement. They found that when the bargaining machinery was used it was difficult to elicit co-operation, and when the consultation machinery was used it was difficult to elicit serious consideration and involvement. To avoid the compartmentalisation, the parties have experimented with the use of the consultation machinery on an informal basis for as many issues as possible.

A similar evolution is taking place at I.C.I., where all subjects are initially introduced into the consultation machinery at the local level. Either side has the right to take a subject into the bargaining machinery. However, the parties have been able to resolve most disputes via consultation and it would appear that problem solving is capable of coping with most difficult issues.

The experience of the Dunlop Company is also instructive on this point. Historically, as in many other companies, the consultation machinery considered issues introduced by employees in the general realm of worker welfare. Sometimes the machinery was used for making awards under the suggestion system, but very few issues of a monetary nature were considered in this forum. More recently, plant-level bargaining has led to the development of a two-tier system of consultative committees on productivity questions. Within a number of the Dunlop plants, departmental committees have been responsible for negotiating agreements relating to changes in working practice, subject to ratification by a plant-wide committee. Both the departmental and the plant committees have powers to co-opt expert representatives from technical, engineering, work study and accountancy functions, to assist in negotiations.

6. EVALUATION OF THE DIRECT VERSUS INDIRECT APPROACHES

At this point it is appropriate to stop and to take stock of the material presented in this and the preceding chapters. While the

parallel is not perfect, in the assessment of immediate results presented in the previous chapter we have generally been examining
the impact of the direct approach – and correspondingly in the
assessment of longer-run cultural and organisational changes we
have been evaluating the indirect approach. This is not to say that
the direct strategy does not produce institutional change or that
the indirect strategy does not, at some stage, result in concrete
economic improvement. Rather the point is that the emphasis of
the direct approach is on immediate results whereas the indirect
seeks organisational changes. In effect, the direct approach resembles conventional productivity bargaining and seeks immediate
improvement through the negotiation of an agreement and its
subsequent implementation. The indirect approach first focuses
on altering styles and attitudes, and then codifies these new
arrangements into working agreements. Before proceeding to
evaluate these respective strategies, it may be helpful to review
more thoroughly the essence of these approaches and to indicate
how they differ in practice.

One key difference between them is the approach taken to the
specification of achievement. In general, the direct approach produces an agreement with considerable detail while the indirect
approach leaves matters to a statement of co-operation, or to such
phrases as 'time, tools, and ability permitting'.

Theoretically, the statement-of-intent approach makes it less
likely that 'hard' results will be realised (at least in the short run),
but if improvement does take place, it is more likely to involve
the complex subject of flexibility, where the payoffs to management may be quite high. On the other hand, the specific approach
has the advantage of presenting a higher probability of successful
implementation but a lower value for the scope and importance
of the productivity improvements actually realised.

Many companies are sceptical of the 'statement-of-intent'
approach to productivity bargaining, feeling that if they do not
get agreement on specific changes, they will achieve nothing in
practice. Consequently, in most cases, it is management that has
demanded that the language be fairly specific. In the case of
Mobil, Coryton, the consultants and the stewards wanted general
language but management preferred the contract to be specific.

A sufficient number of companies, however, have used a general
statement of co-operation to suggest that something genuine is

involved. The companies which have taken this approach tend to be large, 'employee oriented', and practitioners of good public relations, e.g. electricity supply, I.C.I., and Shell. Where there is strong management and a tradition of trust, it appears possible to move forward with a general statement of co-operation. Indeed, this approach may overcome some of the problems involved in an over-specific approach to productivity change. If one accepts the view held by many companies that the most important gains in productivity bargaining come from the improvement in the labour relations atmosphere and the willingness of employees to accept new methods, then the spelling out of specific changes may be unnecessary.

Even where the terms of the contract are fairly broad, a general meeting of the minds usually exists on the actual changes that will occur. For example, in the case of electricity supply, although the productivity changes were not specified, a general consensus existed about the 'details', e.g. eliminating two-man crews on repair trucks.

A practical reason for preferring the 'statement-of-intent' approach is its inherent flexibility; by contrast, a detailed statement of desired changes may only serve to produce new rigidities in the future. Such a document describes, in effect, the next plateau that will have to be abandoned. At one refinery it was only when the company attempted to write down the productivity changes that the relationship altered from one of co-operation to compliance, and the company found it necessary to buy its way into further changes. In an example presented by Kevin Hawkins (Case B), the process of writing down flexibility provisions only made people more conscious of jurisdictional lines.[48]

Writing about management's attempts in the United States to specify and organise, Slichter has observed:

> Few companies have entered into these programs of classification and description with the thought that they would limit their right to assign work or that they would lead to unrest among employees concerning work assignment. Yet in a surprising number of cases these have been the consequences.[49]

---

[48] Kevin Hawkins, 'Productivity Bargaining: A Reassessment', pp. 10–34.
[49] Slichter, Healy, Livernash, *The Impact of Collective Bargaining on Management*, p. 252.

SUCCESS OF THE DIRECT APPROACH

In a number of cases the direct approach has achieved some positive results. The gains may not be large but they have usually been attained in reasonably consistent fashion (with the reminder that many phase II agreements were 'pseudo' and in these cases little was achieved because little real improvement was sought by the parties in the first place).

The Post Office (telecommunications) experience, as an illustration of the direct approach, can best be characterised with the words careful and consistent. The method used by management to estimate actual savings has been described elsewhere (see the discussion in Chapter 4, p. 90. Briefly restated, the method involves calculation of savings based on changes in work organisation. Work study is often involved in specifying the changes and gauging the results.

The results of productivity bargaining in the Post Office, while not spectacular, have been steady. For example, savings in 1965, the first year under a productivity agreement, amounted to 4.6 per cent of the wage bill. In 1968 the savings were 5.0 per cent. During the four-year period 1965 to 1969, management estimated approximately £20 million had been saved, of which 40 per cent had been shared with the workers. As a result, wages increased substantially but not more than in engineering during the same period. On balance, then, management achieved important economic gains while maintaining comparability of pay for its workers with those in engineering.[50]

DIFFICULTIES OF THE DIRECT APPROACH

While the direct approach can create some positive economic gains, it is also likely to create other problems. Some companies have noted that a quick cutback in manpower can produce a variety of operating problems. For example, at one engineering company, management felt that the maintenance of safety standards had been partly jeopardised as a result of unduly emphasising efficiency. Other unforeseen consequences have occurred as

[50] Some observers have interpreted the one-day strike action in 1969 by the P.O.E.U. as stemming from a perceived disparity between 'big accomplishments and only small rewards'. See T. Cliff, *The Employers' Offensive: Productivity Deals and How to Fight Them* (London: Pluto Press, 1970) 208.

companies have become too conscious of short-run efficiency. Tightening up delivery schedules in order to reduce overtime in oil distribution prevented several depots from responding to unpredictable developments, such as cold waves and a rash of absences due to sickness.

More serious, however, have been the attitudinal problems created by management's push for immediate results. Economic gains can be realised but only at a tremendous cost to the long-run 'health' of the organisation. Consider the experience of a large car manufacturer. A group of work-measurement consultants was asked by top management to conduct a pilot project to test the feasibility of applying various industrial-engineering techniques to the clerical operations. The pilot project proved successful and top management 'ordered' the consultants to introduce the scheme in all clerical areas of the company. Lower-level management and union officials were confronted with the programme as a *fait accompli*. When the union objected, top management indicated they intended to proceed unilaterally. Realising the inevitability of the change, the union presented several demands : no redundancy, full information on redeployment, an explicit timetable for implementation, and the guarantee of financial protection. Management at the lower level agreed with several of these proposals, but when the demands were taken to top management, the latter objected to the no-redundancy concept and negotiations were remanded back to the lower level, where an agreement was reached without a no-redundancy pledge and with a sharing formula of less than a 50–50 split for the workers. Subsequently, when top management proposed to formalise the work-measurement programme and to extend it throughout all work areas, local union officials offered little support. Top management then approached district union officials, received their support, and forced the scheme into operation. Worker support for the clerical union in this company has increased dramatically as a result of the introduction of the productivity programme and management's insensitive handling of the matter.

SUCCESS OF THE INDIRECT APPROACH

In a number of cases the indirect approach has set the stage for important improvements and in some of these the longer-term effects are beginning to show. Three cases which we have already commented upon are now considered from this perspective: British Rail, electricity supply, and I.C.I.

British Rail. After a series of attempts, some more successful than others, to develop productivity agreements on a fairly direct and specific basis, British Rail set the atmosphere for a longer-term development involving the use of the indirect approach in 1967, when it began to develop proposals for a continuing programme relating pay and efficiency, envisaged as spanning a period of several years. A first-phase agreement was signed in 1968, after negotiations had reached crisis point, with the unions working to rule and banning overtime. A year later, a second-stage agreement was negotiated, carrying on much of the adaptation set in motion by the earlier deal. Although many of the typical ingredients of productivity agreements featured in these agreements (separate deals being made for the various grades of staff) the objectives of the programme were much wider.

An important aim was for the decentralisation of control and the improvement of morale in an industry that had experienced rapid declines in employment and was not noted as a high-wage employer. Management's plan of attack was to deal first with worker and union concerns, and the revision of the pay structure was the chief element in the strategy. This was followed in the second-stage agreement by progress involving joint studies into labour motivation and participation, an extension of staff status, and investigation of possible arrangements for local bargaining. One of the major derivations of this strategy was that top officials from management and the three principal unions were kept in close contact through working parties, helping to continue the constructive atmosphere that had first been generated in the talks at Penzance and Windsor which had led up to the first agreement.

In terms of concrete gains, a number of important improvements took place : increased versatility for railway workers, consolidation of grades, reduction in overtime, containment of bonus and mileage pay, and the adoption of binding arbitration where both parties agreed in advance. The real significance of the agreements cannot, however, be judged only in terms of these concrete gains : the process of attitudinal change set in motion may be at least as important in the long run. The critical role of trust and changes of attitude was highlighted by Len Neal, the architect of the overall strategy :

> The real point is that by this Penzance agreement we have given birth to productivity bargaining on the Railway, and productivity bargaining (and I have done some) is not a matter of . . . sanctions. Productivity bargaining involves trust and you really cannot have it both ways. You cannot say that you trust people and also say that because people are untrustworthy you must have a copper bottomed clause which says you take the money away if you haven't solved the problem.[51]

The practical consequences of these agreements are beginning to show. In its *Annual Report* for 1970, the British Railways Board comments on the contribution from the productivity agreements to the reduction of manpower, the establishment of a procedure for the communication of management plans and the roles of individuals, down to the level of first-line supervision, and the emergence of 'a welcome willingness on the part of the Unions to join with the management in studying constructively many problems affecting the industry, such as job satisfaction, imbalance of earnings, and recruitment' (p. 5). The same Report also comments on the low level of unofficial disputes, and the progressive implementation of changes in versatility and pay structure already initiated – this despite the fact that a planned third-phase productivity agreement in 1970 had to be postponed in favour of a straight percentage award in line with developments in other industries during the wage explosion of that period.

Thus an agreement that was much criticised in 1968 for its open-ended character is apparently beginning to bring forth positive and worth-while gains – which may at least partly have been reflected in the (unaccustomed) surplus earned by British Rail in 1969 and 1970.

Electricity supply. The cumulative record of success that can characterise the indirect approach is best illustrated by the experience of electricity supply. Results moved from deficit to break-even to substantial gains as the parties proceeded through the various stages of the programme.

In the first agreement, signed in June 1964 (Stage I), both sides agreed to co-operate in changing working practices and improving

---

[51] Len Neal before the C.B.I. Conference, 9 July 1968.

flexibility. To that end, all employees received 'co-operation' payments of from £30 to £80, with an additional £24 for craftsmen. But very little else happened. Management did not take the initiative to explain or to secure the desired changes at plant level. As a result, unit labour costs increased approximately 5 per cent. It should also be noted that agreement on Stage I was reached only after a breakdown in negotiations, a work to rule, and a Court of Inquiry. In respect of these early difficulties, there are strong parallels with the British Rail experience.

The second agreement, signed in January 1965, contained the now famous status agreement that regularised annual earnings, reduced overtime, and instituted a variety of staggered work patterns. Under this agreement, management just about 'broke even', and unit labour costs remained stable.[52] Most of the improvement in productivity occurred on the distribution side where considerable changes took place in operating arrangements. While hours of work actually dropped more on the generating side, there was little improvement in productivity since additional workers had to be used; and since the company maintained take-home pay as hours dropped, this meant higher unit costs. Similarly, on the clerical side, unit labour costs rose – the benefits which the manual workers received were extended to the white-collar workers without any compensating improvements in productivity. These results represented a substantial accomplishment, given the large reduction in working hours from approximately 49 to 41 per week and the maintenance (and, in some cases, slight improvement) of take-home pay.

The introduction of work measurement and payment by results in electricity supply emanated from a joint statement on employee co-operation signed in February 1966.[53] As a result of this programme which introduced incentives on a piecemeal basis, unit labour costs dropped at least 5 per cent per year despite the substantial increase in earnings, which approximated to 8 per cent per

---

[52] This statement is based on calculations made from data on earnings, employment hours, and output contained in R. D. V. Roberts, 'The Status Agreement for Industrial Staff in Electricity Supply', *British Journal of Industrial Relations*, V, 48–62. See also: H. Sallis, *Overtime in Electricity Supply*, B.J.I.R. Occasional Paper (London: London School of Economics, 1970) 40. The same conclusion was reached by the N.B.P.I. See Report No. 36, p. 20.

[53] This agreement prompted a reference to the N.B.P.I. See Report No. 79.

year.[54] Thus, despite early difficulties, progress was gradually made, not only in terms of an extension of the earliest conceptions, but also in concrete terms as measured by improved conditions of employment and better cost efficiency.

It is only fair to add that this record of success came, at least temporarily, to a halt in December 1970, when the trade union side of the N.J.I.C. instructed union members to impose a ban on overtime, a work to rule, and complete withdrawal of co-operation. The disputes procedure which should have led to arbitration was sidestepped, and the Government set up a Court of Inquiry under Lord Wilberforce. In its Report,[55] the Court found that 'over the period since 1964 the industrial staff in the industry have co-operated in major changes in working practices and conditions which have facilitated the effective use of the large capital investment programme, have contributed to a far more effective use of manpower, and have made possible a reduction of nearly 20 per cent in the industrial labour force in the past three years'. However, it was also found that most workers had not been adequately compensated for this co-operation in raising productivity, and that expectations from the introduction of the incentive bonus schemes had not been fulfilled, largely due to slow implementation. It was accordingly recommended that implementation should be speeded up.

It remains to be seen whether this breakdown in relations will mar the future of the productivity and status agreements. What cannot really be in doubt is that, after early difficulties, real progress was made and the desired objectives were achieved, down to 1970 when the momentum of change appears to have been lost, at least for the time being.

I.C.I. Further signs of emerging success from the indirect strategy can be seen in the experience of I.C.I., which yet again began unpropitiously with the M.U.P.S. Trials Agreement of 1966 which proved largely unacceptable to the rank and file. The strategy here was to allow certain agreed general principles to be

[54] This statement is based on calculations made from data on earnings, employment hours, and output contained in Mary McDougall, 'Sharing the Productivity Cake', *Personnel Management*, II, 8 (August 1970) 22–5.

[55] *Report of a Court of Inquiry into a Dispute between the Parties Represented on the N.J.I.C. for the Electricity Supply Industry*, Cmnd 4594 (London: H.M.S.O., 1971).

applied on selected trial sites, leaving it open to negotiators at plant level to apply the principles as they best seemed to fit local circumstances. At the end of the trial stage, the lessons would be incorporated in an improved agreement for the company on a general basis. In view of the basic and comprehensive nature of the changes sought, the reluctance of some plants to go along with the new departure was quite understandable.

The Company attempted to deal with the difficulties by the Weekly Staff Agreement (W.S.A.) signed in July 1969. Most of the achievement objectives remained the same, but significant changes occurred on the reward side, including the introduction of safeguards to protect the crafts – it was made clear that the purpose of the programme was to eliminate wastage and not craftsmen – and additional assurances were given on no redundancy and 100 per cent trade-union membership. Implementation of the new agreement began slowly, but by Autumn 1969 about 15 per cent of all employees were covered by the W.S.A., by early 1971 a coverage of 75 per cent was recorded and completion was expected early in 1972.

Regarding 'hard' results, management's objectives appeared from an early stage to be achieved. Plants operating the agreement were breaking even on direct costs and plant utilisation was increasing – a substantial accomplishment in view of the elimination of incentives and the 20 per cent earnings increase associated with W.S.A. An I.D.S. report in December 1970 further recorded that after eighteen months' experience the W.S.A. target of 15 per cent manpower saving was being met over the company, while in some plants a reduction of as much as 30 per cent in supervisory staff had been achieved as a result of the new freedom from the day-to-day negotiation of bonuses. Supervisors were also experiencing a change in their role, to a much more 'managerial' function, involving greater initiative and activity of the troubleshooting type. More generally, it was reported that there was evidence of improving relations in plants which had previously been notable for industrial relations difficulties.[56]

In summary, one could say that the indirect approach has worked reasonably well at I.C.I. Productivity bargaining has been successful and the parties have brought about some fundamental

---

[56] Incomes Data Services, Report No. 105, December 1970.

changes in their relationship and in the willingness of the respective organisations to accept change.[57]

DIFFICULTIES OF THE INDIRECT APPROACH

While the approach has worked well in some cases, in others it has never grappled with important operating realities. Staff work has been conducted, many meetings have been held, position papers have been written, but not much more has happened. The approach has been guilty of too much rhetoric; 'talks a good game' but never gets down to the level of day-to-day decisions and the improvement of operating performance. Even where some basic modifications have occurred in attitudes and style, the impetus has diminished over time. Quite typically the parties enter into the process of changing the organisation with a surge of energy and enthusiasm. However, as time passes and the task of reorganisation becomes more and more difficult, the programme loses momentum and the project becomes quiescent.

In the case of I.C.I., the parties have had to push hard to keep the implementation programme on schedule.[58] From time to time 'flare-ups' have occurred in union–management relations. Two examples will suffice. In the now-famous 1971 wage claim,[59] it was argued that I.C.I. had been deliberately misleading in reporting that the decline in profits was due particularly to increased wage and salary costs, and certain aspects of the W.S.A. were strongly criticised, especially the absence of mutual access to

[57] As subsequent discussions in this and the next chapters will indicate, the movement in the union–management relationship at I.C.I. has not been completely to co-operation. Elements of conflict and tension remain, but these occur in a setting of more common understanding about the economic realities and a shared willingness to explore ways of increasing participation and extending the concept of W.S.A.

[58] I.C.I. estimates that 10 per cent of management's total time has been taken up in the implementation of W.S.A., with comparable contributions from shop stewards and employees. (Incomes Data Services, Report 105, December 1970.) It is worthy of note that in the case of Shell, which has also adopted a largely indirect strategy, it has been estimated that managers at senior levels 'had spent on average some 3 or 4 per cent of their normal working hours on planning and carrying out the dissemination programme. An enormous effort had also been put in outside normal working hours, particularly by top managers.' Paul Hill, *Towards a New Philosophy of Management* (London: Gower Press, 1971) 174.

[59] *A Positive Employment Programme for I.C.I.* (written submission by the I.C.I. signatory unions), 2 April 1971.

information on the savings deriving from the agreement. In the same negotiations, John Miller, national secretary for the N.J.I.C., commented in an interview, 'I.C.I. has always bragged about their progressive personnel policy; it has been useful to expose the fact that they are just like every other employer, that they want participation only on their own terms, that every decision they make is for only one purpose – to maximise profits.'

A number of companies that have commenced productivity bargaining on an indirect basis have gradually moved to incorporate some of the 'bite' of the direct method. Electricity supply has found that introduction of payment by results, with the direct pull that goes with these systems, has been absolutely essential to keep productivity moving ahead. Thus, some of the best results appear in those cases where the indirect method has been used to tackle the difficult cultural and organisational changes while at the same time the parties have dealt with the need for impetus and pull via the direct method. In this connection, it is interesting to compare the comments of key management people at companies like I.C.I. and electricity supply over the last decade. During the early 1960s when these companies were pursuing a relatively 'pure' form of indirect change, they placed heavy emphasis on such concepts as participation and staff status. When these same companies were interviewed again in 1971, they said such things as 'We have to be realistic and realise that staff status does not mean a great deal to workers; it is really the direct gains such as job security and increased pay that are important'; and, 'Let's not think that Utopia has arrived; participation can carry us only so far – at some point we have to get down to the nitty-gritty job of using carrots and sticks.' Some implications of these observations will be developed in the two final chapters.

10 Interpretation

1. INTRODUCTION

We have now completed our presentation of the main evidence on productivity bargaining experience both at the national level and in particular cases. In the two final chapters we will attempt to stand back a little further from the analysis, partly to reassess the impact of productivity bargaining on the parties to industrial relations and on the structure of their relationships, and partly to explore the future prospects for productivity bargaining.

Our interpretation is written from two perspectives. One is historical, with the emphasis on the orientation and style of the institutions and the actors, both before and after the emergence of productivity bargaining as a major force on the industrial relations scene. The other vantage point is international. Many of the developments in Britain over the last decade are given added point and interest when compared with experience in the United States. As the United States in turn begins to wrestle with many of the economic problems that have long beset Britain, British experience of productivity bargaining may have increasing relevance for the development of American thinking in this area. The opportunity is taken, where appropriate, to draw attention to important parallels and contrasts in the two situations.

Before we embark on the main themes of these two final chapters, one further task remains. In the course of developing our interpretation, and particularly in assessing the future prospects for productivity bargaining, we have to bear in mind that the evidence we have assembled in this book is largely drawn from a few years' experience of an innovation, and that experience has to a large extent been shaped by the character of the economic problems and institutional arrangements and attitudes of that period. Even in the first two years of the seventies, a number of important changes have taken place in the general environment of industrial relations which may be expected to have an influence on the future viability of productivity bargaining or alternative developments seeking a solution to the same range of problems. Indeed, as gains are made in particular directions, the problems themselves may change. As a backdrop to the discussion which follows, therefore, we will make a brief digression to observe a number of important changes in the environment of industrial relations which may play a significant role in shaping the future. The main issues fall into two main groups. On the *economic* front, inflation, incomes policy and unemployment are the prime concern; on the *institutional* side, the impact of industrial relations legislation, and the differentiation between the philosophies based on greater management initiative and on greater worker participation in industrial affairs, provide the main topics.

THE ECONOMIC FRONT

The terminal date for much of our analysis is the end of 1969. Since then, formal incomes policy has been nonexistent, due to the firmly stated rejection of the desirability of such a policy on the part of the Conservative Government. Exhortations from government have continued to play an important part in the attempt to moderate the wage explosion which began in the latter half of 1969 and continued into the last half of 1971, when some signs of abatement emerged, and the rate of increase of earnings slackened from an annual rate of well above 10 per cent to about 8 per cent per year.

The causes of the wage explosion itself are not completely clear, although various explanations may be advanced. Chief among these are the following: the refusal of workers and unions to tolerate any longer the interference of government and its agencies in the collective bargaining process; frustration at the low level of *real* wage increases over the previous four years or so; and the cumulative build-up of wage expectations (in part due to productivity bargaining) to a point at which the growing fiction of a productivity justification could no longer be sustained. Whatever the reasons behind the development, the first eighteen months of the 1970s saw a virtually unprecedented rise in money wages, paralleled by a correspondingly high rate of price inflation, which largely wiped out the real effect of the rise in money wages. In general, attempts to relate these increases to productivity improvement were extremely rare.

It is doubtful whether the apparent reduction of wage pressure had much to do with the exhortation of government for unions and employers to settle for a slower rate of wage increases. A much more plausible factor was the high level of unemployment which, although coming into play only after a considerable time-lag, eventually had to be taken into the reckoning at the point of wage settlement. At the end of 1969, unemployment had built up to close to 3 per cent, and at least some of the blame for this was put on the effects of productivity bargaining : even if productivity agreements had not, in general, caused workers to be made redundant, the pruning of the workforce across a wide industrial front had substantially reduced the number of job opportunities. By the end of 1971, unemployment had almost reached the one million figure (4 per cent), and factors other than the 'slimming' effects of productivity bargaining were undoubtedly exerting a major influence. Even so, during the debates on the unprecedented post-war unemployment level, it became clear that employers were anxious to maintain the levels of labour efficiency achieved during the recession. From this viewpoint, it would seem that some of the lessons of productivity bargaining experience had 'stuck' and that, having come to appraise manpower requirements more carefully, managements would be more careful than before to avoid building up slack in the labour force during the recovery period.

The unexpected combination of augmented inflation and high unemployment was accompanied by two other changes. First, productivity growth increased during 1970–1 although, no doubt because of the heavy unemployment, the rate of growth of G.N.P. remained moderate. Secondly, the balance-of-payments position, which had been nurtured back into surplus by the end of the 1960s, remained in a healthy state but the improved international competitiveness which had been achieved by devaluation was in danger of being eroded by the rise in wage costs.

The overall economic situation, therefore, had changed in some important respects, yet the earlier problems of inflation and low growth persisted. Despite some picking up of productivity growth on a short-term basis, the 'productivity gap' observed in the 1960s was still present in many industries, as were many of the under-lying problems associated with it on the labour side – such as inappropriate piecework systems and disorderly pay structures. From this viewpoint, scope could still be seen for the future appli-cation of productivity improvement programmes of the kind that had been associated with productivity bargaining. The unemploy-ment position has given added point to some other needs in the wage–work system which had gained prominence during the 1960s : notably issues relating to income and employment security, and the procedures to be adopted at the onset of recession. For example, increasing attention was being paid to redundancy pro-cedures, and to the feasibility of including in new collective agree-ments a 'threshold' clause to permit an automatic increase if the cost-of-living index rose by more than a stipulated minimum during the period of the agreement : this latter aspect featured prominently in C.B.I.–T.U.C. discussions in 1971, and provisions against cost-of-living increases were included in a number of agree-ments (e.g. British Oxygen and electrical contracting).

INSTITUTIONAL DEVELOPMENTS

On the institutional side, the major development was the passing of the Industrial Relations Act in 1971, and the introduction of the associated Code of Practice for industrial relations. This is not a proper place for detailed discussion of the Act, but its impact on the atmosphere and attitudes in industrial relations cannot be ignored. It is likely that only after several years' experience will it be possible to evaluate the working of the Act, but in the shorter run the *expectations* about its effects – especially on the trade-union side – may be the primary influence.

It has seemed to many union observers that the new legislation is aimed at a change in the balance of power in industrial relations, in favour of the employer. For instance, in so far as certain issues, conventionally regarded as proper for resolution by joint negoti-ation, become matters for settlement by tribunals, the Commission on Industrial Relations and the National Industrial Relations Court, it will seem that essential rights of the unions are being eroded and the power of the trade-union movement reduced. If early experience confirms the unions in that view, it is likely to strengthen the defensive tendencies which have already been revealed in response to some aspects of productivity bargaining.

Two aspects of particular importance for the future require comment in this context of the emergence of defensive attitudes on the part of trade unions. The first is the emphasis which is placed by the new legislation, and especially the Code of Practice, on the importance of bargaining below industry level. If the principles inherent in the government's thinking are successfully applied, there is little doubt that the existing trend toward increased company and plant-level bargaining will be reinforced. If, however, trade unions find their position weakened below the industry level, there may be something of a retraction to negotiation at industry level, where the full weight of union power can more readily be deployed. In this connection it is worth observing that during the wage explosion of 1970–1 many of the largest increases were won at national level, where bargaining power could be most effectively used.

The second aspect highlighted by the conflict between positive and negative tendencies is the extension of collective bargaining, especially where extension relates to the subject matter of agreements. Here again the greatest scope for development lies at the company or plant level, including items such as improved representation of the workforce by stewards enjoying facilities for communication and consultation, enhanced security, adequate grievance procedures, checkoff, and the evolution of a series of norms relating to working hours, shiftwork, earnings protection, holidays and sick pay. Whether this sort of extension and consolidation, which is already established in the sights of some unions, will materialise, depends once more on the willingness of the unions to decentralise collective bargaining. The risk in following that policy is that employers may gain greater control over the wage–work situation at the expense of the mutuality principle discussed earlier. If to that risk is added the possibility that litigation under the new Act may supplant negotiation, the pressure to return to a more centralised form of dealing may be too great to resist.

These positive and negative influences correspond to the themes that have been traced in our previous analysis : the themes of increased participation and the fear of management encroachment and initiative. Productivity bargaining proved capable of

winning important results for the unions by engaging them and
their members in greater participation in the shaping of the pay–
performance relationship, but it also showed, on occasion, that
managements could use this device to resume some of the 'rights
to manage' which they had ceded to joint regulation and negotiation. Similar conflicts no doubt exist on the management side,
the advantages of improved performance and possibly enhanced
(or more certain) control having to be weighed against the costs,
such as the greater risk of inter-company and inter-plant leverage
on wages. But the real decision may lie with the unions. In the
last resort, it is no use management taking the initiative in the
exploration of productivity problems if the workers and their
representatives suspect that employers are concerned only to extend control into new areas.

The purpose of this cursory review of economic and institutional
development is not to forecast but rather to observe some developing tendencies that may influence judgements about the meaning
of past experience and future prospects in the productivity bargaining field. What emerges is a conclusion that the problems
which gave rise to productivity bargaining in the 1960s are still
very much present, although some progress has undoubtedly been
made in particular areas. Given the obstinacy of these problems,
some of them reinforced by the continued inflationary situation
and by the growth of unemployment, we must expect that efforts
will continue to be made to find means for their solution, whether
by productivity bargaining or by some alternative route. In the
remainder of this book we will see at a number of points how
interpretation and prognosis are influenced by the factors discussed
in this section.

Our general thesis is that the real significance of productivity
bargaining is to be seen in the cultural and organisational effects
it has produced at the operating level. The emphasis of this discussion is, therefore, on the impact of productivity bargaining on
management and union organisation and on the institutional
framework in which these primary parties to industrial relations
come together. This is not to say that some important economic
gains for workers and management may not result from productivity bargaining. However unsatisfactory the evidence on economic gains, there is no doubt that in a substantial number of cases,
important advances in productivity and in worker rewards have

been made. To disregard these achievements would be misleading, especially in the context of an evaluation for the short term, but the further we move in the direction of a long-term perspective, the less the relative importance of the purely economic effect would appear to be.

Our earlier analysis suggested that whether or not economic objectives were the prime concern during the negotiation stage, the most useful results have often come in other forms, especially in the shape of changes in bargaining structure and institutions and improvements in the cultural background to labour–management relations. It is this 'non-economic' theme that we now wish to pursue further. In the remainder of this chapter we examine in greater detail the way in which the productivity bargaining experience has affected the orientation of management and unions, the structure of collective bargaining, and the nature of plant-level relationships.

2. THE MANAGEMENT FUNCTION

Three aspects of the impact of productivity bargaining on the way in which management operates provide the focus for the following discussion. First, it has changed the orientation or outlook of management towards its relationships with labour. Secondly, it has advanced the professionalisation of the industrial relations function and brought new status to the field. Thirdly, it has brought within the purview of industrial relations all items of cost and has broadened the concern of management from a preoccupation with wage rates to one of the overall cost performance of the organisation.

These factors have not featured in every case, of course. But where genuine attempts at productivity bargaining have been made, and particularly where a comprehensive approach has been adopted, strong indications of changes in these directions are generally observed, and it is in the light of this that we give special consideration to each of these characteristics.

CHANGED ORIENTATION

From a historical perspective the impact of productivity bargaining on management style and outlook has been nothing short of revolutionary. Without labouring the well-worked theme of 'weak management', it is well to remember the state of the art in this field during the 1950s and early 1960s.

Prior to productivity bargaining, management in most situations took a defensive approach to matters of unit labour costs, taking the existing low level of effort as an uncontrollable datum and paying the level of wages which could be afforded in the light of this low productivity. Table 10.1 presents a sketch of the two main strategies and their implications in terms of worker response.

Table 10.1. *Strategies on Labour Costs*

| | | WORKER RESPONSES | |
		Low effort	*High effort*
COMPANY STRATEGIES	*Low wage*	Average unit labour costs and low rewards	Not a realistic possibility
	High wage	High unit labour costs and high rewards	Low unit labour costs and high rewards

By using the low-effort/low-wage strategy,[1] management ensured that unit labour costs would not rise unduly; in other words, management guaranteed itself a minimum return or security level. But in so doing it eliminated the possibility of the superior solution inherent in the high-wage strategy, namely, high wages for the workers and low unit labour costs for the company.

By paying high wages, management satisfies the reward side of the equation, thereby leaving itself 'free' to tackle the achievement side. If the high wages bring to the firm high-quality employees who are easily trained and exhibit low turnover, then unit labour costs might be low – possibly even lower than the alternative of paying low wages and attracting 'higher cost' employees. On the other hand, if management does not have control over its workforce, unit labour costs under the high-wage approach will be higher than under the low-wage/low-effort strategy. This is the

---

[1] 'Low-wage' in this context need not necessarily imply that *all* workers were on relatively low wages. Not infrequently, *some* workers would be on high wages, but the general level of wages over the workforce could still be characterised as low.

liability side of this strategy : the danger that the workers might take their high wages and not respond with commensurate efforts. It is due to this possibility of 'default' that the high-wage strategy can be labelled 'high risk'.

The challenge of the high-wage/high-effort strategy is that management has to be 'on its toes' to ensure that the workforce gives its best efforts throughout the working week. Over the long run, economic results may be superior on a high task basis, but for some companies such an operating mode has been viewed as very overwhelming and somewhat risky, at least in the short run.

Companies that have engaged in genuine productivity bargaining are generally those that have been willing to accept this risk. *In a very important sense, then, productivity bargaining is intimately concerned to bring about a shift from a low-wage/low-effort strategy to a high-wage/high-effort strategy.* A good illustration of this move can be seen in the experience of Rootes at Linwood. When the plant was initially opened, management decided to pay area wages, and as a result it received only 'area' effort, which was considerably below the effort which the company was accustomed to receiving in the Midlands. As a first step in productivity bargaining, the company installed a Scanlon Plan which increased wages and greatly simplified the rate structure. The wage effect of the Plan was not strong – in the Press Shop, for example, pay rose from £15 to £17 a week, with the prospect of added bonus – but it did produce some gains which proved beneficial even when the Plan lapsed in 1966. Thus despite the overall failure of the Plan, it provided a setting in which management could institute some controls, and in this sense it provided a platform from which the next stages in productivity bargaining could be launched. This was achieved, though not without difficulty and the need for a Court of Inquiry, in the 1968 agreement which introduced work study, three-shift operation and greater flexibility of manpower : these changes were in turn further consolidated in the 1971 agreement. By means of these successive stages, the company was able to move effort close to the best levels in the industry, and overall labour efficiency was increased to a point where, on balance, the Linwood operations were almost as competitive in terms of productivity as any in the company.

Managerial initiative. The shift to a high-wage/high-effort strategy involves management taking the initiative and abandoning a defensive posture. Productivity bargaining has provided management with a concept, as well as with a programme of action, for realising important changes in the work system. This managerial initiative can be described in various ways : eliminating inefficiency, gaining control over 'drift' , and installing administrative tools – but, regardless of the theme in the particular situation, the managerial posture has moved decisively in the direction of planning and promoting improvement rather than just reacting to events.

In instances where management has chosen not to exercise the initiative, the results have not been completely satisfactory – consequently, the lesson has been learned that more direct involvement by management is required if productivity bargaining is to be successful. We have encountered situations where stewards were held responsible for recruiting manpower when unforeseen absences developed or new schedules were required; and in another case, this time in printing, the following clause was included in the agreement : 'The Chapels will undertake to provide comprehensive coverage for holidays and sickness throughout the year'. Reliance by management on the union's handling of the manpower function led in these instances to poor results for both sides : the workforce was not effectively deployed and even if the union leadership had been skilled in manpower matters, the role conflict which was involved could have resulted in repudiation by the rank and file.

Emphasis on planning.   By far the most important impact of productivity bargaining on managerial style has been the emergence of planning as a key function. Planning can be seen both as a necessary prerequisite for productivity bargaining and as an important result of the exercise itself. For example, the use of activity sampling has served the important purpose of identifying areas of the enterprise where manpower utilisation can be improved. The information provided by this technique also enables management to plan and co-ordinate the flow of work more efficiently.

The planning theme naturally embodies more than physical arrangements and involves a heavy emphasis on manpower planning. Productivity bargaining necessarily grapples with the *impact* of productivity change as well as with the creation of productivity change in the first instance. Consequently, it forces management to be concerned with the manpower planning implications of change, and employment guarantees and retraining arrangements may be built into the programme so that workers can respond to the changes in a confident and enthusiastic manner.

An important concomitant of productivity bargaining has been the term agreement[2] which allows the planning horizon to be extended for several years rather than being limited to a year-to-year basis. This longer duration enables both parties to implement their sides of the productivity bargain within a common framework. This allows relatively large-scale changes to be implemented smoothly and in stages, while providing at the same time a fore-knowledge of expected changes in unit labour costs.

If a company knows that major negotiations will not recur for another two years, it can proceed in a deliberate way to institute improvement schemes with a higher degree of certainty. By the same token, the expectation that at a specified future date management will have to renegotiate employment conditions with the union, leads management to formulate long-run policies. Planning only makes sense and is only possible in an environment of reasonable stability and in which unforeseen developments such as impromptu claims or 'quickie' strikes are unlikely events.[3]

A very clear view of this has been advanced by Esso, one of the pioneers of productivity bargaining :

> Productivity bargaining starts from the assessment of an operating problem and the statement of objectives based on careful management study. It is more susceptible to systematic treatment. It can only come through management initiative and study and must be a success in the eyes of both the Company and unions. It results in a bargain which produces benefits for both sides, instead of one side gaining at the expense of the other.[4]

The reference here is really to total systems planning, a linking together of considerations for worker needs with the economic

---

[2] B. C. Roberts and J. Gennard, 'Trends in Plant and Company Bargaining', *Scottish Journal of Political Economy*, Vol. XVII (July 1970) 160–1.

[3] We are indebted to W. McCarthy for stimulating our thinking on this point.

[4] *Evidence to the Royal Commission on Trade Unions and Employers' Associations*, May 1966, p. 2.

purposes of the organisation. By designing productivity agreements that enable workers to improve their rewards while they are solving some of the operating problems of the business, the parties have engaged in an exercise of joint optimisation.

In passing, we might note that this new attribute of British industrial relations places many British companies in the forefront of industrial relations thinking around the world. Viewed in terms of the American experience, the record of many British companies in synthesising the various strands of the pay–productivity picture has been quite *avant-garde*. By comparison, many American companies have tackled productivity problems in a piecemeal and *ad hoc* fashion. If a problem develops, for example, with piecework, then the system gets revised without any company analysis of employee needs or the consequences for other parts of the system such as product quality or timely delivery. It has been one of the special functions of comprehensive productivity bargaining as practised in Britain that all these elements tend to be looked at simultaneously. This is essential if a plan is to be developed that has some chance of dealing creatively with both the achievement and reward dimensions of the work system.

PROFESSIONAL ENHANCEMENT

Probably the most important result of productivity bargaining for British management has been the elevation of the industrial relations function.[5] In many companies it now stands on a par with the other key functions of finance, production, and marketing. And where this has not yet occurred, the development may not be long in coming, given the thinking of key authorities : 'The first need is for management at the highest level to accept the same degree of responsibility for industrial relations as for other essential functions such as finance, marketing and production.'[6]

The increased professionalism combined with the critical role

[5] In many companies the status of the personnel director as chief negotiator of productivity agreements has risen. A recent survey of salaries in Britain showed the rate of salaries of personnel managers in 1968 increased faster than that of any other managerial specialist. See B. C. Roberts and J. Gennard, 'Trends in Plant and Company Bargaining', p. 153.

[6] Department of Employment, *Code of Industrial Relations Practice, Consultative Document*, June 1971, p. 6.

of the manpower function[7] has meant that in a number of British companies the industrial relations role has entered the councils of top-management decision-making. The significance of this point about the increased stature of the industrial relations function within a number of key British companies can be gauged by comparison with the American scene. In American companies industrial relations is typically not viewed as a key function. Long-range planning gives more weight to product and financial considerations than to issues of industrial relations. This means that competitive problems get solved via product innovation, plant relocation, and technological change rather than through labour–management negotiations to improve worker productivity. Since industrial relations is not a key input to corporate planning but tends to be more a facilitation for policies arrived at on the basis of other criteria, it has been difficult for managers of industrial relations in American companies to take the initiative and begin any type of labour–management process capable of dealing with some of the underlying problems of the enterprise.

SUBSTANTIVE EXPANSION

The preceding themes concerning managerial orientation and competence are important, but if they existed in the absence of any concrete changes in the substance of industrial relations, they would merely be interesting characteristics which would have little meaning for operating results. What is especially significant about productivity bargaining is that in addition to the qualitative change in industrial relations, such as the fostering of improved planning, it also has brought about a distinct increase in the quantitative dimension of the function, namely, in the range of subjects and issues for which industrial relations personnel have assumed responsibility. For example, the planning and execution of a productivity agreement typically involves management in an analysis of the enterprise that goes well beyond just a concern for labour costs and labour productivity. Productivity bargaining can lead to comprehensive analysis of manpower planning requirements, the utilisation of materials, the role of man–machine systems, and a general appraisal of all items that affect operating

[7] The generally tight labour market in Britain after the Second World War has also called for the incorporation of the manpower function into central corporate planning and strategy.

costs. Productivity bargaining has focused attention on the fact that some of the areas of greatest potential accomplishment lie beyond a mere increase in output and involve such activities as utilising materials more effectively, accepting new machinery, and increasing the co-ordination between various work-groups. Productivity bargaining enables attention to be directed to the total cost picture and brings into consideration those aspects of the operations which can make a direct contribution to increased efficiency.

Indeed, such a broadened emphasis on cost reduction is a theme that has special relevance in a period of rising unemployment. As we have already noted in the introduction to this chapter,[8] the spectre of unemployment exerts a very direct influence on the prospects for productivity improvement and, precisely because of this threat, other ways of reducing costs and providing opportunities for rewards need to be found in the future. One way of doing this is to emphasise those forms of achievement that do not heighten concern for job security – and these are precisely such themes as better utilisation of materials, reduction of waste, and the like.

3. UNION ORIENTATION

As we noted in the last chapter, productivity bargaining has proved both an unsettling as well as a positive experience for trade unions. On the positive side, many unions have come away from productivity bargaining with gains quite apart from financial rewards for their members. They have won facilities for stewards, closed or union shop clauses, recognition, check off and other arrangements that have strengthened their organisational position. For the union leaders themselves, productivity bargaining has fostered, as it has on the management side, increased professionalisation. Increased attention has been given to training, new staff positions have been created, communications have been improved, and a general betterment has come about in the calibre and organisational effectiveness of union leadership. Yet it would be misleading to suggest that these changes have been universal. A report from Incomes Data Services in 1970 found that 'In 1966 few unions had the tools to do the job, neither had they the resources nor the

[8] See also Chapter 11, section 4.

structure to take the initiative themselves to promote productivity bargaining. This is still largely true."[9] While some unions have made quite substantial changes, others have done little to adapt to the demands of the new situation, although even the more reluctant productivity bargainers have found some sort of adjustment necessary. Despite the difficulties of generalisation, a few salient developments which seem to have reasonably wide application may be observed.

INVOLVEMENT IN INTEGRATIVE BARGAINING

By far the most important change has been a shift in the outlook of many union leaders away from what might be called a 'win–lose' orientation to one that is more receptive to integrative bargaining, based on a willingness to use the participative opportunities opened up by productivity bargaining. This is not to say that unions have abandoned the use of power or believe that the end of conflict has been reached in the industrial relations field. Rather, it means that in addition to the use of pressure tactics they have been much more willing to engage in problem-solving and other mixed strategies.

A good illustration of this can be seen in the tenor of the 'Positive Employment Programme' (P.E.P.) submitted to I.C.I. in the Spring of 1971. (It is worth noting that one of the prime movers in this claim on behalf of the I.C.I. signatory unions was the T.G.W.U., which has in general been particularly wary of elements in productivity bargaining that might result in a yielding up of shop-floor control to management.) The special feature of the proposal to I.C.I. is that, in addition to asking for a large wage increase and basing it on many of the conventional arguments, such as cost-of-living changes and ability to pay, it also sought increased participation, development of a plant productivity-reward system, and an extension of the Weekly Staff Agreement. Some impression of the flavour of this document can be derived from the following quotations.

On participation :
We have decided quite unequivocally to increase our par-

---

[9] Incomes Data Services, *Study on Unions and Productivity Bargaining*, January 1970, p. 3.

ticipative role as trade unionists and as members of the public in I.C.I.'s corporate planning.

On social responsibility :

We need to beware of meeting the 'no redundancy' pledge by an arbitrary curtailment of recruitment (particularly of young workers) which may have damaging social consequences in areas such as the North East where I.C.I. is a major employer and the range of alternative employment is limited. This points to the need for a wider process of joint review of manpower requirements, with respect being paid to the social responsibilities of such a large firm.

On the national interest :

As part of this settlement let us enter into a joint declaration on planned growth, on a high-wage/high-productivity economy. . . . It is vital that we break out of the current mentality of retrenchment and depression.

On the range of issues on which the signatory unions felt they should be allowed to make a distinct contribution by means of joint working parties :

1. Review of Job Assessment
2. Control Data on Savings (from improved efficiency under W.S.A.)
3. Job Enrichment and Employment Opportunity
4. Investment and the Attack on Unemployment
5. A General Information Agreement
6. Planned Plant Performance Incentive
7. Harmonisation of Staff Conditions
8. Environmental Studies
9. Worker-Directors

These excerpts reveal something of the breadth of interests embraced in the claim, which undoubtedly finds its roots in the implementation of the earlier Weekly Staff Agreement of 1969. There is nothing negative in this approach, which seeks to extend the scope of collective bargaining and joint management–labour activities into new areas.[10]

---

[10] In fact, the subsequent agreement at I.C.I. involved a straight increase of 10 to 14 per cent and none of the special features in the claim came to fruition, though some further progress was promised in the realm of participation. This does not reduce the importance of the overtures made by the unions in this case.

CHANGE IN SHOP-FLOOR RELATIONSHIPS

While the I.C.I. example may represent an exception, even in more moderate form such an embracing orientation, recognising the opportunity for collaboration as well as for conflict, can be seen as leading to a changed relationship between the union, the union member, and management. Prior to productivity bargaining the typical relationship was directly between the union and management, perhaps between union steward and foreman, with the worker being primarily viewed as a union member and not as a worker with any direct line of contact to management.

As a result of productivity bargaining and the gains that have come to workers, as well as an increased emphasis by management on direct communication between foremen and workers, a new and more complex paradigm has developed. Rather than a worker's outlook toward management and toward his union being one of 'either/or' it tends to follow a more complex pattern : it is quite likely that where a worker's attachment and identification toward his employer have been increased, then his attachment toward his union also will have been increased.

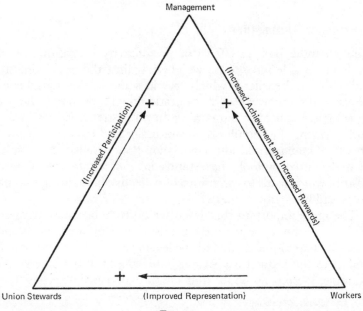

Fig. 10.1

This chain effect of positive attitudes can be presented schematically as in Figure 10.1.

The point of the diagram is to emphasise how positive relations among the three groups are mutually reinforcing – and how productivity bargaining can create improved shop-floor relations along three axes.

The diagram, however, describes relationships only at the level of shop-floor activities. Whether the secondary effects of such closer working relations among men, foremen, and stewards inevitably bring about a loosening of the linkages to the local union branch and local labour market depends on other considerations. Where a co-operative relationship has emerged, such as at Mobil Coryton, it is clear that the stewards, after productivity bargaining, think of themselves less as a part of the local branch and more as a part of the plant community.[11] This same shift in orientation also characterises rank-and-file workers. But where the introduction of a productivity agreement has unsettled relations, as has been the case in some white-collar installations, the likely result is a strengthening of ties between the 'inside' and 'outside' union structures.

MIXTURE OF TENDENCIES

The generally positive effects of productivity bargaining on the trade-union side have to be weighed against the conflicting attitude, observed earlier,[12] which sees in some of the ingredients a threat to the *raison d'être* of the trade-union movement, the principle of free collective bargaining on all matters relating to work and payment. The emphasis on mutuality and the concern over a growth of managerial control over shop-floor activity have resulted in a defensive outlook that stands in contrast to the offensive posture which leads to extensions of collective bargaining into new areas and new subject-matter.

The more important this defensive attitude becomes, the less is likely to be the scope for further major developments in the productivity bargaining field, and the less necessary does it become for unions to think out their strategy for collective bargaining. For example, there is no doubt that union experience of productivity

[11] Cf. Chapter 9 above.
[12] Chapter 9, see Section 4, and the introduction to this chapter.

bargaining has been one of the moving forces behind the decision of unions like the T.G.W.U. to embark on a policy of pursuing plant-level negotiations in preference to industry-wide bargaining which has resulted in many of the gains for the trade unions as an institution.

Yet the T.G.W.U. itself has been to the fore among unions in recognising the dangers in the extension of productivity bargaining if those involved in negotiation are carried away by the immediate gains and lose sight of the long-term implications. Consider the following examples, taken from recent T.G.W.U. pamphlets[13] and no doubt aimed primarily at their own negotiators :

> Managements are increasingly attempting to use work study, job evaluation, share of production schemes, etc., in order to limit the bargaining powers of trade unions. Not only should such attempts be strongly resisted, but also every effort should be made to extend the subjects that shall be determined by mutual agreement between employers and employees through their trade unions.

> The policy is not one of a once-for-all bargain, but a continuous process of bargaining in which the union keeps open all its options to deal with new circumstances and opportunities for gains for its members as and when they arise. It is equally important that every member understands this principle of mutuality and the objectives of employers in trying to buy it out.

And on job evaluation :

> Job evaluation, if left unchallenged and if not considered very carefully, represents a major threat to freedom of trade unions to negotiate their conditions of employment in changing circumstances.

> No scheme should ever be accepted on a permanent basis, and all should be regularly reviewed and re-negotiated on the basis of comparability with other employers.

The net outcome of these positive and negative influences is not yet clear, as we indicated in Section 1 above, where some of the

---

[13] *Plant Level Bargaining* and *Plant and Productivity Bargaining* (London : Transport House, 1970).

major determining influences were discussed. Both effects, however, have already made some impact on the shape and structure
of collective bargaining.

ORGANISATIONAL DEVELOPMENTS

Regardless of whether unions see productivity bargaining as a bad
or good thing, it is clear that productivity bargaining has wrought
some important changes in style and structure. One such development, mentioned earlier, has been the thrust towards professionalism. For example, many stewards find themselves becoming
more and more involved in work measurement studies or in job
assessment schemes and other techniques which require special
training and professional knowledge. The approach that is required under these new systems involves (at least initially) more of
a rational discussion than the typical tactics of pressure and haggle.
Practically speaking, this point suggests that unions will be prevented from becoming deeply involved in the implementation
experience until they are able to support sufficient full-time staff
and until these staff are properly trained in the procedures and
techniques commonly associated with productivity improvement.

A second development has been the use of officials, generally at
headquarters, to act as co-ordinators and advisers to representatives involved in plant negotiations. Sometimes these officials
are concerned with productivity bargaining developments as a
specialist activity, sometimes they have particular expertise in
certain techniques, such as job evaluation or work measurement.
Again, these developments are by no means universal, and while
many unions have taken steps to improve the training of their
district and workplace representatives, the wholesale adoption of
a professional approach has not occurred. Yet if some of the
tensions that may occur at plant level are to be avoided, an increased number of 'permanent', specialist staff may well be necessary. As it stands now, very few union leaders can adopt the
long-term view that productivity bargaining requires. Most
stewards run for re-election every year; yet the time period of a
productivity agreement is much longer. Consequently, they find
themselves identifying with a development that is hard to defend
on a year-to-year basis. Politically speaking, they are often very
vulnerable to charges of having 'sold off the rule book' or having

made 'a bad bargain'. The presence, even in the background, of knowledgeable and responsible officials, secure in their appointments, may help to relieve some of these difficulties and provide greater continuity of purpose.

A third development – perhaps only a straw in the wind at the present time rather than a solid trend – is union consolidation. Precisely because productivity bargaining can heighten coercive comparisons and provoke all of the inequity issues discussed in the preceding chapter, pressure may emerge to bring all of the contending faces within the same organisational unit. In practice, the extent of union amalgamation has been relatively slight, though some important developments have occurred: for example, the expansion of the Amalgamated Engineering Union to take in first the Foundry Workers, and subsequently the Draughtsmen's and Allied Technicians' Association and the Construction Engineers; the link between the Electrical Trades Union and the Plumbing Trades Union to form the E.E.T.U./P.T.U.; the merger of the Scottish Commercial Motormen's Union with the T.G.W.U.; and the absorption of the Lace Makers' and Textile Workers' Union by the National Union of Hosiery and Knitwear Workers. In these and a number of other cases, especially in the white-collar sector, productivity bargaining has not been the only force at work, but some of the influence in this direction is likely to have come from the problems highlighted by productivity bargaining experience.

4. THE MEANING OF PRODUCTIVITY BARGAINING FOR THE INSTITUTION OF COLLECTIVE BARGAINING

Not only has productivity bargaining drastically altered the style and outlook of management and trade union officials, it has also exerted a profound influence on the institution of collective bargaining. We will examine this subject in several respects: the new emerging principles and the new shape of bargaining at the local level.

THE 'NEW' PRINCIPLES

Productivity bargaining has fostered the explicit recognition of several underlying assumptions about the employment relationship. Perhaps these themes were previously acknowledged tacitly by the parties, but productivity bargaining has raised them to the level of full-fledged principles. A number of these, embodying assumptions about full exchange, equality of treatment, and protection of earnings, were discussed in Chapter 9, in connection with the subject of pay parity.

A second, and perhaps more important, doctrine emanating from productivity bargaining is that workers have a right, deriving from their being part of the work situation, to participate in the design of any new work system.[14] The point may seem quite obvious since the word 'bargaining' connotes mutual activity, but this is not necessarily the case and the real import of this point can best be seen by reference to the historical perspective of British industrial relations.

While the phrase 'joint consultation' has been frequently used during the post-war period and machinery embodying this concept has operated in many industries, the fact is that in most cases only 'pseudo'-participation[15] has occurred. Where some form of real participation emerged, usually it was over peripheral issues such as health and safety.

By contrast, productivity bargaining has brought participation into the centre of the picture in two respects. Participation has been a necessary prerequisite as well as a resulting condition of productivity bargaining. Such basic changes in the work system as elimination of overtime, institution of shiftwork, or revision of demarcation rules cannot be handled by fiat. They must be tackled on a joint basis, and to the extent that this joint approach has proved successful, the importance of participation has been reinforced.

While participation has been a pervasive theme of productivity

[14] Nora Stettner sees increased worker participation as one of the main accomplishments of productivity bargaining: *Productivity Bargaining and Industrial Change* (Oxford: Pergamon Press, 1969) 168–80.

[15] An example of such rhetoric, or 'participation on paper', was embodied in the recommendation of the National Joint Advisory Council to the Minister of Labour in 1947, which proposed that consultative machinery be set up 'for the regular exchange of views between employers and workers on production matters'. For a discussion of such synthetic joint consultation – what he terms the 'unitary view' of industrial relations, see A. Fox, *Industrial Sociology and Industrial Relations*, Royal Commission Research Paper No. 3 (London: H.M.S.O., 1966).

bargaining, it has not taken the same form in all cases.[16] In some instances, participation has involved 'clearing things with the union', wherein management checks with the workers before taking action, or perhaps develops a plan and then presents it to the workers and their leaders for discussion and eventual agreement. This approach is in line with the British tradition of consultation and the belief that change should go forward only after some contact with all concerned has taken place. It is also in line with the thinking of the Industrial Relations Act and the associated Code of Practice, which states that 'consultation should involve an "exchange of views", not just passing information on decisions already taken'. And the process should 'enable the committee to discuss the widest possible range of subjects of concern to employees, paying particular attention to matters closely associated with the work situation'.[17]

In some situations, participation has been more extensive and the involvement of workers and their union representatives has occurred at the very beginning and throughout the exercise – there has been a process of *joint* design and execution of the productivity improvement programme.

The general movement towards greater participation in the design of the affairs of the workplace has not emanated just from the management and government sides. In some important respects, the trade-union movement has pushed actively for greater and greater participation. In many instances, the quest for full participation has come under the banner of 'mutuality' or alternatively under the theme of '*status quo*'. Carried to its fullest form, such emphasis on mutuality means that the workers and union representatives have a veto power over any changes in the employment relationship. This is the negative aspect of participation from management's point of view. But as we have seen, participation produces important positive benefits. How these positive and negative elements might be reconciled is an issue to which we now turn.

---

[16] For an analysis of various participation modes, see A. Globerson, 'Spheres and Levels of Employee Participation in Organizations', *British Journal of Industrial Relations*, Vol. VIII (July 1970) 252–61.

[17] Department of Employment, *Code of Industrial Relations Practice Consultative Document*, para. 8.

THE DILEMMA OF PARTICIPATION

The dilemma for British industrial relations is that the need for management initiative, which gives day-to-day meaning to the planning function, clearly conflicts with the emphasis on mutuality and full trade-union participation. One avenue to reconciliation derives from the experience of U.S. industrial relations. In brief, the principle is that management has the freedom to initiate, but the workers and their representatives also have the right to challenge and to take a dispute through the steps of the grievance procedure, eventually leading to third-party arbitration. This does not mean that management has a right to change basic conditions that have been negotiated, but it does have a right to take the initiative in certain areas that have been set out in the basic agreement. One such area of initiative is technological change. Another is the introduction of new job classifications or new piece rates. These subjects are placed within a framework of principles and guidelines that are spelled out in the collective bargaining agreement, and disputes are resolved in the light of these guidelines.

Two British examples of this form of approach to reconciling the need for management initiative with the right of labour to participate can be cited. The first comes from an agreement signed in 1971 by Albright and Wilson with the G.M.W.U. and a number of craft unions :

> It is agreed that there shall be no delays or interruptions of work while discussions on any dispute are taking place, and that an interim management decision will be accepted on any immediate issue until the matter has been resolved, if this is necessary to ensure continuation of work.

The second example comes from the motor car industry, specifically Rootes :

> The A.E.F. insisted that standards established by work study must be mutually accepted and agreed to before they could be implemented on the shop floor. The Company, on the contrary, could not accept that standards established by work study should be the subject of shop floor bargaining, although they did not deny that, if sound reasons could be produced, such

standards might be challenged through the procedure for avoidance of disputes. In the final Agreement, they had gone as far as they could to meet objections by the Unions, first by providing that cases of disagreement should be investigated jointly by management and a representative nominated by the Union concerned, and secondly by accepting the insertion of the words 'as near as possible to' in the final sentence of the clauses which now read : 'During the operation of this procedure, normal working will continue at or as near as possible to standard performance.' The Company was fully prepared to train in work study techniques employees selected by the Unions for this purpose. The Agreement as finally formulated had proved acceptable to the major Unions representing production workers.[18]

While these two illustrations are isolated examples of what may become a new model in the British industrial relations system, they represent the typical case in U.S. industrial relations. Having noted this, several caveats are in order. The advantage of such clauses is that management is free to initiate change and is in a position to create the circumstances for constant economic progress. The other side of the picture is that the 'freedom to manage' is preserved at the cost of more elaborate contracts and complicated procedures for resolving disputes over whether actions in particular instances were proper. This is the well-known formalism and orientation to procedure that has characterised American industrial relations. It would be unfortunate if the emphasis on managerial rights brought about a weakening of one of the important strengths of British industrial relations, namely, their informality and the willingness of the parties to use genuine integrative bargaining in the solution of persistent problems.

In this respect the American system has a good deal to learn from the British system, especially the latter's emphasis on participation. In the American system, much more attention is given to management initiative, with union involvement, during the life of the contract, limited to challenging such management actions. To the extent that many problems can be solved only by joint design and careful execution of the plan by both sides, the British experience is a very important fund of knowledge for the American

[18] Taken from the *Report of the Court of Inquiry into a Dispute at Rootes Motors Ltd., Linwood, Scotland*, Cmnd 3692 (London : H.M.S.O., 1968) p. 13, para. 41.

scene, especially for those industries that are deadlocked over problems of productivity improvement.

In the United States, worker participation represents more of an *opportunity* for management whereas in Britain it is a *necessity* to any kind of progress. In Britain unions occupy such an important place in the plant-level industrial relations system that their role is crucial in determining the success or failure of productivity agreements. In the United States, where unions are less strong, management may be able to gain its own way in the absence of union support. For example, most companies would not think of asking union approval before introducing work measurement techniques, in contrast to the British situation where such agreement is absolutely essential. But the question for the U.S. industrial relations system is whether such participation would not be an important way of increasing the gains to both sides.

PLANT-LEVEL BARGAINING

Perhaps of equal importance to the practice of increased participation has been its inevitable consequence, the decentralisation of industrial relations. Genuine involvement of the workforce in the problems of the work system can only take place at the level where these problems exist, that is, at the level of the plant or work-group. One of the most important and perhaps lasting benefits of productivity bargaining is that it has brought stewards, foremen, and other representatives of the local scene together to grapple with the substantive problems of the workplace.

This emphasis on plant-level bargaining has been made up of two separate and distinct movements.[19] One trend has been the movement of collective bargaining activities from the industry and company level to the plant level because of the participation factor just mentioned. Another has been the movement of collective bargaining away from the work-group and its consolidation at plant level. This latter trend has been fostered by a general desire for order and procedure as well as by the introduction of the 'rational' techniques such as work measurement and job evaluation. The hiring of staff groups to administer these systems has resulted in the consideration of these important items on a plant-level basis rather than at the level of the work-group.

[19] We are indebted to Andrew Thomson for this important distinction.

The importance of plant-level bargaining has been dramatised by the experience with sectional agreements. As we noted in Chapters 2 and 3, a significant number of agreements were focused on one department or occupational group rather than the entire plant. Such sectional arrangements have accentuated the problem of pay disparities (discussed in the preceding chapter). As a result there has been a strong push, especially on the management side, to encompass all workers in co-ordinated agreements at the plant level.

As the parties have gained experience in handling matters of substance at the plant level, a new dimension and capacity has been added to the collective bargaining machinery. Stewards who have participated in developing job descriptions, for example, have developed important knowledge about wage and job relationships. Similarly, where changes have been made in wage-payment systems, a knowledge and a willingness to deal with this complex subject has emerged.

Thus, we argue that productivity bargaining has been the vehicle which has given substance to plant-level negotiations. In other words, productivity bargaining has provided the focus and content which has made plant bargaining a reality. To reverse the sequence, as some companies have done, confuses desirability with feasibility.[20] Merely setting up plant procedures can be a sterile exercise. We have noted in our fieldwork a number of companies that have moved quite hastily to 'plant bargaining' with very disappointing results. One reason is that they have adopted the form and not the substance. In an extreme case, some fourteen committees were established and many procedures put on paper, but in practice very little happened because the parties did not grapple with the important problems of the workplace. The general point is that plant bargaining without any substance is form without content. A decentralisation of collective bargaining takes place only because the parties see mutual advantage in discussing and resolving local problems. Thus structure has to adapt to need, rather than vice versa.

---

[20] Some of the recommendations of the Donovan Commission and other study groups appear to suffer from this defect; it is assumed that because plant bargaining is a good idea (desirability), merely urging the parties to establish local procedures will accomplish the result (feasibility).

CONTINUED RELIANCE ON INDUSTRY BARGAINING

Despite substantial movement away from industry bargaining, the centralisation of joint negotiations has remained the most common practice. Some important reasons exist for this extensive and continued emphasis on centralised bargaining. In particular, it has been much easier for key negotiators to strike one bargain and have it implemented across an industry, thereby preventing smaller plants from being pressured into unfavourable settlements. With lucrative settlements taking place (in part, due to productivity bargaining), ample opportunity exists for unions to create cross-pressures within an industry if centralised arrangements are not present.

Thus, an important function for industry-level dealings has been to control earnings and labour costs. To the extent that 'drift' through whipsawing has been a force to be reckoned with, it is more likely that it can be controlled via the central setting of rates and the monitoring of results than would be the case with separate bargaining on a company-by-company basis.[21] On exactly this point, the Engineering Employers' Federation has recently shifted its position markedly from that advocated in the late 1960s. In contrast to its former encouragement of plant-level bargaining, the E.E.F. has argued in its Annual Report for 1971 that national, industry-wide bargaining needs to be firmly re-established. Although acknowledging the difficulty of quantifying the point, it maintains that the trend to decentralisation has weakened the bargaining power of firms, and finds that comparability has entered into plant bargaining – in the case of engineering, contrary to the national framework agreement. The following passage puts the case clearly :

> The more decentralisation the greater the number of comparisons that can be made, the greater the number of disparities,

---

[21] Turner makes the point this way: 'It is probably a sound observation that, other things being equal, the more decentralized the bargaining system, the faster wages are likely to move in whatever direction they are moving anyway. That is why national agreements were so important in the inter-war depressions ; because they reacted less promptly than wage-rates determined at the workplace level, they set a "floor" to the general tendency of wages to fall.' H. A. Turner, 'Collective Bargaining and the Eclipse of Income Policy : Retrospect, Prospect and Possibilities', *British Journal of Industrial Relations*, Vol. VIII (July 1970) 206.

anomalies and inequities that can be pointed out, and individual firms can be 'picked off' in strategically more-or-less well organised local wage rounds.[22]

Aside from these objective factors, many institutional reasons can be cited for the persistence of centralised dealings in Great Britain.

Even if local dealings are theoretically desirable, a complete movement to this structure would be hard to institute because of strong traditions. As a result productivity bargaining probably has to accommodate itself in some degree to the practice of centralised negotiations. Centralised bargaining has been a natural development in a country such as Great Britain characterised by many small employers, by an active role of the government in the economic system, and by a cohesive workforce that demands comparability in compensation. This fixation on uniformity carries throughout much of British industry. Examples have come to our notice in several industries examined in the course of this study, notably in oil refining. Even in a situation like the motor industry where, for many reasons, major differences in earnings levels and structures have been the rule, great pressure has been exerted over a period of years to achieve equality of earnings. This objective (still not fully achieved) has been sought in the face of dramatically different labour markets and local operating conditions.

Centralised dealings also manifest important values, such as equity and the notion that everyone within a company should be treated similarly. For example, I.C.I. has spent a lot of time convincing each employee that he is treated like everyone else at I.C.I. and is a member of the 'family'. As one of the managers expressed the point, 'We have been fighting for the policy of central rates all of these years – we can't go back on it now'.

Centralised dealings have also been a necessity, particularly on the union side, because, historically, the only leadership responsible and secure enough to be 'confronted' existed at the top. Typically, union leadership at the plant level was inexperienced or non-existent and once such centralised dealings develop, labour leaders guard these arrangements quite protectively. For example, the T.G.W.U. official responsible for oil distribution has been reluctant

---

[22] Engineering Employers' Federation, *Wage Inflation and Employment* (London: E.E.F. Research Dept, 1971).

to allow local dealings with respect to productivity. He has spent years developing a conciliation machinery that facilitates quick and efficient negotiations. Any decentralising of negotiations would be a diminution of his authority.[23]

Similarly on the management side, a strong preference has existed for centralised dealings; they are defensive and safe. Most line managers prefer to relegate matters of labour relations to the central staff group or the employers' associations. In many large companies centralised dealings have emerged only after a long period of transition. Many staff and line people have become committed to centralised bargaining for the same reason that the T.G.W.U. official has clung to the arrangements in oil distribution : however inappropriate centralised dealings may be for pay and productivity negotiations in a particular setting, the existing staff have devoted their careers to bringing this about or to maintaining it and are not readily persuaded to change their overall strategy.

EMERGENCE OF A SYNTHESIS

Within the context of centralised dealings, the need for more local determination has been accommodated in a number of ways. One such device is the framework agreement. The major advantage of the framework agreement is that by providing a form of enabling authority *from* the central machinery, it is possible both to allow companies to engage in enterprise bargaining and to remain in membership. In this sense, the framework agreement can be seen as a defensive response either by the members of the joint negotiating body or by an employers' association unilaterally. The possibility that important members will leave and so remove their support (or their funds) may be too serious to be countenanced, since it would leave the remaining members in a weak position.

An important feature of the framework agreement is the specification of general principles or guidelines to individual members so that some of the traditional parity between them is preserved. Thus, it is a fairly common feature of such agreements at

---

[23] As we have noted elsewhere (Chapter 9), the T.G.W.U. has emphasised the desirability of plant bargaining. The point of the above example is that while policy may favour decentralised collective bargaining, in terms of tradition and prestige there may be substantial inertia in favour of centralised dealings.

national level that they should be accompanied (as in the case of the Chemical Industries' Association) with an explicit set of guidelines;[24] or that some advisory committee should be set up either to provide guidance to those conducting individual bargaining or to examine the possibility of developing adequate principles. For example, the N.J.I.C. for the paint, varnish and lacquer industry spent over a year trying to develop guidelines similar to those of the chemical industry agreement, but experienced considerable difficulty because of the large number of small firms. Eventually, in November 1968, it decided to establish a Productivity Bargaining Joint Advisory Committee.

Also, there may be a more positive motive involved in the move to accommodate decentralised bargaining. For there is no doubt that in many industries the real relevance and importance of industry agreements had been decimated – even in advance of productivity bargaining – by locally negotiated additions, by slack incentive-payment schemes, and other well-known methods of drift. By openly embracing the principle of plant bargaining, some of the central bodies and employers' associations (and perhaps some unions also) may have hoped to find a means of regaining some control over what was occurring at local level. While we have not found any explicit statement of this intent, some of the measures taken, especially by employers' associations, in the setting up or strengthening of central advisory services to provide guidance on the negotiation, implementation, and monitoring of agreements at plant level would fit this hypothesis.

Areas in which this advice could be particularly relevant include systems of work study and job evaluation, the modification of wage-payment methods and wage structures and the centralisation of knowledge and techniques used in the industry to solve common problems. It was openly recognised by the C.B.I. in its 'second thoughts' on productivity bargaining that employers' associations would both have to equip themselves better for the task by acquiring increased and more specialised staff resources, and to adapt to the 'different role which this approach to bargaining will require

---

[24] Significantly, in 1971, the employers' panel of the Chemical Industries J.I.C. became increasingly worried that companies were paying increases twice over – as a result of industry-wide increases, supplemented by increases for productivity improvement at plant level. As a result, the J.I.C. reviewed the two-tier structure and introduced modifications designed to reduce the risk of double-payment. See Chapter 9 (pp. 298–9).

of them'. In passing we might note that the future role of employers' associations with respect to productivity bargaining may be more as service agents than as the designers and implementers of change. The role of the industry association becomes one of establishing principles, collecting and disseminating data, conducting research, running conferences – a facilitator rather than an operator of productivity bargaining.

Similarly, on the other side, no doubt some of the same pressures have been felt in trade-union circles, where the growing power of stewards engaging in plant bargaining has been recognised as a threat to central authority in the union organisation. In this light, the steps taken by certain unions to improve the training given to their officials at all levels down to the stewards, and to improve the communication channels within the organisation, can be seen as a parallel to the employers' associations' moves to regain an important role.

As the preceding paragraphs have shown, productivity bargaining has served to strengthen both tiers in the bargaining machinery. It has fostered both more local determination, and more central control – though not always in the same industries. In many respects, these developments are in line with the recommendations of the Donovan Commission, and there can be little doubt that the analysis and findings of that body have added strength to the reshaping of the collective bargaining system and the institutions concerned in its operation. But many of these developments were taking place while the Commission was deliberating and before it had reported, and it seems probable that a good deal of the change in bargaining structure during the latter half of the 1960s was precipitated not by Donovan, but by the growing experience of productivity bargaining and the perceived needs of different groups to explore its potential or to introduce safeguards against a threat to their own role. In this sense, it might be no great inaccuracy to say that productivity bargaining acted as a catalyst for the kinds of change that have been discussed above, while the Donovan Report both conceptualised and confirmed the developments already taking place on a broad front.

The future trend of bargaining structure is not easy to discern. We have already seen that the movement towards more extensive plant bargaining and the strengthening and adaptation of central agencies has been somewhat moderated by the more pressing requirements following the collapse of incomes policy in 1969 and the new problems created by the prospect of legislation on industrial relations. But it has not stopped altogether. The main problem now is to reach some new equilibrium in which the proper weighting is given to both the industry agreement and the plant-level settlements – a weighting that will undoubtedly vary among industries.

5. CONTROL OF PLANT-LEVEL RELATIONS

Accepting the premise that productivity bargaining has fostered more plant-level dealings, we still face the question : has the tenor of plant relations shifted under the impact of productivity bargaining? This brings us back to the control issue discussed in the last chapter, where we concluded that productivity bargaining has changed the form but not the locus of the control function. That theme may now be stated rather more formally : the change in plant-level relations resulting from productivity bargaining can be characterised as a shift from a *craft* system to an *administrative* system for controlling manpower utilisation. The term 'craft system' refers to an external labour market approach to selecting, training, and allocating workers to employment opportunities. By contrast, the 'administrative system' relies upon procedures and rules that have their origin in the particular firm – hence, the characteristics of an internal labour market. The principles undergirding the administrative approach are those of classical bureaucracy and modern-day management theory.

FEATURES OF THE CRAFT AND ADMINISTRATIVE SYSTEMS

The craft system is essentially an external labour market mechanism for recruiting, training, and allocating workers. If, from a theoretical point of view, work can be organised either according to the management principles of engineering economy or according to established occupational lines, then the craft system represents the most notable example of the latter approach. The essential feature of a craft-type occupational system is that each single craft maintains a considerable degree of autonomy in regulating the standards and conditions for the performance of particular tasks. The base of this autonomy is the skill and specific knowledge required to perform the tasks. Since it usually takes considerable time and effort to become proficient in performing such tasks, it is more economical to grant monopoly over the service to a certain group which, in return, guarantees certain standards of performance by apprenticeship, certification, and self-supervision.

The administrative system handles most of the steps (and decisions) involving training and placement within the confines of a particular employer. Rather than allowing job design to be determined by occupational definitions existing in the local labour market, management packages job duties based on technology, scale of operations, and other economic considerations *internal* to the firm.

The organisational principles[25] of the craft and administrative systems can be summarised and compared as follows :

Craft System	*Administrative System*
clearly defined work jurisdiction	more flexible work jurisdiction
mobility within the occupation and across firms	mobility within the firm
regulated socialisation and conduct	conduct on the job governed by plant rules
few levels in the management hierarchy	many levels in the management hierarchy
supervision specific to craft	supervision by 'generalists'
decision-making decentralised to first-line supervision and craftsmen	decision-making more centralised
performance standards self-regulated	performance standards specified by the 'tools' (e.g., work measurement)
few staff personnel	many staff personnel

The administrative approach overcomes many problems inherent in the craft system. While the genius of the craft system is its ability to 'manage' the work system on an *ad hoc* basis on the

[25] These generalisations have been adapted from several studies : A. L. Stinchcombe, 'Bureaucratic and Craft Administration of Production; A Comparative Study', *Administrative Science Quarterly*, Vol. IV (September 1959) 168–87, and 'Social Structure and Organizations', in *Handbook of Organizations*, ed. J. G. March (Chicago : Rand McNally, 1965) 165–6; and H. A. Turner, *Trade Union Growth, Structure and Policy* (London : Allen and Unwin, 1962).

shopfloor, it represents a delegation (some might say 'abdication') of management authority to the workers possessing the experience, who make 'on-the-spot' decisions; consequently, it often performs inefficiently. Workers wait for other workers to complete their tasks, and required materials are often in short supply. In the absence of an overall 'guiding hand' considerable inefficiency can exist in the system.

The main shortcoming in the craft system is not with the *quality* of the work but with the *quantity* of the work. Indeed, quality of work can be high, given the professional standards of most craft workers. Thus, the move to administrative style represents an attempt by the organisation to make it possible for workers to apply themselves over a longer period of the working day. The assumption is that quality of work performance will not drop as opportunities are provided to increase the quantity of output.

THE HISTORICAL EVOLUTION FROM CRAFT TO ADMINISTRATIVE SYSTEMS

For the early portion of the Industrial Revolution, the craft system represented a viable and perhaps the only feasible manpower system. From management's point of view, it was acceptable because employment was intermittent and management was not in a position through its own devices to wrestle with the issues of manpower utilisation. The small firm employing workers for short periods of time had to hire skills that were available in the labour market. Even where employment tended to be more stable and workers were retained for extended periods of time, management was not in a position to establish its own occupations or skill clusters because it did not possess the expertise required to design and administer a special wage structure. It was much easier and, indeed, in most instances, absolutely essential to employ workers within the established craft lines.

Moreover, the craft system represented an economical system for management in that training costs were largely borne by the labour market. To the extent that training under the craft system took place as workers moved from site to site, the costs were absorbed by many employers. Occupational lines might not always have been appropriate for the needs of particular employers, but distribution of workers and skills into more specialised clusters would have required considerable training; and with employment somewhat intermittent, a sufficiently long 'payout period' was not available to make such an investment worth while.

From the workers' point of view, the craft system also held many advantages. The training and exclusiveness that went with membership in a craft group provided workers with good pay and considerable status. Since their training was of a general nature, workers were able to sell their skills across the labour market and consequently did not become dependent upon any particular company for employment – which is the case with the specific training that accompanies a particularised clustering of skills and job duties.

Likewise, trade unions found the craft system compatible with their own needs for sovereignty and control of their membership. Workers did not become attached either economically or psychologically to any employer and gave their primary allegiance to the union as the protector of group interests.

However, as significant changes took place in the economic and technological environment, the craft system, which once was the only way of organising work and workers, became less appropriate in many situations. Growth in the size of product markets and the movement to larger-scale production made it possible for employers to hire workers for extended periods of time and to take advantage of the economies of scale that generally resulted from a high division of labour. Also, as management's competence improved, it became possible to organise new skill groupings and worker job assignments.[26] Therefore, from management's point of view it became both feasible and desirable to move toward an administrative system.

From the workers' point of view, if employment were stable, employment in semiskilled tasks rather than in highly skilled jurisdictions of the craft system might be acceptable. And, if the increased economies and productivity that went with a rationalised workplace made it possible for the workers to generate earnings that were as high as those enjoyed by craft workers, the economic needs of the workers could also be met.

In line with these new realities, some industries steadily shifted

[26] Clegg identifies growth of unit size and development of professional management as two key factors behind the emergence of rules and bureaucratisation. H. A. Clegg, *The System of Industrial Relations in Great Britain* (Oxford: Blackwell, 1970) 158.

away from the craft system and moved toward a more rationalised arrangement of jobs.[27] In some cases the change may have been swift enough for particular craft workers to feel the brunt of the change as they were forced into the background, into the maintenance departments, and into the speciality areas. But generally as the mass production and semiskilled portions of the enterprise developed, the transition was gradual and the changes in skill patterns took place as the industry expanded and new workers were hired.

ROLE OF PRODUCTIVITY BARGAINING

While in many instances this movement toward an administrative mode proceeded steadily and inexorably, in other instances little change occurred in the style of the manpower system – and yet the external circumstances had changed dramatically. In many industries, prior to productivity bargaining, technology had moved to the point where new skill groupings were required. Specialised equipment made it desirable for a company to hire workers at the bottom, train them, and move them to higher positions during their tenured careers. And yet the craft system which persisted prescribed inviolate occupational lines and emphasised horizontal mobility among firms within the jurisdiction of the union branch rather than vertical mobility within the establishment.

Shipbuilding and printing are two industries that, prior to the advent of productivity bargaining, were organised strictly according to the craft system but where the technology and the economics of production required a different manpower system. The craft system had persisted in part due to tradition, but mainly due to a lingering concern over job security. Unlike engineering, where employment was relatively stable, employment in these industries, for particular sections of the workforce, was intermittent and uncertain.

A shift away from the craft system was only possible after the parties in productivity bargaining came to grips with the question

[27] Space does not permit a discussion of this historical evolution from the craft to the administrative system on an industry-by-industry basis. The engineering industry represents one such case and several studies clearly document the gradual transition over the last fifty or sixty years. See J. B. Jefferys, *The Story of the Engineers, 1800–1945* (London 1946). For the cotton industry, see H. A. Turner, *Trade Union Growth, Structure and Policy.*

of job security and after the unions had participated fully in discussions about the appropriate redesign of the manpower system. It became the special function of productivity bargaining, therefore, to bring the design of shopfloor relations more into line with the requirements of the work system.

From this interpretative standpoint, productivity bargaining represented a device for introducing and accelerating certain historical processes affecting the organisation of work. This aspect of productivity bargaining, allowing the work organisation to catch up with the environmental requirements, is seen most strongly in the industries cited, but there seems little doubt that this characteristic was present in many other industrial situations. The common condition for these developments was the presence of inertia and insecurity (in a variety of forms), and it was the special contribution of productivity bargaining that it suggested methods of overcoming these problems via new forms of work organisation.

Moreover, even where the gap between organisational needs and the existing structure was not so great, the general approach to change was still frequently constrained by the conventional view of workforce alignment. Here, too, productivity bargaining served to widen the perspective and to create the climate for a cultural change which could, for example, provide the opportunity for a continuous up-dating and realignment of work organisation as the need emerged.

This view of productivity bargaining as a device to restore equilibrium or to provide the means to achieving a moving equilibrium through time – and these really have to be seen as distinct possibilities, involving different strategic approaches paralleled in our direct/indirect dichotomy – is thus seen to be quite general. While it may be too much to ask of this interpretation that it should be sufficiently general to embrace all cases, we would argue that it provides an important and widely applicable principle that has been implicit in much of the recent history of productivity bargaining in Britain.

11 Implications for the Future

The purpose of this chapter is to look ahead and to consider, for the next decade, what are the prospects for productivity bargaining as weighed against those for other approaches that might be addressed to the same set of problems. The main burden of the chapter is, therefore, to assess the present standing of productivity bargaining, and to observe the emergence of other possible approaches. The chapter closes with a view on the role of productivity bargaining in the United States and in Britain in the foreseeable future.

1. THE OUTLOOK

DIMINISHED ROLE FOR PRODUCTIVITY BARGAINING

Productivity bargaining of the traditional sort has lost its momentum. This conclusion relates to the increased difficulty with which *de novo* agreements are being negotiated, as well as to the emergence of counterproductive forces in situations where second and third generation agreements have been negotiated.[1]

The background factors which have been responsible for the growth of resistance to new agreements have already been sufficiently spelled out in the introduction to Chapter 10. Both economic forces and changes in the institutional environment have brought about a change in the atmosphere of collective bargaining,

---

[1] It should be noted that the discussion in this section relates to the *direct* approach to productivity bargaining. As Chapter 9 indicated, the experience with indirect approaches, though limited, does not suggest diminishing returns.

resulting in a shift away from the favourable conditions which existed for much of the 1960s. To some extent, these factors also help to explain the diminishing success of second-generation agreements, but a few specific points may usefully be spelled out a little further.

The smaller size of potential achievement. The cream has been skimmed off many situations by the first agreements, and subsequent exercises have generated only small savings. Productivity bargaining has tended to work best when the utility matching that is involved identifies working practices worth a lot of money to the company and not too much to the workers (for example, abandoning jurisdictional restrictions). At some stage, productivity bargaining must reach the end of the line for such attractive exchanges. This is particularly true in cases where the main breakthrough takes the form of a revision of wage structure or the introduction of work measurement. At the end of the first round, a certain amount of rectification may be needed to remove anomalies, but the scope for major changes producing large-scale savings is likely to be limited. Much the same conclusion applies where some major deficiencies in work organisation have been eliminated during the first or second round of negotiations, and further changes of significance prove hard to identify.

Even if 'bothersome' practices still persist, their abandonment may be very costly to the workers, and in some cases unacceptable to them. On the obverse side, we have encountered a number of situations in which union officials in secondary productivity bargaining talks offered up practices thought to involve very significant concessions on their part, only to be told by management (after costing estimates had been prepared) that the savings were relatively small. Such developments not only make productivity bargaining economically difficult, they also discourage the unions when they realise their proposals are so inconsequential.

Pressure for larger rewards. As productivity bargaining has proceeded, pressures for larger rewards have mounted from the workers' side. This can mean larger rewards in an absolute sense, as well as their relative share of the generated savings. Several factors have been responsible for this development. Perhaps the most important has been the calculating mentality that inevitably develops as workers learn the rules of the new game. In negotiating an initial productivity agreement, workers may be quite happy to settle for a wage increase in the range of 5 to 10 per cent since this would be well above their aspirations. However, as they become more sophisticated, as productivity bargains develop elsewhere and produce handsome returns, their own aspirations move upwards. Thus, they are influenced both by developments elsewhere as productivity bargaining diffuses throughout the economy, and by their own experience under productivity agreements. Further impetus may derive from growing awareness that while a first-round agreement may have brought them substantial gains, the rewards to the employer have been much greater, and pressure for a larger share to the workers, or for more knowledge on the magnitude of the overall savings, may well come into play at the second round.

This tendency for productivity bargaining to induce a more calculating approach has been cited by many authorities. In its testimony before the Royal Commission, the C.B.I. said that, 'If restrictive practices were bought out, productivity bargaining could lead logically to the creation of new practices, which the workers would then want to sell as a saleable commodity'.[2] Some empirical evidence supports this point. For example, Esso at Fawley found that as they progressed from the Blue Book to the Orange Book, workers became quite concerned about the value of restrictive practices and entered into negotiations with a very calculating attitude.[3]

Diminished incentive. The net effect of the two preceding trends is that there has been less enthusiasm on both sides to enter into productivity bargaining because the *quid pro quo* has become less attractive. From management's side, the proportion of savings which can be retained has diminished, as a result of increased emphasis on the principle of personal parity and the requirement that the earnings position of each worker should be maintained. From the workers' side, the return to the contributing group has been lessened to the extent that the savings are shared with comparable workers : in other words, the emphasis on outcome parity has limited the amount of rewards left for distribution to the

---

[2] George Cattell, *The Times* (3 July 1969). K. Jones and J. Golding, *Productivity Bargaining*, Fabian Research Series, 257 (London : Fabian Society, 1966) 49–50, also observe this tendency.

[3] Hawkins also presents an example of the same calculating orientation in his Case Z. See K. Hawkins, 'Productivity Bargaining; A Reassessment', *Industrial Relations Journal*, Spring 1971, pp. 10–34.

primary group. As long as the principle of exchange parity remains dominant (that is, big gains to those who make big contributions), productivity bargaining retains a high incentive for the primary parties, but as the other industrial relations principles come into the picture, productivity bargaining becomes less attractive.

Increased conflict. As would be expected, given the diminished scope for achievement and the demands for higher rewards, the negotiation of new productivity agreements has been accompanied by considerable conflict and other evidences of difficulty.

In the late 1960s during negotiations for a new agreement at Mobil Coryton, the craftsmen worked 'unenthusiastically' and stuck to the old rule book as a way of putting pressure on management to adhere to their demands. The experience of Otis Elevator also illustrates the difficulties encountered along these lines as a result of successive productivity bargains. In a series of agreements signed in 1961, 1964 and 1967, good progress was made in overhauling the incentive system and wage structure as well as achieving greater flexibility in the utilisation of worker skills. However, in 1969 when the company proposed more improvements in flexibility and the use of work measurement techniques as well as the ability to schedule overtime as required, negotiations stalemated and stewards, under pressure from district officials, refused to engage in any more productivity bargaining.

More generally, the period from late 1969 to 1971 was characterised by a rise in industrial unrest, much of which could be traced to difficulties over the continuation of productivity bargaining. A few examples will suffice to illustrate. In the case of British Rail, only six months after a 5 per cent increase related to efficiency in August 1969, the Associated Society of Locomotive Engineers and Firemen sought to break away from productivity bargaining and to pursue a 10 per cent increase across the board; 750,000 local government manual workers demanded a 20 per cent increase in basic pay and another 10 per cent for those not on productivity schemes; London dockers *refused* a 25 per cent increase in earnings conditional on co-operation in modernisation plans; and even late in 1971 the Union of Post Office Workers, still bitter at the memory of the earlier postal strike, rejected proposals (backed by the executive) that would have involved the introduction of a new work and staff measurement scheme in sorting offices. Thus, quite apart from the growing unwillingness of workers to engage in productivity bargaining for reasons of reduced return, and the consequential resort to 'pressure' tactics in negotiations, there were signs that the presence of productivity 'strings' were themselves becoming objectionable in some sectors.

Finally, to these sources of resistance, there has now to be added the fear that further productivity deals will only worsen the already gloomy unemployment situation by introducing further manpower economies.

OPTIONS FOR THE FUTURE

In view of the diminished attraction of productivity bargaining for tackling some of the persistent problems of the workplace, what other options are available? While many contenders can be listed, only four candidates will be discussed: scientific management, technological change, manpower planning, and participation-achievement-reward (PAR) systems. The first two options follow logically from the theme of management initiative, while the second two follow from the other theme developed in the last chapter, namely, the importance of satisfying workers' needs and recognising the importance of participation and mutuality. In this sense, the first two options take the defensive posture of trade unions as a datum and assert that management must use the 'new tools' and technological change to improve the operating situation; while the second two options work from the assumption that unions and workers want to be involved and will play a constructive role in the design of workplace relations.

2. THE SCIENTIFIC MANAGEMENT OPTION

Many companies feel that the solution for achieving improvement on a continuing basis falls within the exclusive domain of the company, namely, better management. Productivity bargaining, from this perspective, represents an opportunity for management to recast the organisation into a form that is capable of adapting to change. According to this view, effective management, efficiently organised, and equipped to instal and monitor the latest techniques for the improvement of managerial control, is the only sure answer to improving worker productivity and employee relations on a long-term basis.[4]

ASSUMPTIONS

Several important assumptions underlie the scientific management option. One is that many major hindrances to increased productivity lie within the management realm. For example, inadequate scheduling (a management weakness) with a resultant lack of raw materials and unnecessary downtime may exert a much more devastating impact on the overall effectiveness of the plant than excessive breaks from work on the part of the workers. A second assumption is that workers are not concerned about the ideological issues of control and participation, and are willing to go along with good management in a programme of productivity improvement – which is, on this view, essentially a process of solving day-to-day problems with competent leadership. If management has the competence and the right framework for action, workers will accept the system. Moreover, the economic results for both sides will be more than satisfactory.

LIMITATIONS

While the scientific management approach holds some promise, it also contains some inherent limitations. One important problem is that foremen may lose position relative to staff groups who handle the new tools. Specifically, job evaluation and work measurement require the guidance of specialists and consequently first-line supervisors are not at the centre of the picture.

A second drawback is that scientific management does not represent an open-ended or ongoing system. Management may, for a period of time, be able to operate effectively with the new tools, but eventually they have to go back to the bargaining table. Our investigations have revealed that in a number of companies where

---

[4] One of the clearest statements of this is quoted by E. O. Smith, in *Productivity Bargaining* (London: Pan, 1971). In the view of one junior manager at the Steel Company of Wales, the Green Book productivity proposals were superfluous: 'The existing labour force could have remained if only management could have organised itself in a more efficient manner. Involving junior management, but at the same time maintaining the necessary amount of authority, seems to be a growing problem in industry' (p. 414).

productivity bargaining has led to the installation of payment-by-results schemes as short-term arrangements for increasing effort, revisions have now become desirable, and this requires a return to negotiations.

Beyond this 'plateau effect' of scientific management, there is the additional possibility of drift 'back down the slope'. For example, it is not clear that management on its own can maintain the integrity of an incentive system. The inevitable pressures towards demoralisation are too strong for management to withstand by itself. Similarly, the use of job evaluation is no guarantee that drift and disorder will not gradually re-enter the wage structure. While in the short run job evaluation may eliminate some coercive comparisons, over the long run persistent pressures due to shortage of labour, and militant unions, may once again produce a breakdown of orderly relationships.

The most serious drawback to the scientific management approach is that it assumes that management can organise and administer the affairs of the work place unilaterally. While in some cases this 'unitary' view[5] may be viable, in most instances it overlooks the necessity and even desirability of worker participation.

3. TECHNOLOGICAL CHANGE

A second strategic option depends on the elimination of inefficiencies stemming from poor labour utilisation and protective practices by means of a thorough-going programme of technological change. More capital-intensive methods of production, including advanced automation techniques, can be deployed in such a way as to cut out completely some production stages in which low productivity or difficult industrial relations have persisted. In some respects, such a strategy has much to recommend it in the British context where, by international standards, the amount of new capital invested in advanced technology appears to be on the low side for many industries.

American experience suggests that, aside from increased productivity directly stemming from labour-saving devices, the introduction of new technology should also eliminate many other

[5] A. Fox, 'Managerial Ideology and Labour Relations', *British Journal of Industrial Relations*, Vol. IV (November 1966) 366–78; and *Industrial Sociology and Industrial Relations*, Royal Commission Research Paper No. 3 (London: H.M.S.O., 1966).

productivity problems. Summarising the U.S. experience, three experts concluded :

> It should be observed that managements do not remain passive in the face of restrictive practices. Years may be required, but most (not all) restrictive practices are eventually discontinued or their application substantially narrowed. Technological change is the most effective . . . weapon against them.[6]

But what has been the British experience? The introduction of technological change in several industries has been characterised by union opposition and an atmosphere of deadlock. Whether we are referring to the use of containers for cargo on the docks, larger truck capacities in distribution, 'liner trains' on railways, or a variety of new devices in printing, the road towards the introduction and utilisation of new equipment has been long and tortuous. Even where technological change has taken place, it does not appear universally to have swept away outmoded practices. Indeed, it would appear that these are precisely the industries where problems have arisen in the greatest intensity : disputes over crew sizes, skill jurisdictional battles, prohibition on increased driving speeds, and temporary bans on operating new equipment. Some confirmation for this association can be seen in the data presented in Chapters 4 and 5, where (admittedly weak) relationships were discovered between capital intensity (implying greatest historical experience of technological change,[7] and (1) the coverage of productivity bargaining; and (2) the prominence of skill utilisation features on the achievement side of the agreements.

Additionally, this provides further support for the general proposition that the main function of productivity bargaining in many situations has been to update the work organisation to match the existing technology. In effect, productivity bargaining has provided the means, though delayed in time, of establishing more appropriate crew sizes, skill jurisdictions, and shift schedules

---

[6] Sumner H. Slichter, James J. Healy and E. Robert Livernash, *The Impact of Collective Bargaining on Management* (Washington : The Brookings Institution, 1960) 333.

[7] We do not have a direct measure of the rate of technological change occurring on an industry-by-industry basis. Instead we have assumed for purposes of argument that the degree of capital intensity mirrors the amount of technological change that has occurred over an extended period of time for a given industry.

– arrangements that might have been introduced when the new technology was initially installed.

The two processes of technological change and productivity bargaining have been relatively divorced from one another, in British experience. An illustration comes from one of our case studies on Fleet Street, where despite vast technological changes, some already installed and others on the horizon, productivity bargaining has surprisingly steered clear of this subject. To be sure, the focus of the agreement on demanning could be explained in terms of the labour-saving equipment that had been installed, but the emphasis was on the *implications* rather than on the introduction of the new technology, *per se*,[8] and this is typical of several other cases.

The reluctance to make productivity bargaining a vehicle for technological change has perhaps stemmed from a fear on the part of the parties of overwhelming productivity bargaining with a complex and imposing issue – with the result that no agreement would take place. Just this has happened in the newspaper industry in New York City, where little progress has been made with productivity bargaining due to the importance given by both sides to getting acceptance of new technology, such as computers and photo-electric type setting; while in London, where the subjects have been separated, considerable progress has been made with productivity bargaining.

Here, then, is a possible springboard for the future. The experience of productivity bargaining in working out acceptable arrangements for change could be used to foster the introduction of new technology in difficult situations. Rather than having productivity bargaining confine itself merely to updating manpower and skill arrangements for existing technology, productivity bargaining might be used as a device for 'paving the way' for new technology and the associated changes in the work system. This has occurred

---

[8] We do not want to adopt the categorical position that an issue such as technological change has been *completely* absent from productivity bargaining. In several agreements, clauses have appeared with wording such as: 'increased use of computer' and 'operation of new plant and equipment'. But only five agreements out of some eighty or more that were examined carried any mention of this subject and when they did the emphasis was on reaffirming management's general right to introduce new technology. Even in the classic disputes concerning new technology such as at Tilbury over handling containers and at Southwark over web offset, the emphasis has been on manning and payment issues and not on the *fact* of the new technology.

to some extent in the implementation of the Manpower Productivity Plan (the so-called Green Book) at the Steel Company of Wales, where an important element in the overall programme has been the facilitation of the introduction of a massive technological change. Technological redundancy was linked in this case with redundancy due to working practice alterations, and the savings made possible from the two sources being used jointly to finance high, stable earnings and, for those who would leave, enhanced redundancy payments. Even in this case, however, the productivity deal was used as much to make the consequences of change acceptable as to ensure the acceptance of the new technology itself.

4. MANPOWER PLANNING

Any fusion of productivity bargaining with the process of technological change will need to include another element : manpower planning. Indeed, in many situations, technological change has been blocked because of workers' resistance stemming from concern over job losses. It is for this reason that productivity bargaining, as it confronts the need for more technological change, must also embrace a heavy element of manpower planning.

Concern about job security contributes greatly to the current resistance to productivity bargaining, as we have seen, and in the high-unemployment situation of 1972 this concern is inevitably heightened. Workers and union representatives are much less enthusiastic about improving productivity at the cost of fewer jobs, when many people are looking for employment. Several cases can be cited where, after a period of willing acceptance of manpower reductions, handled by means of internal redeployment, a fall in overtime and the deterioration in the general economic situation has led to growing concern about subcontracting and the retention of a full workforce.

In other instances union leaders have not been content to accept the principle of no redundancy. They have been concerned about attrition and wastage which can lead to the diminution of their own organisation as well as the loss of jobs for the 'community'. This has clearly been the fear which caused one union executive in Birmingham in the spring of 1971 to announce that they were 'restricting all productivity agreements which involved any form of demanning, be it by a reduction in labour force or a restriction of jobs created'.[9] Similar examples have occurred elsewhere, notably on Clydeside.

Thus, within a setting of high unemployment and concern about job loss, new productivity agreements that reduce labour requirements are not an attractive possibility. Does this mean that manpower planning is something that has to be placed on the shelf? On the contrary, it can be argued that special manpower programmes are even more urgently required to deal with the 'hangover' effects of productivity bargaining. In many situations where productivity bargaining has been practised, a 'labour reserve' has been created. The productivity programme has moved ahead of manpower adjustments,[10] and the need has emerged for a period of 'digestion', wherein the workers who have been displaced are trained for other employment within the establishment as openings develop. This may entail new training schemes, special efforts at upgrading workers previously thought to be limited in skills, and a much more comprehensive analysis of manpower retention rates, wastage and future manpower needs.[11]

In some situations where excess manpower is on hand, it may be necessary to adopt the Ford approach of temporarily laying off workers. This action represents a modified no-redundancy pledge in the sense that the workers are not severed from the company and receive pay while in layoff status as well as retaining priority for recall. This is the conventional American approach which enables a company to interrupt temporarily the services of workers, meanwhile paying benefits which enable the workers to hold out until they are recalled as employment once again picks up.

While manpower planning is absolutely essential in the short run and comprises a very important element of any future productivity improvement programme, it is not a strategy that in and of itself can create productivity improvement. Rather, manpower planning is a device that facilitates change that has been arrived

[9] *The Record* (April 1971) 6.

[10] In some instances, the improvements in benefits and working conditions created by the agreements have lowered turnover rates, thereby producing a larger labour reserve than expected.

[11] Such careful and comprehensive manpower planning can be seen in the experience of the chemical industry. Using a combination of transfer, retraining, resettlement, early retirement, and redundancy pay, management and unions were able successfully to handle major revisions in manning requirements. See L. C. Hunter, G. L. Reid and D. Boddy, *Labour Problems of Technological Change* (London: Allen & Unwin, 1970) 252–71.

at through other strategies. It is essentially a means of eliminating the negative rather than creating the positive in industrial relations. We now turn to one method for stimulating a positive thrust in the efficiency of the work system and in the character of union–management relations.

5.   THE POSSIBILITY FOR A NEW DEPARTURE

What may be called for in many situations is a formula for the productivity–pay nexus that combines the realism and pragmatism of the direct approach to productivity change with the continuing concern with change and organisational involvement of the indirect approach. Perhaps because of the incomes policy framework in which it thrived, perhaps for other reasons, productivity bargaining as generally practised until now has commonly suffered from the defect of being a short-term measure. In a majority of cases, the open-ended, indirect approach, wherein the parties join forces to improve the work system on a continuous basis, has been disregarded in favour of the direct, short-run approach.

If there are limitations to the potential deriving from this sort of productivity bargaining, so also do these limits exist in the utilisation of wage systems as a means of stimulating productivity achievement. It has been a special feature of productivity bargaining that it has concentrated attention on a wide range of cost items, not just on the increase of output emphasised by most payment-by-results plans. The challenge then is to bring together the encompassing quality of productivity bargaining with the systematic and ongoing quality of wage-payment systems.

The kind of system that we have in mind is not new. It has been referred to by various names : as an efficiency agreement by the N.B.P.I.,[12] as a programme for higher efficiency by Esso, as a company-wide incentive scheme by the C.I.R.,[13] as a long-range sharing plan by Kaiser Steel,[14] and as a Scanlon Plan[15] by a number of companies in the United States and the United Kingdom. All these ideas have three themes in common : participation, achievement, and reward. As a shorthand version for describing this approach we will use the term PAR.[16]

Underlying PAR is the notion that productivity improvement is an organisation-wide task and that important gains – such as conservation of materials, acceptance of new machinery and methods, more flexibility in work arrangements and better co-ordination of work groups – can best be achieved when strong emphasis is placed on common interests and the importance of teamwork.

It is not surprising, then, that PAR-type plans, which place such heavy emphasis on co-operation, are usually formulated in an atmosphere of collaboration. The Kaiser Plan resulted from a two-year study by a joint union–management committee that was established shortly after the 1959 steel strike. Similarly, most of the Scanlon Plan installations have emerged from joint study and consultation. While the concept of total group motivation has theoretical appeal, it can only be made effective when ways are found for involving the energies and interests of a large proportion of the employees. This calls for a structure of committees and communication, both at departmental and plant levels. A number of studies have demonstrated the positive effects on productivity and motivation that stem from participation. A recent illustration of

[12] See N.B.P.I. Report No. 123.

[13] In its report on Clayton Dewandre the C.I.R. commented : 'If the parties prefer some form of incentive system then we would consider it vital that it be a company-wide system. Any form of individual or small group payment by results system is likely to be quickly eroded and end up with the same sort of problems as the present system. The simplest form of collective bonus would be one which was based either on the total output of the company as measured by some agreed method, or on the performance of employees generally as measured by an overall index. This index is derived from work studying a full range of jobs and then noting subsequent increases in output and compositing them.

'A more sophisticated form of company-wide incentive scheme, for which there are a number of precedents, would be a scheme whereby bonus is distributed according to movements in the ratio between the total wages bill and the value of production or the value added in the production process. A drop in the ratio of the wages bill to the value of production produces bonus payments for distribution to every employee in proportion to his pay.' C.I.R. Report No. 15, Cmnd 4640 (London : H.M.S.O., 1971).

[14] For a detailed description of the Kaiser Plan, see Harold Stieglitz, *The Kaiser-Steel Union Sharing Plan*, Studies in Personnel Policy, No. 187 (New York : National Industrial Conference Board, 1963).

[15] For information about the Scanlon Plan, see Fred G. Lesieur, *The Scanlon Plan* (Cambridge : The Technology Press, 1958). Also, for an analysis of the philosophical perspective and managerial style inherent in the Scanlon Plan, see D. M. McGregor, *The Human Side of Enterprise* (New York : McGraw-Hill, 1960).

[16] Some of the material in this section has been taken from previously published work. See R. B. McKersie, 'Wage Payment Methods of the Future', *British Journal of Industrial Relations* (June 1963) Vol. I, 191–212; and G. P. Shultz and R. B. McKersie, 'Stimulating Productivity: Choices, Problems and Shares', *British Journal of Industrial Relations*, Vol. V (March 1967) 1–18.

this has been cited in a study in a British paper mill in which extensive participation was used to good advantage for both sides. The object of the exercise was 'to consider ways in which productive efficiency at the mill could be improved'. The results were summarised as follows : 'The exercise had the substantial morale-building effect that we wanted, in that it established a new understanding among groups and it gave management a new opportunity for improved industrial relations.'[17]

Like any system of incentive wage payment, PAR uses a formula or norm against which improved performance can be gauged. In most Scanlon Plans the ratio relates labour costs to some measure of output, usually the sales value of production. Important changes in technology, product mix, wages, or prices provide the occasion for review of the ratio. Savings are divided in a pre-agreed fashion between the workers and the company – with a small portion of the savings being accumulated for various reserves. The Kaiser Plan goes further in both job guarantees and sources of savings: the problem of potential displacement is met by guaranteeing that no one will lose employment due to the working of the plan or the introduction of new technology; and gains are shared from technological change and the more efficient utilisation of materials, as well as from increased labour efficiency.

PAR plans usually involve the active participation of a union, although in the absence of a union the approach has still been effective. The involvement of the union means that production problems become the focus for joint efforts rather than being left solely to management, and that workers can use the union–management machinery for communicating constructive ideas rather than just for voicing complaints.

EMERGENCE OF PAR

In some respects productivity bargaining has set the stage for PAR by eliminating a number of persistent problems, which tend to inhibit the functioning of a PAR-type system. Overtime is one such example. As long as workers feel insecure or fear that they will be taking money out of one pocket and putting it into another as a result of applying themselves more diligently, they will not be

17 Anne Shaw, 'Participation in a Paper Mill', *Personnel Management* (July 1970), Vol. 2, No. 7, 20.

interested in a PAR-type system. Introducing PAR into a situation of extensive overtime would evoke the following kind of response by workers : 'Why should we work more efficiently, only to lose premium pay and be rewarded with smaller bonuses?' Similarly, if the workers feel that the result of more productivity is redundancy, a PAR approach would not be attractive. Therefore, to the extent that productivity bargaining has established a 'firm foundation' by eliminating overtime, by providing guarantees against redundancy, by dealing with basic problems of insecurity in fluctuating pay and disorganised wage structures, the reward side has been stabilised and a PAR approach can start on a good footing.

Similarly, on the achievement side productivity bargaining has paved the way by eliminating looseness that is more susceptible to a buy-out than to a PAR system. A PAR system does not make sense in the presence of major problems which can be tackled quite directly through the surgery of productivity bargaining, such as elimination of idle time and introduction of work measurement. Once these aspects of slack have been eliminated, the organisation is in a position to tackle those forms of achievement which require increased co-ordination and diligence on a continuing basis.

There are signs already that elements of the PAR approach have begun to emerge. For example, at Fawley a standing joint committee is in operation, the agreements are open-ended and the succession of productivity bargains has begun to resemble an *ad hoc* PAR approach.[18]

> The function of the Joint Productivity Committee is to produce recommendations in the area of Craft/T.G.W.U. flexibility which will be used as the basis for a further agreement.

In other instances, the sharing of benefits 'after the fact' has created a feedback quality characteristic of ongoing systems. For example, in the Post Office (telecommunications) case, savings are calculated regularly and the parties agree once a year on the allocation. The same approach is being taken at B.P. Chemicals.

> The present agreement demands an assessment of savings made at the end of twelve months from the date of implementation

---

[18] For an additional point of view on Fawley, one that also emphasises the movement towards an efficiency approach, see N.B.P.I. Report No. 123, pp. 8–9.

(1 October 1969). The results of the assessment will be used by joint agreement to modify the agreement for its second year of operation. This process of review is expected to continue annually for at least a third year. It is difficult to assess how far beyond the third year the process will be sufficient. It is safe to assume that whatever is decided will be by joint consultation and involvement of the parties concerned.[19]

Perhaps one of the best examples of productivity bargaining evolving into a participation approach is British Oxygen. In the initial phase of productivity bargaining, emphasis was placed on reducing hours and attacking the problems of extra manning. In the second phase, emphasis has been switched to the discussion of principles and the establishment of a productivity committee.[20]

LIMITED APPLICABILITY OF PAR

While the PAR concept has considerable theoretical merit, it is *not* likely to be used very widely. Some of the factors inhibiting the greater use of PAR are attitudinal, such as management's hesitancy to become involved in a full-fledged participation system. Elsewhere, the difficulty stems from the inability of the productivity committees to function effectively.[21] Some of the factors are more inherent in the PAR concept itself. Like any wage-payment system, PAR experiences a continuing tension over the adequacy of norms for establishing the amount and division of the savings. The question then arises of how to re-gear the system. Sometimes it can be done gracefully by the parties; or sometimes it requires protracted bargaining, which may in many respects resemble productivity bargaining.

The technical design of a PAR system is also critical. Adequate rewards must be generated, otherwise the workers will not be interested. On the other hand, if the rewards are too large, man-

---

[19] Based on correspondence.

[20] For elaboration and citation of the emphasis on participation at British Oxygen, see the following: N.B.P.I. Reports No. 36, p. 18; No. 123, p. 6; and Commentary on 'British Oxygen Phase II', *Personnel* (April 1969) p. 3.

[21] In his discussion of Case Z, Kevin Hawkins describes the difficulty encountered in one situation where joint union–management productivity committees failed 'to maintain control over the actual achievement of the productivity targets'. See K. Hawkins, 'Productivity Bargaining: A Reassessment', pp. 10–34.

agement will be reluctant to allow the plan to continue. This requirement of equity extends to the work-group level where any perceived disparities in inputs and contributions to the uniformly shared rewards will create considerable difficulty and disillusionment.[22]

For these reasons both management and union representatives may be reluctant to enter into such a high-risk endeavour. They fear getting locked into something that may not produce equitable results for both sides. Moreover, a poorly functioning plan may not be too easy to abandon. Rather than embarking upon a formal system, the parties may prefer to retain the flexibility inherent in the *ad hoc* approach to questions of efficiency. This is the essence of productivity bargaining.

6. THE ROLE OF PRODUCTIVITY BARGAINING IN THE FORESEEABLE FUTURE

Having outlined the essence of several other options for improving productivity, it is appropriate at this point to return to the subject of productivity bargaining. While its role for the moment is somewhat in doubt, it still merits serious consideration for the future. None of the other options represents an ideal solution and it is unlikely that any of them will be used as extensively as productivity bargaining was during the decade of the sixties. Even a system, such as PAR, which has much theoretical appeal has some very important practical limitations. It is doubtful that PAR will ever be used in more than a small fraction of establishments in Britain. In the United States, the incidence of coverage by PAR-type systems is still well under 1 per cent.

We have seen in Chapter 10 that many of the problems that were in existence at the start of the 1960s are still on the scene. While productivity bargaining has, in general, yielded some improvement, even at its peak its penetration was limited to one-third of the workforce at most, and its real impact was almost certainly much less. Consequently, much of British industry has not been touched by the concept. For this reason, then, considerable potential remains for additional productivity bargaining.

[22] Problems of this sort were in large part responsible for the demise of the Linwood plan.

The need for the extension of productivity bargaining is under-scored by the fact that its incidence, relatively speaking, has been no more extensive in craft than in semiskilled and unskilled situations. Although we noted in Chapter 3 a small positive relation between productivity bargaining and the proportion of craft workers, the result was not significant. And yet, in view of our argument in Chapter 10 that the need for and the potential impact of productivity bargaining is greatest where a shift occurs from a craft to an administrative system we might have expected a bias towards craft-dominated sectors.

The potential is also great for the spread of productivity bargaining to the service sector, to government, and to white-collar employment. The extent to which these industries have been un-touched by productivity bargaining can be seen in the tables presented in Chapters 2 and 3.

And even for those instances where productivity bargaining already has been tried, it is quite likely that additional productivity bargaining may very well be required. As we noted in Chapter 8, overtime has a tendency to reassert itself, sometimes up to pre-productivity bargaining levels; piecework systems often deteriorate over time; and many of the other items that were corrected through productivity bargaining can 'drift' back into difficulty.

Moreover, with respect to the 'catch-up' function that productivity bargaining has performed, there are likely to be many opportunities for recasting the work organisation to meet the changing requirements of technology and production. Thus, in addition to the persistence of long-standing problems and the resurgence of former problems, there is the distinct possibility that a *new* set of problems will emerge in the foreseeable future for which productivity bargaining may be an effective solution. As technical advance continues, we can expect to see a movement in many industries from mass production to the automatic mode of manu-facturing. This transition will carry with it the need further to integrate skills and to emphasise job enlargement, which has already represented an important theme of productivity bargaining. However, where the emphasis has previously been primarily on job enlargement across existing craft jurisdiction or between craft and process work, the new era on the horizon, especially for the process industries, will require the integration of skills across *all* functional categories into composite technician and mechanic classifications.

We are beginning to see evidence of this development in the chemical, oil, motor car, and steel industries where discussions have been taking place over the concept of refinery technician and other industry-specific versions of the 'all-round mechanic'. In some instances, discussions have focused on the complete merger of process and maintenance activities. The direction of all of these developments is towards the creation of new skill clusters that are industry-based and more encompassing.[23] We have already observed the fears that can accompany such a transition – the fears of becoming 'jack of all trades and master of none'. Yet this kind of basic work reorientation and cultural change is the very kind of adaptation which productivity bargaining promises to be able to achieve.

Moreover, we should pause to note a number of advantages that productivity bargaining possesses, which are especially important for repeating the process and for its viability over the long run. It is flexible; it does not have any of the problems inherent in a formal wage-payment system which specifies relationships between achievement and pay on a more permanent basis. The gearing between pay and productivity can be constantly changed under productivity bargaining. It also has the advantage of bringing issues of productivity and pay directly into the collective bargaining arena. Most wage-payment systems (and even PAR) establish a separate machinery and have a tendency to divorce matters of achievement and rewards from the normal collective bargaining process. This has the danger of returning industrial relations to the earlier era in which the consultation compartment was separated from the bargaining compartment. One of the great strengths of productivity bargaining has been the synthesis within the negotiation setting of all important elements of the work system and employment relationship.

One final point in favour of productivity bargaining is the experience that has been built up in a number of important sectors. While it is known that much that has gone on under the guise of productivity bargaining has been far from genuine, there is no doubt that managements and union representatives over a wide

[23] The discussion in the preceding chapter on the nature of the new administrative system bears on this point.

front have developed an appreciation of the potential of soundly based productivity bargaining, and success is liable to create a demand for extension and repetition. Admittedly, the scope for achievement may be smaller and the union may strike a harder bargain, but earlier experience can prove an important factor in the efficient design and implementation of new agreements. Undoubtedly, much of this experience is still capable of being tapped from the ranks of present-day management and union officials.

POTENTIAL OPPORTUNITIES FOR PRODUCTIVITY IMPROVEMENT
IN THE UNITED STATES[24]

This final review of the scope that still seems to exist for the application of productivity bargaining in Britain prompts the question whether at least some of the lessons of productivity bargaining experience might not be applied with some prospect of benefit to other countries, where even if the mix of circumstances is different, some of the main elements have a common character. Here we will limit discussion to the United States situation where events in the first two years of the seventies have suggested the presence of some similarities with the British context in the sixties.

We consider the two categories of industries which showed a particularly high incidence of productivity bargaining in Britain: (1) industries that operated on a craft system of production; and (2) manufacturing industries, where inefficient work arrangements produced discontinuities in production that were especially damaging to productivity.

In the industries based on the craft system, the efficiency problems in Britain and the United States are reasonably similar; and recent productivity bargaining in the U.S.A. has tackled these issues with some promising results – for example, in longshoring, construction, printing, railroading, and the airlines.

American industries involving the craft system represent about 10 per cent of total employment compared to 25 per cent in Britain;[25] and these are, no doubt, the industries that are most afflicted by work restrictions on manpower assignment and mobility. In a number of them, as for instance in construction, the transition from craft to industrialised modes of production had been severely retarded, if not obstructed. However, recent productivity bargaining agreements between the building trades and the modular and systems building manufacturers have bowed to the new technology and this has led to a partial breakdown of the craft system and the emergence of modernised assembly-line manufacturing.

An analogous development appears to be going on in the shipyards. A new production method involving assembly-line production has been successfully tried in Pascagoula, Mississippi, by the Ingalls West Shipyard, a division of Litton Industries. The new method greatly simplifies jobs and reduces skill requirements, training needs, and production time. Labour costs reportedly are 40 per cent below those in conventional shipbuilding.

With respect to manufacturing industries, where productivity deals have been prominent in Britain, there appears to be much less scope for improvement in the U.S.A. One reason for this pertains to differences in bargaining structures between the two countries. In the manufacturing sector of the U.S.A., the collective bargaining structure is relatively decentralised, with the single employer or plant as the prevailing unit of bargaining.[26] This has

---

[24] Much of the material in this section is taken from our paper prepared for the U.S. Productivity Commission.

[25] It is, of course, difficult to develop a precise estimate of the portion of the labour force covered by the craft system. As one approximation of the craft complement in an industry, one might take the percentage of apprentices. If one considers 2.5 or more per cent apprentices employed in an industry as an indication of a substantial craft element, then the following industries in Britain would qualify: metal manufacture, metal goods, engineering and electrical goods, vehicles, shipbuilding and marine engineering, instruments, printing, timber and furniture, and construction. These industries together constitute about 25 per cent of total employment in Britain. In the U.S.A., only construction and shipbuilding meet the criterion of minimally 2.5 per cent apprentices, which makes the total employment organised by the craft system somewhat less than 10 per cent, an estimate that was also obtained by Stinchcombe, by using a different estimating procedure. See A. L. Stinchcombe, 'Social Structure and Organizations', in *Handbook of Organizations*, ed. J. G. March (Chicago : Rand McNally, 1965), p. 166.

The main explanation for the differences in extent of craft organisation is the characteristic mode of work at the time when unionism was developing. Most manufacturing in the U.S.A. was not organised until the 1930s by which time it was at the mass-production stage. By contrast, in the U.K. the unionisation efforts took place earlier when the mode was more artisan and job shop in character – with the craft system remaining even as these industries entered the mass-production stage.

[26] See 'Major Union Contracts in the United States, 1961', *The Monthly Labor Review* (October 1962), Vol. 85, No. 10, 1137.

produced two structural properties significant for productivity considerations. It has led to a formal bargaining machinery at the company or plant level that can bargain effectively and with full and undisputed discretion. And it has focused attention on bargaining issues relating to productivity and originating at the level of the establishment.[27]

A second key difference between the two manufacturing sectors concerns the type of union control. The strongly prevailing craft system in many production industries in Britain[28] has exercised a major influence on the allocation of labour and the operation of the production process. As a result, technological innovations have been retarded and the savings of labour resources they make possible have been reduced in industries where in the U.S.A., by contrast, unions have generally shown a favourable attitude towards technological change and have co-operated in its implementation.

Nevertheless, the potential need for something akin to productivity bargaining in U.S.A. manufacturing should not be ruled out, mainly for two reasons. First, such industries are being increasingly exposed to international product competition; and they find themselves in a position of having to increase productivity to compensate for higher labour costs. Secondly, the growth of capital-intensive industries with process-type production has been accompanied by a concomitant growth of relatively 'closed' internal labour markets in large multi-plant firms.[29] In these industries, manpower adjustments through the incumbent workforces have often become more important than through the 'external' labour market. This has heightened the need for rules and practices that allow a great degree of internal flexibility and mobility.

The steel industry is a case in point. One of the issues in the 1959 steel strike was the demand for modification of the 'local' working conditions clause in all steel agreements. The companies

---

[27] For a valuable analysis of the industrial relations systems of Britain and the U.S.A., see J. W. Garbarino, 'British and American Labour Market Trends', *Scottish Journal of Political Economy*, Vol. XVII (June 1970) 319–36.

[28] A point made by Flanders and Fox, quoted in Chapter 5, bears repetition here, namely that many non-craft work-groups in Britain have increasingly adopted practices during the post-war years that are commonly ascribed only to craft groups.

[29] See P. B. Doeringer and M. J. Piore, *Internal Labor Markets and Manpower Analysis* (Lexington, Mass.: Heath, 1971) Chapter 3.

argued that this clause resulted in unnecessary manpower and prevented flexibility in job assignments. Although the final settlement provided for no change in the local working conditions, a committee was set up to study the problem. Three years later, the 1962 steel contract provided for an inter-regional preferential hiring programme in exchange for improvement in job and income security.[30] The most recent steel settlement of August 1971 includes a provision *for joint management–union efforts at the plant level to increase productivity.*[31]

In some industries, where productivity bargaining has been successfully used in Great Britain, there has been little interest in such bargaining in the United States – and yet a real potential for improvement in efficiency exists in this country in these same industries, which include the service industries and white-collar employment generally. In terms of relative employment, these industries are large and growing larger. In Britain, probably less than 10 per cent of the employees in these industries are covered currently by productivity agreements; however, where agreements have been entered into, the results have been noteworthy; they have brought about such improvements as the introduction of work measurement methods into offices, the development of flexible shifts (e.g. at the Covent Garden Opera House),[32] and the wider use of incentives in the water supply[33] and other local governmental agencies.

Productivity bargaining as practised in Britain has generally shown a certain style and substance that might usefully be transferred to industrial relations in the United States. British collective bargaining has increasingly been characterised by greater emphasis on consultation and worker participation than bargaining in the U.S.A.; and the British productivity bargaining agreements have built on this and have successfully employed joint labour–management design and regulation of the work system to the benefit of both management and labour.

In the United States, on the other hand, the attack on labour inefficiency has typically been through management initiative,

[30] See *Monthly Labor Review* (May 1962), Vol. 85, No. 5, 554.

[31] 'Developments in Industrial Relations' in Bureau of National Affairs, Washington D.C., *Daily Labor Report*, No. 148 (2 August 1971).

[32] G. Wood, 'Productivity Bargaining Encore', *Personnel Management* (November 1970) Vol. 2, No. 10, 48–52.

[33] See N.B.P.I. Report No. 152 (London: H.M.S.O., 1970).

with unions attempting to negotiate ways of coping with the consequences to the workforce and of obtaining a share of the savings. British labour has participated directly in shaping productivity achievements, but such direct participation has – except under the banner of Scanlon Plans and certain other forms of labour–management co-operation – generally been absent from the American scene. And even where productivity bargaining has been employed – as in longshoring – the American approach has tended to be short term, and has lacked the quality of ongoing co-operation between management and workforce more frequently found in productivity bargaining in Great Britain. The American approach has tended to be in the nature of a 'buy-out' – an exchange of money for certain specified concessions. While this approach has also been present in British productivity bargaining, in many instances there has also been an emphasis on continuous change, either through successive agreements or by way of general commitments to continuing co-operation.

As pointed out earlier, British productivity bargaining has also produced some important changes in the industrial relations system. Some of the innovations (such as term agreements and grievance procedures) are well established in the U.S.A., but others – especially in the area of revised bargaining structures – can provide especially pertinent examples of developments needed in the U.S.A. For example, in the American construction industry the bargaining structure has been unduly fractured; in railroading, it has been over-centralised. Both industries could learn something from British experience. The bargaining structure for the construction industry in Britain has been centralised for some time; however, this central machinery has been considerably strengthened through productivity bargaining – primarily so that both sides jointly can control the results and share in the rewards. On the other hand, British Rail, before productivity bargaining, typically decided everything 'at the top'; and productivity bargaining has introduced local working parties to devise methods for improving efficiency.

These two examples suggest that bargaining structures in the U.S.A. need to be both decentralised and centralised. They need to be decentralised for purposes of defining problems and developing solutions for work problems; and they need to be centralised so that both parties can exert proper control over the results.

British productivity bargaining has managed to achieve this mixture of local participation and central control in a number of important industries.

To summarise : both the British productivity bargaining experience and the more limited American experience have significance for American industry and unions today. In both countries there have been favourable results in a number of key industries. The British experience also suggests that the service industries, and those with large numbers of white-collar employees, represent potentially good opportunities for productivity bargaining – although such bargaining has not so far been extensively used in these situations in the United States.

It is true that most American companies have not encountered productivity problems comparable to those of their British counterparts; however, rising foreign competition and pressures for higher wages have intensified the problems of controlling unit costs. Moreover, in Britain where there has been greater emphasis on consultation and worker participation, productivity bargaining has opened the door to new and more co-operative attitudes.

PRODUCTIVITY BARGAINING AS A CYCLICAL PHENOMENON?

Finally, returning to the British situation which has been our main preoccupation in this book, we must ask whether it is realistic to expect the extension of productivity bargaining, which we have argued to be desirable, actually to come about. For the reasons presented in Chapter 10 and again at the beginning of this chapter, a negative answer seems to be in order. Yet on balance we believe that such a conclusion may be unduly pessimistic. We base this view on the scope which seems to exist for what may be termed a 'cyclical' use of productivity bargaining.

Experience to date has been that, after a moderate beginning in the early part of the 1960s, productivity bargaining mushroomed in the final years of the decade, to be succeeded by a period of considerably reduced activity. (This last statement is hard to quantify in the absence of data comparable to those for the years 1967–9, but there is little doubt about its validity : even then, it is important to note that productivity bargaining is by no means at a halt, and some important extensions and developments are still occurring.) These three phases of initial development, wide application and decline may be seen as a 'one-off' experience or as the first occurrence of a series of events which will appear again in the future, when a combination of circumstances materialises similar to that of the 1960s.

Can we then identify the circumstances which encourage the application of productivity bargaining, and can we expect to see such a set of conditions re-emerging during the 1970s? The two critical dimensions for such an exercise are *motivation* and *feasibility.*

Motivation.   For extensive use of productivity bargaining, both trade unions and employers must see some positive advantage in it for themselves. During the 1960s, the motivation on the employers' side stemmed primarily from growing consciousness of inefficiencies, particularly in labour utilisation, leading to poor unit cost performance : this was particularly important in areas of industry where international competition or comparison were operative. On the labour side, the motivation existed initially in the prospects of above-average wage increases. Where productivity levels and growth were low, so also wage levels and wage increases tended to be low, and the productivity agreement offered prospects of achieving a higher rate of improvement of rewards.

These two forms of motivation interacted in a general economic environment in which full employment existed but where policy to contain the growth of prices and incomes was always present. With the progressive development of incomes policy in the mid and late 1960s in the fight against inflation, the motivations of both employers and unions for the pursuit of productivity bargaining were enhanced. Finally, with the fading of incomes policy, and the growth of unemployment, the motivation declined, although in particular sectors and in many companies sufficient incentive remained for the parties to continue their joint explorations of the potential for productivity improvement. In general, however, the level of activity was much more subdued.

This analysis suggests that a renewed vigour in the use of productivity bargaining will require a reduction in unemployment as an essential starting condition. Only once this is achieved are trade unions likely to give general support to negotiations whose outcome may involve a reduction in employment or employment opportunity. On the employers' side, the indications are that at present, during relatively depressed economic conditions, considerable improvements have been effected in manpower utilisation, and again the scope for a general revival of enthusiasm is likely to be limited until the slack in the economy has been taken up. We have noted earlier the view of employers that when activity picks up, a more careful eye will be kept on tendencies to build up a new layer of 'fat' in the manning situation, but how far such pressures could be withstood in a buoyant economy is an open question. To the extent that employers yield to the pressures making for an excessive build-up of their workforce, the opportunities for retrenchment are likely to become available at about the same time as the need for a reimposition of closer regard to cost performance becomes necessary – that is, as the peak of the cycle is approached. This would also coincide with the time at which a renewed interest on the part of the unions might be shown, due to an improvement in the unemployment situation. Finally, if this combination of circumstances brings with it, as it has in the past, an intensification of inflationary tendencies, the probability of a renewal of formal incomes policy will be high. Even if the form of incomes policy differs from that of the late 1960s, which seems likely, some part of it must surely involve control over the wage–productivity relationship.

From the motivational point of view, then, no immediate resurgence of productivity bargaining on a wide front seems probable but, as the peak of the next cycle approaches, the conditions will become increasingly favourable. Whether or not it will materialise would seem, from the standpoint of the present day, to depend largely on the ability of employers to avoid building up employment slack during the upswing, the extent to which unemployment levels in the economy subside, and the timing and form of a re-application of incomes policy.

Feasibility. Motivation in itself may not prove a necessary condition for revival of productivity agreements. It will also be important that productivity bargaining is feasible, and in this connection the two most critical factors will be the suitability of the bargaining structure and the commitment of the necessary resources from unions and management.

The shake-up in bargaining structure achieved over the last few years, generally leading in the direction of increased plant and company-level bargaining, has undoubtedly produced a more favourable environment for productivity bargaining than that which existed in the mid-1960s. At that time, it will be remembered, many employers anxious to pursue a productivity bargaining strategy were obliged to withdraw from employers' associations to achieve the freedom of action demanded by the strategy.

The changes in bargaining structure since then have removed many of the problems, but we have seen some signs that pressures for a return to stronger central bargaining at industry level have been re-emerging. At the same time, there are indications that some employers – especially large employers with a number of separate plants – have been increasingly worried about the decentralisation of bargaining to plant level. The freedom which has previously been given to plant management to conduct their own negotiations may well be more restricted in future as the companies draw back towards greater central responsibility and control for wage negotiations. A further factor in the reckoning is the impact of industrial relations legislation and the implementation of the Code of Practice. We have seen that the expectation from these developments is a strengthening of the trend to plant and company negotiations, but the possibility of a 'backlash' effect should not be ruled out.

The question of resources has also been discussed in Chapter 10 where the point was made that the experience of productivity bargaining, built up in management hierarchies and the ranks of the trade unions over the last five years, is still available to be tapped when the opportunity presents itself. The importance of this can be emphasised by again turning back to the mid-1960s, when, with relatively few exceptions, the know-how of management and unions in plant-level bargaining was extremely limited – aside of course from *ad hoc* negotiations on piece-rates and bonuses. The result, not infrequently, was a series of false steps by participants on both sides, and in some cases it was only in the second-round negotiations that sufficient confidence existed to make real progress possible.

CONCLUSIONS

While some important uncertainties remain, the general outcome of this review of motivations and feasibility relating to a new initiative in the field of productivity bargaining is that a further cycle of activity, similar to that of the 1960s, could well develop later in the 1970s, with the timing depending largely on the timing and character of developments at the macro-economic level. It would be surprising, however, if a second cycle took the same form as the first. Many lessons have been – or should have been – learned from the first experience, and a number of other conditions have changed on both the economic and institutional fronts. Whatever differences might emerge between past and future patterns, however, they are not likely to obscure the presence of a continuing theme centred on the pay, productivity, and working methods nexus.

Finally, even if a more negative view is taken, the disappearance of productivity bargaining from the scene is likely to be delayed yet awhile. Even in the present unfavourable economic circumstances, there is evidence of a small but still important continuation of activity, and the publicity – good and bad – given to productivity bargaining in the last decade has ensured that its potential is known across a large sector of industry and that managements will consider whether an approach embodying at least some of its principles would be of advantage to them. With the passage of time, the chances are that some of the lessons from the experience of the 1960s will become part of the standard package of approaches and techniques to collective bargaining, while others may disappear from the scene. We hope that the foregoing analysis of productivity bargaining will help to ensure that the valuable features for the longer term will be preserved within the armoury of the bargainer.

Index

Abruzzi, A. 237n.
Addison, John 48n.
Albright and Wilson 336
Alcan 28, 33, 246, 296
 difficulties in negotiation at, 167–8
 ex gratia payments, 247
 guarantee of security, 154, 242–3
 worker assignment at, 124
Alexander, D. C. 111n., 167n., 188n., 205n., 242n.
Alexander, K. J. W. 271n., 276n.
Allen, William 10, 11, 12
Attitudes to co-operation (of workers) 95–6, 97, 162, 207–8, 282–4, 302–3, 306
 and staff status, 241
 compliance and internalisation approaches to, 202–3
A.U.E.W. (A.E.F.) 166, 333, 336
Automation 130, 368

Bargaining methods
 integrative, 161, 162, 168–76, 177, 187, 189, 195–8
 mixed, 176–86, 194–5
 pressure, 161, 162, 163–8, 176, 189, 196–8
Bargaining structure
 and overtime pay, 138
 changes in, 106–8, 112, 295–301, 319, 344–5, 378
 design issues in, 177
 effect on operating results of agreements, 260–3
 in the U.S.A., 371–2, 374
Bayley, J. C. R. 172n., 173n., 176n., 179–80, 181n., 182n., 190n., 272, 276n.

Blakeman, Leslie 238n.
Boddy, D. 229n., 361n.
Bodkin, R. G. 104n.
Boilermakers' Society 186, 187, 190, 258n., 263, 276
Bond, E. P. 104n.
Bowers, J. K. 101n.
B.P. Chemicals 134, 365–6
Brechling, Frank 104n.
Bridges, Harry 257
British European Airways 28
British Overseas Airways Corporation 28, 140
British Oxygen Company 37, 59, 366
 cost of living clause, 316
British Railways 28, 273, 280, 354
 crew size on, 141–2, 174, 181
 evaluation of agreements, 246–7, 306–7
Brown, M. B. 206n., 286n.
Buckingham, G. L. 109n.
Buffa, E. S. 237n.
Building industry 106n.

'Call-in' 134, 241
Casual labour 42
Cattell, George 12n., 220n., 286, 287n., 353n.
C.B.I. 51, 52, 110–11, 316, 343–4, 353
Ceiling on wage rises 60, 100
Chemical Industries Association 108, 111, 343
 and plant bargaining, 298–9
 evaluation of agreements, 254–5
Cheshire, P. C. 101n.
Clack, G. 130n.

Clegg, H. A. 8n., 19n., 149n., 254n., 299n., 348n.
Clerical workers 77–9, 157
Cliff, Tony 113n., 215, 238n., 304n.
Coal mining
  job evaluation in, 205
  payment systems in, 238
Coates, K. 206n., 286n.
Code of Industrial Relations Practice 316, 317, 324n., 378
  on consultation, 335
Coercive comparisons 48, 263, 281–2
Collective bargaining
  centralisation, 340–2
  decentralisation of, 338–9
  extension of, 22, 317, 327–8, 331
  in U.K. and U.S., 373
  system in need of change, 56–7, 105–8
Commission on Industrial Relations (C.I.R.) 55n., 316, 362, 363
  on role of shop stewards, 270, 274
Communications 170, 188, 307
  in the implementation process, 207–10, 215–6, 219
  in trade unions, 344
  structure, 363
Comparability 16, 51–2, 55, 93, 106, 163, 263, 340
Compliance 201–2
Consultants
  objection to use of, 168
  use of in productivity bargaining, 108–10, 158, 164, 175, 176, 184, 214, 302
Consultation 180
  separation of bargaining and, 301, 334–6
Control
  administrative system of, 291–5, 345–50
  craft system of, 345–50, 368, 370–1
  of shop floor relations, 284–95, 318, 345–50
  of work by management, 80, 113, 162, 244–5, 286–90, 330, 355–6
  personal v. professional, 287
Corfield, Tony 288
Corina, John 104n., 105n.
Cost of living 16, 51, 55, 163, 316

Costs
  and payment systems, 239
  labour, 40, 149, 157, 164, 186, 245–55, 262, 263, 315
  —— control of, 292–3, 308, 320, 340
  overall performance, 319, 325–6
  reduction of, 227, 235, 236, 248
Council on Prices, Productivity and Incomes 15
Craft labour 41, 70, 74, 118, 128, 131, 294–5, 368
Craftsmen's mates
  abolition of, 122–3, 157n., 185, 252, 294
  redeployment, 235
Craft unions 46, 73–4, 294–5
  rivalry at S.C.O.W., 165–6
  supervision, 292
Cultural change
  in the workplace, 17, 23, 95, 109, 162, Chapter 9 *passim*, 318, 350, 369
Custom and practice 5
  social purpose of, 22

Daniel, W. W. 199n., 241n., 270n., 282–3
Demarcation 17, 18, 20–21, 32, 118–9, 121, 208, 228, 260
  and technological change, 127, 128
Denison, E. F. 12
Department of Employment and Productivity
  Manpower and Productivity Service, 175n.
  register of productivity agreements, 62–4, Chapter 3 App., 81n.
  vetting of wage agreements, 86–7
Devaluation (of sterling) 60, 100, 315
Devlin, Lord 175
Devlin Report (docks) 12, 14, 17n., 123, 170–1, 188
  difficulties of implementation, 261
Docks industry 7, 11–12, 17n., 106–7, 171, 188, 354
  continuity rule in, 19–20
  fall-back guarantee in, 154–5, 171n.
  mixed bargaining in, 180

strike (1970), 155, 261
union 'flying squads' in, 215
union tactics in negotiation, 189
worker assignment in, 123
Doeringer, P. B. 372n.
Donovan Commission (*see* Royal Commission on Employers' Associations and Trade Unions)
Drucker, P. F. 211n.
Dunlop Company Ltd 296, 301

Economist Intelligence Unit 217n., 291n.
Edwards, R. S. 30n., 34n.
Efficiency agreements 61, 94–7
and the indirect strategy, 161, 362
Effort utilisation 117, 139–43, 157, 161, 234–9, 289–90, 347
and payment systems, 238
stability of improvements in, 244–5
Eldridge, J. E. T. 129n., 207, 208n.
Electrical contracting industry
cost of living clause, 316
productivity bargaining in 251–2
Electrical Trades Union 49, 185, 258, 333
training schemes, 220–1
Electricity supply 14, 16, 28, 29, 34–5, 96, 155, 211, 240, 278, 307–9
communications in, 208, 308
Courts of Inquiry, 170n., 308, 309
evaluation of agreements, 307–9
lead-in payments, 279, 308
overtime working in, 137, 231–2, 234, 278
productivity negotiations, 170, 301
scheduling of working hours, 132
Employers' associations 9, 43, 111, 296, 342
advisory function in productivity bargaining, 298, 343
Engineering Employers' Federation 107, 111, 296, 342n.
change of view on plant bargaining, 340
evaluation of agreements, 254, 266

Engineering industry 111, 254, 340
long-term agreement, 25, 261–2, 266
Esso 27, 33, 109, 121–2, 123, 211, 214, 221, 257, 292, 293–4, 296, 323, 353
accelerated implementation of Distribution Agreement, 213
bargaining tactics in distribution agreement, 165, 166, 221, 282
reduced labour costs, 248
results of agreements compared, 264–5
(*see also* Fawley agreements)
Ex gratia payments 247
Expectations (of higher wages) 255, 267, 314

Fairfields experiment 119
and overtime reduction, 137
flexibility in, 276
management reorganisation, 219
role of foreman in, 271
Fawley agreements 1, 6–10, 22, 26, 30, 33, 38, 40, 50, 95, 209, 229, 233, 264, 271, 275, 353, 365
preparation for, 164–5
reduction in personnel staff, 220
Fison's Fertilizer Company 122
Flanders, A. 6n., 9, 17, 50, 95, 109n., 119n., 209, 229n., 271
Flexibility
craft attitudes to, 118–9, 127, 185, 201, 258
horizontal, 121–2
in scheduling, 131–5
in the Post Office, 191
in work assignments, 19–21, 32–3, 75, 118–31, 187–8, 229, 258, 276, 283, 293
vertical, 121, 122–3
Ford Motor Company 119, 272
wage structure revision, 145
—— effectiveness of, 250
Foremen
as 'quasi' shop stewards, 217
effect of agreements on job of, 269–72, 291–2, 310, 329, 356
professionalisation of, 291–2
role in implementation, 211–2, 217, 219, 269, 271

training, 218, 219, 257, 272
Fox, A. 119, 334n., 357n.
Framework agreements 27, 65, 105–10, 111, 113n., 224, 251, 266, 298–9, 300, 340, 342–5
Fraser, R. 150n.
Fringe benefits 81, 152, 158–9, 295
Fullan, M. 116n.

Garbarino, J. W. 372n.
Gas industry 106
Geddes Report (shipbuilding) 11, 12, 14, 126
Gennard, J. 323n., 324n.
Globerson, A. 335n.
Glor, Evelyn 206n., 219n., 222n.
G.M.W.U. 113, 166, 259, 336
  approach to productivity bargaining, 113
Golding, J. 116n., 353n.

Haire, M. 211n.
Hawkins, B. 119n., 137n., 148n., 219n., 242n., 295n.
Hawkins, Kevin 250n., 270n., 274n., 300n., 303, 353n., 366n.
Healy, J. J. 144n., 289n., 303n., 358n.
Henry Wiggin & Co. Ltd
  bargaining tactics, 166
  withdrawal from E.E.F., 296–7
Higgs, P. 150n.
Hill, Paul 311n.
Homans, G. C. 276n.
Hunter, L. C. 229n., 361n.

Implementation (of agreements)
  advantages of rapid, 213–4
  by compliance, 161, 162, Chapter 7 *passim*
  by internalisation, 161, 162
Incentive payments system 4, 9, 23, 144, 145, 148–51, 157, 158, 238–9, 250, 288–90, 308, 310, 312, 343, 354, 363n.
  decay of, 237–8
  industrial incidence of, 149
  union attitudes to, 150–1
Incomes policy 15, 16, 53, Chapters 3 and 4 *passim*, 245, 314, 345
  evaluation of, 97–113
  legislation, 61–2

negative effects of, 172, 197, 266–7
stimulation to productivity bargaining, 64–5, 77, 148–9, 250, 266–7, 362, 376–7
Industrial Relations Act 316, 317
  and worker participation, 335
Industry-wide bargaining (*see* National agreements)
Inflation 55, 315, 376
Information sharing 173, 190, 197, 209–10
  and work measurement, 204
Integrative bargaining 165–76, 195–8, 224, 327–9
International Longshoremen Workers' Union 257–8
Iron and Steel Board 11

Jefferys, J. B. 349n.
Jenkins, C. L. 271n., 276n.
Jensen, V. H. 11n., 171n.
Job design 119–20, 159, 199, 239, 283, 346, 368–9
Job enlargement 33, 283, 368
Job evaluation 22, 77, 79, 109, 110, 144, 158, 239, 279, 288, 290, 338, 343
  as a means of checking wage drift, 146, 293, 357
  cost of, 239
  T.G.W.U. view on, 331
Job satisfaction 120, 199, 201, 239, 282–4, 307
Job security 129, 131, 142, 152, 156, 159, 161, 312, 350
Jones, K. 116n., 353n.
Judson, A. S. 211n.
Jurisdictional issues (*see* Demarcation)

Kaiser Plan 363

Labour Party
  view on information sharing, 210
Larkom, Joy 170n., 181n.
Lawrence, P. R. 120n.
Layoffs (*see* Redundancy)
Lead-in payments 279
Leisure
  increase in, 22, 36–7, 81, 157–8, 280, 284
Lesieur, Fred G. 363n.

'Lightning' strike 19, 323
Lindsay, Isabel 255n.
Lipsey, R. G. 104n.
Livernash, E. R. 144n., 289n., 303n., 358n.
Lloyd, Selwyn 15, 56, 104n.
London Transport 14, 256
Low pay 57–60

McCarthy, W. E. J. 13, 149n., 287, 323n.
McDougall, Mary 309n.
McGarvey, Daniel 186, 190
McGregor, D. M. 363n.
McKersie, R. B. 149n., 163n., 363n.
Management
  and the impact of productivity bargaining, 319–26
  responsibility, 35, 38, 43, 77, 260, 324
  restructuring of, 218–9
  role in implementation, 216–23, 255–7, 268–9
  role in internalising approach to change, 202
  training, 220–1, 257
Management initiative 164–5, 167, 178, 268, 318, 321–2, 336–7, 355
  U.S. and British experience compared, 336–8, 374
Mangum, Garth 16, 17n.
Manning problems 31, 33, 77, 79, 140–2, 168, 234–5, 357–9
Manpower forecasting, planning 38, 156, 269, 322–4, 360–2
March, J. G. 346n., 371n.
Measured daywork 80, 144, 148, 238–9, 288
  advantages of, 238
  supervision requirements, 238
  union resistance to, 148, 150, 288–9
Meyrick, A. J. 104n., 105n.
Miller, C. F. 149n.
Miller, John 312
Ministry of Labour
  powers of delay in incomes policy, 61–2
  see also Department of Employment and Productivity
Mobil Oil 33, 123, 170, 172
  change in foreman's role, 270

Coryton negotiations, 184–6, 218–9, 259, 288, 354
  hours of work patterns in, 136, 232
  manpower reduction at, 249
  overtime elimination, 213, 232, 277
  work measurement in, 147, 288
Molander, C. 270n.
Monitoring of agreements 219, 254
Motor industry
  freedom from demarcation disputes, 130
Mutuality 148, 149, 150, 289–90, 317, 330–2, 335, 355

National agreements 9, 43, 105–8, 111–2, 317
  and advantages of centralisation, 340–2
  as an obstacle to productivity bargaining, 27, 262–3, 265, 295–7
  in engineering, 25, 261–2, 296–7
National Board for Prices and Incomes (N.B.P.I.) 13, 16, 50–1, Chapters 3 and 4 *passim*, 214, 253
  evaluation of agreements in electrical contracting, 252–3
  influence as an outside agency, 175, 252
  on job evaluation, 146, 214, 239
  on overtime, 136–7, 175, 232–3
  on payment systems, 239
  on shiftwork, 230–1
  on work measurement, 147, 214, 236, 252
  tests for acceptability of productivity agreements, 60, 87–97, 282
National Incomes Commission 251
National Industrial Relations Court 316
National Institute of Industrial Psychology 218n.
Neal, Len 307
N.E.D.O. 173n., 209
Newspaper printing 18, 20, 175, 217, 263
  Joint Board for the National Press, 175
  scheduling of working hours, 132

technological change in, 359
N.G.A. 168, 278
Norm for wage increases 57, 59
exceptions to norm, 57–8, 59
North, D. T. B. 109n.
N.U.B. 259

Oil industry 6, 47–8
subcontracting of maintenance,
130
Oldfield, F. E. 184n.
Oppenheim, A. N. 172n., 173n.,
176n., 179–80, 181n., 182n.,
190n., 272, 276n.
Otis Elevator 354
Output
restrictions, 23, 33
Overmanning 14, 38, 377
in office employment, 147, 157
Overtime
industrial incidence of, 46–7,
70–1
limitations on overtime, 138n.
reassertion of, 233, 234, 280
reduction of, 6, 13, 21, 33, 34,
37, 81n., 132, 135, 159, 175,
232–3, 280–1, 306, 364–5
systematic, 22, 137, 284
to supplement low rates, 136–7,
233

Parity 341
exchange, 277–8, 281–2, 354
outcome, 278–9, 281–2, 353
personal, 279–82, 353
Parker, S. R. 13n., 149n.
Parkin, J. M. 104n.
Participation *see* Worker Participation *and* Control
Participation–Achievement–Reward
systems 140, 355, 362–7
Paulden, S. 119n., 137n., 148n.,
219n., 242n., 295n.
Payment by results *see* Incentive
payments
Pearson Report (docks) 155
Philblack 121, 122, 123, 259, 292
Pilot agreements 29–30, 35, 172,
310
and the internalisation approach,
212
Piore, M. J. 372n.

Plant bargaining 7, 9, 11, 26, 34–5,
42, 43, 52, 105–6, 108, 111–2,
260, 296–7, 301, 317, 338–9,
378
in the U.S.A. 371–2
Post Office 28, 30, 90–1, 183n., 354,
365
bargaining tactics in, 168, 172,
182, 190–5
cultural changes in, 273
implementation of agreements,
200, 206–7, 216
results of agreements in, 304
Post Office Engineering Union 28,
90–1, 304n.
case study of bargaining method,
190–5
Pressure bargaining 163–8, 195–8,
224
Printing industry 7, 217
bargaining problems in, 168
craft system in, 349
foremen in, 291
technological change in, 127
Productivity
and work measurement, 236–7
distribution of gains, 89–92, 179–
83, 185, 249–50, 353–4, 364–5
in coal mining, 238
in motor car industry, 12
in shipbuilding, 11–12, 14
in the docks, 11, 14
in the steel industry, 11, 14
low in office employment, 147,
157
of labour, 11, 12, 13, 249
potential in U.S.A., 370–5
reduced scope for improvement,
352
Productivity agreements
change in ingredients, 157–9
coverage by skill groups, 74, 77–9
design of, 30–9, 74–7, 202–3,
281–2, 290
difficulty of economic evaluation,
245–7, 318
economic results of, 247–55
implementation of, 161, Chapter
7 *passim*, 290
industrial incidence of, 39–50,
68–9, 79–80
negotiation of, Chapter 6 *passim*,
264

size distribution of (1967–9), 72–3

Productivity bargaining
and corporate planning, 164, 177, 323–6
and negotiation level, 26–30, 38
conditions for, 376–8
direct and indirect approaches compared, 162, 176–7, 196–8, 225, 301–12, 362
effects on management, 319–26
future of, 367–70
significance of, 5, 23, 40, 318, 321, 351–5
strategy, 28–30, Chapter 6 *passim*, 312
time horizon of, 158–9, 160–1, 162, 197, 246
'Pseudo' agreements 250, 254

Quarterman, W. E. 149n.

Reddaway, W. B. 102n.
Redundancy 7, 22, 142, 360
guarantees against, 37–8, 152–4, 156, 193, 242–3, 281, 305, 310, 328, 360, 365
payments, 38, 101n., 243, 360
voluntary, 38, 243
Reid, G. L. 229n., 361n.
Restrictive practices 42, 353, 357–8
Reuber, G. L. 104n.
Richard Thomas and Baldwin, productivity bargaining in, 27
Roberts, B. C. 323n., 324n.
Roberts, G. 127n., 130n.
Roberts, R. D. V. 30n., 34n., 308n.
Robertson, D. J. 166n., 222, 259n.
Robinson, R. T. 240n., 241n.
Robinson, T. R. 104n.
Rootes Ltd
and *status quo*, 336–7
implementation of agreement at, 219–20, 222–3
wage strategy at, 321
Rowe, P. H. 173n.
Royal Commission on the Press 20n.
Royal Commission on Trade Unions and Employers' Associations 13, 51–2, 57, 77, 108, 278, 339n., 344, 353
Productivity Bargaining, 278n.

Workplace Industrial Relations, 218n.

Rubber industry 209, 296
framework agreement, 299
freedom from demarcation disputes, 128
limited success of agreements in, 251
Rule, H. S. 124n., 187n.

Sallis, H. 137n., 231n., 308n.
Scamp Report (railways) 174n., 181n.
Scanlon, Hugh 150
Scanlon Plan 4, 321, 362, 363, 364, 374
Searle-Barnes, R. G. 148n., 238n.
Selective Employment Tax 102
Shake-out 101
Shaw, A. 236n., 364n.
Shawcross Report (newspapers) 12
Shell 29, 35, 155, 165, 173, 294, 311n.
craft flexibility in, 122, 124
Stanlow agreement implementation, 205–6, 220
Stanlow negotiations, 170, 181, 187–8
training programmes in, 220
Shiftwork 33, 134, 230–2
Shipbuilding industry 11, 48, 49
craft system in, 349
demarcation in, 119, 126–9
job insecurity in, 129
Shop stewards
concern over control, 284, 286–7, 288–9
professionalisation of, 332, 344
role in implementation, 216, 217–8, 258, 322
role in productivity bargaining, 172, 174, 177, 184–6, 188, 222–3, 269, 274–5, 276, 292–3, 329, 339
training, 220–1, 298, 332, 344
Shultz, G. P. 363n.
Skill utilisation 117, 118–31, 156, 161, 358
assessing gains in, 229–30
stability of improvements in, 244
Slichter, S. H. 144n., 289n., 303, 358n.
Sloan, Norman 48

Smith, Adam 130
Smith, D. C. 104n.
Smith, E. O. 235n., 243, 247n., 269, 295n., 356n.
Smithfield Market 33, 59
S.O.G.A.T. 278
'Solidarity' 20
Standstill on prices and incomes (1966) 24, 25, 53, 54, 56, 58
effect on productivity agreements, 59
Stanton and Stavely
introduction of work measurement, 236
Status
enhanced, 161, 170
foreman's loss of, 270, 271
protection of, 152, 154, 237
staff, 240–1, 270, 306, 312
Status agreements 34, 35, 37, 39, 96, 155, 158, 170, 208, 240–1, 306–12
Status quo 17–21, 335
Steel Company of Wales 14, 26–7, 33, 165–6, 183n., 269, 356
Court of Inquiry, 259
ex gratia payments, 247
industry craftsmen in, 295
manpower reduction in, 235, 243, 360
technological change in, 360
Steel industry 11, 14, 27
demarcation in, 128
productivity improvement in U.S., 372–3
Stettner, Nora 260n., 334n.
Stieglitz, Harold 363n.
Stinchcombe, A. L. 346n., 371n.
Supervisors *see* Foremen
Sykes, Andrew 287

Technological change 115–16, 325, 349, 364
and demarcation, 127, 128
and increased productivity, 90–1, 130, 235, 357
and manning standards, 141–2, 235
and skill utilisation, 156–7, 229, 368
management initiative on, 336
resistance to, 7, 41–2, 71–2, 126–7, 142, 359, 360, 372

U.S. and U.K. experience, 358, 370–2
Term agreements 374
advantages of, 323
T.G.W.U. 8, 49, 113, 123, 165, 166, 275, 333
approach to productivity bargaining, 113, 189, 327
criticised, 215
decentralisation in, 258, 331, 341–2
view on information sharing, 210
Thomson, Andrew 338n.
Thomson House 219, 292
cut in manning standards, 225
Threshold clause 316
Time off in lieu (of overtime) 37, 135, 136, 220, 233, 277
Timetable of negotiations 264–5
Topham, Tony 206n., 286, 288–9
Trade union
communications, 208, 326
co-operation, 259–60, 274
defensive attitudes to Industrial Relations Act, 317
gains from productivity bargaining, 241, 326
mergers, 333
participation in implementation, 206, 285, 312
role in implementation, 215–6, 257–60
role in leadership in bargaining, 273, 332–3
tactics in productivity bargaining, 189–90, 327
understaffing in, 216, 332
Trades Union Congress (T.U.C.) 51–2, 54, 316
attitude to plant bargaining, 111–3
vetting of wage claims, 86n.
Training and the craft system, 347–8
(*see also* Management, Foremen, Shop Stewards)
Tubes Ltd
integrative bargaining at, 205
problems in productivity bargaining, 188
Turner, A. N. 120n.
Turner, H. A. 130n., 340n., 346n., 349n.

Two-tier negotiations 224, 300–1, 342–3

Unemployment 101, 104n., 138n., 315–6, 326, 355, 376
  manning changes and, 143, 361
  U.S. experience, 16, 257, 303, 324–5, 336–8, 358–61, 370–5

Wages Councils 300
Wage drift 144, 146, 158, 245, 262, 292–3, 340
Wage payment systems 4, 110, 144, 147–51, 158, 362
  effectiveness of changes in, 237–9
  (*see also* Incentive Payment Systems)
Wage strategy, company 320–1
Wage structure
  and job evaluation, 239
  changing relativities, 277–82, 283
  effect of productivity bargaining on, 92, 283
  in British Railways, 306–7
  rationalisation, 22, 60, 77, 109, 110, 144–6, 155, 158, 352, 365
Walker, M. 167n.
Walton, R. E. 163n.
Webb, A. E. 101n.
Wedderburn, Dorothy 241n.
White-collar workers 30, 61, 97, 110, 368, 373
  effect of productivity bargaining on, 241–2
Whybrew, E. G. 46, 70, 135, 280
Wilberforce, Lord 309

Wilson, C. H. 236n.
Wood, G. 373n.
Woodward, J. 116n.
Work group, structure influenced by productivity agreements, 275–7, 330, 338
Work measurement 22, 76–7, 79, 109, 112, 113, 144, 147, 158, 203–4, 235–7, 255–6, 288, 290, 308, 338, 352
  for white-collar workers, 30, 79, 110, 147, 157, 183, 236, 237, 305, 354
  shop steward involvement in, 332
Work rules
  origin of, 21–23, 40–1, 200
  updating of, 18, 19, 21, 31, 334, 358–9
Worker participation
  and wage payment systems, 149–50
  forms of, 334–5
  in collective bargaining, 22, 317, 328–30, 338, 373–4
  in implementation, 204–7
  in regulation of work, 284–5, 288, 290, 334–8, 355, 357, 364, 366
Working hours
  changes in, 32–3, 37, 75, 131–9, 230–34
  in British Rail, 175
  in electricity supply, 308
Working practice
  changes in, 6, 41, 235, 301, 309

Zweig, F. 17n.